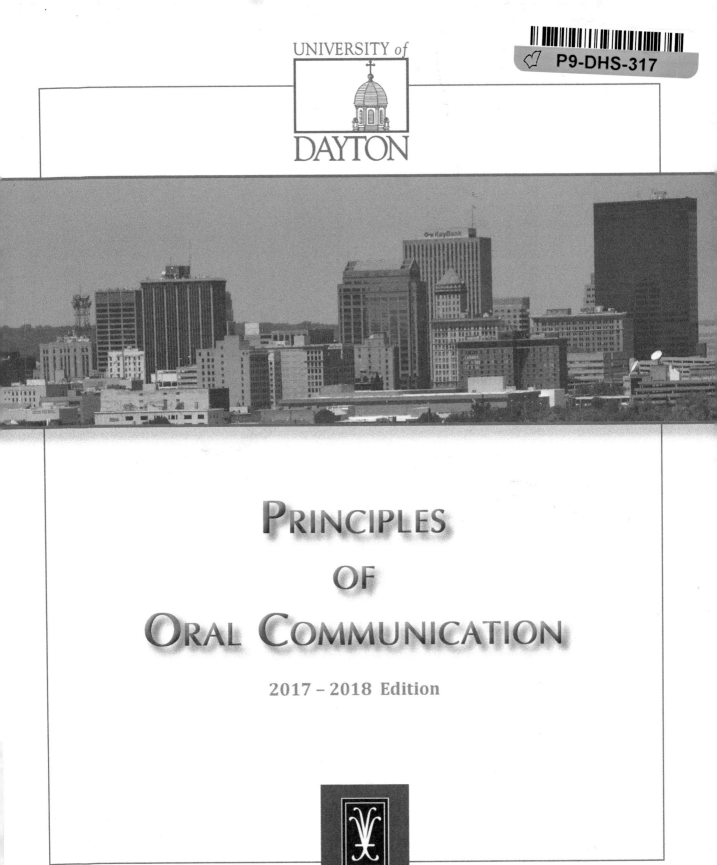

UNIVERSITY of
DAYTON

P9-DHS-317

PRINCIPLES

OF

ORAL COMMUNICATION

2017 – 2018 Edition

FOUNTAINHEAD
PRESS

Our "green" initiatives include:

Electronic Products
We deliver products in non-paper form whenever possible. This includes PDF downloadables, flash drives, and CDs.

Electronic Samples
We use a new electronic sampling system, called Xample. Instructor samples are sent via a personalized web page that links to PDF downloads.

FSC Certified Printers
All of our printers are certified by the Forest Stewardship Council, which promotes environmentally and socially responsible management of the world's forests. This program allows consumer groups, individual consumers and businesses to work together to promote responsible use of the world's forests as a renewable and sustainable resource.

Recycled Paper
Most of our products are printed on a minimum of 30% post consumer waste recycled paper.

Support of Green Causes
When we do print, we donate a portion of our revenue to Green causes. Listed below are a few of the organizations that have received donations from Fountainhead Press. We welcome your feedback and suggestions for contributions, as we are always searching for worthy initiatives.
    Rainforest 2 Reef
    Environmental Working Group

Designer: Susan Moore

Copyright © 2017 by University of Dayton

The Speaker - Copyright © 2015 Fountainhead Press

For information, please call or write:

        1-800-586-0330

        Fountainhead Press
        Southlake, TX 76092

        Web Site: www.fountainheadpress.com
        E-mail: customerservice@fountainheadpress.com

Fall 2017 Edition

ISBN: 978-1-68036-544-3

Printed in the United States of America

The Department of Communication would like to thank the Basic Course Advisory Board for their help in developing this edition of the textbook:

Shawn Swavey, Department of Chemistry

Heather McLachlan, Department of Music

Peter Titlebaum, School of Education and Allied Professions

Thomas Whitney, Department of Civil and Environmental Engineering

Jamie Longazel, Department of Sociology, Anthropology, & Social Work

Nancy Mohan, School of Business Administration

Danielle Poe, Department of Philosophy

Katy Kelly, Roesch Library

Ryan Allen, Learning and Teaching Center

Gov. Robert Taft, School of Education and Allied Professions

Letters from Provost Benson, Dr. Valenzano & Dr. Wallace and Humanities Commons Intro

Prep Questions

1. Describe the Common Academic Program (CAP) and explain how CMM 100 contributes to the learning objectives for UD undergraduates.

2. Explain three skills that CMM 100 is designed to help you develop. Provide two examples of how these skills could potentially be useful to you in your field of study/future career.

3. What is civil dialogue? Compare and contrast dialogue with the type of communication that is commonly practiced on news programs and talk shows.

4. What are some of the benefits of receiving training in civil dialogue? How could this type of training enhance your undergraduate experience in the UD community? How could it enhance your professional life?

5. What are the primary goals of CMM 100 and how do they compare and contrast with those of a course designed to teach public speaking?

6. What four courses make up the Humanities Commons and what are the six Student Learning Objectives in those courses? How do they connect with CMM 100?

LETTER FROM THE PROVOST

Dear CMM 100 students:

This textbook is designed and written specifically for the University of Dayton's new Communication course, CMM 100. This course delivers a required component in our new Common Academic Program (CAP) and promotes important learning objectives for all UD undergraduates. Because CAP seeks to embody fundamental goals for an undergraduate education at a Catholic and Marianist university, this textbook also reflects UD's broader educational mission, to link learning and scholarship with leadership and service.

"That is all well and good," you may think; "it's just the sort of thing that an academic administrator would say. But why do I have to take this course, when there are so many other things that I want to study before I graduate?" This is a fair question. I would note, first, that oral communication skills are highly prized in any professional field or area of academic study you may pursue. These are foundational skills, essential for a high quality liberal education and pursuit of your personal aspirations, whatever they may be.

CMM 100's focus on skills of civil dialogue and persuasive argumentation is especially relevant to the world you will inhabit as a UD graduate. In our time, the inevitable disagreements and conflicts that arise among human beings are more often addressed through emotionally combative, disrespectful, and poorly reasoned verbal attacks than through serious dialogue and even-handed, reflective exchanges of persuasive evidence. Persons educated to resist incivility and demagoguery through careful understanding of others' standpoints and thoughtful exchanges of reasons for their own judgments and actions will be sought after and admired as wise colleagues, influential leaders, responsible community members, and trusted friends.

The skills that you will gain and refine in CMM 100 are also particularly important for UD's mission to educate leaders who serve and build community among diverse people, advancing the ends of social justice and the common good. As our *Commitment to Community* (C2C) document emphasizes, striving to live in community on campus and to experience community living as a central ingredient of your education requires that you embrace certain ethical principles and develop certain habits. As you will see, the ethical principles and habits necessary for community living also are important to the subject matter of CMM 100.

This course is vitally important to your UD education—as important as any you will take—and it should be fun besides. Any UD student should enjoy thinking through controversial, contemporary issues, crafting clear, well-reasoned explanations of complex ideas, and attempting to persuade fellow UD students. Regardless of other courses you want to take during your UD career, CMM 100 should be personally engaging and practically useful.

I hope that the course is at once stimulating and challenging for you, and that this book is a valuable resource for your future studies at UD. I look forward to hearing your reactions to our new Communication course.

Paul H. Benson
Provost, University of Dayton
June, 2013

Letter from the Chair

Dear CMM100 Student,

Welcome to CMM100 Principles of Oral Communication! I want to take a moment and share with you how unique this class is. You may hear your friends at other schools refer to their communication course as "public speaking," but at UD that is not what the class is—in fact there is no course like this one around the country!

When we designed this class we met with departments across the university, from Business, to Engineering to Education, and identified key oral communication skills that your faculty felt were essential for your success. What we have done is create a class that shows how the skills of effective oral communication are about so much more than just traditional public speaking. In CMM 100 you will learn how to deliver a speech, but more importantly you will begin to develop the ability to explain complicated information to non-experts. You will also develop effective problem solving and communication skills within small group contexts. Perhaps the most unique part of this class is the emphasis on civility and how to disagree with others without being seen as disagreeable or offensive. These are all things your faculty and prospective employers believed needed to be emphasized in this class.

CMM100 has been designed specifically for UD students. You will notice that in each chapter specific events and concepts central to UD are highlighted as examples. You will also be asked from time to time to think through challenging issues pertinent to the UD community that relate to course content. In fact several chapters of the book were written by your UD faculty so that they were more relevant to you—and this just heightens the special nature of the course which you are about to take.

From the interteaching sessions, to the content of the book, to the performative assignments and in-class activities your instructor will facilitate, all of the distinctive elements of CMM100 are the product of adapting the course each year based on student and instructor feedback. Much like communication itself, this course is not static. In fact, thanks to your fellow students and your instructors, the course has changed for the better each semester we have offered it. While the syllabus, all of the graded assignments, and course policies are the same for every section of CMM100, the lectures and discussions will be specific to the learning community in your classroom. You will even have the opportunity to help your instructor tailor review sessions by giving feedback regarding concepts on which you need more information. Besides the valuable critical thinking skills you will learn, one of the best parts of CMM100 is that you get to pick your own speaking topics within the semester theme so you get to play a role in how you experience the course!

One final aspect of the class that bears noting is its connection to the rest of your education here at UD. You will note that in the first chapter we discuss some foundational figures in communication, people like Plato and Aristotle and Cicero. What is interesting is that you will also encounter many of these great thinkers in other classes, such as History or Philosophy, but from a different perspective. These connections will help you see how your classes support and complement each other, because we have made a conscious effort to build a cohesive UD education that integrates different disciplines and ways of understanding the world.

I hope that you enjoy your semester in CMM100 and that you find new ways to think about the world around you. Throughout the semester, you will notice that you are constantly engaging with new people and new ideas. The more you open your mind to these new opportunities, the more you will find this course useful and enjoyable. I invite you to let CMM 100 be the beginning of a long conversation, one that continues in every class you take at UD from here on out!

Joseph M. Valenzano, III
Chair, Department of Communication

LETTER FROM THE UNDERGRADUATE DIRECTOR

Dear CMM 100 Student,

Congratulations on your decision to enroll in CMM 100 this semester! Not only will this course fulfill a University requirement, but it will allow you to gain essential knowledge and practical skills in explanation and advocacy as practiced in civil dialogue. Those people trained and experienced in civil dialogue tend to be much better listeners, better analysts, better at building the relationships that are critical in organizations, and they are perceived to be more informed and more competent professionals. As we continue to move toward becoming a culture of specialists, the ability to explain complex and specialized knowledge to non-specialists is a necessary ability.

Along with training in oral communication, the Department of Communication offers courses and concentrations in Journalism, Public Relations, Communication Management, and Electronic Media. Please let me take a moment of your time to describe some of the opportunities available if you choose to major in Communication, concentrating in one of those four areas.

The field of *Journalism* is becoming more complex as the news industry continues its transition. The industry is heading toward *media integration* which will create a multiple-platform industry with newspapers, web news, broadcast television and radio, and cable outlets rolled together into a new "shape." Even so, the skills of this 21st century organization will continue to require strong writing skills and a solid foundation in the legal, ethical, and social issues essential to the professional journalist. Students in the journalism concentration are exposed to writing, editing, design, research, and production experiences with special attention to detail and accuracy. Our journalism students graduate prepared to enter careers with newspapers, television and radio outlets, wire services, magazines, web publishers, book publishers, corporations, and nonprofit organizations.

Public Relations students learn how corporations, nonprofit groups, organizations, and individuals manage their public image, control internal and external communication, and establish themselves as good and productive citizens in a community. PR training in the Department of Communication includes both theory and professional skills based on a solid foundation of strong and precise writing, strategic planning, message design, ethics, and research. Our students have established careers as media planners, media strategists, event planners, crisis communication specialists, public information officers, public opinion researchers, community affairs liaisons, and many others.

If the thought of telling stories and sharing information across a variety of media platforms sounds exciting to you, then you should investigate our *Electronic Media Concentration.* The focus is on television and radio broadcasting, audio and video production, and multimedia production. You can gain an understanding of principles and get practical experiences through production, script writing, and carefully designed class activities. The program encourages cross training on multiple media platforms to increase adaptability and to make our graduates more attractive in the professional marketplace. Careers include traditional broadcast and cable television and radio, corporate production for training and promotions, independent production and post production, public television, nonprofit organizations, education, advertising, script and screen writing, multimedia design and production, and many others.

Our concentration in *Communication Management* can prepare you for a challenging career: managing people in organizations. Trying to get people to cooperate and accomplish an organization's goals can seem nearly impossible! To complicate matters, you will likely be working with at least some people that you will never meet; people who are in different zip codes, time zones, or even on different continents. Managing people in organization requires keen attention to interpersonal relationships, group decision making, persuasion, cultural differences, clear explanations, and especially conflict management. The Communication Management concentration will help you learn to be an influential and positive presence in your organization through coursework, research experiences, and practical application gained from innovative class projects and internships. Careers include organizational management, sales, staff development, human resources, customer relations, consulting, and a variety of others.

Even if you don't consider a career in Communication, please take full advantage of the CMM 100 class that you are enrolled in right now. The class offers a unique perspective on skills considered absolutely essential by employers for positions in virtually every professional arena. If you find yourself interested in other Communication classes, or even a minor in Communication, please don't be shy! Feel free to contact me at swallace1@udayton.edu so you can meet with a faculty member who can answer your questions.!

I hope you have a great semester in CMM 100!

Sam Wallace
Director of Undergraduate Studies
Department of Communication
swallace1@udayton.edu

THE HUMANITIES COMMONS AND CMM 100:
PRINCIPLES OF ORAL COMMUNICATION

As a student in CMM 100, you may also be enrolled in one or more of the four courses which comprise the Humanities Commons:

English 100 or ENG 200H: Writing Seminars
History 103: The West and the World
PHL 103: Introduction to Philosophy
REL 103: Introduction to Religious and Theological Studies

These are the foundational courses of the Common Academic Program (CAP) which begin the process of integrating all aspects of a student's university experience via the seven mission related Student Learning Outcomes (SLO's). Each Humanities Commons course will emphasize six common learning objectives that have been identified and agreed upon by faculty from each of the four departments. In these courses students will:

1. read a variety of primary texts closely and critically (including self-critically).

2. analyze, in writing, a variety of texts contributing to larger historical conversations, debates, and traditions and as resources for understanding and appreciating the complexities of human identity, dignity, and experience.

3. develop an understanding of their place in community, country, and world in relationship to multiple others, with particular attention to differences–such as class, gender, and race–upon which social inequalities are constructed and maintained.

4. engage central concepts of Catholic intellectual tradition as they contribute to humanistic inquiry and reflection in the relevant academic discipline (English, History, Philosophy, or Religious Studies).

5. examine the question of what it means to be human from a disciplinary perspective, and in the process make connections among disciplines and develop an appreciation for the ways in which learning is a process of integrating knowledge.

6. understand and practice academic honesty as foundational to the making and sharing of knowledge as a community of learners that is both local and global.

Your CMM 100: Principles of Oral Communication course will enable you to participate more fully via oral communication in these courses and beyond, explaining, persuading and dialoguing with classmates, instructors and others, while the humanities commons courses will provide the experiences, subject matter and perspectives about which you will communicate. You may (and should!) see the similarities and differences in oral versus written communication, and the variety of communication models across disciplines and diverse speakers.

SCENARIOS

Scenario 1

You are the Vice President of a marketing consulting firm and you are interviewing three candidates for a managerial position. This person will report to one of the senior partners, and will be responsible for training incoming associates, planning and leading weekly staff meetings, overseeing project management, and daily communication with clients, among other duties. With your group members, devise three interview questions to ask the candidates that would help you assess their communication knowledge and skills. Work to develop questions that would help you to get a sense of the candidate's ability to do each of the following (one question for each would be ideal):

1. Explain complex ideas to non-experts

2. Persuade others by making a compelling case

3. Engage in dialogue with people whose ideas are different from their own

Scenario 2

Who is the best communicator you know? Who is the worst? Why? Work with your group members to generate a list of 5 things that good communicators do well, and 5 things that you wish people would do better when they communicate. Based on these lists, identify what you think are the 3-4 most important communication skills for today's college graduates and be able to provide reasoning for your answer (work to achieve group consensus on this).

Scenario 3

Detail the benefits to an education when classes cover similar material in different ways. What topics might you see covered in both the Humanities Commons and CMM 100?

Scenario 4

According to the *Civility in America* report, 86% of Americans say that it is uncivil when someone you are eating with is on the phone. Almost as many agree that it is uncivil behavior when someone talks loudly on a cell phone in public. A third of Americans believe these problems stand to get worse over time. Identify two examples of incivility that you have recently experienced, and then work with your group members to determine practical ways of responding to and managing these situations.

Scenario 5

In what ways are the skills in explanation, advocacy (the ability to present a persuasive case), and civil dialogue important in your field of study/desired career? Give an example of a complex idea in your area of study here at UD that you may one day have to explain to a non-expert. Give an example of a controversial issue (an idea or subject about which people disagree) within your field of study that you may one day have to discuss with others. Talk with your group to generate and share ideas.

TABLE OF CONTENTS

SPEAKING OF CIVIC ENGAGEMENT BOXES

SPOTLIGHTING THEORISTS BOXES

The Practice of Public Communication

Practically SPEAKING

Imagine being tutored by one of the greatest minds ever to live. Imagine personal attention from the man responsible for some of the most important writings in history. Of course, such an opportunity is not really available today, but it was in the classical world, and one person managed to receive such an education: Alexander the Great of Macedon. From his early teenage years Alexander was personally tutored by Aristotle, the man who wrote books that are still considered foundational texts for communication studies, philosophy, political science and even the natural sciences. You might think that such an opportunity came about largely because of the wealth and power of Alexander's family, and in that you would be only partially correct.

In 343 BC Philip of Macedon, Alexander's father, approached Aristotle with an offer to tutor his son, then thirteen years old. At the time, Aristotle had not written many of his works and had only recently finished twenty years of studies at Plato's Academy. In fact, he was little more than a roaming refugee in exile since Philip himself had ordered the complete annihilation of Aristotle's home city, Stagira.[1] So, the fact that Philip chose him is interesting. There was also a personal connection between Philip and Aristotle in that they knew each other from childhood when Aristotle's father, Nicomachus, was the personal physician to Phillip's father. Perhaps the combination of the childhood connection, Aristotle's education under Plato and Philip's possible desire to extend an olive branch to the remaining people of Stagira led to the choice of Aristotle as personal tutor to Alexander.[2]

It did not take long for Aristotle to accept the offer and begin schooling Philip's son and a few other sons of nobles at Mieza, a spot of land west of the Macedonian capital of Pella.[3] While there, Alexander learned about medicine, ethics, literature, Greek culture and other subjects while sitting outdoors on stone benches. One can easily see the impact these lessons had on the young prince. When he became king and began his conquest of the known world, Alexander would collect samples of flowers and animals and send them back to his former tutor for study.[4] He also carried a volume of Homer's *Iliad* with him that Aristotle had personally edited. An even more practical impact was the fact Alexander used his knowledge of medicine garnered from his time with Aristotle to personally treat wounded soldiers on the battlefield![5]

The education of Alexander by Aristotle provides us with an early example of what we may now call a classroom, and the broad outline of what we call a liberal arts education. Alexander was schooled in a wide array of subjects from ethics, philosophy, and rhetoric to politics, medicine, and physics. Today, universities take a similar approach in designing a general education for students. The lasting impact of the way schools were structured and students taught in classical Greece and classical Rome can still be seen today.

In this chapter we will explore some of the great thinkers of classical Greece and Rome and look at how their schools were structured. It is important to note, some did have schools, like Plato and Aristotle, but others were more like wandering tutors. All of these individuals and groups, however, understood the importance of education and the place of speech in it. To cover this much history in such a short space we will highlight aspects of classical education relevant to our focus on communication and introduce you to figures such as Aristotle and Cicero, whom we will revisit later in the book. We will also discuss some more contemporary contributions to our understanding of message construction and reception. We will conclude the chapter with a brief discussion of different contexts today where the lessons of these ancient Greeks and Romans remain relevant.

PREP QUESTIONS

1. Describe the two differences between education today and education in the Classical Period? Why are rhetoric and speech no longer emphasized in education?

2. Discuss the relationship between civic engagement and public speaking. Provide a historical example of when someone engaged in civic engagement through communication.

3. List and define Cicero's five canons of rhetoric.

4. List the four functions of rhetoric, according to Aristotle.

5. Describe the three component parts of persuasion as defined by Aristotle.

6. Discuss the difference between artistic and inartistic proofs. Provide an example of each.

7. List and define Aristotle's three virtues of style.

8. Define discourse. Give an example of a discourse within your community in which there are diverse viewpoints regarding a specific social identity, such as race, gender, or religion, and explain how some of these views are more dominant than others.

9. What are three specific ways in which students in CMM 100 will learn how to participate in the discourses of their communities?

10. Summarize Isocrates' and Plato's views of rhetoric.

11. List the ten principles for ethical communication given in the chapter.

12. List Stephen Carter's three elements of integrity.

13. How did Aristotle define virtue? List six different virtues that a communicator could exhibit in his or her interactions with others.

14. Define demagoguery.

15. List and define two unethical uses of language.

16. What is dehumanization?

1

Communication as a Force in Our Lives

Right now, all across the country students are sitting down and learning how to communicate better. They are taking a similar class to the one you are enrolled in; some courses are titled Oral Communication, others maybe Introduction to Public Speaking, and others still perhaps refer to the class as Speech Communication. The point is, you are not alone, and what you are doing is nothing new. In fact, instruction in communication is rooted in a long tradition that we can trace back to at least classical Greece (approximately 490–322 BC). There remain, however, two significant differences between your educational experience and those of the Greeks.

The first is in the *nature of education*. For our purposes, the classical period refers to ancient Greece and the Roman Empire, and during that time education was not what it is today. Whereas today there is much government intervention and control over education (public schools, state-sponsored universities, etc.), in the classical period the state had very little influence over the nature of education. In fact, students could only receive an education in one of two ways: hiring a private instructor or attending one of very few schools. These options were only available to the wealthiest and most promising children. This model of education is nothing like what is available to students today.

The second major difference between education today and education in the classical period involves the curriculum. One of the fundamental tenets of an education in the Greek city-states or Roman Empire was *rhetoric*, which for them essentially meant the ability to speak well and persuade audiences. There were some who decried rhetoric in favor of philosophy, but there was no denying the importance placed on teaching people to speak well in the classical period. Today's education system, however, has moved away from this emphasis. Students are often only introduced to formal training in speech at the college level—and even there for only one semester with a focus on public speaking, instead of communication in a variety of contexts. Education today does not emphasize the importance of speaking well, and one of our aims with this book is to show you how speaking well should be as important today as it was in the days of the Greeks and Romans.

rhetoric
the ability to speak well and persuade audiences

Despite their different views about how best to teach communication and the definition and utility of rhetoric, the thinkers and practitioners of classical times would agree on the important role it serves in public life. They all knew public speaking could move people to action, change their beliefs, and educate the masses, and history has proven their understanding accurate. At key moments in our history, speech has helped moved us to war, shaped public attitudes and policies, and enabled us to express a definition of our identity with each other. There also have been important technological advances that have affected our ability to use communication to accomplish those tasks. In this section of the chapter we will briefly discuss the power of communication as a means of civic engagement and address how technology has influenced that power, especially in today's hyper-mediated world. Communication is a primary way of participating in the life of one's community and, through one's words and actions, shaping the thoughts, attitudes, and actions of others.

Public Communication as Civic Engagement

The ability to use symbols to communicate with each other is what makes us human. Even neuroscientists recognize that speech is the one cognitive ability that separates humans from other animals. In addition, communication is the way we negotiate and construct society's rules, values, and beliefs. To a considerable extent, the social world operates on the basis of assumptions that people share regarding what is good, right, or true. Consider the class that you are taking. Your behavior in this class from one day to the next is based on assumptions that you, your classmates, and your teacher share about your respective roles, the purpose of your being in the class, and the manner in which the class should operate. If you were to share different assumptions, then your class might operate very differently from how it does. Social reality, in a sense, is co-constructed by those who participate in it.[6]

civic engagement
acting upon a sharp awareness of one's own sense of responsibility to his or her community

The constructed quality of social reality highlights the degree to which human beings have choice and responsibility for the social world. If people want social reality to be different than what currently exists, then they must take responsibility for making it into what they desire it to be. *Civic engagement* occurs when people act upon a sharp awareness of their own sense of responsibility to their community. Unfortunately, our collective commitment to each other has seen a marked decline in recent years, despite enhancements in technology that make it easier than ever for us to communicate with each other.

For instance, Robert Putnam argued that our sense of community involvement and civic engagement has drastically decreased since the end of World War II, as evidenced by low voter turnout, decreased membership in civic organizations like the Rotary Club and Knights of Columbus, and reduced subscription rates to newspapers. These developments would shock the Greeks and Romans we discussed earlier, who saw civic engagement as one of the most fundamental duties of a citizen.

Even though we may not experience it in the intense way the Greeks and Romans did, communication remains central to civic engagement. Have you ever wondered how to "have your voice heard" on a subject? Perhaps your state is thinking of raising tuition. How do you respond? Communication! Maybe your town wants to raise property taxes. How do you fight such an action? Communication! Or how do you let a congressional representative know that you don't like his behavior? Communication! Communication is central to understanding and participating in public life.

At a meeting of the G-20 in London, England in March 2009, several thousand people rallied against the foreign leaders who gathered to talk about the world's economic troubles. How did they make their voices heard? They chanted, held posters and gave speeches throughout the day. This is an example of civic engagement at its finest. Without communication, all that would have happened would be a bunch of

The crowd at the G-20 protest in London in April 2009

people standing together in the middle of the street. Communication provided meaning for them, their purpose, and their protest. It allowed them to take an active role in the well-being of their community.

Communication also allows us to create and maintain relationships with each other. Language provides us with an opportunity to connect with others and find out what they like, what they don't like, and whether or not we have things in common with them. Language is a creative—and also potentially destructive—part of our lives, but it is central to all things that make us human. It can create strong relationships, and also, if used without care, can destroy associations with others. It can influence and evoke emotions and move us to action. It can teach us things about ourselves, others, and the world around us. It is the cornerstone of community.

Many classical scholars recognized the relationship between communication and civic engagement. They understood that rhetoric was central to a thriving democracy and that people needed to be taught how to effectively and ethically communicate their ideas to others. Good people who spoke well could create a healthy and thriving community. That belief still holds true today, and many contemporary communication scholars continue to explore ways to speak well and encourage civic engagement.

Cicero: An Example

One scholar who exemplified civic engagement was Marcus Tullius Cicero. Cicero was one of the most influential figures in the history of rhetoric. Born in 106 B.C. near Rome, he received a strong education in Roman schools and began a career in the courts, later moving into the Senate. Eventually he rose

Cicero

to the highest position in the Roman Republic, that of consul, and developed a reputation as a well-spoken champion of the people. Like many people in today's world, Cicero lived during tumultuous times, watching the rise and fall of Julius Caesar and the subsequent establishment of the Roman Empire under Octavian. Throughout his career, Cicero fought against the nobility and the threat of military dictators, and it ultimately resulted in his death.

Cicero contributed much to our understanding of communication, and he himself was a gifted orator, but eventually his speaking ability got him into trouble. During the Roman Civil War between Octavian and Marc Antony which followed the death of Julius Caesar, Cicero vocally fought against a dictatorship and found himself at odds with Marc Antony. Eventually, Antony had him killed and nailed his tongue and hands to the door of the Senate as a sign for all those that might have aligned themselves with Cicero against him. The hands and tongue were symbols of Cicero's ability to persuade others, and the nails a warning to those who followed in his footsteps. Such was the death of Cicero, and the beginning of the Roman Empire.

Despite Cicero's unfortunate and untimely end, his story is an example of civic engagement. Cicero used his words to persuade others to adopt what he believed was good and right for his society, even in the face of strong opposition. In doing so, he was acting upon a sharp awareness of his own responsibility for his community. We as practitioners of communication can follow Cicero's example and even use some of the methods and approaches that he advocated.

invention
••••••••••
the first canon of rhetoric in which you choose the best possible arguments for your case

In his works, notably *De Oratore* and *De Inventione*, Cicero explored what he called the five "canons" of rhetoric. A canon is a principle, rule, or criterion by which something can be judged or assessed. Cicero's five canons provide a structure for developing a strong speech or any other complex message that you might wish to deliver to an audience or listener. The first is *invention,* which is when you identify the best arguments for your case in a given situation. This is the creative dimension of message construction where you find the best possible way to convince someone to agree with you. If you wanted to argue that Mickey Mantle was the best baseball player of all time, you would invent, or choose, the way to support your case by deciding what to present about Mickey Mantle that supports your position and what not to present. You might need to do some research about Mickey Mantle to know what you could present in the first place, especially if initially you do not know much about him.

arrangement
•••••••••••••
the second canon of rhetoric in which you determine the most effective way to organize your case for the topic and the audience

The second of the five canons concerns organizing your arguments in the most effective manner. *Arrangement*, or finding the most effective way to organize your case for the topic and the audience, can be done in a variety of different ways. To arrange points in the best possible way requires that you understand your topic and your audience, because the most effective arguments on a given topic may not be the same for different audiences hearing a speech on the same topic. For example, political candidates make different arguments to different audiences when trying to get each group to vote for them. In some cases, you might choose to organize your message in a predetermined manner and might even create an outline of your main points. In other cases, you might decide to create a less rigid structure consisting of a number of talking points, which you could discuss in the moment, if your interaction with the audience seems to warrant addressing those points in a given order. We will look at various arrangement options available to you when we look at how to craft the different types of messages later.

Cicero's third canon refers to how you design the specifics of your speech. *Style* involves your word choices, phrasing, and the level of formality in the language you use to present your case to the recipient. All speakers have their own language style, and discovering yours will make this creative stage much easier and more enjoyable. Of course, style must also fit the situation and the audience. We cover the nuances of style in greater detail when we discuss language in a later chapter.

style
the third canon of rhetoric; involves word choice, phrasing, and the level of formality in the language you use to present your case to the audience

Today, people tend to place the most emphasis on the fourth of Cicero's five canons. *Delivery* refers to the manner in which you physically and vocally present your message. Although it has now become erroneously equated with an effective communicator, for Cicero, delivery was part of the process of delivering information or an appeal to others, but not the sole determining element of its effectiveness. In this way, he recognized the power of good delivery, but also by connecting it to the content itself cautioned against the dangers of overemphasizing physical and vocal delivery.

delivery
the fourth canon of rhetoric; the manner in which you physically and vocally present the speech

The final canon of rhetoric proposed by Cicero is less important today than it was during his time, but still remains a part of the communicative process. *Memory*, according to Cicero, refers to one's ability both to use memory to recall names and important information in the middle of an interaction as well as to deliver a cogent message without notes. The ability to speak without notes is less of a concern today thanks to things like PowerPoint and teleprompters, but in Classical Rome performing speeches without notes was a sign of eloquence and intelligence. That said, the ability to recall information relevant to a conversation or meeting and incorporate it into a response is still a valued skill today, and communicators must make decisions about how they will help themselves to remember the message once they begin interacting with the audience.

memory
the fifth canon of rhetoric; refers to one's ability to recall names and important information in the middle of a speech as well as to deliver a cogent speech without notes

Cicero's five canons provide communicators with a general structure that they can follow as they craft a message for an audience. Each canon can be understood as a set of interrelated tasks that a communicator must carry out as she or he prepares to engage an audience. One need not go through these tasks in a strictly linear manner. One can move back and forth among tasks as one makes decisions about the message that one is crafting and the manner in which she or he is planning to deliver it. Nonetheless, these tasks are likely to follow more-or-less the order in which Cicero lists the five canons, with invention coming first, arrangement and style following it, and delivery and memory being addressed last.

Aristotle and the Practice of Communication

Another contributor to the long tradition regarding communication as a form of civic engagement—perhaps the greatest contributor—was Aristotle. Aristotle lived in ancient Greece during the Fourth Century B.C., several hundred years before Cicero. Aristotle defined rhetoric as the means of identifying probabilities inherent in an issue or interpretation. When the truth of a matter could not be settled through philosophical means because the premises on which people might reach a decision were not known with absolute certainty, Aristotle believed that people could approach the good and true through rhetoric. He focused on rhetoric as a persuasive process. This is an approach still taken by scholars today. Despite his more favorable view of rhetoric, Aristotle understood the dangers inherent in a purely technical understanding of speech, so he conducted an exhaustive analysis of how persuasion works. In this analysis he determined three sources of persuasion, recognized two forms of proof for arguments, and identified the stylistic virtues for speech.

Aristotle taught his students about the interconnection of three component parts of persuasion. The first part he called *ethos*, or the credibility of the speaker. He felt that the more believable, honest, and learned on the subject a speaker was, then the more persuasive the message. In addition to ethos Aristotle proposed that *logos*, or the logical dimension of the appeal, contributed to a message's persuasive effect. Aristotle believed that persuasive messages must follow a logical order (which we will discuss in greater detail later in the book) that makes the case in a clear and cogent fashion to the recipients of the message; without this orderly argument, persuasion is much less likely to occur. The third source of persuasion Aristotle called *pathos*, which referred to the audience's disposition toward the topic. He said that language can be used by a speaker to emotionally connect audience members with a topic and thus move them to an ethical and correct action. Ethos, pathos, and logos each focus on a different dimension of persuasion: the speaker, audience, and message, respectively.

Aristotle referred to ethos, pathos, and logos as *artistic proof*, or something created by the speaker for the presentation. The speaker's credibility is dependent on the occasion and topic, and the emotions of the audience are also directly related to the message and thus both are crafted for the specific moment by the speaker. Likewise, you develop the logic in a message that is meant to sway an audience. The other form of proof identified by Aristotle, *inartistic proof*, concerned all the evidence, data, and documents that exist outside of the speaker and the audience but nevertheless can aid in persuasion. Inartistic proofs are not manufactured by the speaker in the same way as artistic proofs, even though a speaker might make use of them in the interaction with the audience.

Aristotle also understood that style played a part in the ultimate success or failure of persuasive appeals, and so he laid out three virtues of style by which *rhetors*, or speakers, should abide. These virtues of style stand as ideals that speakers should strive to attain in their efforts to communicate. The first stylistic virtue is *clarity*, or the ability of speakers to clearly articulate what they wish to say. Clarity manifests itself with simple, direct sentences, and we will discuss more about how to construct such messages in the chapter on language. For the moment, however, take note that the ability to develop clear messages is essential when speaking to one or one hundred people. Aristotle's second stylistic virtue, *correctness*, relates to the accuracy of information presented and the honest representation of the speaker. Quite obviously, this virtue is intimately tied to being an ethical speaker, which will be discussed further later in the book. Finally,

ethos
the credibility of the speaker

logos
the logical dimension of the appeal

pathos
the emotional dimensions of the appeal that can influence an audience's disposition toward the topic, speaker, or occasion

artistic proof
constructed by the speaker for the occasion; concerns ethos, pathos, and logos

inartistic proof
all the evidence, data, and documents that exist outside of the speaker and the audience, but nevertheless can aid in persuasion

rhetors
speakers

clarity
the ability of speakers to clearly articulate what they wish to say

correctness
the accuracy of information presented and the honest representation of the speaker

SPOTLIGHTING THEORISTS: ARISTOTLE

Aristotle (384–322 BC)

Born in the village of Stagiros, near what was then considered Macedonia, in northern Greece, this Greek philosopher and teacher was responsible for many contributions to rhetoric and public speaking. During his life he accomplished a great many things, including mentoring Alexander the Great of Macedonia.

Due to Aristotle's close connection to the kingdom of Macedon, many Greeks, especially those in Athens, probably viewed him with a great bit of suspicion. In 367 BC Aristotle moved to Athens to study under Plato at the Academy. Despite his fondness for Plato, Aristotle was much more realistic and practical in his approach to philosophy than his teacher. Aristotle used his education and exposure to great thinkers of his time while at the Academy to guide his academic pursuits. He was the first to outline what we refer to as formal logic, and he crafted an ethical code grounded in living a happy life rather than adhering to religious codes. Further, he developed a political philosophy vastly different from Plato's that found as its inspiration the democratic and constitutional governments of his time— approaches Plato clearly held in disdain.

In the 350s BC Aristotle taught rhetoric at the Academy, largely as an attempt to compete against the school opened by Isocrates. Aristotle's rhetoric courses focused on logic, in direct contrast to what Isocrates and his Sophistic plan of study offered. In 347 BC, just around the time Plato died, Aristotle left Athens and went abroad where he studied other subjects, like biology. Around 343 BC, however, he moved back to his roots at the request of King Philip of Macedon in order to educate the prince, Alexander.

Within eight years, but well after his tutelage under Aristotle ended, Alexander conquered Athens and Aristotle returned to the home of his mentor. In 335 BC Aristotle opened the Lyceum—his version of the Academy—and taught students there until the death of Alexander the Great in 323 BC. When Alexander passed, Aristotle gave his school over to his most prominent student, Theophrastus, and died a year later on the island of Euboea.[11]

Aristotle wrote extensively on a variety of subjects and remains one of the most influential philosophers on oratory, philosophy, logic, and politics in all of history. He serves as an excellent example of the importance of education. Even today he is one of the most recognized of all classical Greek thinkers and figures.

Aristotle emphasized the virtue of *propriety*, or good behavior and faithfulness to what one considers moral and just. Propriety, therefore, relates to the idea that a speaker should be both ethical and clear in content, but also in delivery. It is an overarching virtue that essentially encompasses both clarity and correctness, and is an important part of developing healthy relationships with other people.

propriety
good behavior and faithfulness to what one considers moral and just

Aristotle viewed rhetoric as an important component of civil society. Specifically, he noted that rhetoric, as a means rather than an end, fulfilled four functions in an open society. First, rhetoric allows for true and just ideas to prevail through open discussion, because he noted all things in debate are not equal and capable speakers need to advocate for them to win out. Second, in addition to the preservation of truth and justice, Aristotle also believed rhetoric offered the ability to instruct people on how to connect their ideas with the experiences of their audiences; in short, it allows us to teach others. Keep in mind, teaching, for Aristotle, occurred in a much smaller context than today with "classes" of only a handful of students. Third, Aristotle saw rhetoric as the means of analyzing both sides of a question—similar to the view taken by Protagoras. Finally, Aristotle understood rhetoric as a means to defend oneself, noting that speech and rational thought are abilities unique to human beings.[7] He understood communication as one of the most important tools a person can possess for engaging in civic life. Table 1.1 notes how these four can pragmatically be used today:

Table 1.1

Aristotle's Four Functions of Rhetoric	
Function	Example
Upholding truth and justice	In a courtroom
	In a legislative body
	In a classroom
Teaching to an audience	Classroom
	Encouraging civic engagement
	Pulpit
Analyzing both sides of a question	Jury
	Voting decision
	Making a final decision
Defending oneself	Personal or public disagreement
	On the witness stand

Aristotle felt that through the use of ethical and proper speech people could search for truth. Further, societies would become more open and therefore a sense of justice and fairness would be encouraged. He trained his students to examine arguments, defend themselves, and ultimately be able to teach the next generation these important skills. It is safe to say that Aristotle saw good communication skills as the foundation of a lasting productive civil society.

PARTICIPATING IN THE DISCOURSES OF ONE'S COMMUNITY

Today, scholars and students explore communication in a wide range of contexts. Cicero, Aristotle, and other early Greek rhetoricians were interested especially in speeches that members of a given community would give in public forums. Although many scholars and students today still examine political figures and their comments, others analyze the messages that everyday folks create in the context of their professional work and their involvements in the community because their words, more than any others, create the fabric of our society. For example, how people discuss race, ethnicity and even sports represents their understanding of the ties that bind us as a community. As people craft messages and transmit them to others, these others have an opportunity to respond to the views that they have expressed. They might agree with some of those views and might question others. As people express their understandings and respond to what others have expressed, a conversation results that shapes the social reality that these people share.

Accordingly, conversations such as these and other interactions between people, whether they take place in the context of one's professional life or in one's relationships with others in the community, are not simply empty talk. Through these interactions, people negotiate what is real and what is not, what is good and what is bad, what is right and what is wrong, and what ought to be done and what ought not to be done in given situations. Earlier in the chapter, we described the constructed character of social reality. The communication that we have with others might seem to be mundane and unimportant, yet each interaction is a site where people determine many aspects of the world in which they do live, as well as what sort of world in which they want to live. Conversations and other forms of communication are important contexts within which people figure out what it means to be members of a given community.

When many people talk about social reality in a similar or even shared way from one conversation to the next, a *discourse* exists. Metaphorically, a discourse can be understood as a stream of talk that flows throughout society, through which that society's members negotiate their social reality. Such talk consists not only of statements that people make about a given topic, but also practices in which people engage that have significance for themselves and others. On a college campus, such practices might include how people dress, with whom they sit when they visit the cafeteria, how they interact nonverbally with people whom they pass on their way to class, how they decorate their dorm rooms and houses, and even the classes that they take—any of which might communicate something to themselves and others about the social order. In any given community, there are many discourses, including discourses relating to race, ethnicity, gender, socioeconomic class, religion, politics, and age. A community such as the University of Dayton campus can be understood as a "field" where many different discourses converge, intersect, flow together, and even move against each other. Within any of these discourses, there might be different, even competing views of what is true and what is not, what is good and what is not, and what should be done and what should not be done. There also might be certain voices within a given discourse that carry a lot of influence, even authority, while other voices speak from a more marginalized place. As these streams of conversation flow within this field, people come to understand in particular ways the social world that they share and make decisions about how to live and act.[8]

discourse
communication of thought by words; talk; conversation

For instance, at the University of Dayton, there are many discourses of religion. One dominant discourse on campus is a discourse of Catholicism. This discourse is often reflected in the messages that University administrators craft and transmit to the campus as a whole and the conversations that occur in official events and activities on campus. Administrators use words such as "Marianist," "faith," "social justice," and "service." There are also other discourses of religion on campus, ones that reflect the concepts, ideas, values, and experiences associated with other faith traditions, such as Judaism, Islam, Hinduism, Parsee, and Bahá'í. Moreover, there are secular discourses that form the basis of people's sense of morality and purpose but are not associated with any religious tradition. Such discourses, while often viewed with some respect, have a more peripheral status in the overall discourse of the University. The holy days associated with some of these traditions, for instance, are not officially observed on the campus calendar. Many of the concepts and ideas that have significance to the followers of these traditions are typically not expressed in official documents or statements at the University as prominently as those that have meaning within the dominant Catholic discourse. Within each of these discourses, whether dominant or peripheral, people strive to understand their everyday lives and to decide how they should conduct themselves from one situation to the next, and not all adherents of a particular discursive tradition speak and act in the same ways. For instance, not all Catholics share the same beliefs or attitudes regarding their faith, nor do they practice their faith in the same ways. Sometimes people speak and act from a place that straddles two different discourses—for instance, if they identify with or have experience with two different religious traditions, perhaps because of diverse experiences within their family. When people participate in multiple discourses, they often can ask questions and contemplate possibilities that might not be visible to people speaking and acting from within any one of the discourses alone.

A good communicator in today's world, just like those in the days of Aristotle and Cicero, needs to be knowledgeable about the discourses within his or her community, so that she or he can create and deliver messages that will have the greatest potential for shaping the social world in ways that are both effective and ethical. There are many ways in which one might participate in the discourses of the community—or even the society—in which one lives and potentially have some influence on how others understand and act with regard to their shared social reality. In this course, you will learn about three of them.

public speaking
speaking where communication moves typically from one speaker to an audience of many

One way in which people participate in the discourses of their society is through *public speaking*. In public speaking, communication moves typically from one speaker to an audience of many. Certainly, you will give many presentations during the course of your professional life, regardless of the field that you enter. You also might be called upon by friends and neighbors, community organizations, or local governing bodies to present to audiences in the local community as well. Your purpose in giving a presentation can be informative or persuasive in nature; there are also other purposes as well. In this course, you will create and give a persuasive speech. In doing so, you will have an opportunity to contribute to the discourse here at the University and potentially influence people's beliefs, attitudes, and actions regarding some topic or issue.

A second way in which people can participate in the discourses of their society is by engaging another person in *one-to-one conversation*. A one-to-one conversation is similar to a speech in that the speaker might have prepared in advance what she or he wants to say and might be expected to take a leading role in the conversation that ensues. However, it differs from a speech in that conversations have a give-and-take quality, for participants share responsibility and ownership for the interaction in a manner that is more equal than in a speech. Accordingly, no one has full control over what happens. The listener might have questions or ideas or opinions to offer, which can change the trajectory of the interaction. Understanding needs to be created through the ongoing exchange between speaker and listener, even if the speaker and listener still expect to participate in the interaction to differing degrees. Similar to a speech, a one-to-one talk can have a variety of purposes, and one of the participants might play a more directive or leading role in the interaction. In this course, you will learn how to plan for and lead a talk to explain to your listener some concept, idea, person, place, process, or thing. An explanation involves giving information to a listener and helping him or her to understand that information. In this regard, it differs from persuasion in that your goal is not to change someone's attitude or to prompt them to take action in some way, but rather to help them to understand. What they do with that understanding is theirs to decide.

one-to-one conversation
a talk in which participants share responsibility and ownership for the interaction in a manner that is more equal than in a speech

A third way in which people can participate in the discourses of their society is to engage in *dialogue* about some controversial issue, especially within a group of peers. In dialogue, the primary goal is not to persuade or to explain, but to achieve mutual understanding. A dialogue is not a debate, so the aim is not to "win" or otherwise overcome the arguments that others put forth. Rather, the goal is to explore some topic on which there are different views, in a manner that allows the participants to understand each other's perspectives regarding the topic or issue at hand. Dialogues can be powerful spaces for ensuring that different perspectives within a community can be heard alongside each other without those who hold those perspectives falling into opposition. A dialogue also can be a space in which discourses that are more marginalized or peripheral have a greater opportunity to be explored than they otherwise might be.

dialogue
an interaction in which people with different perspectives seek to understand each others views; speaking so that others want to listen and listening so that others want to speak

Throughout this book, you will encounter excerpts of communicative events accompanied by a brief discussion of the issue the speaker addressed and how she or he approached it. The issues and speakers all vary, from as famous as Dr. Martin Luther King Jr., to as classical as Pericles of Athens, to as obscure as Newton Minow. What they all have in common is a genuine appreciation of the power of communication to affect their communities and the lives of their fellow citizens, and they all demonstrate an effective reading of the discourses already occurring within the communities that they addressed. For instance, take a look at the box in this chapter that discusses a speech by former First Lady Michelle Obama in which she sought to motivate the NAACP to get behind her fight against childhood obesity.

As the Greeks and Romans taught, exposing yourself to a great many ideas and examples of good communication is essential for learning how to become a better communicator. Even though the importance of communication as a means of civic engagement has remained constant throughout history, there have been some

Speech to the NAACP Comparing Improving Childhood Obesity to the Civil Rights Movement
by Michelle Obama

Delivered July 13, 2010, Kansas City, Missouri

First Ladies in the United States generally have a national agenda. Michelle Obama's cause is childhood obesity and she established a program entitled "Let's Move" to promote efforts to reduce childhood obesity.[20] She announced the program in early 2009 and it has remained a focus of her time as First Lady. She has delivered many speeches on the topic and in doing so she has kept a focus on the health of America's children. One of the reasons for her success is that she has what Aristotle would have termed strong ethos.

When Mrs. Obama spoke to the NAACP in Kansas City, Missouri, she had ethos, or credibility, not only due to the fact that she was the First Lady, but also because she was a working mother who had faced the task of feeding her children. She used this ethos effectively to reinforce her message.

Mrs. Obama noted some troubling statistics and spoke of the necessity to act immediately. She noted actions the government was taking but called on communities to get involved and individuals to exercise personal responsibility. Perhaps most importantly she told her audience that the battle could be won. In the conclusion of the speech, Mrs. Obama called for action from the NAACP by linking the childhood obesity problem to the struggle for equal rights. Here is an excerpt from her address that shows how she did just that: "Surely the men and women of the NAACP haven't spent a century organizing and advocating and working day and night only to raise the first generation in history that might be on track to live shorter lives than their parents. And that's why I've made improving the quality of our children's health one of my top priorities."[21] Her speech in Kansas City is an example of ethos, but more importantly of how speech is central to civic engagement and can be a source of positive change in society.

developments that have changed the way we use it to enact change and send messages to audiences of which we need to be aware. We especially need to be aware of certain ethical considerations as we craft and deliver our messages in order to shape social reality in particular ways.

SOME ETHICAL CONSIDERATIONS IN COMMUNICATION

Scholars and practitioners in ancient Greece noted the importance of ethics in communication, although they focused their attention on providing speakers—rather than audiences—with guidance for ethical message construction. They understood the immense power speech had over the actions of the public, and so in their schools they often took care to teach not just the skills of message construction and delivery, but how to wield them for the public good. For them, and for us today, why you say something is just as important as what you say and how you say it.

Isocrates and Plato: Two Early Advocates

Like Cicero and Aristotle, Isocrates was early advocate of communication as a form of civic engagement. He lived in ancient Greece during the Fourth Century B.C.. He opened a school where rhetoric and speech were core components of the education his students received. The School of Isocrates was expensive and highly selective. Isocrates was one of the first scholars to offer a view of communication as a form of ethical participation in the life of the community.

Isocrates taught his students that a person's capacity to know things was limited, and therefore to expect to know the right course of action in every situation and on every issue was impossible. For Isocrates, only a well-educated man could determine the best course of action through a well-informed, yet incomplete, opinion. He believed that "it is much better to form probable opinions about useful things than to have exact knowledge of useless things."[11] Essentially, Isocrates felt that in order to speak well in any context people needed to be well learned on a variety of subjects.

Isocrates also believed that good speakers were morally sound individuals who could discern right from wrong. He felt that education on many subjects was the best way to ensure ethical goals for a speaker. He also believed that ornate language and lofty sentence construction within a message about a worthy topic—which could only be identified by well-informed individuals—evidenced an ethical and moral person. This emphasis on style and content represents a sort of fusion of the approaches taken by Gorgias and Protagoras, two well-known teachers of rhetoric. It also illustrates an emphasis on teaching people to think before they speak, and not to profess to know things which they do not know.

Isocrates believed you could not teach people the appropriate thing to say in any given moment with a handbook, only through extensive repetition and exposure to civic life. This exemplifies Isocrates' approach to education commitment to the strength of community. He recognized that communicating effectively and ethically with one's own neighbors and fellow citizens was the bedrock upon which a thriving and vibrant community was built. That said, Isocrates influenced many great orators in his time and in the years that followed, especially those in the Roman rhetorical tradition.

A contemporary of Isocrates, Plato held a less than favorable view of the practitioners and writers in his time who advocated what has become known as the Sophistic approach to communication. The *Sophists* were itinerant teachers who traveled from city-state to city-state in classical Greece, training people in public speaking. While there was little unity to their various approaches, the Sophists focused principally on technique. Plato was skeptical of this approach. First, he believed that a focus only on technique was dangerous and not conducive to living what he termed "a good life," where understanding, justice, and living a just life were the ultimate goal for an individual. Plato referred to rhetoric as "a knack,"

Sophists
•••••••••
itinerant teachers who traveled from city-state to city-state in classical Greece, training people in public speaking

The Struggle for Human Rights
by Eleanor Roosevelt

Delivered September 28, 1948, Paris, France

Former First Lady of the United States, Eleanor Roosevelt, lived a privileged existence. Despite her well-off origins, however, she witnessed much hardship and human suffering during her life: the Great Depression and World War II. To her, human rights were a fundamental issue worth fighting for. After her time in the White House alongside her husband, Franklin Delano Roosevelt, she confronted her growing concern over the expansion of the Soviet Union and how its policies infringed on human rights.

Mrs. Roosevelt became an advocate for human rights and delivered many speeches on the subject. One of the more notable of these speeches was given at the Sorbonne in France, where she noted: "It was here the Declaration of the Rights of Man was proclaimed, and the great slogans of the French Revolution—liberty, equality, fraternity—fired the imagination of man."[5] Speaking at virtually the front door of the Soviet Union and its allies on these issues would have been a risky proposition for any speaker, but Mrs. Roosevelt found it important and necessary to do so.

Mrs. Roosevelt noted that the charter of the recently formed United Nations concerned human rights and that the Human Rights Commission was working on language concerning those rights. She also commented on the objections of the USSR and a few other countries and outlined differences between the United States and the Soviet country.

Mrs. Roosevelt recognized that achieving universal human rights would be difficult, but she concluded her speech with a prayerful message of hope: "I pray Almighty God that we may win another victory here for the rights and freedoms of all men."[6]

or trick and felt that the Sophists trained people in how to achieve personal goals through the use of persuasion that used language to manipulate public opinion. He believed, instead, that education should focus on philosophy, or the search for truth, rather than persuasion. Additionally, Plato felt not everyone was capable of conducting the arduous task of seeking and knowing the truth. He believed that the only people capable of doing so, and thus the only people who could tell the difference between good and bad, were philosophers, and therefore they should lead the people. In his famous book *The Republic*, Plato argued that leaders of this kind might still need to employ the knack of rhetoric to deceive the public for its own good. Rhetoric in a just society, for Plato, was an advocacy tool for the philosopher, nothing more.

Plato was skeptical, at best, regarding the use of rhetoric. He understood the way it was employed during his day as an evil, but when used properly in his vision of a just society, it became a utopian tool for philosophers. Regardless of the debate over which was better or more important—rhetoric or philosophy—Plato foreshadowed discussions about the power and purpose of speech that last to this day. He understood its power and, more importantly, its relationship to shaping the world around us.[12]

Some Principles of Ethical Communication

The ethical principles and duties laid out by classical thinkers, such as Isocrates and Plato, still apply today. Just as it was then, when we speak to the public today—be it to your fellow students, your church congregation or at a rally—we are asking them for their time, attention, and trust. Whenever we speak, we want someone's attention; thus, we ask them to place value in our message by committing time to listen to us. That value rests on their trust that we are interacting with them with more than our own self-interest in mind and that we are using ethical means in communicating with them.

Ethical communication requires, first, that the speaker is seeking a goal that has the audience's best interests in mind. One such moment when a speaker addressed a group with the global community's best interests in mind came following World War II when Eleanor Roosevelt spoke about human rights to a group in France. The issue of basic human rights is something that affects all of us, and speaking on behalf of protecting those rights represents a good and ethical goal. If we have good goals, we should also share our intentions with the audience honestly, and acknowledge any personal interests or biases we may have related to the topic.

As a more current example, let us take a look at charity work here on campus. Every December as the semester ends, UD delivers "Christmas on Campus." This celebration symbolizes the Catholic and Marianist tradition of the University of Dayton by inviting local families to campus to celebrate Christmas early. UD students "adopt" a child from the Dayton community and bring them to a decorated campus for an evening of fun and celebration. Every year students seek support for Christmas on Campus in the form of donations of time, treasure, and talents from members of the UD community. Talking to your friends to encourage support for Christmas on Campus would fit this description of ethical speaking because you would be seeking a good goal, and good speakers must have good goals. They must have more than their own self-interest in mind.

But ethical speaking is not just about achieving good goals or ends; it is also about the means we use to achieve those ends. Let's suppose you are seeking donations from your classmates for breast cancer research. As a piece of evidence, you state that there is a 75% chance that the other person's mother will develop breast cancer—except this data is not accurate and you do not even provide a source for the information. In fabricating the statistic, you would violate the principles of ethical speaking because you would not be defending the truth. Despite the fact this story may help your case and move someone to donate for a noble cause, the ends were achieved through deception and manipulation—two things not characteristic of ethical action. Additionally, it will damage your ethos, if the audience were to discover that you were using such means to convince them.

In this book, we offer ten principles for ethical communication. These principles provide a framework within which you as a speaker can make decisions about how to engage in the conversations that are taking place not only here on campus, but also in the wider community, in a manner that adheres to standards of ethical conduct on which there is a broad consensus among scholars within the field of communication. In this sense, these principles can help us to understand what constitute ethical means for communicating our message to others:

1. Speakers will respect all audience members, including those who may advocate different opinions from the one which they are advocating.

2. Speakers will not claim to be informed or an expert on a topic when they are not.

3. Speakers will ensure research sources are accurate and will not use false, fabricated, or irrelevant information in their presentations.

4. Speakers will not use demagoguery to move the audience.

5. Speakers will not use material from sources without giving them credit.

6. Speakers will not manipulate the audience solely by playing on their emotions.

7. Speakers will not have an agenda and will not advocate for something they do not believe in or would not do themselves.

8. Speakers will not deceive their audiences by concealing a hidden agenda.

9. Speakers will respect the amount of time they are given to deliver their message.

10. Speakers will not claim certainty when it does not exist.

integrity
a quality of discerning and acting on one's ethical principles

Acting in accordance with principle is fundamental to conducting oneself with *integrity*. Law professor Stephen Carter describes integrity as having three elements: "(1) *discerning* what is right and what is wrong, (2) *acting* on what you have discerned, even at personal cost, and (3) saying openly that you are acting on your understanding of right from wrong."[15] These principles require that you give thoughtful attention to the question of what makes something high or low in ethical quality, and that you then act in an ethical manner. The latter can be difficult to do, because others may disagree with your ethical judgment or may want you to act differently, even if they know it is not right. For example, if a professor asks you directly if your friend cheated on an exam, your guilty friend will likely be unhappy with you if you tell the truth, even if that friend recognizes truthfulness as the moral response. So, Carter acknowledges that doing the right thing won't always work out so well for you. But, if you are to maintain integrity, you have to accept those consequences. Living with integrity means sometimes suffering for doing what is right.

Communicating in a principled way demands that one develop certain qualities of character. One of the greatest lessons you can learn about communication is that your communication is shaped by your character. Various religious and secular perspectives throughout the ages have invoked the concept of character in their efforts to describe what constitutes ethical conduct. In his book *Nicomachean*

SPOTLIGHTING THEORISTS: RICHARD M. WEAVER

Richard M. Weaver (1910–1963)

Richard Weaver was born in North Carolina. Five years later his father died and his mother moved the family to Lexington, Kentucky. Weaver worked his way through school at the University of Kentucky and graduated with a degree in English in 1932. Upon graduating, Weaver was unable to find work given the poor economic climate created by the Great Depression. The young graduate was bitter and joined the Socialist Party, but after a few years its ideas fell out of favor with him and he left the party.

He eventually received a scholarship to Vanderbilt University and studied under John Crowe Ransom, where he was introduced to southern agrarianism, an anti-progress movement. In 1942 Weaver achieved a Ph.D. at Louisiana State University and began a career teaching and writing about rhetorical theory and composition.[6]

Weaver was very interested in the nature of human beings and how language was used in expression. Weaver became known for describing such ways of knowing as argument by definition. He was enthralled with orator Edmund Burke and the Lincoln-Douglas debates of 1858. Weaver was also interested in understanding how orators could use loaded words to make a point. He labeled these "god terms" and "devil terms." Weaver noted that god words, such as science, progress, freedom, and democracy, had positive cultural connotations, whereas devil words, such as communist and fascist, had negative connotations.[7] Weaver later declared that no words are value-free, because each contains a worldview.[8]

Weaver also wrote about culture and rhetoric's place in it. He felt that society in general was declining. Weaver noted that scientific progress was not all that should be considered when analyzing culture. He pointed to things such as scientism and cultural relativism as warning signs in the structure of societies.

Weaver died at age 53 in 1963.

Ethics, Aristotle defined character as a form of moral excellence. One's character can be described in terms of specific *virtues,* or personal qualities that manifest moral excellence and make one capable of performing noble deeds.[16] Aristotle explained that virtues are expressed when one finds the mean between extremes as one takes action. He identified several, including generosity, courage, temperance, gentleness, friendliness, truthfulness, fairness, and magnanimity. For instance, the virtue of courage is the mean between cowardice and foolhardiness. If one leans too far to one extreme as one responds to a situation, then one has failed to be courageous by acting out of fear. One, however, can lean too far towards the other extreme and act in a manner that is rash or reckless. This too is not courage. To be courageous, Aristotle argued, one must find the middle way between the two extremes. Only then could one's actions within the given situation be understood as virtuous.

virtues
....
personal qualities that manifest moral excellence and make one capable of performing noble deeds

Accordingly, you'll have to think carefully about what values you hold and how you live those values if you want to develop the type of integrity necessary to be effective at communication in a manner that goes beyond technical proficiency. Fortunately, UD offers many opportunities for you to do this through many CAP courses, co-curricular programming (such as through the Fitz Center or Campus Ministry), and elsewhere. Take advantage of this time to consider your values and develop your integrity, and it will serve you well in the workplace as well as in your personal life.

Some Unethical Means of Communication

When people do not approach their communication with others on the basis of principle, they are likely to resort to various means of unethical communication. One of these means is demagoguery. Unfortunately, many speakers today rely primarily on demagoguery when crafting appeals, even if they do not communicate outright mistruths. *Demagoguery* refers to speech that attempts to win over an audience through appealing to their prejudices and emotions, particularly those of fear, anger, and frustration. Unfortunately, the practice of demagoguery has become even more common with the advent of mediated communication and 24-hour news channels.

demagoguery

speech that attempts to win over an audience through appealing to their prejudices and emotions, particularly those of fear, anger, and frustration

Demagogues originally referred to leaders of the common people in classical Greece, but like today, the term carried a negative connotation that implied deceit, selfishness, and a desire to create mischief in the population. Demagogues typically seek to gain power for themselves by activating and exacerbating the darker side of human emotions. For example, Huey Long, governor of Louisiana in 1928, won election by demonizing the wealthy and corporate interests while promising a utopian community where "every man is a king, but no one wears a crown." He referred to the wealthy as "parasites" and used them as a target for the anger of the Louisiana public that had begun to feel the effects of an economic downturn.

Perhaps the most famous demagogue in American history was Senator Joe McCarthy who, in the 1950s, accused high-ranking officials, Hollywood celebrities, and even newsman Edward R. Murrow of being either communists or communist sympathizers bent on destroying the fabric of American society. This period, now referred to as the Red Scare, saw many people lose jobs and suffer damaged reputations that could not be repaired, even after McCarthy's accusations were discovered to be baseless and unfounded. His accusations created a public frenzy by playing solely on the public's fears of communism.

Emotions are an important part of effective message construction, but when speakers use emotions to further their own ends, or fabricate evidence to create particular emotional reactions in others, appealing to someone's emotions becomes unethical. There are plenty of emotional appeals that are both ethically constructed and designed to achieve ethical ends, but as a speaker we must be cognizant of both the means we use to move people to action and the action toward which we move them. Demagogues violate both of these principles by capitalizing on an audience's emotions to achieve personal, rather than communal, goals.

Those who resort to demagoguery in communication recognize the power of language in shaping people's perceptions. Language is a creative—and also potentially destructive—part of our lives, but it is central to all things that make us human. It can create strong relationships, and also, if used without care, can destroy associations with others. It can influence and evoke emotions and move us to action. It can teach us things about ourselves, others, and the world around us. It is the cornerstone of community. Language is a powerful tool that helps you accomplish the goals of any presentation or interaction. As the adage goes, though, with great power comes great responsibility, so you must be careful not to abuse language when interacting with other people.

Two ways in which communicators can use language that crosses the line from helpful to abusive are profanity and hate speech. The first of these ways, *profanity*, consists of coarse and irreverent language. To "profane" something is to treat something that is held to be sacred or worthy of reverence without any respect. Profanity is all around us—in movies, on the street, within songs and in many other places. Oftentimes we use this language because we let our emotions get the best of us, but that does not make it right. Comedian George Carlin had a routine in which he identified "the seven filthy words" that one could not say on public airwaves. Those seven words are common, but in some areas and within some cultures, other language that you may not believe to be offensive may be considered profane, so it is important to know your audience when making language choices. You would be less likely to use profanity in discussions at work or with your parents than with your friends, for instance. Monitor your own environment and word choice to avoid creating an uncomfortable atmosphere through your language choices.

profanity
coarse and irreverent language

Using profanity is seen by many people as unethical, unprofessional, and damaging to a person's credibility. If you use profanity in any situation you run the risk of aggravating and alienating those around you. Some instances may call upon you to use profane language, such as explaining George Carlin's monologue to a friend or group, and in a case like that it is important to let the other people know that some language you will use is necessary but is not meant to offend them. When you issue advance warnings of this form of language it makes you appear much more considerate and shows your understanding of the appropriate use of language.

The second way in which language can be used unethically is *hate speech*. Hate speech attacks or demeans a particular social or ethnic group, many times with the intent of inciting action against that group. Hate speech uses offensive and emotional language to incite anger in the audience, and neither the language nor the goal it is used to achieve is ethical. In the 1930s and 1940s Adolph Hitler used such language to move his country to war. He blamed the ills Germans faced on the Jewish community and began a program of systematic elimination of that group that we now refer to as the Holocaust. Kenneth Burke, a rhetorician who lived in the twentieth century, published an essay in 1939 that pointed out the power rooted in Hitler's unethical language.[17]

hate speech
rude and crude speech that attacks or demeans a particular social or ethnic group many times with the intent of inciting action against that group

Burke's analysis of Hitler's rhetoric provided the foundation for quite a bit of scholarship on similar language. Burke noted that Hitler's hate speech followed a particular structure whereby a social ill is found, a cause is identified, a defense of the good qualities of society is presented, and then action must be taken to rid society, or purify it, of the ill. One especially damaging quality of hate speech is the *dehumanization* of a particular social group. Dehumanization means making people seem less than human in order to more easily motivate action against them. For Hitler, Jews were portrayed as less than human, thereby making it easier to purge them from society. In other cases people compare enemies to rats, insects, or even diseases to make the audience appear better than the hated group and more willing to take action. Scholar Robert L. Ivie later took Burke's work and expanded it to illustrate that dehumanizing enemies in a battle makes it easier to motivate people to fight wars. Hate speech dehumanizes a particular group of people to make it easier for an audience to agree to action against them. For this reason it is often much more dangerous than profanity.

Rhetorician Richard Weaver also built upon the work of Burke by noting an additional way in which dehumanizing language manifests itself. He labeled certain loaded words "god terms" and "devil terms" and argued that society imbued such terms with positive and negative connotations that can affect the meaning of a message. He argued "god terms" like "science," "progress" and "democracy" always conveyed something positive to people, whereas words like "communist" and "tyranny" always connoted something negative. When someone or something was described using these words it circumvented arguments and immediately promoted a positive or negative view of an object or person. In hate speech, devil terms are prominent and help to bypass reason to capitalize on a person or group's emotions. Such efforts are both uncivil and unethical.

In general, we believe that practicing communication with civility is fundamental to conducting oneself in an ethical manner. We will explore civility in much greater depth in Chapter 11; however, it is valuable to take a moment to reflect on civil discourse as it relates to listening and speaking. Based on what you have already read in this chapter, it is easy to see that using language in ways that do not offend, alienate, or dehumanize others goes hand-in-hand with civility. We have all probably witnessed behaviors we would not call civil such as name calling, lying, gossiping, or even judging others based on gender, race, socioeconomic status, and/or age, just to name a few. We may have even engaged in some of this behavior ourselves. If we, as individuals, lived according the "Golden Rule" (do unto others as you would have done to you) perhaps we would all speak ethically and thereby help to create discourses that are edifying rather than debilitating in the communities of which we are part.

SUMMARY

In this chapter, we discussed how fundamental communication, understood as rhetoric, was to education in the classical period. We considered how communication can serve as a primary way of participating in the life of one's community and explored how two classical scholars, Cicero and Aristotle, contributed to a long tradition of understanding communication as civic engagement. We identified three ways in which people can participate in the discourses within their community through which people negotiate and co-construct their social world. Communicators must strive to communicate with audiences on the basis of certain ethical principles, while avoiding certain unethical communication practices. These practices include demagoguery and two unethical uses of language: profanity and hate speech.

KEY TERMS

arrangement 8

artistic proof 10

civic engagement 6

clarity 10

correctness 10

dehumanization 24

delivery 9

demagoguery 5

dialogue 15

discourse 13

ethos 10

hate speech 23

inartistic proof 10

integrity 20

invention 8

logos 10

one-to-one conversation 15

pathos 10

profanity 23

propriety 11

public speaking 14

rhetoric 5

rhetors 10

Sophists 17

style 9

virtues 21

REVIEW QUESTIONS

1. What is civic engagement?

2. What are three elements of persuasion identified by Aristotle?

3. What are the five parts of a message as proposed by Cicero?

4. What are the two major ways in which a greater emphasis on rhetoric in today's curriculum would improve our abilities?

5. What are some key principles for ethical communication?

6. What does it mean for a speaker to act as a demagogue?

7. What are two unethical uses of language?

ENDNOTES

1. Peter Green, *Alexander of Macedon: A Historical Biography* (Berkeley, CA: University of California Press, 1991), 54–56.
2. Ibid.
3. Ibid., 54.
4. Paul Cartledge, *Alexander the Great: The Hunt for a New Past* (Woodstock, NY: Overlook Press, 2004), 84.
5. Philip Freeman, *Alexander the Great* (New York, NY: Simon & Schuster, 2011), 24.
6. Peter L. Berger and Thomas Luckmann, *The Social Construction of Reality: A Treatise on the Sociology of Knowledge* (New York, NY: Anchor, 1967).
7. James A. Herrick, *The History and Theory of Rhetoric,* 4th ed. (Boston, MA: Pearson, 2009), 39.
8. Stanley Deetz, *Democracy in an Age of Corporate Colonization: Developments in Communication and the Politics of Everyday Life* (Albany, NY: SUNY, 1992).
9. http://blogs.abcnews.com/politicalpunch/2010/07/michelle-obama-to-the-naacp-now-is-not-the-time-to-rest-on-our-laurels.html (accessed April 30, 2017).
10. Ibid.
11. Quoted in Thomas M. Conley, *Rhetoric in the European Tradition* (Chicago, IL: University of Chicago Press, 1990), 18.
12. Herrick, 72.
13. http://www.americanrhetoric.com/speeches/eleanorroosevelt.htm (accessed May 9, 2011).
14. Ibid.
15. Stephen L. Carter, *Integrity* (New York: Harper Perennial, 1996), 7.
16. Aristotle, *Nicomachean Ethics* (Indianapolis: The Bobbs-Merrill Company, Inc., 1962).
17. Kenneth Burke, "The Rhetoric of Hitler's Battle," *The Philosophy of Literary Form,* 3rd ed. (1941; Berkeley, CA: University of California Press, 1973), 191-220.

SCENARIOS

Scenario 1

There are many recent social issues within the news media. Name a few. Discuss how specific groups or individuals are using communication as a form of civic engagement with regard to these issues. How would it be different if we lived in a society that didn't allow for the freedom of speech? How would this change our ability to enact social change?

Scenario 2

You are asked to give a speech to a group of high school students in a government class, explaining the contributions of four classical thinkers to understanding communication as civic engagement: Cicero, Aristotle, Isocrates, and Plato. Prepare the speech. Make sure to include an explanation of the terms and examples of each. Also, go through the five canons of rhetoric. How would you apply all of them when designing and presenting your speech? What types of artistic and inartistic proofs can you use to strengthen your argument?

Scenario 3

A company that handles the adoption of orphaned children comes to you for help in creating a strong persuasive commercial. Construct a brief commercial for the company that uses all three component parts of persuasion as introduced by Aristotle. Be creative!

Scenario 4

In 2010, MSNBC news commentator Keith Olbermann delivered a strongly-worded criticism on his show of Scott Brown, then a candidate for the open Senate seat in Massachusetts. Olbermann called Brown an "irresponsible, homophobic, racist, reactionary, ex-nude model, Tea Bagging supporter of violence against women, and against politicians with whom he disagrees." Initially refusing to apologize, Brown added "sexist" to the list of complaints in his following broadcast. After being criticized for the comments by other media outlets, including by comedian Jon Stewart, Olbermann apologized for the remarks.

1. Is Olbermann's remark an example of demagoguery? If so, explain why.

2. What are three specific examples of demagoguery you have heard in the media in the past year? Explain why each appeals to the prejudices of their potential audience.

3. While Olbermann was eventually let go by MSNBC, he soon found a job on another news network. In your own opinion, why do you think these kinds of messages keep finding their way onto the air?

Communication as a Transactional Process

CHAPTER OVERVIEW

2

- Explores two contemporary models for understanding communication as a process
- Examines the role of listening in the process of communication
- Covers the concept of communication apprehension and its relationship to the process of communication

Practically SPEAKING

Many people suffer from phobias of one sort or another. For example, those who suffer from arachnophobia fear spiders of all shapes and sizes. Then there are those who fear animals, who suffer from zoophobia. Perhaps you know someone with aerophobia, the fear of flying. Maybe one of your friends has nyctaphobia, the fear of the dark. There are other more unique fears, like triskaidekaphobia—the fear of the number thirteen— or the fear of old people (gerontophobia). One of the most debilitating fears happens to be agoraphobia, or the fear of public spaces that comes from a feeling of inescapability. People who suffer from this fear cannot even go outside their own homes without risk of severe anxiety.

Fear is as human an emotion as love or happiness, and so it is not a bad thing to be afraid of something. In fact, it can make you function better. Take the example of Oscar-winning actor Sir Laurence Olivier. Olivier, named to the American Film Institute's list of Greatest Male Stars of All Time,[1] suffered from debilitating anxiety attacks before performances.

From as early an age as five or six, Olivier demonstrated a penchant for drama and acting, creating a makeshift stage in his parents' house from window curtains and a wooden chest to perform for his sister, visiting neighbors, or extended family members. Olivier's formative years took place during World War I, a time when England's image of itself as Europe's dominant force came under fire. Despite his commitment to the lines of each of the plays and roles he would perform, Olivier still suffered stage fright, or performance anxiety.

One of the more poignant insights he offers to this fear was, "It comes in all sorts of forms; I suppose it's always there, but most of the time it hovers unseen."[2] Olivier also suffered from fear right before going on stage, describing it as "nothing like first-night nerves . . . the breathing becomes affected: the breath becomes shorter when you want it to become longer and deeper . . . you try to calm down but the sweat breaks out again. The voice in the head starts to ramble."[3] Do any of these feelings and emotions sound familiar when you prepare to deliver a speech? Well, fear not, because Olivier mastered his fear, made it work for him, and went on to become a world-renowned performer.

In this chapter we will first define and discuss exactly what performance anxiety is, as it goes by many names. We will then talk about the causes of it and provide strategies for managing it so it can help rather than hurt your efforts. We then talk about one of the skills we can develop as speakers and audience members that can help diminish our fear when we speak, and the fear of others when they speak: listening. If we can practice becoming courteous and effective listeners then we can create a more comfortable environment for speakers, no matter how nervous they are and no matter the situation in which they find themselves. Finally, we discuss the foundations of ethical message construction provided by the Greeks and Romans, and how those principles are manifested today.

PREP QUESTIONS

1. Compare and contrast the linear and transactional models of communication.

2. What is the difference between hearing and listening?

3. What are the three types of listening? Explain how they differ from each other.

4. How are active and passive listening different? Give an example of when you might engage in each type.

5. What are the three primary sources of distraction during a speech?

6. What are the four types of non-listening? Give an example of each.

7. Define communication apprehension.

8. What is self-fulfilling prophecy? Explain how it works with regard to public speaking.

CONTEMPORARY VIEWS OF COMMUNICATION

The classical scholars whose views we explored in the previous chapter represent a small sampling of those who contributed to the long tradition of understanding communication as civic engagement. They tended to focus on formal presentations because that is the type of communicative event that dominated the time in which they lived, but their contributions provided much of the foundation for the study and practice of communication today. Throughout this book we will introduce you to various other noteworthy figures and their contributions, some from the classical period and others from more contemporary times. The important thing to understand is that the practice of good communication between people and our understanding of rhetoric, speech, and persuasion have evolved over time. That evolution began with the works of these important individuals from classical times, yet today it has come to include the concepts and insights that innumerable contemporary scholars have offered through their own original research. In fact, contemporary scholars have developed different models that help explain the communication process that the Greeks first studied. Let's take a look at these more modern models and explore the components of the communication process as we understand it today.

The Linear Model of Communication

One of the first models that scholars and practitioners advanced was the linear model of communication. The linear model essentially describes communication as a process much like injecting someone with a drug. There are seven components to this model of communication. First, there is a *sender*, or the person who desires to deliver a message to another person or group of people. That person uses a symbol system, normally language, to encode the subject matter they wish to send. *Encoding* is the process of attaching symbols to your ideas and feelings so that others may understand them. The subject matter that is encoded is the *message,* or the actual content you send to an audience, and it can be both intentional and unintentional. That message is then sent through a *channel*, or the modes through which it is conveyed to another party. The traditional modes for transmitting messages is the voice or the written word; however, in today's society we also send messages through electronic channels like the radio, television, or the Internet.

sender
the person who desires to deliver a message to another person or group of people

encoding
the process of attaching symbols to ideas and feelings so that others may understand them

message
the actual content you send to an audience, both intentional and unintentional

channel
the mode through which the message is conveyed to another party

noise
......
anything that interferes with the encoding, transmission, and reception of a message

As the message travels through its channel it competes with other forces that sometimes disrupt its transmission. These disruptive forces are broadly referred to as *noise.* This term constitutes anything that interferes with the encoding, transmission, and reception of a message, and it can take many forms. When you think about noise, don't simply assume it is auditory, or the result of some loud "bang" or "boom." Noise certainly can include sounds, but it also includes environmental distractions such as scenery and temperature, personal biases and predispositions, anxiety, and confusing word choice by the speaker. It is an umbrella term for elements outside the message that can hamper its transmission from one party to another.

receiver
....
the person or persons who receive the en-coded message sent by the sender

The sixth and seventh components of the linear model of communication involve the party opposite the sender of the message. The *receiver* is the person or persons who receive the encoded message sent by the sender. Receivers are not always those for whom the message is intended. Think about when you have conversations with friends in Kennedy Union, or at a coffee shop. Yes, they will hear you and they are to whom you are speaking, but the workers and others in the room will also hear parts of, or even the whole conversation you have with your friends. They will not care much about it, but they still receive the message. There are always unintended recipients to messages we send, which only underscores our duty to pay close attention to what we say and where we say it. After all, how many times have you overheard something from a nearby conversation and then told someone else what you heard? Or, perhaps someone told you about a conversation they overheard.

decoding
....
the process of taking a message that has been sent and using one's own experiences and knowledge to give it meaning

Unintended receivers are only one of the potential issues that we need to be aware of when it comes to this part of the communication process. We also must understand that receivers decode messages using their own knowledge and experiences, and so they may not decode the same message you encoded for them. *Decoding* is the process of taking a message that has been sent and using one's own experiences and knowledge to give it meaning. Think about times when you have listened to a lecture in class and thought you heard the teacher say one thing, when they actually said something else. Sometimes this is due to words sounding alike, other times it is due to not paying close enough attention, and yet other times it happens when a speaker misspeaks or mispronounces something. Ultimately, we cannot control how an audience will decode the messages we send, but we can maximize the potential for their doing so accurately.

linear model of communication
....
communication process that involves a sender who encodes a message and sends it through a channel where it com-petes with distracting forces called noise while on its way to a receiver who then decodes the message

In summary, there are seven components to the basic *linear model of communication*: a *sender* who *encodes* a *message*, sends it through a *channel* where it competes with distracting forces called *noise* while on its way to a *receiver* who then *decodes* the message.[4] (see Figure 2.1). This model of communication is very speaker centered, as it puts the focus of communication on the sender and places the receiver at the end of the process.

For an example of communication situations where the linear model best explains what is happening, think of a YouTube video that broadcasts a taped message or presentation. In this context, the speaker sends a message through two channels (voice and video) to you as a receiver and there is no further interaction. It is

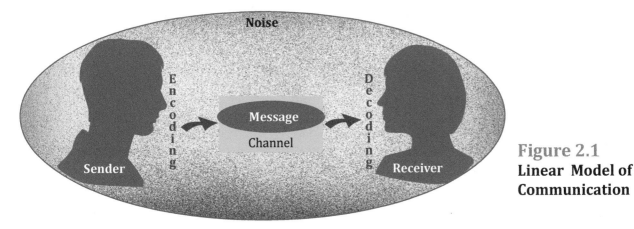

Figure 2.1
Linear Model of Communication

important to know that the model for understanding presentations like these is the Shannon-Weaver, or linear, model of the communication process. This model also serves as the foundation for understanding the other model of communication contemporary scholars have developed.

The Transactional Model of Communication

The linear model of communication, despite offering a clear explanation for the process of transmitting a message, does not adequately explain how all communication occurs—especially not even how most conversations take place. In fact, most communication does not occur in a one-way manner, but rather involves a constant exchange between the speaker and the audience. A more accurate model for this process is the *transactional model of communication*, which expands upon the linear model by recognizing and incorporating the notion that we serve as sender and receiver of messages simultaneously.[5] To do this, the transactional model adds an eighth component to the communication process.

transactional model of communication
recognizes that we simultaneously send and receive messages; a cyclical model of the communication process

This new component occurs after the receiver decodes a message, and is called feedback. *Feedback* consists of the responses and reactions to the messages transmitted by the sender and is itself a new message delivered to the original sender. The notion of feedback allows the both parties in the message process to simultaneously serve as sender and receiver of messages (see Figure 2.2). Feedback can be verbal, nonverbal, or both and it plays an important role in

feedback
the responses and reactions to the messages transmitted by the sender; is itself a new message sent back to the original sender

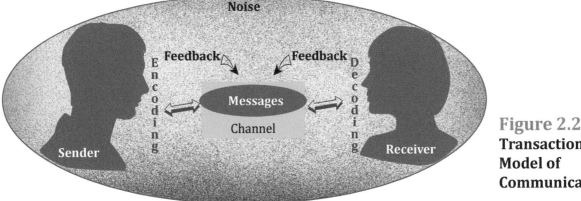

Figure 2.2
Transactional Model of Communication

any interaction, thus making the transactional model of communication a more appropriate explanation for communication.

The feedback we provide in a communication situation can alter an unfolding interaction and can let senders know about our impressions of the speaker and their message. Confused looks from a message recipient can tell a speaker to slow down and more thoroughly explain a concept, while head nods alert a speaker that the recipient agrees with what the speaker is saying. We will further explain audience feedback, what it means to you when delivering a speech, and how to adapt to it as a speaker when we cover audience analysis.

There is one very important aspect to take away from the transactional communication model of communication. We must always keep in mind that communication is an ongoing process, meaning that even as you deliver a message to an audience, the audience members communicate with you as well. Paying attention to the dynamics of the communication process when interacting with others will help enable you to better adapt to the moment and increase your effectiveness at getting your messages across to an audience.

Both the linear and transactional models of communication provide us with a logical way of understanding the communication process, but they cannot be understood as the "be all, end all" of the study of communication. In fact, several scholars have warned against emphasizing the development of models to the detriment of the more creative aspects of communication like language. Most notable among these contemporary thinkers is Marie Hochmuth Nichols, a former president of the Speech Association of America (now the National Communication Association) who called on her colleagues to understand the power of the spoken word. Hochmuth Nichols can best be understood as someone who defended the roots of the discipline found with Aristotle and the other classical figures we discussed earlier, but who also understood the potential of speech to change and affect the world around us. Both her understanding of the power of language, and the models developed in the middle of the twentieth century, provide important insight into how to craft effective messages in any context.

LISTENING AND COMMUNICATION

hearing
the physiological process of processing sounds, conducted by one's ears and brain

listening
the psychological process of making sense out of sounds

Understanding communication as a transaction between sender and receiver emphasizes the central importance of listening in communication. People often confuse listening with hearing when in fact they are quite different. *Hearing* is a physiological process of capturing sound, conducted by ears and brains. *Listening* is the psychological process of making sense out of sounds, and involves paying attention to the external world. Listening is an important skill for both speakers and audiences. For some rhetors, knowing that many people will be paying attention to them when they speak causes a high level of anxiety and is a contributing factor to their fear of public speaking. For others, the intense focus of one person in an interaction can also cause discomfort. But like many things, once we understand what listening is and how people use it our level of discomfort in either situation will lessen. This part of the chapter will help you understand the

SPOTLIGHTING THEORISTS: MARIE HOCHMUTH NICHOLS

Marie Hochmuth Nichols (1908–1977)

Marie Hochmuth Nichols's influential career covered more than three decades. She was one of the more preeminent rhetorical scholars, teachers, and leaders in the communication discipline during the twentieth century. She was the first female president elected by the entire membership of the Speech Communication Association in 1969 and shepherded the discipline through a tumultuous period of transition.[15] Nichols also served as editor of the most prestigious periodical of rhetoric and public address, *The Quarterly Journal of Speech*. In 1976 she was awarded the Speech Communication Association's Distinguished Award.[16]

Nichols was a scholar of both theory and criticism in the neo-Aristotelian tradition. She also was heavily influenced by the work of Kenneth Burke and I. A. Richards.[17] Nichols published many essays; two of the most prominent were "Lincoln's First Inaugural Address" in 1954 and "The Criticism of Rhetoric" in 1955. In these and other essays she argued in defense of the discipline of communication and called on people to focus less on developing models and paradigms, and more on the ends and purposes of speech.

Specifically, she contended that the communication discipline is, and always will be, about understanding the uses and power of verbal symbols.

So highly regarded was Dr. Nichols that the National Communication Association (formerly the Speech Communication Association) named one of its most prestigious awards, the Marie Hochmuth Nichols Award, in her honor. It is awarded for published works in public address. In 1983 Kathleen Hall Jamieson issued the highest of praises for Nichols: "Some of us command an encyclical; some of us command a single rhetorical theorist; some of us command a rhetorical period. Marie Hochmuth Nichols commanded the tradition."[18]

complex nature of the different types of listening audiences employ, as well as discuss the importance of listening for all parties in a communicative interaction.

Listening for Speakers and Audiences

Both senders and receivers engage in listening, and it is important to understand the importance it holds for both parties. Speakers use listening as a means of measuring whether their audience receives their message, and how to adapt if they determine people are not getting the intended message. Audience members use listening to gather information and form judgments; however, listening properly is far more difficult for them than for speakers.

Listening should be thought of as more than simply making sense of sounds, as it encompasses paying attention to nonverbal messages and processing them as well. Speakers listen both to the audience's verbal responses to statements—which can be as simple as making grunts of agreement or disagreement, or shouts of praise, or as complicated as logical expressions of agreement or disagreement—and their nonverbal actions which can include leaving the presentation, staring off at something else, or even nodding off during a conversation. All of these actions indicate to a speaker who listens that changes need to be made in order to return the audience's attention to the message.

One way in which listening skills are exceedingly helpful for speakers is during a question and answer session or informal discussion. In fact, more is said about how much an audience learned by the questions they ask than from any statement they may make. Questions can be quite telling about a recipient's retention of the message. In ancient Greece, Socrates knew this all too well, as he developed a method of inquiry that balanced speaking with listening. *Socratic questioning* is the process of asking questions of a speaker focused on their responses to previous questions; its ultimate goal is to uncover the truth.

Socratic questioning
the process of asking questions of a speaker focused on the responses to previous questions; its ultimate goal is to uncover the truth

Audience members face a harder time listening than speakers do because there are so many distractions that can keep them from focusing on the message. After all, the average human attention span is not very long and ranges anywhere from a few seconds to about 10 minutes, depending on the subject to which they are paying attention. When audience members do not pay attention to a speaker and the speaker notices, it may heighten the speaker's level of anxiety as they may believe the speech is boring and lose confidence in their speaking ability. It also may aggravate the speaker. Consider a phone call with a friend or family member when you suddenly feel like the person on the other end is not paying attention. Or, think about a moment when you told someone a story and the listener started to check their phone or look around the room. These are evidence of not only poor listening, but incivility and a lack of respect toward the speaker. It is, therefore, an audience's ethical obligation to maintain attention to the speaker and the message as much as possible.

Types of Listening

Often when people speak before an audience, they feel a considerable amount of anxiety. One of the main reasons audience listening makes speakers nervous is because they are afraid the audience will catch them making a mistake or saying something inaccurate and call them on it. Although that is a possibility in some situations, it is not common and only reflects one form of listening. There are, in fact, three listening purposes and two listening types audiences employ, and each engenders a response by the audience to the speaker and the message.

listening for appreciation
listening for enjoyment; not high in cognitive commitment

The first listening purpose is for appreciation. *Listening for appreciation* encompasses activities where you listen for enjoyment. Starting your favorite playlist on your way to work or listening to the radio is an example of listening for appreciation. It also occurs in the company of friends and family when you are joking around and relaxing. People often listen

SPOTLIGHTING THEORISTS: SOCRATES

Socrates (469–399 BC)

Virtually all we know of Socrates comes to us by way of his student, Plato, and his contemporaries Xenophon and Aristophanes, because he himself did not write any philosophical texts. Socrates perfected the art of listening to criticize through what we now call the Socratic method and Socratic questioning. In Ancient Greece, Socrates would wander through the marketplace questioning the political and moral positions of people in Athens. He did so by carefully listening to them and then asking questions about their statements. His questions almost invariably illustrated significant problems with the philosophies of his contemporaries. This would not have been possible had Socrates not carefully listened to, and critically analyzed, the positions they took. He can rightly be considered the father of modern logical intellectual inquiry, but even more to the point, he demonstrated the power and purpose of listening carefully to the messages of others.

Socrates was an Athenian who devoted his life to teaching philosophy, although according to Plato he did not accept payment for his educational services. He went through life financially poor, but was highly regarded by his students. In addition to his teaching efforts he also served in the military during three Athenian campaigns.

Socrates lived in Athens during a time of turmoil, when neighboring Sparta and its allies defeated Athens. After this defeat, Athenians seemed to have doubts about democracy, and from Plato we can see how Socrates may very well have shared those doubts. One of his greatest roles during this time was as moral and social critic of the city he loved, leading to eventual problems with those in power at the time. Greeks at the time held a "might makes right" philosophy toward justice and governance and Socrates vehemently disagreed with this position.

Plato called Socrates the "gadfly of the state" because he spurred Athens into action through his various encounters with leaders, philosophers, and politicians. The story goes that one of Socrates' friends asked the Oracle at Delphi who was wiser than Socrates, and the Oracle responded that no such person existed. Upon hearing what he believed to be an erroneous statement, Socrates set out to show that there were wiser people throughout Greece by entering into dialogues with politicians and philosophers.

He used a dialectic method of discussion in these conversations whereby he would solve what he saw as problems by breaking problems down into a series of questions that eventually produced the answers sought by those around them. These discussions almost always centered on moral and social dilemmas and the concepts of justice and goodness.

Socrates' questioning agitated the leaders of Athens because he often made them look foolish. They eventually had him arrested. When convicted he was sentenced to death, and despite the opportunity to flee and escape prison, he decided to stay and face judgment. Socrates was forced to drink a cup of hemlock, a poison, and died in his cell. His philosophy, however, has survived 2,400 years and greatly influenced Western thought.

for appreciation when others tell stories that resonate with and move them. In these moments, audiences are not waiting in the wings to pounce on an incorrect statement or to disagree with a speaker; they are listening to relax. Audiences often do not employ high levels of cognitive commitment when they are listening for appreciation, though they might be highly engaged emotionally or in other ways—for instance, if they too are participating in the telling of a story or are contributing to the enactment of a particular episode, rendering, or performance.

listening to comprehend
....
listening to understand a concept or message

A second purpose of listening is *listening to comprehend*. When we try to understand a message or learn about something we do not know we listen to comprehend. This listening purpose involves a higher level of cognitive commitment than listening for appreciation because we pay attention to the message in order to gather and store information about a topic. Think of classroom lectures, business meetings, discussions about household matters with a spouse or partner, or watching news broadcasts as examples of listening to comprehend. We do not look for things to argue about in an instructor's lecture; rather, we take notes so we can learn about something with which we are unfamiliar. It is about understanding the messages presented by others, and obtaining clarification if there is confusion after the speaker is finished. We do this in a variety of ways:

- Asking specific questions about the parts that were confusing
- Paraphrasing the speaker's message in a response
- Qualifying your response with statements like "Correct me if I am wrong," or something similar
- Like listening for appreciation, this type of listening by an audience is not combative.

listening to criticize
....
listening to make a judgment about a message; involves a high level of cognitive commitment on the part of the audience

The final purpose of listening is the one we almost always ascribe to audiences, even when it is not what they are doing. *Listening to criticize,* or listening to evaluate, entails paying attention to the information and the argument presented by the speaker so that we can make a judgment about the message. Listening to a political candidate's speech is a prime example of listening to criticize, as can be disputes with friends over their beliefs or ideas on particular subjects. The word criticize holds such a negative connotation, however, that most people fear this type of listening because they equate criticism with negative attacks, when in actuality it is simply the expression of an analysis or interpretation of data. Unfortunately, the negative perception distorts the true benefits of this type of listening by an audience, such as encouraging debate and dialogue. Critical listening is a fundamental part of any thriving democracy and is not something to fear. When we listen to criticize we are not looking to attack speakers or even make negative judgments about them; we are merely evaluating their message on its merits, and sometimes people simply must agree to disagree. To properly employ critical listening, however, requires that as message recipients we understand the ideas presented by the speaker and reflect upon them before issuing any assessment of them.

active listening
....
listening to understand a message by processing, storing, and potentially evaluating a message; also involves reactions by the listener in some form

In general, people should strive to engage in what is called *active listening*. Active listening occurs when audiences have high cognitive involvement with the speaker's message, and seek to understand the message. In other words, they are processing, storing and potentially evaluating it as it is being delivered. In this regard, active listening is most likely to occur when someone is listening to comprehend or listening to criticize. Moreover, active listening also involves some form of reaction by the listeners to demonstrate that they are gathering the data being presented. In contrast, *passive listening* is listening without reacting, although the listener may well receive the information presented. Passive listeners do not raise hands or inquire during a presentation, and typically show no reaction in a conversation either. This is the "sponge" approach to listening and can be risky if you do not understand something being said. Listeners are more likely to take a passive approach if they are listening to comprehend or listening for appreciation. When it takes place during the latter then the sounds are often referred to as background noise. While in some cases, it might be safe to put less energy and attention into the listening process, if it is important to understand the message accurately, to make a critical decision about what is being said, or to have a deep appreciation for the message, then one must resist the temptation to be passive, given the many obstacles that one is likely to face when listening to others.

passive listening
listening without reacting

One reason why active listening is important is because there is a difference between how you speak and how your brain functions. You speak at a rate of approximately 120 to 150 words per minute, but your brain processes words at over 600 words per minute, resulting in lots of time for your mind to wander. This time is referred to as *spare brain time*, or the time available for your mind to wander due to your ability to process messages faster than it takes to construct them. Be aware that spare brain time makes it easy for your mind to wander to other things when you should be listening to a conversation. Spare brain time refers to concentration, which is necessary for sending and receiving messages successfully.

spare brain time
the time available for your mind to wander due to your ability to process messages faster than it takes to construct them

Some noise, like background noise, does not affect a person's ability to concentrate or listen attentively; however, other noise can interfere with a person's ability to receive a speaker's message. These noises are distractions, and in the next section we will discuss several different types of distractions that can negatively impact someone's ability to listen and thus create a more challenging atmosphere for successful communication to take place.

Overcoming Distractions

Distractions can engender an uncomfortable atmosphere for senders and receivers. Some of these distractions occur because of a person's reactions to fear, while others are external to the people involved in the interaction. Nevertheless, all of these can inhibit a person's ability to listen.

Biological reactions to the environment in both speakers and audience members can distract them from listening. Think about a situation where you are in a room that is too cold, or perhaps too hot. How hard is it to pay attention to the lecture in that room? It is likely difficult. Or perhaps you are ill, have a headache, or are hungry—all biological responses that diminish your capacity to pay attention to a message. Such experiences also can interfere with people's efforts to speak. When some people get hungry, their mood becomes irritable, and if this is a spouse or partner it creates a delicate communication situation. So, how do we overcome these distractions?

Table 2.5

Dealing with Distractions	
Type of Distraction	**Coping with Distractions**
Biological	Be sure to get enough rest and food and water, and if ill let the audience know
Environmental	Clear focus and acknowledge them to the audience
Hecklers	Ignore them Directly address them The audience may support the speaker

Unfortunately, there are few remedies other than concentration and focus. You could try and eat or drink before a speech if you are hungry, and in fact if you are the speaker you should go into the presentation with a satisfied stomach. If you are ill, you could take medication, but even then the best course would be to acknowledge the illness to the people you are interacting with at the outset so they are aware of it and do not spend time distracted by your reactions to the affliction.

In addition to biological distractions, there may be environmental occurrences that draw attention away from the presentation. Airplanes flying overhead, cars driving by, people coughing or sneezing, and even the howling of the wind can all cause both speakers and listeners to turn their attention somewhere other than the message. Again, the best answer to these distractions is to focus on the interaction and not the environment. After all, the brain is physically incapable of multitasking, so choose which is more important to pay attention to: the conversation or the airplane flyingoverhead.

The final type of distraction we will cover is the rarest of them, and predominantly concerns the context of public speaking: hecklers. Hecklers are those individuals who seek to interrupt a presentation to inject their own viewpoint, either through insult, unsolicited questions, or unwarranted commentary. Heckling could quite possibly be the most unethical behavior an audience member can display. Hecklers have appeared at political speeches, guest lectures by faculty, and even during comedy shows. In fact, comedian Louis C.K. called out a heckler during one of his live albums, explaining that the person was destroying the experience for everyone else.

There are two ways speakers can deal with hecklers, and two ways audience members can help deal with hecklers as well. Speakers can choose to ignore hecklers in the hopes that they will eventually quiet down because they are not receiving attention. Rhetors also can acknowledge the hecklers and ask them to be quiet or face removal from the area. Audiences can also help control hecklers by ignoring them, especially if this follows the lead of the speaker. They also can confront the heckler and express their displeasure with that person's behavior. Either way, hecklers can make both speakers and audiences uncomfortable for as long as they are making their unwanted intrusions loud enough that people can hear them. Choosing to be an attentive listener who allows speakers the opportunity to say their piece prevents this type of behavior from occurring and contributes to creating a more comfortable atmosphere for a presentation.

Types of Nonlistening

Oftentimes we think we listen, when in fact we do not. What we are doing is called *nonlistening*, or providing the appearance of listening without actually paying complete attention to the message. Nonlistening comes in a variety of forms, and in each instance we believe, or pretend, that we are listening, but in fact are not.

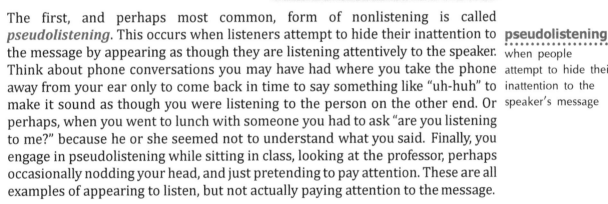

nonlistening
providing the appearance of listening without actually paying complete attention to the message

The first, and perhaps most common, form of nonlistening is called *pseudolistening*. This occurs when listeners attempt to hide their inattention to the message by appearing as though they are listening attentively to the speaker. Think about phone conversations you may have had where you take the phone away from your ear only to come back in time to say something like "uh-huh" to make it sound as though you were listening to the person on the other end. Or perhaps, when you went to lunch with someone you had to ask "are you listening to me?" because he or she seemed not to understand what you said. Finally, you engage in pseudolistening while sitting in class, looking at the professor, perhaps occasionally nodding your head, and just pretending to pay attention. These are all examples of appearing to listen, but not actually paying attention to the message.

pseudolistening
when people attempt to hide their inattention to the speaker's message

A second form of nonlistening is *glazing over*. At some point in all our lives we started to look out the window or stare at a wall during a lecture in school, only to realize later that we missed important information. This daydreaming is a form of nonlistening common to situations where the audience is not enthralled with the topic. Although it may appear somewhat benign, speakers may internalize this as their poor speaking skills creating boredom in their audience. Your lack of focus thus can negatively impact the other person in ways you may not intend.

glazing over
daydreaming instead of hearing the message

Ambushing is a third form of nonlistening in which audiences may engage. This involves selecting only the weaknesses of a message and ignoring the strengths of the speaker's argument. It is a negative form of nonlistening that can encourage a hostile atmosphere that increases a speaker's anxiety toward participating in an interaction. It is important to listen to someone with an open mind and judge the message on all its merits, not only on selected points that are made. This is the listening version of the straw man fallacy in crafting a logical argument, which we will discuss later.

ambushing
selective listening in which the audience ignores the strengths of a message and hears only the weaknesses

prejudging
....
entering into a presentation with a judgment already formed about the message being delivered

Prejudging is the last form of nonlistening we will explore. It is dangerous and a potentially negative form that stems from an audience member's inability to enter the presentation with an open mind. Audience members have an ethical obligation to enter into any interaction with an open mind and allow a person to make their case. If you have already formed an opinion prior to the event and are unwilling to change it, then the interaction is pointless. For example: Suppose your university has been raising student fees quite often. An SGA representative is coming to your organization and you know they support yet another increase in mandatory student fees. Your passion and attitude about the topic would make it easy for you to already have a decision made before they even begin their speech.

Most times a speaker can easily determine whether people have prejudged the speech and the speaker before a word is spoken, which is not fair to the audience or the speaker. Listen for the evidence and the argument and then make your judgment.

Listening is an important skill for communicators and it should be treated as such. When both sides are attuned to the message, they create a more comfortable speaking situation and help to reduce speech anxiety for everyone involved.

MANAGING COMMUNICATION APPREHENSION

For many people, communicating with others can evoke feelings of intense apprehension. These feelings can constitute a significant element of noise in the communication process, which can affect how one participates in the communication process overall. Communication apprehension can affect how people encode messages, how they transmit those messages, how they decode messages, how they perceive the context of the interaction, the channels that they select for transmitting a message, and how they send and receive feedback from others. Speaking, especially in front of a group, represents one of the most frightening experiences possible for a great many people. The fear of speaking in front of a group, also called performance anxiety or stage fright, is a specific manifestation of *sociophobia*, or the fear of people and/or social situations. The fear of speaking is essentially a combination of any of the following fears: fear of rejection, fear of criticism, fear of judgment, and fear of failure. In this section we will illustrate the academic definition of the fear of speaking and then learn about what students fear most when they speak in front of audiences.

sociophobia
....
the fear of social situations or people

communication apprehension
....
the fear or anxiety associated with real or anticipated communication with another or others

Academics call the fear of speech *communication apprehension* and define it as "the fear or anxiety associated with real or anticipated communication with another or others."[9] Communication scholars apply this definition to a variety of speaking situations, as it also helps to define shyness in interpersonal situations. Here you see why there are multiple ways of describing fear of public communication. People often use the terms fear and anxiety to mean the same thing, even though academics might use these terms to refer to different experiences.

What is important to realize is that everyone experiences both fear and anxiety in their lives. Perhaps things get really busy at work and you become easily agitated over things that normally do not bother you. Some individuals experience abnormal

levels of anxiety, or who become anxious for no reason at all. These people have what psychologists call an *anxiety disorder*. A perfect example of someone with an anxiety disorder is the fictional character Sheldon Cooper from the CBS award winning show *The Big Bang Theory*. Sheldon suffers from multiple phobias as well as obsessive compulsive disorder, significantly hampering his ability to function in mainstream society. His anxiety prohibits him from functioning, whereas normal anxiety does not do that, although it does cause a level of discomfort.

anxiety disorder
abnormal mental outlook in which individuals experience high levels of apprehension that keep them from living life

Causes of Communication Apprehension

Communication apprehension is often the result of a variety of factors, ranging from specific fears about the situation, aspects of a person's personality, or the physiological make- up of an individual. Environmental factors concern those things in the physical situation in which you find yourself. Psychological factors that influence speech anxiety include your approach to everyday life and how you handle stress. Finally, different people have different physiological reactions, in which their bodies involuntarily respond to stimuli that are present in their surroundings.

Three environmental factors influence a person's level of anxiety when speaking, and each stems from fundamental differences in the nature of the communication situation. The first two involve the audience. An audience for a speech is typically much larger than that of any conversation, and so we often find groups intimidating. That intimidation can sometimes increase even more when we are not as familiar with the people to whom we are speaking. For example, you probably feel more nervous talking to a group of strangers than you would to a group of friends. The third environmental influence is *spotlight syndrome*, or the perception encouraged by the room setup that all eyes are focused on you as the speaker. This can affect students in a classroom by inhibiting them from asking questions or making comments.

spotlight syndrome
the belief encouraged by the room setup that all eyes are focused on you as the speaker

Environmental factors don't only manifest when we're delivering presentations or are in front of large, unfamiliar crowds. Consider a first date. The audience for the evening is just one person, but the desire to connect with and impress that person can cause a great degree of pressure. The same effect is what causes nervousness in job interviews and in meeting roommates for the first time. So, just as large audiences can intimidate people, smaller and more intimate environments can as well.

The public speaking environment is different from the atmosphere for most conversations in other ways as well. Public speaking uses more formal language, has a very structured format, and involves more than just a few people. Conversations are less structured, often employ slang, and typically involve only a few people. Differences aside, the two situations share certain characteristics, and understanding those common components can help reduce anxiety over speaking in public or interpersonally.

Conversations and public speaking share several elements that make them more similar than they are different. Both entail extensive nonverbal communication when delivering messages and receiving feedback. Both call on you to logically organize your thoughts. Public speaking and conversation also require you to adapt to audience feedback in order to tell a story in the most effective manner possible. Finally, in both situations you need to tailor your message to the audience. All told, conversations and public speaking have far more commonalities than differences! So, just think of public speaking as having multiple conversations at the same time and your anxiety will be dramatically reduced. Or, think of conversations as different formats for presentations and put as much preparation into what you say in those situations as you would preparing to deliver formal remarks.

Table 2.2

Differences and Similarities in Conversation and Public Speaking	
Differences	**Similarities**
• Public speaking has more formal language • Public format is more structured • Public speaking involves more than a few people	• Use of nonverbal communication • Logic is needed • Must adapt to feedback • Message is tailored to the audience

The environment is only one set of influences on people's anxiety; their mental approach also can contribute to heightened stress in advance of an interaction. Thus, some psychological factors may cause us apprehension, as well. Many people believe that effective communication is a talent and not a skill. The fact is communication is a skill, something that can be learned, and not a talent that they're either born with or not. They enter into a speaking situation under the false assumption that they lack the tools necessary to effectively deliver a message to another person. In other cases, they falsely believe they are naturally good at persuasion or explanation and so become too overconfident in their abilities. Through practice and experience you can become a very effective communicator.

self-fulfilling prophecy
believing that something will happen before it actually does, and then when it does come true it reinforces the original expectation

Psychological elements can also contribute to a person's reluctance to engage others in conversation. Many people, especially as their time to speak draws near, allow worrisome thoughts to creep into their mind, creating a *self-fulfilling prophecy*. If you convince yourself that you will not perform well, you will invariably not practice well, and then the performance will be poor, resulting in the original expectation coming to fruition. This and other forms of worrisome thoughts can cloud a speaker's mind to the point where it increases their anxiety and gets in the way of a successful performance or interaction.

Nerves are not merely psychological; they appear in physical ways as well. When we get nervous we experience involuntary physiological reactions like an increase in heart rate, blushing and perspiration. These are our bodies' ways of responding to stress, and often we jump to the conclusion that 1) everyone around us notices, and 2) everyone is attributing them to our nervousness. Neither of those beliefs, however, is necessarily always true. Often, people do not see perspiration, or notice our blushing, or even see our hands shake. The truth is that we can hide the physiological manifestations of nerves without even trying; other people see only a fraction of what we feel, and usually do not attribute it to anxiety.

Now that we are aware of the environmental, psychological, and physiological factors that affect speech fright we can address how to manage performance anxiety and eventually make it work for us. In the next section we discuss several strategies for handling and reducing the anxiety present before and during a speech.

Coping Strategies

Fear is one of the most potent human emotions, and when you are afraid of something fear grips you and controls your thoughts and actions. It can be paralyzing, but it does not need to be so. Many people feel the best way to overcome a fear is to confront it head on and immerse yourself in it until you realize that there is nothing to fear. For example, they would tell someone who is afraid of heights to climb to the top of the tallest building around and stare out over the edge of the roof. Do that until you get used to it. Although this immersion technique sounds logical, albeit a bit cruel, there is some truth to it.

Experience with that which makes you fearful will ultimately help you manage your fear. Unfortunately, this technique fails to address how you handle the fear while it is still present. Thankfully, overcoming performance anxiety entails both immersion and incremental management techniques. On the one hand, the more experience you get interacting with others in a wide array of contexts, the less nervous you will become with doing so in the future. On the other hand, there are several strategies for helping you manage the fear if it manifests itself during a communicative event, because you will not manage or master your fear overnight.

One of the ways you can combat the worrisome thoughts and self-fulfilling prophecy we mentioned earlier in the chapter is through visualizing success. Thinking positively about the interaction and imagining yourself successfully handling the situation will increase your belief in your ability to do so. A positive approach and visualizing the event without any problems will also allow you to practice more comfortably.

Changing your mental approach also can minimize the influence of physiological factors on your anxiety levels. Understanding that people cannot see your nerves, and that there are a multitude of other reasons why you might sweat or blush, alleviates the worry that people might see that you are nervous. You might be perspiring because the room is hot, or blushing because of the same reason. Your shakes might be because you are sick, or the room is cold. Just because you know that you are anxious does not necessarily mean others know that too.

Table 2.3

Manifestations of and Reasons for Stress		
Physical Manifestations of Stress	**Could Be Caused by . . .**	**But It Might Be Caused by . . .**
Perspiring	Nervousness	Room temperature
Blushing	Anxiety or embarrassment	Illness or room temperature
Trembling	Apprehension	Room temperature or illness
Breathing heavily	Anxiety	Physical exertion

Breathing can also help you combat nervousness and get more comfortable in front of an audience. You do not need to start to speak immediately when the other person finishes, or even once you get behind the podium. If you are feeling tense then take a deep breath or two before you begin speaking. If you find your nervous state is still there, or that it returns during the delivery, do the same thing. Breathing increases your intake of oxygen, reduces blushing, and calms your nerves, so always remember that stopping and taking a breath is an option available to you when you get nervous before or during an interaction. During meetings you might be more willing to contribute if you take notes so that you can refer to them when it is your turn to speak. Having your reactions written in front of you reduces the risk of forgetting what you want to say, or saying the wrong thing, and makes it more likely that you would contribute to the discussion.

Table 2.4

Strategies for Dealing with Speech Anxiety
• Directly confront it by presenting speeches and interacting with others
• Visualize success
• Realize the audience only sees a portion of what you feel
• Take deep breaths for calmness
• Adequately prepare and practice
• Take notes

Finally, and perhaps most importantly when it comes to public speaking contexts, proper preparation will undoubtedly make you more relaxed when you deliver a speech. The easiest thing you can do to gain more confidence in your ability to speak is to practice often, in advance of a speech. The more you practice, the more comfortable you get with the material, and the more comfortable you get with material the more you know it when you get in front of an audience. Practice and experience breed confidence, and confidence is the strongest tool you can develop to fight your fear. Realize that you do not have to present the message using the exact same words each time. Focus on the content. As an example, you may talk to one friend about a date you just had, then talk to a different friend about the same experience but not relay the content using exactly the same words, tone, or even content. You may not say the same thing as word choices may vary, but the content, or purpose, will be the same.

SUMMARY

In this chapter, we explored two models of communication that contemporary scholars use to understand communication as a process: the linear and the transactional models of communication. Many scholars today see the transactional model as being more able to account for the complex and dynamic quality of communication. Understanding communication as a transactional process highlights listening as a key process whereby people attend to and interpret the messages that others send to them. Avoiding nonlistening behaviors, overcoming distractions, and actively paying attention to the speaker's message will help the listener to make sense of the speaker's message. Many people, as they communicate with others, experience communication apprehension, which can interfere with their ability to understand the messages that others send. Thankfully, there are a variety of ways to counter and manage this feeling so that any interference that it might introduce into communication is minimized.

KEY TERMS

active listening   40

ambushing   43

anxiety disorder   45

channel   33

communication apprehension   44

decoding   34

encoding   33

feedback   35

glazing over   43

hearing   36

linear model of communication   34

listening   36

listening for appreciation   38

listening to comprehend   40

listening to criticize   40

message   33

noise   34

nonlistening   43

passive listening   41

prejudging   44

pseudolistening   43

receiver   34

self-fulfilling prophecy   46

sender   33

sociophobia   44

Socratic questioning   38

spare brain time   41

spotlight syndrome   45

transactional model of communication   35

REVIEW QUESTIONS

1. What are the components of the linear and transactional models of communication?

2. What are the three listening purposes and the two listening types?

3. What are the common forms of nonlistening?

4. What are three factors that can cause communication apprehension?

5. What are some strategies for combating communication apprehension?

ENDNOTES

1. American Film Institute, "AFI's 100 Years... 100 Stars," http://www.afi.com/tvevents/100years/stars.aspx (accessed June 25, 2008).

2. Laurence Olivier, *On Acting* (New York, NY: Simon and Schuster, 1986), 181.

3. Ibid., 183.

4. Claude E. Shannon and Warren Weaver, *The Mathematical Theory of Communication* (Urbana, IL: University of Illinois Press, 1949).

5. For example: Michael Dunne and Sik Hung Ng, "Simultaneous Speech in Small Group Conversation: All-Together-Now and One-at-a-Time?" *Journal of Language and Social Psychology* 13 (1994): 45-71.

6. Marie Hochmuth Nichols. http://natcom.org/Default.aspx?id=73&libID=94 (accessed June 11, 2011).

7. Marie Hochmuth Nichols. http://blog.umd.edu/ncapublicaddress/2011/03/09/call-for-nominations-2011-nichols-award/ (accessed June 11, 2011).

8. Ibid.

9. James C. McCroskey, "Oral Communication Apprehension: A Review of Recent Research," *Human Communication Research* 4 (1977): 78-96.

SCENARIOS

Scenario 1

Using the following terms, and without looking at your book or notes, draw a model of both the linear and transactional models of communication.

Terms: Sender, Receiver, Noise, Feedback, Encoding, Message, Channel, Decoding

After drawing the models, answer and complete the following:

1. Which component is used in the transactional model but not in the linear? What difference does this present between the two models?

2. Explain whether the following are best explained using the linear or transactional communication. Justify your answer:

    Television Shows

    Classroom Lectures

    News Programs

    Debates

    Online Chat Programs

    Mealtime conversation

    Blog Posts

    Email

3. Is it possible that any that you explained using one model could be explained by the other? Discuss your answer.

Scenario 2

You are planning on giving a speech to a gathering of UD alumni before an important UD basketball game. The speech is to take place in a meeting hall in a convention center across from the arena with a major highway dividing the two buildings. The hall is crowded with alumni enjoying themselves, and since they are sitting at round tables the audience members are mostly facing each other. Even though the room is air-conditioned, it's a particularly hot spring day outside. Additionally, the room adjacent to the hall is occupied by fans of the opposing team that UD is playing that day. The opposing team's fans are starting to spill over into UD's hall, and some of them look like they have been drinking.

1. Think about the characteristics of the room and the area surrounding it. What are the obstacles that you will have to overcome in your speech? What are some ways you can overcome them?

2. Suppose you are feeling stressed or nervous before your speech? What are some ways that the room's characteristics can be used to your advantage? Consider the layout of the room, along with the way stress manifests itself during speeches.

3. Using the three types of distractions listed by the textbook, identify all of the potential distractions that might occur in your situation, and specific strategies you can use to deal with each.

Scenario 3

Below is a list of responses to presentations, each demonstrating poor listening. Choose the type of non-listening that best fits each comment and justify your answer.

1. "Her speech on human trafficking seemed okay, but my mom told me that it's being overblown by the media."

2. "The lecture was boring. Hey, check out this doodle I drew in my notebook!"

3. "He can hardly even speak English. This guy doesn't know what he's talking about."

4. "Of course I was listening. I raised my hand like three times during the lecture."

5. "I'm a republican. What's the point of listening to what a democrat has to say on creating jobs?"

6. "Huh, what? I'm sorry, there was a butterfly outside the window."

7. "Forget what she said about keeping tuition rates down. She didn't even know where the student neighborhood was located."

Audience in Context

CHAPTER OVERVIEW

- Discusses how audiences can be classified and analyzed
- Explains how audience analysis can be employed in developing points and using language
- Outlines how to effectively adapt during an interaction

Practically SPEAKING

The 2008 presidential primaries represented the first time in over a half century when neither a president nor vice president sought his party's nomination for president. The campaigns for both the Democratic and Republican contenders were bitterly divisive, and each candidate needed to find a way to appeal to groups that normally would not support them. For instance, Republican Senator John McCain needed to quell criticism over what some party members saw as his questionable conservative record.[1]

In 2007 the Conservative Political Action Committee (CPAC) invited all the major candidates to speak at the conference and McCain was the only one not to attend.[2] As a result, he was crushed in the straw poll by his competitors and many conservatives refused to support him.[3] As the year progressed, McCain took further criticism from the right for his immigration policies, refusal to vote for the Bush tax cuts a few years prior, and his maverick nature. The criticism became so severe for McCain in 2007 that his campaign almost went bankrupt.[4]

The Arizona senator's fortunes changed, however, in 2008 when voting began. By the time he reached the podium at CPAC he was the likely Republican nominee for president. He had won significant election victories the previous week, and just a few hours before his speech his chief rival, Mitt Romney, announced the suspension of his campaign. McCain could now attempt to unite the party behind him. Unfortunately for the senator, the audience still viewed him with skepticism at best, and hostility at worst.

McCain needed to tailor his speech to the scene he faced. He knew he faced conservatives, but what kind? What was their age? Where did they come from? What was their economic status? Would race play a part in their perceptions of him? Were they ready to believe in his candidacy? Which political principles did they espouse? The answers to these and other questions influenced the word choices within his speech and the evidence he chose to use to deflect their potential criticisms. But even with knowing these things in advance, McCain still needed to be attuned to his audience while delivering the speech. All of these assessments are part of audience analysis, an essential skill for any communicative situation.

This chapter will show you the various elements of audience analysis that can help you craft and deliver messages tailored to your listeners, whether they consist of one person or one hundred people. It begins by discussing the various dimensions of a communication context that influence your message, and then discusses how that information can be used to inform your decisions on phrasing and organizing your message. Finally, we will explain how audience analysis continues during the interaction, and is not restricted to advance preparation. The chapter provides tips and suggestions for how to gauge the affectivity of your message while delivering your positions to listeners.

PREP QUESTIONS

1. Define context.

2. Provide 5 examples of demographic categories.

3. How do you think stereotyping might inhibit transactional communication?

4. Discuss the two components of the 'what do they know?' dimension of context. What are the dangers in both overestimating and underestimating what your audience knows?

5. Explain how the location of an interaction can influence the exchange between people.

6. Define larks, owls and hummingbirds. Why do you think it would be useful to know which of these categories your audience falls into?

7. Differentiate between open-ended and fixed response questions. Give an example of each question.

8. Compare and contrast the two types of meetings people engage in. Do you think the expectations of civility change depending on which type of meeting you're in? Why or why not?

9. Explain what was meant when Marshall McLuhan said "the medium is the message."

10. Define the rhetorical situation and exigence, as they were understood by Bitzer.

11. Explain how and why Vatz disagreed with Bitzer. Who do you agree with – Vatz or Bitzer? Why?

12. List ways you can use audience analysis information to identify with your listeners and construct messages that appeal to them.

13. How is using information gathered through audience analysis different than stereotyping? How do you think you can draw a distinction between the two?

14. Describe some benefits and challenges to polling an audience in the middle of delivering a message.

15. Discuss how you might use space to adapt to feedback during message delivery.

CONTEXT AND AUDIENCE

The first step to any effective conversation with one or more people is understanding the *context*, or the circumstances in which an event occurs that influences the meaning of the moment and the message. In determining the context of the interaction you are better able to adjust your message to your audience, thus, you increase the chances of successfully accomplishing your goals for the interaction. In this section of the chapter we will discuss the various components of context and identify the different communication situations you will encounter in which you may need to adapt to an audience.

context
the circumstances in which an event occurs that influences the meaning of the moment and the message

COMPONENTS OF CONTEXT

Context refers to everything outside of the message or interaction itself that influences how you understand the situation. To that end, it contains the who, what, when, where, why, and how of an interaction between people. In this section of the chapter we will discuss each of these elements in detail and explain how each one plays a role in defining context and influencing how and what we say to other people.

Who Is the Audience?

No matter what situation you find yourself in, knowing to whom you are speaking is essential for successfully developing and sending messages. The "who" refers to both the identity of the other person or people in an interaction, as well as an appreciation of them in relation to you. It is important to understand the term *audience* as meaning those who are listening to you in a given context. Therefore, you can have an audience of one other person, or an audience of many other people. Throughout this chapter think about audience in both ways so that you better appreciate how audience analysis is a tool to be used in any communication situation—not just public speaking. In today's society we often break down individuals and audiences into *demographic* categories, or groups determined by select population characteristics. Such an approach is both positive and negative.

demographic
groups determined by select population characteristics

Demographic categories measure a variety of different aspects of a population. They detail observable and identifiable characteristics through survey techniques.

Every time you place a check mark next to your race or provide your age on a document you are contributing to demographic information databases. Think about your college applications: You checked these off and sent them back to the universities of your choice. The universities then used this information to examine the appeal of their colleges to certain populations they targeted. Demographic information is powerful, and for that reason the use of it for anything other than description is prohibited by law.

In the United States most demographic categories are protected by law from discrimination. Race, age, sexual orientation, and religious affiliation represent specific groups shielded from discrimination. So, on the aforementioned college application you could not be rejected from a school for checking the box next to, say, "African American" or "Hispanic" or "Caucasian." So, demographic information—understood as a piece of data—can be helpful to corporations, universities, and other groups when trying to tailor appeals to large segmented parts of the general public.

Market researchers make use of demographic data all the time. In one clear ethical violation of the use of such data, Camel cigarettes was fined for targeting young people with their cartoon based advertisements. More common and appropriate, however, is how universities collect demographic data from their applicants to devise recruiting strategies for future classes. Demographic data are immensely useful when tailoring messages to specific audiences.

stereotyping
assuming qualities in a specific individual because of membership in a larger group

Just as the Camel story from a moment ago illustrates, demographic data can be dangerous. When we use one piece of demographic data to assume qualities in an individual because the larger group exhibits a tendency or preponderance for that particular belief we run the risk of *stereotyping* a person. That is to say, we assume qualities in a person based on qualities of a larger group to which they belong. These types of generalized assumptions are risky, and often wrong. The fact of the matter is that people belong to numerous demographic categories at the same time, and each of these groups may exhibit opposite trends, so it is important to remember to be careful when making assumptions in the face of possible conflicting data.

Take the case of Mary Church Terrell, a nineteenth-century social activist who spoke out against gender and racial discrimination. Terrell often had to balance her speeches with examples that appealed to women and African Americans at a time when the experiences of both had some commonalities, but also some significant differences. Terrell needed to pay attention to the racial demographic of her audiences each time she gave a speech to make sure she used the best possible examples.

In large companies, different divisions need to communicate effectively with each other for projects to be successful, so again a proper understanding of "who" the other party is becomes essential for success. Take the case of a large international engineering firm tasked with creating a proposal for a client's new building. Obviously, engineers develop the plans, but accountants are responsible for purchasing and pricing the materials needed for the job. Neither

SPOTLIGHTING THEORISTS: MARSHALL MCLUHAN

Marshall McLuhan (1911–1980)
Media analyst and theorist Marshall McLuhan was born in Edmonton, Alberta, Canada, on July 11, 1911. He earned a B.A. and an M.A. at both the University of Manitoba and Cambridge University. He taught at, among other places, the University of Wisconsin–Madison and St. Louis University.

In 1963 the President of the University of Toronto appointed McLuhan to develop a Center for Culture and Technology.[9] The center studied the relationship between technology, media, and human cognition. McLuhan had many other appointments in business and government throughout his storied career. In addition to these jobs, McLuhan wrote *Understanding Media: The Extension of Man*, which challenged the assumptions many had of media and its uses and powers in a technologically advancing society. He was also concerned with the consequences of media on society. McLuhan is perhaps best known and remembered for this statement that "the medium is the message." This phrase is used in various contexts in academe, including but not limited to media studies, rhetorical studies, film studies, and English.

of these two professions likely understands the details of the other, but they need to communicate with each other to finish the building. Engineers thus need to appreciate where the accountants come from when talking about money and financing, while the accountants also must appreciate the expertise of the engineers in identifying proper materials. These types of meetings are only successful when both parties understand the "who" dimension of the context when they interact with each other.

What Does the Audience Know?

Demographic data about an audience can be pretty easy to determine, but another part of the context is a bit more difficult to identify. In any speaking situation it is important to understand, to the best degree possible, what an audience knows about you and your topic. Are they unfamiliar with the topic under discussion? Do they know a little about it, or do they know a lot? What do they know about you? Answering these questions before and during an interaction can often make the difference between success and failure in a meeting. If you assume they know nothing, when they actually have some knowledge of a topic, then you might come across as condescending and arrogant. If you assume they know more than they do, then they might not be able to keep up with or understand what you're trying to say. It is also important to understand that just because people are unfamiliar with you or your field it does not make them unintelligent. You most likely do not know much about their area of expertise.

Your instinct might tell you that you can assume knowledge based on the person or group's level of education, economic status, or even other demographic categories. However, if you're assuming qualities about a people based solely on the demographic groups they belong to, you are stereotyping.

As an example of audience analysis crossing over into stereotyping let's take the case of a possible classroom interaction at UD. You know that UD is an expensive school and that most people in the class probably have some disposable income. Furthermore, you look and see that the majority of people wear clothing from well known brands. You take this information and then assume the entire audience shares these qualities, when in fact, that is not true. In saying something that implies everyone has name brand clothes, you might be offending or alienating

What It Means to Be Colored in the Capital of the U.S.
by Mary Church Terrell

Delivered October 10, 1906, to the United Women's Club, Washington, D.C.

In 1906 the United Women's Club invited African American advocate and teacher Mary Church Terrell to speak, and she delivered a scathing commentary on racial equality in Washington, D.C.[5] Terrell noted in her opening that the nation's capital had been labeled the "colored man's paradise" but declared such a title must have been bestowed out of irony, because "it would be difficult to find a worse misnomer for Washington."[6] Terrell also argued that conditions for African Americans had worsened in the 15 years of her residence there, and that although many other minorities could find lodging, unless a black person had acquaintances they likely could not find a bed. She noted that if she resisted current standards then she would be "cast into jail and forced to pay a fine for violating the Virginia laws."[7] Such issues reflected the direct experiences of African Americans of her day, but her speech was not simply about race—after all it was delivered at the women's club!

Ms. Terrell vividly described the limitations on the possibility of education, specifically that black school children received a lower quality education than that of white children. Within her speech she also referenced many more examples of injustice and discrimination, all designed to connect the causes of women and African Americans, as the causes of these two groups were priorities in her life.

In the closing paragraph of her speech, Ms. Terrell made a statement of a stern tone: "It is impossible for any white person in the United States, no matter how sympathetic and broad, to realize what life would mean to him if his incentive to effort were suddenly snatched away."[8] Mary Church Terrell lived to see the successes of the women's suffrage movement and the significant victory of Brown v. Board of Education, dying shortly thereafter at the age of 90. In recognition of the power of her voice on civil rights issues, the United States Post Office honored her with a stamp in 2009.

classmates who do not. That said, sometimes knowing the position of the individual or individuals you are speaking to can help you determine what they know about a topic—especially if the topic relates specifically to their area of expertise. For example, speaking to pre-med students about privacy you might infer that they know something about the subject, specifically as it relates to doctor-patient confidentiality.

One of the best ways to determine audience knowledge of a topic is to check your perceptions before and during the interaction. This is particularly useful with smaller audiences, but can also work in larger situations. Simply asking people how familiar they are with something can help circumvent needless background information and allow you to get right to the point of the proceedings. If, however, they admit to not knowing something, then you are prepared to elaborate on it for them. The topic, though, is not the only thing with which they need to be familiar.

Another key component of the "what do they know" part of context is knowing what the audience is aware of about you. In some instances, like interviews, your conversational partner knows a bit about you thanks to your resumé. In other instances, such as sales calls to potential new clients, the other party may be completely unfamiliar with you and your company and so you need to spend time introducing yourself and your company. If there is any question about what the audience knows about you going into a discussion, it is a good idea to open by asking them. That way you can establish a baseline for what the audience knows about you.

Where Is the Meeting Taking Place?

A third factor in determining context involves the place in which the meeting or presentation takes place. Where the meeting occurs can be informative and can significantly alter the dynamic of an interaction. Certain topics and relationships lend themselves to specific locations. When delivering more formal presentations the scene of the interaction can provide insight into the other party's disposition and interests.

It is not a stretch to call your own space, be it a home or an office, your "home field" as you feel most comfortable there. Meetings in your office or home provide you with an advantage, especially when discussing business with other people. You can control the setup of the room to influence the flow of a conversation. On the television show *30 Rock*, the company's vice president, Jack Doneghy, played by Alec Baldwin, changed the chairs in his office in advance of a negotiation with an agent. The agent's chair was uncomfortable and smaller than his, which created a situation more amenable to achieving his goals in the exchange.

Your professors at UD also arrange their offices to either encourage or discourage interaction with people. Desks can serve as barriers for discussions with people. Some professors put their desks in corners of offices and create more open and inviting spaces for an interaction, thus making office hour visits and conversations much more comfortable. Even open and closed doors play some role in how we interpret a person's availability and interest in conversation.

Office and home setups can also provide a great deal of information about a person. Many people choose to decorate their office space in a way that reflects their personality and interests. Even those who occupy cubicles hang posters or put pictures up that show support for issues or even sports teams. Paying attention to such surroundings can help you find ways to identify with the other party in an interaction.

Not all meetings and interactions take place in an office or a home. In fact, off-site meetings in local coffeeshops or diners have become more and more common in our culture. These meeting places can provide an atmosphere more conducive to a relaxing interaction where neither party has the "home field advantage". Off-site meeting places are also helpful when the topic of a discussion is sensitive. Public places, in this way, provide an ironically more private setting because those around you do not know who you are or what you are talking about.

When Is the Meeting?

It may sound strange, but the time of day, month, or even year influences the context of an interaction in several ways. Research actually shows that different people function better at different times of day, and understanding this will help you in any interaction. The amount of time you have before a meeting, presentation, or conversation can also influence the different tools you can employ to gather information about your audience.

In his book *Brain Rules*, molecular biologist John Medina explains the three different types of people in terms of when they function best. The first group, called larks, consists of those of us who function best in the morning and are often early risers. This group represents about 10% of the population. For our purposes, these people would prefer to meet and discuss issues in the morning. The second group, called owls, often works best in the evening and late night hours, staying up often until early in the morning. Owls, obviously, do not function well in morning meetings and may, in fact, become irritated more easily if they are asked to do so. This group represents roughly 20% of the population. The final group, hummingbirds, leans more toward either larks or owls, but generally functions fine during "normal" daytime hours.[9] Knowing to which one of these groups you and your audience belong can be immensely helpful in determining when to schedule meetings with other people. Of course, this is not always possible.

open-ended questions
....
items on a survey that allow room for the person taking the survey to answer in his/her own words

fixed-response questions
....
items on a survey that allow only for prescribed answers

In addition to the influence of time of day on an individual's focus, knowing how much time you have before a meeting or presentation can also affect your preparation. With enough time you can conduct research into your audience to learn how they feel about you and your topic, or even collect demographic data about them that can influence your message construction. You can use surveys that contain *open-ended questions* or *fixed-response questions*. Open-ended questions can be useful tools for gaining depth of understanding about particular issues, while fixed-response questions help gather specific data. Surveys are quite useful if you have the time, but a lot goes into their creation, distribution, collection, and analysis.

Another technique for discovering information about your potential audience when you know you have time before the meeting to do so is through interviewing. If you have enough lead time and some knowledge of who is in the group with whom you will be speaking, you may try and arrange appointments with them to gather specific information you need to help you determine the best ways to approach the meeting. Interviews primarily consist of open-ended questions because demographic questions are simply not suited for conversation, and the answers to some of them (like race and gender) are readily identifiable without asking the person. An added advantage to the interviewing strategy is that throughout the course of the interview you will develop a relationship with one of the people who will attend your talk later, thus increasing your comfort level when you actually deliver the address. They are much more personal than a survey and if used correctly and creatively, interviews can provide extremely useful information.

Time is an important part of context both in understanding when you and your audience function best, but also in determining how much time you have to find out information about your conversational partners.

Why Are You Meeting?

There are many reasons why people get together and communicate, and these reasons play a role in determining the context of the interaction. In this section of the chapter we will identify two common reasons why people get together and talk, and illustrate how the reason for the conversation influences the meaning of what is said.

The first reason why people engage in a discussion is to develop personal relationships. That is to say, it is not related to business, but rather developing or maintaining a personal relationship. In these instances we tend to use less formal language, focus on topics of common interest and disclose personal feelings, emotions, or experiences to others often in the hope they reciprocate. Think about your personal lives and the language and topic choices you make. They surely differ from when you talk to people at work or in a business setting.

The second reason people engage in discussion is to advance business goals. In business settings we typically refrain from colloquial language and avoid the use of slang. We also focus on more task-oriented topics that relate to the business at hand. In many business meetings an agenda needs to be accomplished. This is not to say that "small talk" is out of line; in fact, most meetings begin with it to establish a rapport between the parties, but it rarely, if ever, goes deeper than superficial topics.

Now, things can be complicated when business partners develop friendships, and so in these moments it becomes essential to pay attention to why the meeting is taking place. If the motive is business, keep your language and discussion topics limited to business, but if the main reason for getting together is personal, then you can relax your expectations a bit. Just remember that if the person you are with is a supervisor or even someone whom you supervise, then you still need to pay careful attention to what you do and do not say. Remember that civility requires us to not speak ill of others, whether the meeting is for business or personal relationships. This rule becomes especially important when we are with colleagues who are also our friends.

How Are You Meeting?

For much of human history face-to-face interactions were the only way to communicate; however, recent technological achievements changed this quite a bit. We still meet in small intimate settings with another person, or even a group of people. We also still engage in presentations and public speeches to larger groups, but these are increasingly rare for the average person. Some of the more common ways we interact with people today are through the telephone, web, e-mail, and streaming video. We can send quick text messages, write a somewhat longer e-mail to one or more people, or even have live video conferencing with multiple groups at once.

The late Canadian communication scholar Marshall McLuhan once wrote that "the medium is the message," meaning that the manner in which you choose to deliver your message tells the audience just as much as the content of what you say. By "medium" he referred to technological media, and primarily television; however, the principle still stands with other manners of interaction. The environment you choose to speak through—the "how" you plan on meeting with other people—can send as powerful a message as the content of what you say.

For example, an IT support staff member for a company may choose to send a mechanical expert to a client to demonstrate how the product works to a client, thus making it seem like a more important and personal investment; or, they may simply create a DVD of the presentation and send that to the client. The same message can be delivered both ways, but the manner in which it is packaged sends another message to the audience as well. You must pay attention to the medium through which you communicate with another person, and how you and your surroundings may be perceived through that medium.

There are some pitfalls and potentially hazardous dimensions to the seemingly wonderful ability to communicate with people across the globe so quickly through media. Text messages work best when the person you text knows who you are, and the messages are short. In fact, there is a specific language code for text messaging that allows for shorter written words—but this type of writing does not translate well to other written forms of communication, even e-mail. Keep in mind that there are plenty of situations where delivering a message face-to-face is much more effective than through text or email.

For example, in business settings e-mail may not always be the best mode of communication, especially when trying to build trust and relationships between yourself and a client or colleague. The more personal touch of individual meetings over coffee may work better because they tell the other party you care about them and want to develop a relationship. Sometimes, you may also be asked to deliver a presentation regarding a product, so being prepared to do so also demonstrates interest and ability to the recipient.

One final issue to appreciate is technology's ability to allow us to create visually stimulating presentations using PowerPoint, Prezi, and even Skype. In 2013, former Federal Reserve Chairman Ben Bernanke used technology to deliver prepared remarks to attendees at the RISE Forum hosted by the University of Dayton in association with the United Nations Global Compact.

However, just because technology allows us to use mediated images and messages in the manner Ben Bernanke did does not mean we should do so because images are no substitute for individual attention and actual content. Regardless of whether you are speaking to one person or one thousand, you need to actually present a logical well-developed message.

All in all, how you choose to engage another person sends a very important message about your feelings regarding the relationship. Mediated avenues create an aura of interest and intimacy, but be judicious in choosing when to use them and especially careful in how you deliver messages through them.

CREATING AN AUDIENCE AND CONTEXT

As much as situations seem to call for specific types of language, we have a degree of control in creating the context in which we communicate. There is a very specific connection between rhetoric and the situations in which we speak, and this connection allows us to construct much of the context by interpreting what is going on around us. In short, we can actually use language to create the situation in which we are speaking and the audience we are addressing. The way we describe a situation, in other words, creates our perception of the situation. This idea, however, has been met with some debate in the communication discipline.

In 1968 Lloyd Bitzer published an essay that proposed a specific relationship between rhetoric and situations.[11] Specifically, he said that situations called rhetoric into being. Put another way, each moment in which you find yourself invites you to speak using a specific vocabulary. When you respond to a situation what you say alters the reality of the moment. By way of an example he argued that when presidents are inaugurated they confront a situation that invites them to speak. They do so, thereby changing the reality of the moment, redefining it for the audience and themselves.

Another aspect of these *rhetorical situations*, according to Bitzer, is that each is different. If a person does not respond to it, the moment is lost. Each moment presents a different *exigence*, or urgent moment in which a response is invited or required, and thereby requires a different vocabulary for the speaker. For instance, when you see a meteor streak across the night sky the moment invites you to describe it in a particular way. There are only so many ways you can describe the beauty of such an event, and if you don't do it as it happens then you lose the ability to do so. Even in talking about it later, you are in a different moment that invites a different vocabulary. When seeing the meteor you might say "Wow! That's awesome" but later when describing it to friends you detail how it looked like a "streaking laser across the sky," because they did not see the event and cannot share in the awe the initial moment inspired in you.

rhetorical situations
moments that call for a rhetorical response

exigence
a decisive point at which a response is invited or required

Bitzer also states that rhetorical situations require an audience that demands speakers to craft their messages using a specific vocabulary. Finally, each rhetorical situation contains constraints that limit the ability of the speaker to respond only to the situation at hand. Not everyone, however, agreed with Bitzer when he published this argument.

Where Bitzer saw meaning as inherent in the situation and understood rhetoric as a way to define it, Richard Vatz argues that meaning exists only when rhetoric provides it.[12] That is to say a crisis is not actually a crisis until someone calls it a crisis. We do not find meaning; we create it through our speech. For Vatz, situations are defined by the speaker; the situations do not define the speech. This perspective essentially takes a position completely opposite that of Bitzer, but also puts more of an emphasis on the power of language to define and create meaning for audiences, events, and contexts.

The view advanced by Vatz allows us more creativity in defining the scope and impressions of our interactions with others. With the advent of Facebook, the way we communicate the meaning of a relationship changed. People now do not see themselves as "in a relationship" unless their Facebook page says they are. You, as an individual, have the power to name your relationship and thus make it official, The situation does not demand you do so, as Bitzer would argue, but rather you have the power to name the situation as a relationship or not. In not making a relationship Facebook official, you might believe you could date other people, but in giving it that label you close off that action. The key thing to remember is that, for Vatz, you are not in a relationship until you say you are.

We will now discuss how we can analyze our audiences in any setting and adapt our messages to them and the context in which the conversation happens. This adaptation, coupled with the appreciation that we can create an understanding of that context through our messages and statements—or define the rhetorical situation, rather than be defined by it—is an important tool for successful communication in any venue with any audience, large or small.

Audience Analysis and Message Development

When you know the makeup of your audience it becomes much easier to construct appeals to them. Speaking in terms your listeners know, using examples designed to resonate with them, and referencing statistics they are more likely to care about becomes easier when you know who they are, what they care about, what they believe in, and what motivates them. After all, why talk to an audience of senior citizens about buying a cell phone when your research tells you they are resistant to new technology? It makes no sense. Understanding your audience can help you create a more effective message.

This section talks about two ways to make use of audience analysis information. The first is through verbal appeals, or the specific construction of what to say so you can better identify with your audience. The second strategy is through how to say it, or the organizational structure of your message. Both the content and structure of any missive can be modified and magnified based upon information from an analysis of the audience.

SPOTLIGHTING THEORISTS: LLOYD BITZER & RICHARD VATZ

Lloyd Bitzer

Lloyd Bitzer, a longtime professor at the University of Wisconsin, published several important pieces of rhetorical scholarship, but none more controversial or widely read than his 1968 piece "The Rhetorical Situation." For Bitzer, situations hold inherent meaning that speakers identify through their responses. Situations essentially call rhetoric into being.

This position posits that rhetoric is a reaction to situations and that the power of meaning lies with context and not the speaker. Speeches are essentially predetermined responses to existing situations. They are descriptions of meaning and are not meaningful in and of themselves. As an example he wrote that presidential inaugurations are situations that invite a specific form of speech from a president. The inauguration is why they speak and what they speak about.

Bitzer's essay has been widely cited and used as a foundation for rhetorical studies since its publication, but not everyone agrees with its propositions.

Richard Vatz

In 1973 Richard Vatz, a professor at Towson State University in Maryland who primarily studies the intersection of rhetoric and psychiatry, published a response to Bitzer's essay entitled "The Myth of the Rhetorical Situation." Vatz contended that situations do not invite rhetoric, but rather rhetoric creates situations.

For Vatz meaning is created by the speaker through his or her speech, not through the situation. Situations therefore, lack meaning until it is defined for them by the speaker. Speakers, according to this position, hold the power to use rhetoric to define situations.

To illustrate this point, Vatz points to crises. He says that there is not a crisis until the situation is defined as such by a speaker. He also points to the fact political candidates often seek to "control the agenda," implying speakers define the campaign and not vice versa.

Scholars often cite Vatz's essay as an attempt to spur debate over the concept of the rhetorical situation.

Implications of Bitzer vs. Vatz

Bitzer takes a passive view of rhetoric, arguing that it merely describes situations. Vatz believes rhetoric has a more active role and is not simply derivative of situations. In fact, Vatz goes so far as to call the rhetorical situation "anti-rhetorical." The National Communication Association still convenes panels to discuss the debate between these two scholars, with the most recent at the 2008 annual meeting in San Diego.

Content Strategies

There are three main ways of making use of your knowledge about an audience to augment your ability to successfully appeal to them.

- The first involves using the data as part of a strategy for identifying with your listeners, or making you seem as though you are one of them.

- The second thing audience analysis information allows you to do is incorporate knowledge of the audience into your message.

- Third, you can use clear descriptive statements. This allows you to choose more appropriate examples, statistics, or testimonials for the context in which you find yourself.

Each of these builds upon the others to help you establish a strong rapport with your conversational partners.

Identifying with your audience is possibly the most important result of conducting audience analyses. The information you found can help you understand who your audience is and when you know that you can find things you have in common with them. Once you determine what you have in common you can immediately stress those common bonds, thus making you appear similar to the the other party. Such an approach enhances your ethos, or credibility, and strengthens your ability to appeal to them.

For example, Anya is a 21-year-old college senior at New York University with a major in sociology. She plans to go to law school so she can eventually work in the district attorney's office in St. Petersburg, Florida, where she grew up. When she was younger she watched the riots of 1996 that followed the death of a black man after a routine police traffic stop, increasing gang violence. She decided to pursue a career that would enable her to prevent those things from happening again. Now, as valedictorian of her senior class, she is addressing commencement on her campus. She is at a ceremony celebrating graduation at a school in a different area of the country than where she grew up, so how can she identify with her audience immediately? There are several ways.

First, like her audience, she is graduating and thus roughly the same age as many of them. Second, she knows that many of those in the audience live in New York City, which is no stranger to occasional social unrest. This information can help her develop a presentation that celebrates the joy of graduation while also calling on her audience to help improve society. This can be done quickly in the speech by telling an abbreviated version of her story and linking it to New York. She could, perhaps, cite examples from the class' days at the school when fellow students may have been victims of crimes, or just mention they have all watched the news about crime in the city for the last four years. By making such references in her speech, Anya becomes more credible when calling on her audience to be more socially conscious. Audience analysis helps you find strategies for connecting with your audience in a very real way.

Think of the information you glean from audience analysis as contributing to the relationship between you and your audience. Picture a triangle where you are one corner of the triangle, the audience is another corner, and the message is the third corner (see Figure 3.1). You need to find a way to connect with the audience, and the best way to do that is through the message. The audience also wants to find a way to connect with you, and that also occurs through the message. The stronger your message appeals to the commonalities between you and your listeners, the stronger the connection between you both.

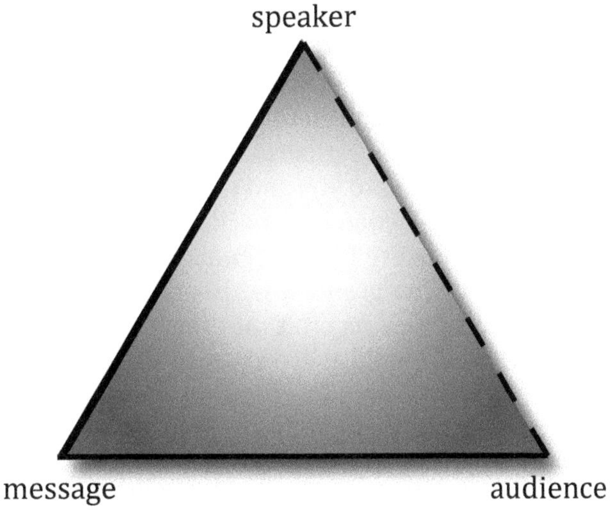

Figure 3.1
Connecting with the Audience

There is another way to identify with your audience through the use of words, but it can only happen after you establish common ground with your listeners. *"We"* language allows you to speak as if you are a member of the group, and once you establish a connection between yourself and your listeners this type of language should be used often. Instead of saying "I," say "we." Instead of saying "me," say "us." This approach enhances your connection to the audience, but if you use it too early without creating common ground, it will actually diminish your credibility. People need to know how you are one of them before you declare that you are one of them. This approach to language works in small groups as well as larger settings. Be careful not to assume a "we" when it has not been demonstrated.

A second way to use audience analysis information to enhance your connection with the audience is *through incorporating what you know about your listeners into the message.* We do this in daily conversations with each other when we state that we know what other people like or believe. Be sure when you do this, however, that you actually do know it as true and are not making an assumption based upon little evidence. In interviews this tactic helps establish that you sought information about the interviewer by demonstrating some knowledge about what they do, produce, or are otherwise interested in. In larger settings, speakers often will use one person as a representative of an entire group in the audience to help make a point. Using knowledge about the audience within a message helps build bridges between people; just make sure what you use is positive in nature and meant to help create rather than damage your association with the other party.

Another way to incorporate information about your audience into the speech is through descriptive statements. At graduation and convocation, University of Dayton President Dan Curran might describe the demographic characteristics of the graduating or incoming class. This illustrates knowledge about the group to whom he is speaking and demonstrates that he cared enough about the group to "do his homework." Citing statistics alone probably will not do much, but creatively incorporating this information into a message can go a long way to establishing a bond with an audience.

The third and final strategy for using audience analysis information to enhance the content of your speech involves the selection of stories, statistics, and examples that will resonate with your listeners. When you know who your audience is it becomes easier to reference things that are familiar to them. The more you appear to know about them, the more you appear as one of them. For example, if a roommate comes to you and tells you her grandfather just passed away, and you recently lost someone in your life, you might tell that story to help comfort your roommate. You also might remind your roommate of some experiences they may have had with her grandfather to help her feel better as well. Narratives, stories, and examples help us craft messages that connect us with others so long as we know where to build those connections. Even Aristotle would recommend you select the appropriate inartistic proofs so that they help enhance your ability to connect with the audience.

Information about your audience helps you make informed choices about the content of your message. It ultimately helps you find ways to identify with your audience members through incorporating that information into your message through the use of specific examples, statistics, and stories that are more likely to appeal to your listeners. Content, however, is not the only area where this information can help improve your communication skills.

Organizational Strategies

Knowledge of the audience can influence the way you organize your messages, specifically the order in which you present main points in a speech or discussion and whether you reference members of the audience as well. The organization of points is one of the most important parts of the developmental process, and information about your audience can help you choose the best arrangement for your information. Traditionally there are three ways to organize points. You must use knowledge about your audience to decide which one will be a better fit for your situation.

One way to arrange main points for maximum effect involves delivering your strongest point first. Each point that follows builds off the foundation of the first main item. This allows you to draw your audience in immediately with a strong start and then build your case from there. In some ways this method serves as a "backup" or secondary attempt at gaining the attention of the audience. This organizational approach typically works best when an audience is not already prone to believing or agreeing with you. A strong first point then helps draw them in and helps them realize that you have a valid argument worth hearing out. So, when you determine there is initial dissonance between you, your audience, and/or your topic through audience analysis, consider arranging the points so that you deliver the strongest first. In a conversation this may also help convince people quickly, rather than having to present more data and evidence later.

Quintilian taught his students to both make their strongest point first as well as to treat the strongest points in great depth. In other words, spend more time on the strongest arguments than the weaker ones. In fact, he advised students to ditch the weakest parts of the argument if need be. This approach to crafting and delivering points makes as much sense today as it did when Quintilian lived.

Another traditional way of organizing points places the strongest at the end of the body of the speech. This pattern puts less powerful points at the beginning and builds toward the most important main point in a *crescendo* pattern. Such an organizational approach could enhance the pathos of an appeal by building excitement, interest, and emotional attachment to the argument made by the speaker. This approach typically works best when you know the audience already agrees with, or is prone to agree with, the position. Crescendo patterns can also be useful in debate settings as a strategy for holding your strongest claim until the last possible moment so the other side cannot or does not have the time to adequately respond to it.

crescendo
an organizational pattern in which the strongest point is placed at the end and is built up to by smaller main points

In addition to a strong organizational pattern, knowing who, how and when to reference audience members can also be helpful. Carefully planned references, and even the occasional impromptu nod while speaking, can augment the appeal of your speech. If certain points within a speech will be magnified by relating them directly to the listeners, or to a characteristic of a larger group, then it makes sense to do so. Only when you are aware of those characteristics through survey information, or know members of the audience by working the room and interviewing, can you make proper use of this technique.

Creating your message is not simply an effort in putting words to paper, but it also involves using audience analysis to choose the proper words to put to paper. When time allows, analyzing the audience before delivering a message is an invaluable tool for any speaker. There is one approach to audience analysis, however, that does not involve extensive advance preparation and is, in fact, available to every speaker in every communication situation.

Analyzing the Audience During the Interaction

In any interaction we can watch, learn, and adapt to the statements, actions, and reactions of those involved. There are also several tactics you can employ to maximize your ability to connect with and influence an audience based upon that constant feedback. This section details two ways you can analyze the audience while speaking, and offers some suggestions as to how to adapt to them based upon that information.

Observing the Audience

As we illustrated in Chapter 1 with the models of communication, we play the role of both message deliverer and message receiver during an interaction, and so in some ways we are also an audience. A majority of the time speakers do not listen to verbal responses while they are speaking, but receive nonverbal messages from the audience. They can then use that nonverbal feedback to change their delivery and measure the effectiveness of those changes.

One key nonverbal activity you should be attuned to is eye contact. Not only should speakers themselves make significant eye contact with their audience, they also should monitor the amount of eye contact they receive from their conversational partners. If the audience or other person is looking away, at a wall, or reading, then chances are they are not paying attention. Speakers can then make adjustments to regain the audience's focus.

Audience members may also shift in their seats, look at their watches or move around during an interaction. Sometimes this may be due to the discomfort of the chairs they are sitting in or the need to be somewhere very soon, but other times it may indicate boredom. Be attuned to both the potential restlessness of your conversational partners as well as the very real possibility that they need to move on to something or be somewhere else. Be judicious when asking people to give of their time and only expect them to give as much as you might in a given situation. Knowing how long you spent with a person or group may help tell you if the movement you see is boredom or an indicator that time is up.

Polling the Audience

Another useful way to gain information about an audience is through impromptu polling. The results are not scientific, nor are they generalizable, but they do provide immediate information for you and your listeners. We poll people in interpersonal contexts when we ask friends or family if they know something or if they have been someplace before. We also poll people in business settings and public speaking situations to gather targeted information useful to making a sale or identifying with a new group. For example, a supervisor may start a meeting by asking how many people are familiar with the policy change under discussion.

Polling in this manner can also help you learn about whether or not the other people comprehend the information which you provide them. Oftentimes, stopping to ask listeners if they understand or if they need something repeated or said in a different way can be a useful tool. It allows the audience to consider the information they have been given, determine if they need clarification, and play an active part in the interaction. In short, it encourages the audience to be interactive. Polling can occur in small groups where you may just be asking everyone you are with for their thoughts on something, or it might occur in a more formalized setting such as in a speech or classroom.

Many classrooms are moving in the direction of incorporating electronic polling to gauge student understanding and interest, and yours may even be one of them. They use classroom response systems, or clickers, which are two-part devices. The first part includes clickers that audience members (students in this case) use to answer questions posed through PowerPoint presentations. The second component is the software that allows for tabulation of the poll results so the presenter can gather immediate feedback on audience comprehension, agreement, or even enjoyment regarding the speech or portions of the speech.

As you can see, audience analysis can and should be conducted during any interaction. Just as preparatory audience analysis allows you to design messages for maximum impact, audience analysis during a speech or conversation also allows you to make adjustments in an effort to maintain attention and even increase your ability to identify as one of the group. We now turn our attention to methods of adapting to audience feedback during a communicative event.

Strategies for Adapting to Feedback During Delivery

Audience analysis during your interactions with others can help you determine how to proceed. Those adaptations can occur immediately or later, after you come to a realization about something, but it is important to be aware of what you can do to increase the impact of your messages based on the audience's reaction to them. There are also two things you can do from the very beginning to increase the likelihood that others will pay attention and not get distracted or bored when you speak.

The first thing you can do in reaction to the audience's behavior at the beginning of the interaction is make sure you effectively use the space in which you are speaking.

- make sure there is adequate seating to seat everyone in the meeting, if not, try to find more seats or an alternative space that has the necessary number of places to sit.

- make sure tables are relatively clean and clear so that people can use the space by them to take notes or lay out materials.

- make sure the lighting is appropriate, and that the place where the interaction takes place is accessible to disabled people if necessary.

Space usage responsibilities extend to the audience as well, so when you are listening to someone or even attending a movie, it is not civil to "reserve" more space than you need by placing your items on seats so no one takes them. Of course, if you are in a group and you will be using the seats, then that is different, but "clogging" space just so you can have more is rude.

The second action a speaker can employ either at the outset of the speech or at some point during the meeting, involves eliminating a barrier between you and your listeners. To increase the intimacy of the speaking environment, and to demonstrate your comfort among the audience (thus increasing your ability to appear as one of them):

- move out from behind your seat

- walk amongst the group

- call for a break so people can get up and interact with each other in a more relaxed manner.

These actions can make an audience feel more at ease with the other people in the room, making them more receptive to the messages of others.

Other adaptation strategies work better when you are speaking. If, for instance, you notice people look confused or seem to be lost, stop and ask them if they understand, or if they need something repeated and/or clarified. Revisit points through the use of impromptu internal summaries of the information if the group appears not to understand a connection you made.

Sometimes people can seem bored or uninterested, and in this case it becomes important to vary your actions. Remember, people's attention spans are not very long, so you need to change things up every once in a while to "restart" their attention span. This can involve changes in the rate or tone of your speech, a noticeable change in the volume of your voice, going off on a short but interesting tangent, or inviting comments and questions from others at the table. It may also indicate people need a break. These surprising changes will work to counteract negative audience behaviors you may notice. Adapting to the audience based on how they react to you as speaker is an important element of being a successful and effective communicator.

SUMMARY

This chapter explained the importance of audience analysis before and during an interaction. We also discussed the different types of information you can and should try to find about your audience and provided several methods of gathering that data. Finally, we learned about what to look for in your audience and how to adapt to their reactions. Remember, there can be no message without an audience and no effective communication without understanding who the audience members are, where they come from, and what they care about.

KEY TERMS

context 61	fixed-response questions 66
classroom response systems 76	open-ended questions 66
crescendo 75	rhetorical situations 69
demographics 61	stereotyping 62
exigence 69	

REVIEW QUESTIONS

1. What do demographic data consist of?
2. What are some useful methods for researching demographic psychographic data?
3. What audience characteristics would lead you to consider placing the most important main point first? Last?
4. What are some ways of measuring audience responses during a speech?
5. What adjustments can you make at the outset of a speech to help you identify with an audience and increase their attention?
6. What were some of the challenges Mary Church Terrell faced when speaking?

THINK ABOUT IT

1. Is there a difference between audience analysis and stereotyping? If so, what is it?
2. Are there any ethical considerations for audience analysis?
3. Do we rely on survey information too much when developing speeches in today's society?
4. How could an unethical speaker use audience analysis to his/her advantage?
5. Is it possible for a speaker to overuse audience analysis?

1. Once you have a speech topic in mind and you know where you will deliver your speech, devise a list of questions regarding demographic and behavioral or attitudinal beliefs. Format these into a survey for your audience to take in advance. Use a Likert scale for attitudinal questions, and phrase them as statements rather than questions.

2. Go to a website for a popular dating service, such as http://www.match.com or http://www.eharmony.com, and look at a handful of profiles. Take a look at the questions the site asks and the options from which people can select their answers. Determine if these are demographic or attitudinal questions.

3. Watch a few films where characters deliver speeches, such as *The Contender, City Hall, Remember the Titans*, or *Mr. Smith Goes to Washington*. Listen to the speeches in these films and identify how these speeches are designed to reach the audiences in the film. Do they employ inclusive language such as "we" or "us"? Do they use a crescendo pattern to conclude the speech? What is done to make the speeches effective? This also can be done with contemporary speeches, but films are fun and effective to look at in this manner.

ENDNOTES

1. Michael Grunwald, James Carney, & Michael Scherer, "A Right Fight," *Time*, February 18, 2008, 37.

2. June Kronholz, "Will McCain Make Nice to the Right?" *Wall Street Journal*, February 6, 2008, eastern edition, sec. A.

3. Ivy J. Sellers, "CPAC 2007 Hosts Record Crowd of Enthusiastic Conservatives," Human Events, March 19, 2007, http://findarticles.com/p/articles/mi_qa3827/is_200703/ai_n18755647 (accessed May 23, 2008).

4. Robert Novak, "Fred Thompson's Progress," Human Events.com, July 21, 2007, http://www.humanevents.com/article.php?id=21616 (accessed May 23, 2008).

5. Mary Church Terrell, "What It Means to Be Colored in the Capital of the U. S.," www.americanrhetoric.com. http://www.biography.com/articles/Mary-Church-Terrell-9504299 (accessed June 11, 2011).

6. Ibid.

7. Ibid.

8. Ibid.

9. John Medina, *Brain Rules* (Seattle, WA: Pear Press, 2008), 156–158

10. Lloyd F. Bitzer, "The Rhetorical Situation," *Philosophy and Rhetoric* 1 (1968): 1–14.

11. Richard Vatz, "The Myth of the Rhetorical Situation," *Philosophy and Rhetoric* 6 (1973): 154–161.

12. http://marshallmcluhan.com/biography (accessed May 10, 2010).

13. Ibid

SCENARIOS

Scenario 1

You are a part of a committee that is exploring possible solutions relating to parking on campus. The committee has been charged with gathering feedback from students, faculty, and staff members on campus and making some recommendations to the administration about improvements. The committee is made up of fifteen members of students, faculty, and staff. Outside the main group, you and the other students on the committee have decided to work together to explain students' perspectives on this topic to the larger committee of faculty and staff, so that the committee as a whole might give due weight to these perspectives as it contemplates possible reforms.

1. What assumptions can you make about the members of the committee that will guide you in crafting your explanation (i.e. attitudes, beliefs, values, priorities, demographic data)? Please be specific regarding the assumptions of faculty, staff and your fellow students. Why do you believe your assumptions are accurate?

2. What do you need to know about your fellow students who are helping you prepare an effective explanation? Again, please be specific!

3. Devise a ten question survey that uses both fixed-response and open-ended questions that you could give to the committee members to better understand their perspectives.

a. How would the information that you gather from this survey be used to create a logical and persuasive message about your views regarding parking on campus for this particular group (the committee)?

b. How else could you go about collecting this information?

c. Can you (or should you) continue to gather information about this group as you are delivering the message? At what point would it be too late? Why?

4. Please describe how the message that you prepare will be shaped by the size of this particular audience? How might the message or your explanation strategy be different if the group was 25-30 members?

Scenario 2

Continue considering the case discussed in Scenario 1. At this point, you and your fellow students have finished preparing your message to the committee. Now, you must set up a meeting time so that all committee members can attend.

1. Considering all the members' schedules, the possible meeting times are 8am on a Monday, 12pm on a Tuesday, and 4pm on a Friday. Compare the advantages and disadvantages of meeting at each time. Based on your discussion, which time would you prefer? Why?

2. Make a list of 5 potential meeting places on campus. Compare the advantages and disadvantages of meeting at each venue. Based on your discussion, which place would you prefer? (Note: Remember to consider the meeting time you chose when making your decision.)

3. One of the faculty members in the committee has proposed having this meeting via Skype or conference call because it could be more convenient for everyone. What do you think about this potential change? How would it affect the communication? In this situation how would you respond?

Scenario 3

Look at each of the following scripts for advertising messages. For each one, identify 1) who their target audience is, 2) as much demographic information as you can infer about this target audience, 3) the beliefs that the company thinks target audience holds, and 4) the values the company thinks the target audience holds. *Beliefs* consist of what the target audience holds to be true or false: e.g., Bigfoot is real or Bigfoot is a hoax. *Values* consist of what they hold to be important: e.g., low cost and resale value are important concerns for students when buying textbooks.

Radio broadcast commercial for Columbia Cornell Heart Institute:

Just months after the birth of her daughter, Melissa suffered a massive heart attack. Her heart was destroyed, and her only hope was a transplant. Melissa was brought to the Columbia Cornell Heart Institute of New York Presbyterian. New York Presbyterian is a leader in LVAD technology, a remarkable innovation that kept Melissa alive until a transplant was available. Eventually, she got the transplant she needed. And now, Melissa's not only caring for her two small children. . . . she's swimming 50 laps every other day!

- Audience/s:
- Audience Demographics:
- Audience Beliefs:
- Audience Values:

Radio broadcast commercial for the L'Oreal "Visible Lift" makeup product:

New Visable Lift Line Minimizing Makeup with Pro-Retinol A. Finally, a makeup that really covers those little laugh lines. And really helps them disappear. With soft, line-minimizing coverage instantly, and actual line reduction in 30 days. So now when you put on your makeup-the years don't come back. Now that's a Visible Lift. You can see it, you can feel it, and you're worth it.

- Audience/s:
- Audience Demographics:
- Audience Beliefs:
- Audience Values:

Commercial for Lean Extremes fitness club:

When we moved this summer, we had to say goodbye to our house, old neighborhood, and (gulp) our fitness instructor! Luckily, we work out at Lean Extremes, a national chain with over 300 locations across the country. When we arrived in Maryland, it was so easy to settle in . . . We love our new home, hit it off with the neighbors and didn't miss a set thanks to Lean Extremes. To find out where the nearest Lean Extremes location is to you, visit their website at website.com and click on their directory. That's website.com, your #1 club for fitness across America.

- Audience/s:
- Audience Demographics:
- Audience Beliefs:
- Audience Values:

Commercial for a landscaping company:

Still trying to get that yard into shape? Enough is enough, I say! A real man isn't afraid of asking for a little help, is he? Well, I know when I called Landscape 911, they helped me out of a real bind. You see, my in-laws were coming from overseas and were expecting to see a garden paradise. With weeds everywhere, yellow grass and a lump of who knows what in the corner, I needed help, and fast. Because it was an 'emergency' as they called it, they arrived almost immediately with a crew that would've impressed Napoleon. Needless to say, calling Landscape 911 saved my yard, my skin, and probably my marriage. Check'em out at www.website.com. Landscape 911, 'cause you never know when you'll need them.

- Audience/s:
- Audience Demographics:
- Audience Beliefs:
- Audience Values:

Commercial for Green Gables Retirement Community:

You've always wanted to retire in style. The residents of Green Gables Retirement Community enjoy 25% more life and easy living! There's no need to cut the lawn, shovel the driveway, or climb unnecessary stairs—you'll have more time, more energy, and more life! Those are just three great benefits of living at Green Gables. Green Gables, the world at your doorstep with all the amenities!

- Audience/s:
- Audience Demographics:
- Audience Beliefs:
- Audience Values:

Scenario 4

Marshall McLuhan said that "the medium is the message." With your group members, come up with two example situations in which each media type below would be appropriate for someone to use and two for which it would be inappropriate to use. For example, it's appropriate to use a text message to tell someone you're running late for your meeting but not when you want to break up with your significant other. Be creative!

- Phone calls
- Text messages
- Facebook statuses
- Emails
- Face-to-face conversations

Scenario 5 (Performance)

You work at an advertising agency, and your clients need you to design TV ads that will help them sell their products. You realize quickly this will take some creativity since their products are rather obscure. It's up to you to find a way to advertise each of the products in a way that will appeal to their target audience/s. Design TV commercials that will effectively market each of the products listed below. Decide who the character/s in the commercial will be, write the script, describe the setting, identify the narrators, select background music, and/or anything else you might need to sell the product.

- The "Tough Love" app: a smartphone app that you can program to keep you from calling or texting your ex.

- The "iBaby": a robot baby that you can rent for a short period of time to let you know if you're ready to have a child. It requires regular attention, will wake you up in the middle of the night, needs to be burped, etc.

Explaining Complex Ideas to Non-Experts

CHAPTER OVERVIEW

4

- Discusses the foundations of effective explanations in a variety of contexts
- Details the components of explanations that facilitate understanding by an audience
- Provides tips and suggestions for delivering effective explanations in multiple speaking situations

Practically SPEAKING

On March 8, 2014, Malaysia Airline Flight 370 disappeared while en route from Kuala Lumpur to Beijing, China. The story captured the attention of the globe as it took weeks for investigators to determine where to search for the plane. Ultimately, the search narrowed to a remote and portion of the Indian Ocean off the coast of Australia. Even still, search teams encountered tremendous challenges while looking for signs of the plane's whereabouts and news media covering the story quickly turned to experts in fields like mathematics, aeronautical engineering, terrorism, oceanography and computer science to help explain the intricacies of this mystery to the viewing public. All of these experts were tasked with talking about complicated equations, concepts and ideas from their fields of study in terms non-experts in the audience would understand—and to do so in only a few minutes!

For example, The Royal Aeronautical Society convened a panel of experts that included pilots, manufacturers, policy regulators and airline executives in London on April 2, 2014 to help explain the potential utility of the myriad theories about how the plane could have gone off course and disappeared. This group went through six possible explanations for the diversion and disappearance and analyzed them all. They determined that, of the six, there were three (depressurization, deliberate sabotage, terrorism) possible scenarios but one of them (terrorism) was increasingly less likely. To help explain both the theories and their evaluation of them the panelists needed to relay complex information in a way the audience could understand.[1]

When the search turned to a more restricted, albeit deep, part of the Indian Ocean and it became clear the plane's black box was no longer sending out a location signal, the authorities turned to a specialized submersible vehicle called the Bluefin-21 to help them scour the ocean floor. The unmanned submarine is a product used by the US Navy that runs missions as long as 24-hours, mapping the ocean floor and using sonar to look for objects. The Bluefin-21 is an enormously complicated machine, but nevertheless experts in its use and development needed to help audiences understand what it was, what it did, and how it would help locate the remains of the plane.[2]

This example illustrates that explanation of complicated objects or concepts to non-experts is a central task regardless of what field you are in. There is no way we can understand everything in our own field of study, let alone things that emanate from another discipline, so it is important to develop the skills to help others understand things with which they may not be familiar. In this chapter we will help you acquire these skills by first discussing the foundations of explanation and how they are intertwined with how every individual makes sense of the world around them in different ways. Finally, we provide some practical and useful tips for explaining complicated subjects to non-experts in a way that helps listeners remember what it is you explained to them.

---

1 "Experts give six reasons to explain disappearance of MH370, says report," TheMayasianinsider.com, (April 2, 2014), http://www.themalaysianinsider.com/malaysia/article/experts-give-six-reasons-to-explain-disappearance-of-mh370-says-report, Last Accessed April 29, 2014.

2 Xu Geng, "Experts explain how Bluefin-21 works in search for MH370," CCTV.com, (April 16, 2014) http://english.cntv.cn/2014/04/16/VIDE1397600401238183.shtml, Last Accessed April 29, 2014.

PREP QUESTIONS

1. Define schema. Why are they helpful in explanatory speaking?

2. How do schemas develop? How do they change throughout time?

3. Why is it important to present information to your audience at an optimal speed?

4. List three ways you can help your listeners remember your information. Give an example of each.

5. Define the two techniques useful in providing the information listeners need.

6. Define the three techniques useful in helping the listener understand the ideas.

7. What can you do to be most effective when using visual aids on the fly?

8. How do you maintain visual contact with your audience when writing on the board during a presentation?

9. What three steps are needed when presenting information that helps explain an idea?

10. What is the difference between information and explanation?

4

FOUNDATIONS OF EXPLANATION

Explanation is a process of making information clear to a person who previously did not understand it. The ability to explain clearly is an essential element of almost every job, as well as a key tool for communicating in social contests as well. Although you would be hard-pressed to find a job for which explanation was never necessary, there are many careers where people's success is *especially* tied to their ability to explain complex ideas to non-experts. The STEM fields (science, technology, engineering, and math) are one group of professions for which explanation is critical. In each of these professions, people with specialized scientific knowledge must coordinate their work with, or advocate ideas to, those who lack the same expertise in order to successfully obtain funding, receive support, facilitate implementation, or allow others to use the products of one's work. An engineering firm has to explain a proposal it entered in a competitive bid for a contract; a pharmaceutical researcher might need to explain a proposed project to supervisors to receive approval to do research on a drug; and a geologist may need to explain to a city planning commission how roads and buildings could be affected by an earthquake.

explanation
a process of making information clear to a person who previously did not understand it

But the STEM fields are not the only professions for which explanation is an essential job skill. In education, the ability to explain ideas is one of the primary tasks for a teacher on a daily basis. In other professions like business, politics, and law, people's job success often hinges on the ability to explain ideas to those lacking specialized knowledge. A financial analyst must explain to managers the impact of a proposed fiscal plan; an elected official will need to explain the effects of a change in regulations, and an attorney must be able to explain how the law applies to a policy an organization is considering adopting. In short, the ability to explain complex or advanced ideas to non-experts is important in the majority of professions.

The most important point about explaining new ideas is the goal of the activity— it is to *elevate the listener's understanding, not to dumb-down the message*. In that regard, explaining ideas is the act of teaching the listener some new information. To do this well, the speaker needs to know the audience's level of knowledge on the topic, understand how people learn, and then apply principles of communication that will help listeners easily process and understand content. Explanation is a listener-focused activity, not a speaker-centered task. To put it another way, explanation is a transactional process, not a linear one.

Because explanation requires that listeners learn new information, we must first offer a basic introduction to how people understand the world around them. This topic is far bigger than could be covered in a chapter, course, or even undergraduate degree program, so we will focus on one particularly useful concept—the *schema*.

Schemas

A *schema* is a mental representation that organizes information about a subject. We use schemas to make sense of the information we encounter. We *have* to use schemas because our brains are bombarded with more information than we could make sense of without a guide to process it. Schemas give us a template for processing all the information we encounter. They allow us to know exactly what to do with the majority of information we encounter, and to respond to it with little cognitive effort. Without them, we would have to actively consider and evaluate every sensory input we encounter, and that would overwhelm our cognitive abilities.

Stop reading and take just a few seconds to consider your environment right now: What do you see? What do you hear? What do you feel, smell, or even taste? The details you could report would fill many pages. Now consider this: Does all this information challenge your ability to make sense of it? The answer, as you sit in a familiar location reading a textbook, is probably not. It is likely that virtually everything you are sensing fits so nicely into a schema, you don't even feel like you're being exposed to anything that requires cognitive effort.

Schemas are very helpful with regard to processing information. One theory that helps detail this is called the *Elaboration Likelihood Model (ELM)*. Developed in the 1980's by Richard E. Petty and John Cacioppo, ELM proposes two primary cognitive processing paths we use to make decisions. The *peripheral path* is quick, relying on schemas and prior experience to guide expectations and decisions. We typically use the peripheral path when we have little interest in a topic or are already positively disposed to it. The *central path*, on the other hand, involves careful thinking and evaluation of the messages we receive. When an issue is unclear but relevant to us, we tend to employ the central path. Although Petty and Cacioppo used ELM to explain persuasive messages, the same routes apply to receiving, evaluating and understanding explanations. We will be more apt to rely on schemas and prior experience when the topic being explained is of little interest to us, while we will pay much closer attention to explanations about things that affect us.[1]

Consider this story from the mid-1990s. A few days after a man moved to a new town, he heard a radio contest on a classic rock station while driving home from work. In the contest, listeners had to name a Led Zeppelin song being played by another group, such as a marching band, and the winners would get tickets to a Led Zeppelin tribute band. Led Zeppelin was a staple on classic rock stations at that time, and listeners of that station should have had little difficulty identifying their well-known songs. The listeners, however, did not do well. The next day, the DJ announced that he was repeating the contest but making it easier. Again, he asked listeners to name the song. This time he played a lengthy excerpt from Led

Zeppelin's greatest hit, "Stairway to Heaven," a song about as familiar to classic rock fans as "Happy Birthday" is to the average American. The contest was now ridiculously easy, but caller after caller guessed the wrong song and in several cases they weren't even guessing songs by Led Zeppelin and others weren't even guessing classic rock artists. What made the whole thing truly bizarre was that the DJ did not seem surprised at these outrageous answers. What was going on? The man had just moved from a major city to a smaller town in a different region of the country. Was there something about this place he didn't know about? He became so perplexed by the time the third caller guessed an artist who hadn't even had a hit in the same decade as Led Zeppelin that he actually pulled over. This situation was so inexplicable that for a few seconds he couldn't make sense of it and drive at the same time.

What explains the man's confusion? People have many schemas that help them understand all the information their senses provide—what the objects you see are used for, how people interact with each other, how objects should be arranged (e.g., chairs and podium in a classroom), and an endless list of other things. Most Americans have a schema for a call-in radio show. In one common form, the DJ asks a question, people call in with their best attempt to answer, and the winner gets a prize. In some variations, the winner must be a certain number caller, or DJ's playfully make fun of wrong answers. But when the contest asked listeners to guess the Led Zeppelin song, and fans of that music fail so miserably, the information cannot be explained with any schema a person is likely to have—particularly when the DJ reacts as if the responses are to be expected. Unable to explain this situation with an available schema, the observer has to abandon the shortcut to making sense and evaluate a wide range of possibilities. That generates enough of a cognitive load that it interferes with other active cognitive processes, like driving a car.

What does a schema look like? In general, they may best be thought of as networks of association. Imagine a web of ideas, concepts, and attributes that are linked based on association. Your schema for a college class probably includes elements like listening to a professor talk, having a class discussion, reading a textbook, writing a paper, and taking tests—but not, dancing, eating snacks, and playing loud music. Likewise, you have a schema for what makes a good birthday party, Thanksgiving dinner, or attractive outfit. The filing system for documents you have on your computer's desktop is a type of a schema—it is a schema for classifying the types of documents you regularly save.

Figure 4.1
Example of a schema

Scripts

Sometimes a schema includes a sequence of behaviors. This type of schema is called a *script*. Scripts include both the activities associated with an event, and also the order in which they should be done. The script for dinner at a sit-down

script
when a schema includes a sequence of behaviors

restaurant includes being seated by a host, getting drinks and a menu, ordering food, receiving a check, and paying the server before leaving. Think about a restaurant experience you may have had where it did not follow this script. Perhaps the server forgot to offer you drinks before taking your order, or delivered the bill before the meal. If this happened, you likely had an averse reaction because it did not follow the script that typically occurs in these situations.

Many schemas are unique to each individual. Throughout your life you have created your own understanding of the world and developed your own schemas. Characteristics of an ideal romantic partner form a schema that is different for each person. However, many schemas are shared among members of a culture. Proper behavior at an orchestra concert, what to do at a church service, or what should be served at Thanksgiving dinner are all schemas widely shared among Americans. Scholars have documented many socially shared schemas and scripts, such as ordering at a restaurant and even what happens on a first date.[4] Part of becoming a member of a culture, whether as a child growing up or as an adult moving to a new country or region, is learning those socially shared schemas.

Because many schemas are shared among members of a culture, they provide shared understanding for those people, but, they can also be confusing to outsiders, because their schemas are likely to be somewhat different. For example, every culture has a schema for family, but, the exact nature of that schema varies across cultures. Many cultures consider family to be based on a husband and wife, but there are polygamous cultures whose schema for family includes the possibility of multiple married partners. In American family schemas most children are of similar status, while many Eastern cultures specify different status levels based on age or sex. These differences in status may determine how the family members are to interact. So, while some schemas are widely shared, the more diverse your listeners' cultural background is, the greater the chance that audience members won't always share identical schemas. Assuming the audience shares your schema can often inhibit effective explanation.

It is also worth noting that socially shared schemas often change over time. The increasing prevalence of single-parent or unmarried-parent families and growing acceptance of gay and lesbian marriage is challenging the expectation of married heterosexual parents in many western cultures. Sometimes schemas vary across generations. For instance, the millennial generation may, in general, have a different schema than their parents for the qualities of a good job. Experts have noted, "This new crop of employees is far more motivated by their mission than by the money they make. They want to transform a broken industry, save the planet, feed the starving, etc."[5] For today's college students, making a difference may be a more significant part of the schema of "a good job" than making a lot of money.

EXPLAINING IN A WAY THAT SUPPORTS UNDERSTANDING

Prior to formulating an explanation, speakers need to attend to two tasks: Establish a clear purpose, and learn about the audience. The former is necessary, because speakers must have clear boundaries on what exactly they are explaining. Without a clear purpose and scope, the explanation will likely wander and confuse the audience.

Audience analysis is also essential. Imagine you are an accountant and have been asked to offer some basic financial principles to an audience. Do you think you know what you might say? Without knowing what the audience knows and doesn't know about your topic, you probably cannot offer an answer to that question. If your audience is a kindergarten class, your points are likely to be simple comments about making sure you save some of your money instead of spending it all the day you get it. If your audience is a group of college students, you might wish to offer some guidance on how to pay off school loans. If your audience is a group of accountants, you might explain how a new legal ruling will affect how their company should handle certain receipts. In each instance the purpose, scope and even strategies for explaining the issue are very different.

In some cases, you can reasonably guess what your audience knows just by looking a few simple demographics like age and education, or perhaps you might know the other person well to begin with (i.e. family and friends). But for others, you may need to do some specific analysis before speaking. Having a chance to survey audiences or find other ways to learn about their knowledge prior to offering an explanation may allow you to do a much better job.

When a person understands an explanation it means they have learned it, but unfortunately there is no one way to guarantee learning occurs in a listener. That said, although different people seem to learn better with different methods, some fundamentals of learning apply the same to almost everyone. In particular, presenting information in a manner that helps people cognitively process it tends to increase understanding for almost everyone. Here are four tips for presenting information in a way that helps audiences process what you are saying as accurately as possible.

Start with the Big Picture

One of the most important things a speaker can do to help the listener understand a new idea is to begin by presenting a brief, easy-to-follow overview of the big picture. This approach essentially provides a general schema for understanding all the details to follow. When people begin by jumping right into details, the audience has no sense of how those elements relate to each other or the larger concept being explained, and that makes it difficult to process that information.

Suppose a speaker wants to explain some basic exercises people should do, and then begins to give lots of specific instructions on each move. The audience could easily be confused. But, if the speaker first organizes the information by letting the listeners know there will be exercises for the upper body, legs, and core, and then offers some general principles about doing all of these moves, the listener now has a mental framework into which they can easily put the specifics. Until people know what to do with information, they have to store it in their short-term memory, which is very limited in space (only about three to seven items). When they try to put too much in, earlier information gets pushed out to accommodate newer information, and it is lost forever. This overload makes learning difficult.[6]

It is important when presenting the big picture that you make it as simple as possible, leaving out all non-essential information. You can fill in the important details later, but the big picture should present a simple framework so everyone gets that part right. Extraneous information is often interesting, but it can actually decrease learning. Bits of interesting information associated with your topic, but not part of it, are called *seductive details*. Researchers have found that people are often so fascinated with seductive details that audiences focus on them, rather than the idea you are trying to explain.[7] While interesting information or stories can have an appropriate role in an effective explanation (such as grabbing a listener's attention at the start of a presentation), speakers just need to be careful not to place them in a location where they cause a distraction.

seductive details
bits of interesting information associated with your topic, but not part of it

Pace Information Appropriately

In addition to structuring information in a manner that makes it easy to process, it is also important to present the information at an optimal speed for the audience. This "Goldilocks zone" of information flow should be neither too fast, nor too slow. If you present too much information too quickly people cannot keep up, and even those trying their hardest to follow will eventually be overwhelmed and lose track of your point. On the other hand, if you present information too slowly, people will start to lose focus and think about other topics. Their minds will often be elsewhere when relevant information is presented.

The trick is to present a steady flow of information, and keep it within the limits of what people can process. A few techniques can help keep you from going too fast. First, if a point or a question will require some time to think about (perhaps because audience members lack a schema to process it), pause briefly to allow the listeners to think. The same is true if listeners are trying to take notes so they can follow or retain information. Second, appropriate repetition of core information can be helpful in pacing, because it can buy the listener time to process existing information while emphasizing an important point. Repetition should not be over-used, because it can reduce information flow to a point that is too slow, but strategically repeating a main point can allow time for it to sink in and can signal to the audience that this information is especially important. Plus, repetition by itself can enhance retention of information, and if that information is central or foundational, you will want to be sure the audience retains that point.

Choose a Manageable Amount of Information

Related to pacing, consider the total amount of information that a listener will be able to process in the time you have allocated to explain something. While the human brain is an amazing device, it still has limits on how much it can add to its storage at one time. So, when explaining something, you need to consider not just how quickly people can absorb the information, but also the total information that can be retained at one setting. Exceeding that limit by trying to cram too much information into one message is a common cause of people forgetting.[8] The over-exertion of trying to follow too much information may even cause a *reduction* in learning, compared to what a person could retain if trying to learn a more manageable amount.

Here is the important implication: *You need to begin by deciding what is most important, and make sure you present only that information.* If time permits elaboration on some of those ideas, you can then select the next most important information and add that layer. But you're better off picking a smaller amount of information and have the audience retain all of it, than to try to cover too much and have them retain little or none of it. Aside from hurting your audience's ability to retain information, presenting too much information can obscure what is really important. When a person is exposed to too much information it can be difficult to know what is most significant, and that person may focus effort on retaining material that is not the most important. When explaining a subject to another person or group of people it is imperative you know what you want them to understand when you are done, and not obscure that information from them under layers of interesting, but tangential information.

Use Presentational Aids When Possible

When helping someone understand a new idea, speakers need to consider all channels of communication. While our spoken language can convey amazing amounts of information in a fairly concise form, many ideas are better understood if they are not just heard, but also seen, smelled, tasted, or felt. Are you trying to help the audience recognize important smells, like a natural gas leak? Much better to let people smell it than just try to describe it. Do you want your audience to know how much fish sauce to put into Vietnamese soup? Let them taste too little, too much, and the right amount. Do you want them to be able to find a location? Showing a map will make it easier than just describing it.

Presentation aids can be used in a variety of settings and are not simply restricted to PowerPoint or Prezi. Home Interior Designers, which can be found independently or in stores like Lowes, use engineering programs to draw scale pictures of designs for rooms in a house requested by clients. You might then explain the very same design to a friend at lunch and sketch it on a napkin. The napkin and engineering software program are just as much presentation aids as a PowerPoint, and just like PowerPoint, if they are not necessary they will detract from understanding. Consider  drawing on a napkin when the person you are speaking to already understands what you are drawing. That could come across as doodling and be perceived as rude by the other person. So, presentation aids take many forms, but should only be used when they are needed.

Don't waste time preparing presentational aids if they aren't necessary, but if any other senses can help people understand what you're explaining, then engage those senses in addition to offering a verbal explanation. The added layer of stimulation will enhance the probability that you effectively explained the subject to the audience.

Helping Listeners Remember Your Information

Have you ever forgotten something important that you knew you should have remembered? Perhaps you had even heard it more than once, and still forgot. Your answer is sure to be "yes," because all of us forget things we wish we'd have remembered. On the other hand, are there things that you remember well, even if they aren't that important or you haven't heard them in a long time? Again, your answer should be "yes," because latching onto certain memories is a universal human experience.

Brothers Chip and Dan Heath asked the question, "Why do we remember some ideas but forget others?" They found six principles that account for much of why certain ideas stay with us better than others, and presented them in a book called *Made to Stick*.[9] Although they were not asking how to explain complex ideas to non-experts, it turns out that these are overlapping questions—people better recall information they easily understand, and retaining information on a topic helps people better understand complex ideas. Three of the principles they suggested are particularly useful in helping people process new ideas.

Making it Simple

In order for something to be memorable, it must be easy to comprehend. To do this, a speaker must find the core of the idea, and present it in a compact manner that listeners understand when hearing it for the first time. So, a simple message has two qualities: *Core* and *compact*.

This concept is easily illustrated with corporate mission statements. If you look up an organization's mission statement, you'll normally find long complicated sentences, full of abstract language and big concepts. As an illustration, take a look at the UD Mission statement:

> As a vibrant academic department in the College of Arts and Sciences grounded in the Catholic and Marianist character of the University of Dayton, we actively serve our various and multiple communities, we produce high quality scholarship within the broad contours of our discipline. We provide an academically rigorous, critical, intellectually diverse, and praxis-oriented set of educational degree programs in political science, human rights studies, and public administration intended to properly educate and equip our students for life-long learning, faithful citizenship and positions of conscientious leadership and service to their professions, community, and the world.

After reading such a statement several times carefully, see how much you can recall an hour later. Odds are, not much. These statements cover a lot of ground, but they rarely present a core idea in a compact manner.

In contrast, consider one of the more successful U.S.-based airlines, Southwest. They have made a point of summarizing their mission in one sentence: "We are THE low-fare airline."[10] That simple presentation of mission has more impact than an entire page of fancy lingo because it is easy to understand and recall.

For Southwest, that simple idea has guided decisions and actions for over three decades to great success. Hearing that sentence, you immediately understand the business plan of Southwest Airlines.

How do you make an idea simple? Heath and Heath explain, "'Finding the core' means stripping an idea down to its most critical essence. To get to the core, we've got to weed out the superfluous and tangential elements. . . . The hard part is weeding out ideas that may be really important, but just aren't *the most important* idea."[11] Speakers often want to pack a lot of information into a presentation, but trying to cram too much in prevents simplicity, and makes a message hard to understand and retain.

Contained in Heath and Heath's procedure for making a message simple is an important truth: *Clearly explaining an idea requires that you have thought and planned carefully before speaking.* Achieving clarity isn't something you can do off the cuff. You need to understand what is most important, because that determines the starting point of your explanation. Then, you can start to fill in other important information that supports that core idea. A common cause of confusing explanations is trying to describe something that has not been carefully thought through. People often fail to start with a clear presentation of the core, mix important and tangential information together, present information in illogical sequences, use wording that sounds contradictory, and often run over their allotted time—all because they tried to talk before fully thinking about and planning their message.

One final but important note about making explanations simple bears mentioning. Just because you are making the explanation simple, does not mean the topic is itself simple. Remember, complex things which people do not understand require explanations they can understand in order to learn the subject. The explanation must be simpler than the subject and placed into terms the audience understands, but it does not mean the topic's importance or core need to be dumbed down.

Making it Concrete

Consider an important research article on how people think, which leads with this sentence: "A fundamental tenet of all recent theories of comprehension, problem-solving, and decision-making is that success in such cognitive arenas depends on the activation and appropriate application of relevant pre-existing knowledge."[12] Read that again. Was it easy to understand? Will you remember it tomorrow? Unlikely. There are many reasons this sentence is difficult to understand, but one is that the language is so abstract. Now consider that it could have been said this way: "People understand more and make better decisions when they use schemas properly." You likely found that easier to follow.

Heath and Heath use the product Velcro to explain why we process and recall concrete ideas better than abstract ones. Velcro has two sides—one with lots of loops, the other with lots of hooks. When you press the two sides together, the hooks slip into the loops to form its grip. Memories seem to work that way as well—the more hooks they have, they more easily they are retained. Try to recall this information: (a) The house you spent most of your childhood in, and (b) the definition of "satisfaction." Which was easier for you to remember? Which brought multiple thoughts to your head at once? Most likely it was your childhood home. That residence offers lots of memories—events, smells, sights, sounds, and more. These are all hooks that make something memorable. You might be able to think of some words to define satisfaction, but it is probably harder to do as there are fewer "hooks." Concrete ideas seem to have better hooks than more abstract ideas. There is more there for us to mentally "grab hold" of.

When explaining complex ideas to non-experts, if you begin with—or rely heavily on—abstract ideas, your listeners will probably not fully grasp your ideas. The more you can offer explanations grounded in concrete ideas, the more effective you are likely to be. One of the best ways to provide hooks for your loops and engineer effective explanations is to tell stories.

Using Stories

Finally, one of the most important ways we can help people understand an idea is to share a story that illustrates the idea. While we often think of stories just as a fun diversion, they are actually much more important. Some experts go so far as to suggest that stories are one of the more common ways people make sense of the world around them.[13] While meaning is partially created by knowing the definition of words being used, much more of meaning is made by understanding the story in which those words play out. For example, your religious faith is a story which not only guides your actions, but also helps you make sense of events you experience. In a sense, a story becomes a schema for events you experience.

Stories have substantial impact on understanding ideas. Consider Aesop's fables, such as the boy who cried wolf. The story makes an important point (don't ruin your credibility), and it offers an easier way to understand and remember than an abstract statement of ethical theory would do. Stories need to be used appropriately when supporting an explanation. Used poorly, they can run on too long, contain ideas irrelevant to the core (likely to be seductive details), or be so emotional that they distract cognitive processes. But, if a story is told sharing only elements that are related to the point being made, it can offer insight that would otherwise be missed. When telling a story, it is essential that you clearly state how the story sheds light on the point you are explaining. If you don't do that, people might enjoy the story, but won't connect it with what you want them to understand.

Stories also capture the attention of listeners, and thus present an opportunity to reach an audience with a memorable way of understanding a key point in your message. Stories, though, should be focused, short and concrete. You also should tell the listener the point of the story explicitly either before or after telling the tale, or else they may very well take a meaning from it that is not what you intended.

Stories are also not necessary for every explanation, but if a story truly enhances a listener's ability to understand the idea you are explaining without distracting from the main point, then including it can add impact what would otherwise be missed.

SPOTLIGHTING THEORISTS: CHIP AND DAN HEATH

The authors of the *New York Times* bestseller, *Made to Stick: Why Some Ideas Survive and Others Die,* Chip and Dan Heath have contributed much to our understanding of how to explain complex subjects to audiences of one, one hundred or one thousand people. While neither is a communication scholar, they understand the way in which ideas from different disciplines like Business and Psychology intersect and influence how we can construct effective explanations.

The brothers have also co-authored two other popular press books that take academic research and explain it in a way the general public can understand. In 2010 they released *Switch: How to Change Things When Change is Hard*, which debuted as #1 on both the *New York Times* and *Wall Street Journal* bestseller lists. Recently, they completed another book, *Decisive: How to Make Better Decisions in Life and Work.* All three of their books help people understand how both their own minds and the minds of audiences work when processing complicated information in an effort make good decisions.

Both brothers have strong pedigrees. Chip is a professor at the Stanford Graduate School of Business, while Dan is a Senior Fellow at Duke University's CASE Center, which focuses on social entrepreneurs, and also the founder of Thinkwell, an innovative publishing company. Chip has done extensive consulting with companies such as Google, Gap, and the American Heart Association. Dan previously worked as a researcher for the Harvard Business School, where he earned his MBA. Together, their works have been translated into 28 different languages.[14]

TOOLS FOR EFFECTIVE EXPLANATION

The principles discussed above offer some general approaches to explanation. People understand best when presented with a schema to organize the information they encounter, and with a manageable amount of information to process in the time allotted. They understand better when the message appeals to the appropriate senses, and, they understand better when information is simple, concrete, and illustrated with a story. These principles alone provide useful guidance for decisions you will make in crafting an explanation. There are also some basic techniques that you can use when applying those principles that make implementing them more effective.

This first pair of techniques add clarity to an explanation. In a situation where explanation is needed, the audience has less understanding of the topic than the speaker, and so listeners will not understand important information if it is not provided clearly. Two techniques are especially useful in providing the information listeners need: Definition and vivid description.

Definition. Any time a word is used which a listener might not know—especially if that word has a specialized meaning in that instance—then the speaker needs to define the word. Imagine a company's Chief Financial Officer (CFO) is presenting a financial report to employees. In the report, she talks about *operating margins, beginning net assets, hedge fund investments, real assets*, and *private equities*. Will the audience know what the financial figures mean? They are likely to understand the math, which is very simple, but without definitions they are unlikely to know what those numbers mean. Thus, she will fail in her goal of explaining the company's financial situation. If the CFO offers a definition of each concept that is easy to understand, her explanation of the company's financial situation has a good chance of being clear to the audience.

Vivid description. If a listener needs to visualize something in order to understand it, then a vivid description may be necessary. Such a description includes a wide range of details, perhaps relating to many different senses, which allows the listener to understand better. If you have ever watched a TV show about food, you know that a talented host will describe food using vivid descriptions that appeal to sight, taste, feel, and sound. Andrew Zimmern and Adam Richman use vivid descriptions, full of concepts the viewer understands to describe foods that viewers may never have eaten. For example, what do you think kangaroo tail soup tastes like? If you have no idea, Andrew Zimmern describes it in *Bizarre Foods:* "It smells like beef and barley . . . Winey, deep, and aromatic . . . Kangaroo tail tastes like braised beef. It's kind of crunchy and smooth, all the same time." Getting a better idea? More description could give you even a better idea . . . if that sounds like something you'd want to eat. For another example of the power of vivid description, look at the testimony given by Fannie Lou Hamer in 1964 on racial injustice.

The next set of tools are important techniques you can use to help listeners understand ideas they are not currently familiar with: comparison, contrast, and metaphor. These each involve creative uses of language to make concepts more relatable for audiences. Like stories, description and definition, the key is knowing when they are appropriate to employ, and what comparisons and metaphors will work best with a given audience in a specific context.

comparison
connecting new information with something a person already knows

Comparison. One of the more common ways people learn is by connecting new information with something they already know. Comparing something new with what is known allows a person to use all or parts of an existing schema. That means that the information that is part of that schema can be applied. So, an apt *comparison* allows a lot of information transfer to happen at one time. For example, if you want to explain the experience of being stung by a jellyfish, comparing the experience with sensations a person might have experienced will make it easier to understand. Comparing a complicated idea or item to a more commonly understood concept helps people appreciate the foundation of the more complicated subject by identifying characteristics it shares with something they already know.

Contrast. In some cases it is what is *different* between the new information and what is known that is most important. For example, piloting a large sailboat has some similarity to driving a car, in that both use a wheel of some type, but that's where the similarities end. When sailing a boat, there is enough lag time between moving the ship's wheel and the vehicle response that beginners overdo almost every steering move. Steering a boat requires small movements and patience, plus knowledge of how much a steering adjustment will move the craft. Likewise, changes in speed happen very slowly using the sails, not quickly like they do with an accelerator or brake pedal. So, while driving a car and commanding a sailboat both involve controlling speed and direction, it is the contrast, not the comparison, that helps explain the experience and process to the listener.

Comparison and contrast are often most effectively used when paired together. Because few things are identical in every regard, a comparison of what is similar followed by a contrast of what differs may offer the most helpful route to a more thorough understanding. Explaining how to drive a riding mower might involve a more balanced presentation of comparison and contrast from driving a car than the example of a sailboat. But, both pairings (car-boat, car-mower) can benefit from comparison and contrast in the explanation.

Metaphor. In the chapter on Language we will define metaphor and provide you with different types of metaphors that could be employed in a message. For the purposes of our discussion here, know that metaphors are very effective and efficient tools for explaining complicated subjects to listeners. In fact, they are so prevalent in our everyday language you probably don't even notice you use them. Metaphors help us extend meaning to things with which people are not familiar by connecting them to things they know very well. In fact, one of the most common ways to expand our language is to develop new meanings through the metaphorical extensions of existing words. Computer technology provides an obvious example.

With the invention of new technology, we suddenly needed language to describe a lot of new hardware and software. Most of those words were metaphors. Consider the origins of words like *mouse*, *tablet*, the *web* (on which you can *surf*, so how is that for a mixed metaphor!). These words, along with hundreds of others, are metaphors used to make new complicated concepts and things familiar. Our brains are wired to understand new ideas as metaphorical extensions of existing knowledge, providing us with a useful and creative shorthand for making new things understandable for an audience.

PREPARING AND TAKING NOTES

Language skills are not the only elements of an effective explanation. In professional settings where explanations are called for, such as a team meeting, briefing on a policy, or performance review, it is immeasurably helpful to prepare notes before the meeting. Taking notes helps you organize the explanation before having to provide it.

Comments Before the Credentials Committee
by Fannie Lou Hamer

Delivered August 22, 1964, at the Democratic National Committee, Atlantic City, New Jersey

Fannie Lou Hamer, the granddaughter of slaves, was born in 1917 in Mississippi. She became a sharecropper on a plantation, and in 1962 when members of the Student Nonviolent Coordinating Committee (SNCC) came to town to hold a voter registration meeting, Hamer didn't even know that she had a constitutional right to vote. Once she knew she could, she volunteered to help register others to vote and was later jailed, beaten, and driven from the farm where she was a sharecropper as result.[3]

Hamer went on to become secretary of the SNCC and traveled to various places registering people to vote, spoke about voting rights, and cofounded the Mississippi Freedom Democratic Party (MFDP). The Credentials Committee of the 1964 Democratic Convention asked her to speak about racial injustice.[4]

Hamer told the committee about the treatment she had received from the police, how the plantation owner had pressured her to withdraw her registration request, and that when she refused he told her to leave his property. She also recounted the resistance at registration drives and how she and others with her were not allowed to eat in some restaurants or use restrooms.[5] She told of black prisoners ordered to beat her with blackjacks and of the terrible names the police called her. Here is an excerpt from her informative and emotional testimony:

"I was carried out of that cell into another cell where they had two Negro prisoners. The State Highway Patrolmen ordered the first Negro to take the blackjack. The first Negro prisoner ordered me, by orders from the State Highway Patrolman, for me to lay down on a bunk bed on my face. As I laid on my face, the first Negro began to beat me. And I was beat by the first Negro until he was exhausted."[6]

As the sender, notes allow you to recall the important points of the explanation without having to rely on memory. Notes also can provide you with multiple ways of explaining a particular point, depending on how well the other party seems to understand your explanation. For instance, consider a doctor explaining the survival rate of a particular cancer to a patient. They might begin with talking about the data on how many people survive for a particular period of time, but the patient may not understand what this means for their specific case. So, the doctor then might resort to telling a story or comparing the numbers to something that might make the data more understandable. Now, if the patient understands the numeric information the doctor initially explained, these other methods of explanation are not necessary—but it's good to have them in case you do need to employ other ways to unpack complex information for the other person.

Now, what do good notes look like for an explanation? First, they need to be somewhat structured, meaning the important takeaway points need to be clearly delineated on the notes, while the methods you might use to explain each point is under the point which they help explain. So the example of the doctor above might look something like this for the first point:

The survival rate for patients with this particular cancer is excellent when caught this early.

- ***Data****: 90% of patients survive this cancer when caught at this stage.*
- ***Story****: Patient named Jim had similar diagnosis to me last year*
- ***Analogy****: Like those toothpaste commercials/9 out of 10 dentists recommend*

Let's look at another example: a performance review by a boss. The supervisor has three categories to evaluate the employee, and so the overall rating in each category constitutes the three main points of the explanation. For each category the supervisor may have several types of evidence to support their conclusion, but may not have the time nor the need to explain all of them. Nevertheless, they have them prepared in their notes in case they do need it.

Ultimately, a speaker's notes have the following qualities:

1. Main take-away points are on one level while evidence supporting those points is on another level

2. There are several different ways to explain the takeaway point, but they all do not necessarily need to be covered

3. They are extemporaneous, and are not meant to be read, but rather used as a method to ensure recall of salient information

4. They contain citations for relevant information gathered from external sources because you never know when you might be asked to provide the source

We have included an example of explanatory notes as an appendix at the end of this book, for a hypothetical explanatory talk on ideology, an important concept from the fields of communication, sociology, political science, and philosophy. Note that there are three sections to the notes:

- **A brief introduction** that leads into the talk by introducing the topic and purpose of the conversation, building rapport with the listener, gauging his or her experience with the topic, and establishing the speaker's credibility,

- **The body of the talk**, in which the speaker shares information about different points relating to the topic and includes different tools for explaining that information for each of these points, and

- **A brief conclusion** in which the speaker reinforces the main ideas from the talk—often by asking the listener to give a summary of what she or he understood and reaffirming or clarifying key ideas—and brings the conversation to an end.

The body of the talk is organized into multiple "talking points," each of which can be covered or not covered depending upon what the listener already knows or does not know about the topic. Each talking point uses the three-point structure covered at the end of this chapter, in which the speaker (1) states the overarching point (takeaway point), (2) provides information from her or his research and helps the listener to understand that information through use of explanatory tools from this chapter, and (3) connects this information back to the overarching point. For each talking point, the speaker has prepared multiple ways of explaining the same overarching idea, using the tools for explaining in this chapter—which might or might not be used once the conversation begins. The notes are written in an extemporaneous fashion; they do not include full sentences except for direct quotations. Note that citations are given in the notes, so that the speaker can verbally attribute the sources for the information that she or he gives as the conversation unfolds. The notes also contain some cues helpful to the speaker, such as markers to indicate when particular video clips could be shown to the listener and start times for these videos.

The notes are structured but flexible enough that the speaker can adapt to the listener's needs and experience as the conversation unfolds. To learn what experience the listener has regarding the topic and to identify what points are most important to cover once the conversation begins, the speaker should ask questions throughout the conversation, some at the beginning of the talk, some during the middle of the talk, and some at the end of the talk before bringing the talk to a close.

ASKING QUESTIONS TO CHECK PERCEPTION

Asking questions is a primary way of learning about what a listener already knows about the topic, gauging how clearly she or he is understanding the explanation once it begins, and determining what points might need to be reinforced before ending the talk. Often, complex information takes a few minutes to unpack for a listener—even when the explanation is clear. The appropriateness of questions relates both to their timing and how they are worded. A poorly timed question may come across in a way that insults the other person, too many questions may detract from the explanation, while a poorly worded question may not get you the information you seek.

There are three periods of an explanation when you might ask questions of the listener: near the beginning, in the middle and towards the end. The goals of each of these questions are slightly different, but all should provide you with information that helps you adjust the explanation in a way that makes it clearer for the other party.

Asking early questions: Near the beginning of an explanation you might want, or need, to ask the other person what they know regarding your overall topic. The answer to this question will help you gage where to begin the explanation, because if a person is not familiar with the topic you might need to provide a little more information than if they had some idea of what you are talking about. These questions should be specific, because just asking a "yes or no" question does not tell you what the person knows. Therefore, you should ask them to briefly explain what they know about the topic.

If you walk into a situation where the overall concept is something you believe the other party has some understanding of at the start, you don't need to ask a question early on. Take the case of the aforementioned performance review. The supervisor does not need to find out what the employee knows about the categories or performance review process, and so they can just get started explaining the review. They might, however, need to ask questions in the middle of the explanation.

Asking questions in the middle of the explanation: These are the most common questions that take place during an explanation. Their goal is to make sure a main point is understood, and these questions can be either planned or prompted by the listener's behavior. Sometimes when the topic is pretty complex and unfamiliar to the other person you might want to plan a question to gage their understanding after explaining a key point. If the person does not seem to get it, you can try another method of explaining the same point to help them understand.

Other times it may seem from the nonverbal behaviors of the other person that they either have stopped paying attention or do not understand the material you have explained. In this scenario you would ask a question to see if they are, in fact, paying attention and understanding the content. The box to the right

> Shaking head from side to side
>
> Looking down or away from the speaker
>
> A furrowed brow
>
> A frown
>
> Shrugging shoulders

contains some nonverbal behaviors that might hint that the other person is lost or does not understand what you are saying.

Just like questions you might ask at the outset of an explanation, these questions should not be of the "yes/no" variety. Rather, they should ask for a specific response from the other person that demonstrates understanding. One of the best ways to do this is to ask them to apply the content to something else and have them relay it back. Here are some examples of good perception checking questions in the middle of an explanation:

- Can you give me an example of this from your life?
- What does this sound like to you?
- How might you explain this point to someone else?

These types of questions force the other person to demonstrate their understanding by verbalizing a coherent application of the material you just explained. If they do so accurately, you can move on to the next key point—if they do not, you need to *both* correct their misperception and explain the material in a different way to ensure understanding. When we ask someone questions like "Do you understand this?" and "does this make sense to you" the other person will most often say "yes" even if they do not and thus no understanding is achieved.

Asking questions at the end: The third period of an explanation where questions are helpful. Whereas questions at the beginning are used to help identify where to begin the explanation and those in the middle serve to identify understanding of a specific complicated key point, questions near the end of an explanation help to pinpoint how well the other party understands the topic now that you have explained it. Ideally, these questions give the other party an opportunity to extend the conversation by asking them to think about issues which the topic might relate to now that they understand it.

Take the case of a student explaining hydroponic farming to a friend. After detailing the reasons why it is becoming more popular and relaying the ways in which is can be beneficial to the environment the person may ask the listener to think of other ways this type of farming might help. Or they may ask them what they see as the potential drawbacks or benefits to hydroponic farming. The answers to these questions will help the explainer see how well the other party now understands the concept by seeing if they can now think more deeply and critically about the subject.

Asking appropriate questions at the right time during an explanation is key to facilitating understanding. It is also not as easy as it might seem because knowing when to ask questions and phrasing those questions in a way that provides you with actionable information takes practice and requires paying attention to the context in which the communication takes place. In addition to language skills and questions there is one more strategy we will discuss that aids in achieving understanding in an explanation.

VISUAL SUPPORT FOR EXPLANATION

When you prepare an explanation, you should consider not just the words you use, but also what other means of communicating information will help. Presentational aids—especially visual aids—are one element you should always consider in advance. Guidelines for how to prepare and use them effectively are presented later in the book. However, sometimes in the course of an explanation, you discover that some visual representation might be helpful, for reasons you could not have foreseen before speaking.

What can you do to be most effective when using visual aids on the fly? There is no simple or complete list of rules, because each situation is different. However, we offer a few general principles here that are worth keeping in mind. In all cases, the question is *"What will help the listener understand, without becoming a distraction?"* The guidelines presented below are often useful, but always go back to this question rather than mindlessly following a rule. And the more you know about how listeners process information, the better you can answer this question.

Keep your visual aid simple and as neat as possible. Drawing or writing while speaking takes time and focuses audience attention on the visual element. Adding tangential information takes additional time away from your message—giving listeners' minds time to wander—and can be confusing. Listeners will naturally try to understand why each detail is there, so unnecessary information becomes a distraction. Fun, but seductive, details are also distracting, and can take listeners' minds away from your point.

While you want to write or draw quickly so as to keep audience members attentive to your points, going so quickly and sloppily that your audience cannot read your writing or understand something you've drawn undermines the point of having done it in the first place. So, only go as quickly as you can write legibly.

Maintain visual contact with the audience. When writing on a board, the natural position is to turn your back to the audience—which is one reason why speakers should always prepare visuals in advance when the need can be anticipated. However, if the need to produce a visual on the fly comes up, speakers should write and then turn back to the audience as soon as the writing or drawing is done. Always talk to the audience, not to the presentation aid.

Explain what you write or draw. A list, chart, drawing, or some other visual aid may be essential to your explanation, but just putting it out by itself may create more questions than it answers. Always be sure to offer a clear explanation of what your visual is and how it contributes to understanding the point you're making.

Be attuned to the listener's response. If you have discovered the need for unplanned visual support of an explanation, you have now moved "off the script" and are engaging the audience directly on something that you just discovered is causing difficulty in understanding. Take care to watch their nonverbal and listen to verbal responses to gauge whether or not the visual aid helped them overcome their confusion. Head nods, smiles and raised eyebrows can indicate they have achieved understanding, while shrugs, furrowed brows and open mouths can indicate they still do not get it. Watching your listeners' reactions allows you to make sure the audience understands the important point the visual conveyed before you move on.

STRUCTURING EACH POINT IN THE CONVERSATION

You may have heard it said, "The facts speak for themselves." This may be true, but if you let the facts speak for themselves, they can say anything they want to the audience . . . which might be different from what you want them to say. For example, here is a fact: A recent study suggested that texting results in more injuries per mile traveled for pedestrians than for drivers.[14] Now, what is that fact saying? It may be telling us that we should not text while walking. It might be telling us that preventing texting while driving should not be a policy concern. It might be telling us that self-driving cars will reduce injuries . . . or that more money should be spent on mass transportation. Or, it might say something else entirely. It also raises the question of whether we should trust the study, whether the severity of injuries should be considered in addition to just the number of them, and more. Think of all the ways we could go with this simple statement! Without an explanation of the fact, it does not speak with one voice, but with many, and is thus terribly confusing.

Texting while driving

Speakers sometimes state information, assuming that listeners will all make the same use of that information as the speaker. That does not ever happen. All listeners interpret that information with the schemas, values, and biases they have, so, just putting some information out there is a sure way to *not* make your point clear. Instead, some other approach is needed.

In general, three steps are needed when presenting information that helps explain an idea. These steps don't have to be enumerated or highlighted, but they should all be present:

1. State the point
2. Present the material using the principles and tools in this chapter
3. Make the connection between the support (step 2) and your point (step 1)

Consider this example. In explaining the search for the missing Malaysia Flight 370 a speaker might tell the audience that in early April 2014, ships hunting for wreckage detected underwater pings. That seems like useful information. But what does it tell us in explaining the search? That could vary widely. Here is one possible way it could be used to clarify a point:

> Searching for the underwater wreckage of a plane is very difficult. The plane's flight data recorders, also called "black boxes," are the most important piece to find, because they contain a complete record of flight information. These black boxes make a pinging noise after a plane crashes in the water to help searchers locate the wreckage.
>
> 1. In early April 2014, ships hunting for wreckage detected underwater pings.
> 2. Hearing these pings might seem like a sure sign that the searchers had located the wreck. However, it is not always that simple. First, pings can sometimes be detected that are caused by something other than black boxes. Sometimes a ship's own equipment creates a false signal. Second, even if the pings were from black boxes, finding a wreck on the bottom of a deep ocean can be difficult. Normally sonar and other equipment are needed to scan a wide area of ocean floor, which is rarely flat and easy to scan. And the area that must be searched can still be quite large. Even if pings are detected, it can still take months to locate a wreck.
> 3. So, while detecting a ping gives searchers hope, just hearing that noise does not mean that the wreck has been located.

In this example, the takeaway should be clear: hearing pings does not mean a crashed airplane has been located. The story of MH 370 helps make the case and is directly tied to the core topic being explained. It also provides a vivid story in concrete detail that a listener can remember.

SUMMARY

In this chapter we discussed explanation and its various components. We illustrated that in order to effectively explain something to someone you must first appreciate the fact you and the other person have different schemas that help make sense of the world. We provided some principles for explanation that, if followed, help enhance audience understanding and retention of key information in the explanation. We provided practical tips for helping others remember information, and for how you can construct effective explanations. Finally, we offered some guidelines for effectively employing presentation aids in explanations that occur in a variety of different contexts.

KEY TERMS

comparison   100

elaboration likelihood model (ELM)   90

explanation   89

schema   90

script   91

seductive details   94

ENDNOTES

1. John T. Cacioppo and Richard E. Petty,"The Elaboration Likelihood Model of Persuasion", in NA - Advances in Consumer Research Volume 11, eds. Thomas C. Kinnear, (1984) Provo, UT : Association for Consumer Research, Pages: 673-675.

2. Mary Claire Serewicz & Elaine Gale, "First-date scripts: Gender roles, context, and relationship," *Sex Roles, 58*, (2008) 149-164.

3. Brian Halligan, "How Millennials think, and what to do about it" *Inc.* (July 3, 2013), http://www.inc.com/brian-halligan/how-millennials-think-and-what-to-do-about-it.html, Last Accessed April 29, 2014.

4. Sarah Blissett, Rodrigo B. Cavalcanti, & Matthew Sibbald, "Should we teach using **schemas**? Evidence from a randomised trial," *Medical Education, 46*(8), (2012) 815-822.

5. Shannon F. Harp, & Richard E. Mayer, "How seductive details do their damage: A theory of cognitive interest in scientific learning," *Journal of Educational Psychology, 90*, (1998) 414-434.

6. Donald A. Bligh, *What's the use of lectures?* San Francisco: Jossey-Bass (2000).

7. Chip Heath & Dan Heath, *Made to stick*, New York: Random House (2000).

8. Heath & Heath.

9. Heath & Heath, p. 28.

10. Rand J. Spiro, Walter P. Vispoel, John G. Schmitz, Ala. Samarapungavan, & A.E. Boerger, "Knowledge acquisition for application: Cognitive flexibility and transfer in complex content domains," In B. K. Britton & S. M. Glynn (Eds.), *Executive control processes in reading* (pp. 177-199). Hillsdale, NJ: Lawrence Erlbaum, (1987).

11. Fisher, Walter R. (1984). "Narration as Human Communication Paradigm: The Case of Public Moral Argument." in *Communication Monographs* 51. pp. 1–22.

12. Injuries Related to Texting and Walking Increasing," *Claims Journal*, (March 5, 2014), http://www.claimsjournal.com/news/national/2014/03/05/245467.htm Last Accessed April 29, 2014. See their website for even more information: http://heathbrothers.com

SCENARIOS

Scenario 1

Think about a complex topic/issue from your major. For example, if you are a Chemical Engineering major, you could use the example of thermodynamics. Remembering your group members are not Chemical Engineer majors, explain to them the complexity of thermodynamics in layperson terms. Ensure they understand the information given to them by watching for nonverbal cues. Think about the jargon and language you use when explaining this complex topic.

1. After listening to your group members, discuss whether you used peripheral path or central path to understand the message. What is the difference between the two according to Richard Petty and John Cacioppo's Elaboration Likelihood Model (ELM)?

Scenario 2 (Performance)

Imagine it is one year ago today. You may have been thinking about going to college, you may have visited a couple of universities, you may have even decided to go to UD. Think about the schema you had regarding: college life, living on your own, coursework, friends, social life, etc.

1. Why did you have this particular schema about college?

2. Have these schemas changed today? How?

3. How would you explain college life and/or UD to a senior in high school thinking about going to college? How would you explain the same issues to his/her parents? What aspects of UD do you think a potential applicant might not understand? How might you explain these things to them?

Research and Preparation

Practically SPEAKING

Students today typically react to the necessity of venturing to the library with a mixture of dread, loathing, and reluctance; however, that has not always been the case. In fact, there was a time when libraries held an exalted status and represented more than simply storage facilities for the printed word. In the ancient world, libraries were castles of learning and homes to schools, zoos, museums, and the brightest minds of the day. They were, in point of fact, the backbone of empires and kingdoms.

The most famous library in history was located in Alexandria, Egypt, and its history is a mixture of both fact and myth. King Ptolemy I (Soter) and his son King Ptolemy II (Philadelphus) commissioned the Great Library at Alexandria and modeled it after Aristotle's Lyceum in terms of mission, but the Alexandrian library dwarfed the Lyceum in terms of size, structure, and content. This model, however, occurred for good reason.[1]

Ptolemy I was one of Alexander the Great's generals, and after the death of his leader and subsequent partition of the empire, Ptolemy ruled Egypt. Alexander was a student of Aristotle's, and so he made sure his generals were schooled in the same vein. Additionally, through his conquests Alexander attempted to Hellenize the world by spreading the value of the *enkyklios paideia*, or rounded education, which tiered instruction into the *trivium* (grammar, rhetoric, and logic), and *quadrivium* (arithmetic, geometry, music, and astronomy).

The Ptolemys sought to create a universal library, one where knowledge of all things could be found, not just a localized culture-specific repository of knowledge. The Great Library also contained a museum. Together they represented one of the greatest achievements in all of antiquity.[2] The Great Library and Museum worked in tandem to store and develop the wisdom of the ages. Scholars from around the known world lived and worked tax-free at the Library copying scrolls secured by the government. On several occasions, Ptolemy and his successors even brought scrolls on loan from Greek city-states and copied them only to keep both the original and the copy! It was the epicenter of scholarship and innovation because many of those holdings were original Greek works and translations of non-Greek texts of religious, poetic, and political significance.[3]

Unfortunately, nothing much remains of the Great Library and Museum and the histories of it are the product of researching letters and writings that reference it. No one is sure how it was destroyed, but destroyed it was, and many writings contained there are now lost forever. Ironically, we know about the ancient world's research mecca only through research, as it no longer exists and its documents are long gone.

Nowadays we think of libraries simply as places where knowledge is stored, and the university as a whole fits the model set forth by the Great Library. Nevertheless, the Greeks and Romans recognized that libraries and research skills are central to the development of a critical mind, and we should learn from that example.

In this chapter we will explore the very nature of research, and illustrate the importance of becoming information literate. We will discuss different types of sources and how you can find the ones most appropriate to your project. Finally, we will detail the importance of properly citing sources you use and provide three examples as to how you can do so.

PREP QUESTIONS

1. What are the three characteristics of a good research question?

2. List different methods for note taking.

3. Define what it means to be information literate.

4. List the five characteristics of someone who is information literate.

5. What are the three components of evaluating information?

6. Name and define the three different types of plagiarism.

7. State the three kinds of information researchers seek and explain how each can be utilized.

8. Explain the value of using online databases and interviews. When would it be preferable to use each?

9. List the ending URLs from least to most credible.

10. Give two examples of ways that one can word their verbal attributions.

CRAFTING A RESEARCH QUESTION

Once you determine your topic, you need to focus your research around a question about that topic. This question is called your *research question*, and it guides you through the discovery process. Regardless of whether you are delivering a speech or participating in a discussion about an issue, a research question is essential for providing you with a focus for your efforts. It allows you to keep attention on the issue and not get sidetracked with extraneous information. There are three characteristics of every quality research question.

First, a research question is an open-ended question and cannot be answered with a simple "yes" or "no." The answer to the question is complex and requires a level of detail and description that is not necessary for a "yes" or "no" question. If the general topic of discussion is about a famous musician, and the specific topic is Bob Dylan, then your research question might be "What inspired Bob Dylan to write his song "Hurricane"?" Answering such a question calls for you to explore who Bob Dylan was, some history of the song, background on its topic, and even perhaps some cultural issues at play during the time he wrote the song. Of course, you could craft a myriad of different research questions from the specific topic of Bob Dylan, and each would need different data and information to answer, but any question you seek to answer must be open-ended.

In addition to being open-ended, a research question must be tailored to the topic. In other words, it must be relevant to the general and specific topic under consideration in some way. Using the Bob Dylan example again, some other successful research questions might be "What was Bob Dylan's childhood like?" "Why did Bob Dylan choose music as a career?" or even "How has Bob Dylan influenced contemporary musicians?" What would not work in the framework of this general and specific topic would be a persuasive question like, "How can I convince people to listen to Bob Dylan?" or an informative question unrelated to the topic like, "Who else was a successful speaker at the time of Bob Dylan?" This question, though it

research question
the question about your topic you seek to answer

enkyklios paideia
rounded education spread under the reign of Alexander the Great

trivium
grammar, rhetoric, and logic

quadrivium
arithmetic, geometry, music, and astronomy

Bob Dylan

mentions Dylan, is not about Dylan, thereby violating the specific topic and creating a tangent for the discussion.

Rubin "Hurricane" Carter

Finally, the answers to strong research questions will inevitably become the thesis statement or argument you present to others. Look at the Dylan example from a few moments ago. Let's say that your research indicates that Dylan wrote his hit song "The Hurricane" because of a personal sense of social justice, the desire to right a wrong perpetrated on a minority, and to shed some light on the situation in which Rubin "Hurricane" Carter found himself. That presents a strong thesis about the song and how it reflected the plight of Carter, a former boxer who was accused, convicted, and later exonerated for the murder of three people at a bar in Paterson, New Jersey in 1966. This topic is obviously complex and warrants further explanation, hence the need for a longer discussion built on the foundation provided by the answer to your initial research question. See Table 5.1 for some examples of poorly and properly worded research questions.

Table 5.1

Wording Research Questions	
Poorly Worded Research Questions	**Properly Worded Research Questions**
Who is Barack Obama?	What is the history of Barack Obama's political career?
Is it easy to pass Calculus 1?	What are some study strategies to successfully pass Calculus 1?
What is an easy way to break up with someone?	What is an ethical method to end a romantic relationship?
Why do service learning?	What benefits can students receive from engaging in service learning?
Are you a healthy eater?	What are the factors to consider for a healthy diet?
Why did Germany start WWII?	What were the historical, economic, and social events that contributed to Germany's military aggression leading to WWII?
Why play video games?	How can playing video games improve hand and eye coordination?

Refining Your Topic

As you search for the answer to your research question you also must adapt to the results of your research. To do this, you must be prepared to refine your specific topic and even your research question to better guide you on your quest for information. First and foremost, when you begin you must be prepared to discover that the focus when you finish researching may very well not be the focus you wanted, or thought you had, when you began. This is only natural, and is the result of good research skills.

One of these skills is note-taking. Good researchers have a method of note-taking that works best for them. This may involve note cards, photocopying information to better write margin notes, keeping a research notebook, or even using Post-it notes to label where you found information. Regardless how you do it, you need to develop a categorizing system that makes sense to you so when it comes time to organize the information you found into meaningful points you can easily do so. Taking good organized notes while you research will help you refine your topic and focus your thoughts.

Good researchers seek information with an open mind, and do not simply look for data that supports their original idea. It is important to allow contrary information to count as much as material that supports your ideas. There are multiple interpretations of a variety of different data, from statistics, to events, to even the lives of people, and good researchers find as many of these as possible to better balance their results. The more relevant information you collect, the stronger your position will become. Let the information be your guide, rather than you guiding the research.

It is tempting for any student to simply go and locate the minimum number of sources to complete the assignment, but that defeats the purpose of expanding your knowledge base and contributing to the research field. If you research properly, sometimes it can take you to places you never thought about. If you research properly, sometimes it can introduce you to a new area of interest. Remember, those who used the Library at Alexandria lived there; they did not just visit. Follow the information, don't simply collect it, and you might just find the experience enjoyable and enlightening. Approach research with a spirit of discovery and adventure, rather than as a chore to be completed.

One final tip for conducting research and developing your topic is to think big initially, then reduce your topic down to something more precise. There is a reason why we talked about a general topic, then a specific topic, and finally a research question. Each step gets progressively more specific and thus smaller than the previous one. As you gather more information you can fine tune your focus and make it more specific, thus helping you determine what you need in your quest for information. Even if you find things that you do not need for the immediate task, you may find that you will call upon those things in a future conversation or presentation. When you know your topic, you then have a better idea of where to look for information; however, you also must distinguish useful and reliable information from useless and unreliable material.

Information Literacy

Literacy refers to the ability to read, while information literacy is the ability to read information. Specifically, *information literacy* is the ability to figure out the type of information you need, find that information, evaluate it, and properly use it. There are five characteristics of an information literate person, and in this part of the chapter we will explain each of them, paying particular attention to understanding the issues regarding the use of information. We will then differentiate between three different types of information researchers encounter and eventually use.

Characteristics of Information Literacy

Just as literate people can read properly, information literate people can successfully research material they need. The five characteristics of information literate people include first the ability to determine what they need information for. They are also able to go out and find that information. Third, they can evaluate the information for accuracy, bias, and relevance to their purpose. Next, they can use the information they find to create new knowledge for themselves or others. Finally, the information literate person understands the issues relevant to using information, such as plagiarism.

When you have a topic and purpose you then begin to research, but for what? Good researchers take an intermediate step between determining the topic and researching the material. They determine their information need. Are they seeking background information? A strong anecdote for an attention getter? Or evidence for their claims? Knowing the type of information you need will determine where you look, because not all types of information can be found in the same place. Depending on your need, you will look at different sources to find the information that best suits your need.

In today's media-rich environment we tend to believe we can find anything we need on the Internet, but the Internet is not a cure-all to the difficulties of research. In fact, it presents some disadvantages along with all the advantages it provides for researchers. Because it is rife with biased and sometimes false information, the Internet should only be considered one of several options for researching materials. Libraries, like Roesch Library at UD, hold vast stores of potentially useful information that might not even be available on the Internet, such as articles from a remote British newspaper during the Nazi's London Blitz of World War II. Knowing where the information is, however, is only one part of finding the information you need. The other part is recognizing which tool (e.g., the Internet or the library; a book or a journal) will net you the best results in your quest.

As an information literate researcher, when you find information you think might help with your project you need to evaluate it for accuracy, bias, and relevance.

Accuracy refers to the source's correctness or truthfulness. *Bias*, or the attempt to unfairly influence someone or the perception of something, is also a concern.

Accurate information can be presented in a manner that unfairly influences how one side is perceived. Information also must be judged for relevance to your topic. Researchers able to evaluate material they find for accuracy, bias, and relevance will create stronger presentations and contribute more to the world around them.

The fourth characteristic of an information literate individual—using the material garnered through research to create new knowledge for others—is associated directly with the contributions produced by research. Information literate researchers use the information they discover to educate and enlighten themselves and those around them. They combine new and old information to create fresh perspectives on topics. They may also provide valuable information about something to a group of people who were unaware of what they needed to know about it.

One way in which you can continually share your own research and learn from the research of others at the University of Dayton is through participation in the Brother Joseph W. Stander Symposium. The Stander Symposium, which takes place every April at UD, is designed to recognize student learning through faculty mentored undergraduate and graduate research, scholarship and artistic accomplishments from all academic units at the University of Dayton. The Stander Symposium represents the Marianist tradition of education through community and is the principal campus-wide event in which faculty and students demonstrate our mission to be a "community of learners." More information on the Stander Symposium can be found at http://stander.udayton.edu. Building new knowledge from old research and information is one of the primary aims of research. Doing so without committing plagiarism is a chief component of the final characteristic of an information literate researcher.

Plagiarism and Accountability in Information Use

In addition to the four characteristics we just discussed, information literate individuals understand the gravity of the issues involved with information use. The most important of these issues is that of giving credit where credit is due. Not to give credit to people whose work you use in a report or speech is *plagiarism*, or to present another person's work or ideas as your own. It is important to understand that intent is irrelevant with plagiarism, so it is better to over-cite sources than not cite them enough.

plagiarism
to present another person's work or ideas as your own

Plagiarism comes in three different forms, but all are equally wrong. The first is *incremental plagiarism*, or failing to give credit for pieces borrowed from a source. Incremental plagiarism is the most common form of plagiarism, as many people fail to reference statements or information they paraphrased or even lifted from a source. In 2005 Republican Nevada Congressman Jim Gibbons ran for governor and delivered a speech that seemed to rail against liberals. In this speech he delivered fifteen paragraphs that were taken directly from a speech delivered by Alabama Auditor Beth Chapman two years earlier.[4] This is a perfect example of incremental plagiarism. Another example is when students use paragraphs from sources in their presentations or papers, change only a few words, and fail to cite the source.

incremental plagiarism
failure to give proper credit for parts of a speech that are borrowed from others

patchwork plagiarism
••••••••••••
stealing ideas from two or more sources without referencing them

Another form of plagiarism is called *patchwork plagiarism*, or stealing ideas from more than one source and pawning them off as your own. Patchwork plagiarism involves lifting whole sections of information from several sources and linking them together without referencing any of them. This may appear to involve using various forms of information to build new knowledge, but it is not, as there is little to no integration of the sources into a coherent argument. This type of plagiarism occurs most often when students list information within a project without referencing where the data came from. Verbally citing your sources is an important component of being an ethical and civilly aware speaker. It also improves your credibility as a speaker.

global plagiarism
••••••••••••
taking an entire speech from a single source and pawning it off as your own

The final form of plagiarism, *global plagiarism*, is the one most people are familiar with. Global plagiarism involves stealing an entire speech or paper from a single source and calling it one's own. Global plagiarism takes many forms, from cutting and pasting, to having someone write a speech for you, to even buying a paper off a website. All of these do not give credit to the source of the ideas and information that became the project and as such represent plagiarism.

Perhaps the greatest problem with plagiarism, aside from the fact it is an ethical and moral affront, is the fact it destroys the fruits of researching. No longer are you able to learn about something, build new ideas, or expose yourself to things you may never have explored if not through research. You lose the opportunity to expand your own knowledge and help others do the same. Plagiarism attacks the very heart of a university's mission, and as a result is typically punished harshly; it is the worst academic crime possible. Information literate researchers are aware of all of this and avoid plagiarism at all costs by properly citing the information they find when researching.

ghostwriting
••••••••••••
to write for and in the name of another person

There is one exception to the rule when it comes to presenting someone else's ideas as your own—but it does not apply in the classroom. *Ghostwriting*, or writing for and in the name of another person, is a fairly common practice among politicians and business leaders. In fact, presidents employ an entire speechwriting staff to write their speeches because they simply do not have the time to write their own speeches. Business executives also have staff researchers who write many of their presentations because of time constraints.

The difference between ghostwriting and plagiarism is that ghostwriters are professionals who still abide by the rules of research and expectations for citations. They also allow the speaker to take credit and accountability for what is eventually said in the presentation, and most importantly, know that their participation in the speech's development is not hidden from the audience. In short, we all know the president uses speechwriters, but in the case we discussed earlier about Jim Gibbons of Nevada, there was no ghostwriter and the material was appropriated from a source without letting the audience know from whence it came.

Ghostwriting is not a new phenomenon. In classical Greece citizens often hired professionals to help them write speeches. The Sophists whom we mentioned in Chapter 1 sometimes fulfilled this role, and made a pretty penny doing so! Clients often sought out professionals to help them write speeches to use in assemblies

SPOTLIGHTING THEORISTS: S. R. RANGANATHAN

Shiyali Ramamrita Ranganathan (1892-1972)

Library scholar, mathematician, and philosopher S. R. Ranganathan was born in Shiyali, India and brought a fresh perspective on librarianship to India and beyond. He wanted to be a mathematician, and earned his BA and MA in mathematics in his home province. He became the University Librarian for the University of Madras despite no prior experience or training in library studies or stewardship. He devised the Acknowledgement of Duplication which states that any system of classification necessarily implies a given item can be classified in in at least two different categories. For instance, a book on the history of China could be categorized under "China" and "history."

He also devised the Colon Classification Scheme in 1933, which uses subject units as the basis for organizing information. This is different from the system used in the United States and the system devised by Melvil Dewey. By 1947, he was known for successfully turning the university library at Madras into a modern research facility. His Five Laws of Library Science help frame the principles behind the management and organization of libraries. According to Ranganathan, the Five Laws of Library Science are:

1. Books are for use, not simply storage and preservation.

2. Every reader his [or her] book, or every patron should be able to obtain what they need.

3. Every book its reader, which suggests each book in the library has a person who would find it useful.

4. Save the time of the reader through business methods that improve customer service.

5. The library is a growing organism and thus must accommodate a growing staff and collection.[1]

Roesch Library is constantly updating its study spaces and accessibility of research sources in order to fit the needs of students, faculty, and staff. Although not a communication scholar, Ranganathan's theories inform the way libraries consider the relationship between the researcher and the sources they need.

1. McCrimmon, Barbara. Encyclopedia of Library History, 1st ed., s.v. "Philosophies of Librarianship." New York: Garland Publishing, Inc., 1994.

or in court, much the same way those business leaders and politicians use ghostwriters today.

Ghostwriters are examples of people who are information literate. A little earlier in the chapter we mentioned that information literate people know their information needs. Specifically, they know what type of material they need to find. In the next section we discuss the three main forms of information used within a speech: background, tangential, and evidentiary.

Using Information

Information contributes to messages in a variety of ways. Researchers sift through the data they find and determine if and how that material can be used. One way information can be used is to provide background for the topic. Another way it can help is by "adding flavor" or color to the message. The third and final form of useful information is evidence, or information that supports main points.

background information
material that provides context for a topic

Background information provides context for your topic. It covers things such as definitions of key concepts, dates of events, and the key players or moments related to the topic. This type of information helps you further narrow your topic and point you in the direction of evidentiary information for your topic. Despite the fact you will undoubtedly not use all of the background information you gather, you should hold onto it as it may be useful later.

A second form of useful information is that which may capture the audience's interest. This type of information may be only slightly related to your topic, but is nevertheless interesting and can be used to draw an audience in through use as an attention getter. It also includes tangential anecdotes that can be used to illustrate a point. The more popular forms of *tangential information* include startling statistics, famous quotations, and unique stories; all should be related to the topic under consideration in some way, but not necessarily directly linked to the topic. Each of these may not support main points you make, but they do help make the message more creative, interesting, and effective by adding unique data.

tangential information
evidence used to provide background and capture an audience's interest

evidentiary information
information that supports main points within a speech and is directly related to the topic

The third, most common, and most important use of information is to support main points. *Evidentiary information* is information that supports main points you make and is directly related to the topic. It allows you to bring the voices of experts to bear through building on their research findings. Without evidentiary information there would be little support for any points you make, thus turning your statements into speculative opinions, rather than informed judgments. It is essentially the "meat and potatoes" of any message. This information can take the form of personal accounts, newspaper stories, or statistics, but all of it has to be directly connected to the main point it is intended to support. One example of effective use of evidentiary information in a speech can be seen in an address given by Reverend Billy Graham to the Empire Club in Canada in 1996 (see the box on page 148).

So far we have discussed both how to create a research question and what type of information we seek to help provide answers to those queries. In the next part of this chapter we will cover how to find information, because knowing how to find information is an essential characteristic of an information literate researcher.

FINDING SOURCES

Finding information is no longer as difficult as it was during the days of the Great Library of Alexandria. Advances in technology and access now allow researchers to gather plenty of materials for projects without even leaving the comfort of their own office. In this section of the chapter we will discuss three places the contemporary researcher can explore when seeking information: libraries, personal correspondence, and the World Wide Web.

Libraries

Even with the advent of the Internet the library still represents the largest and most reliable source for research materials. Every college and university still maintains a library, and many towns and cities also have public libraries that are easy to access. Libraries store books according to the Dewey Decimal System or a similar system, and many allow for searches according to that classification system or by identifying other search criteria. Libraries also typically hold subscriptions to many different research databases that can also help researchers find information they seek. Above all, the most practical and useful tool in a library for assisting in research is the staff. Library staff can answer questions about your research in a variety of ways, such as e-mail, phone, text, and in person.

Libraries catalog and store books, magazines, and journals using either the *Dewey Decimal Classification System* or the Library of Congress Classification System. Depending on the country, other classification systems are used, such as S. R. Ranganathan's Colon Classification System in India (see the Spotlighting Theorists for this chapter). The Dewey Decimal Classification System has been revised 22 times since it was developed by Melvil Dewey in 1876. The Library of Congress Classification System was developed in the late nineteenth century and early twentieth century to organize the Library of Congress book collection. It is the most widely used library classification system in the world and is used here at the University of Dayton's Roesch Library. Classification systems like these allow for researchers to locate several sources related to the same subject just by initially finding one. Now, libraries allow users to search for materials via library websites or online catalogs according to keyword, subject, author, and more.

Dewey Decimal Classification System
the coding system for books, magazines, and journals used in libraries

Getting Research Help at Roesch Library

E-mail: ref@udayton.edu
Text: 937-369-OLIB (0542)
Chat: udaytonlib (Google Talk)
Phone: 937-229-4270
Twitter: @roeschlibrary

Visit the Information or Roesch Help Desk on the first floor of Roesch Library for in-person assistance. Library staff will assist you in finding sources for your speeches and other coursework.

JSTOR
an electronic database for political journals

Communication/ Mass Media Complete
an electronic database for academic journals and popular sources related to communication and journalism

The same types of searches are also available for databases to which a library subscribes. These databases allow for specified searches of discipline or source specific material. For example, databases such as *JSTOR* allow a researcher to explore only academic journal articles related to politics. *Communication/Mass Media Complete* allows the same for journals and mainstream references related to communication and journalism. While those are examples of discipline specific databases, *Lexis-Nexis* is a source specific database available to many researchers.

Lexis-Nexis
an electronic database for newspapers and magazines

Leadership in the Third Millennium
by the Reverend Billy Graham

Delivered June 6, 1995

The Reverend Dr. Billy Graham presented an invited speech to the Empire Club in Toronto, Canada.[5] Reverend Graham is a well-known author and evangelical Christian minister who has promoted a message of redemption through Jesus Christ since the late 1940s. In this address Graham spoke of the importance of leadership in a world fraught with challenges. Graham utilized multiple sources of information to support the main points in his speech—all of which emphasized what he saw as the five attributes needed for contemporary leaders: integrity, personal security, sense of priority, sacrifice, and commitment.

Graham quoted numerous people throughout the address, ranging from Alexander Solzhenitsyn and George Washington to Queen Elizabeth. He quoted the Bible several times, particularly passages in the New Testament. Additionally, he quoted writers and reporters, as well as data on suicide rates in Canada. All of these various forms of evidentiary information provided data in support of his claims.

Graham's conclusion included a quotation from Sir Edmund Hillary, the famous mountain climber, who during a London speech when he reflected on his latest attempt to climb Mount Everest stated: "'I tried to conquer you once and you beat me. I tried to conquer you the second time and you took the lives of two of my best friends. But Everest, you will not be victorious. I will be victorious because you can't get any bigger, but I can." This piece of information fit perfectly with Graham's message of what it takes to be a leader in the third millennium and serves as an example of how speakers can wield information in different ways to maximum effect within a speech.

Lexis-Nexis allows people to sift through newspaper and magazine articles from publications around the world, thereby limiting its reach to newspaper and magazine sources. There are many, many more databases of which researchers can avail themselves, and the best way to find out which one best fits your needs is to make use of the most approachable tool in the library: librarians.

Even with the advances in organization and technology that revolutionized the research process, it is important to remember that librarians still remain one of the best resources for locating information. Librarians know where to go to find information on many different topics, and the chances are high they know how to help you as well. They also have that human knack for thinking on their feet and trying different tactics if initial lines of thought do not prove fruitful. It is important to talk to librarians when starting your project because they will be able to cut down on your research time and assist you in finding the most accurate, unbiased and relevant information for your project. They also will counsel you on how to find information from more places than databases and the full-text information found there. They will open doors to print sources that are not uploaded on the web, but are just as relevant to your project, sometimes even more so.

Personal Correspondence and Interviews

Libraries often carry special collections of materials previously owned by private citizens. Within these collections are personal correspondences such as letters and diaries. These materials, as well as more structured personal correspondence like surveys, make up yet another potential resource for researchers. Additionally, communications such as interviews and e-mails also can be used for background or evidentiary information, and can sometimes be used to provide a colorful anecdote or clever attention getter.

Researchers survey groups of people to find out their moods, feelings, or characteristics. These surveys can take two forms, the first being formal surveys. *Formal surveys* employ scientific methods to ensure random sampling, reliability and validity. These take time to administer, and oftentimes in preparing for a formal presentation, a person will not conduct an original survey, but rather find the results of one conducted by someone else that provides insight into the topic on which they are speaking. The second form of surveying is an *informal survey*, whereby the researcher asks a handful of people their opinions on a topic to add context to their work. These surveys are not reliable or valid, but can still yield useful information.

formal survey
a time-consuming way of gathering data on a population which employs randomized sampling to ensure reliability and validity

informal survey
polling a few people based on convenience

Informal surveys sometimes morph into another method of gathering information, especially when conversations become deeper than the planned survey questions. This method, *interviewing*, allows for more information from an individual than a survey, which aggregates group responses. Interviews follow a specific format that respects both the needs of the interviewer and the rights of the interviewee.

interviewing
a direct method of gathering information from a human source that allows for questions to adapt to responses

When conducting an interview it is important to first identify what you hope to learn from the interview. After developing these goals, set out to find the person to interview who will best help you achieve those information gathering goals. Once the person is contacted and agrees to the interview you develop the questions in advance for the interview. During the interview, you must allow for the possibility of asking questions you did not initially plan for based on the responses provided by the interviewee. Following the interview it is important to take your notes from the conversation and translate them to source material as quickly as possible, because memory fades and becomes unreliable the longer you wait to record information.

undercover interviewing
when the interviewer disguises either himself or his purpose in an effort to trick someone into sharing more information than they may have if the interviewee knew to whom he or she was speaking

One ethical issue related to interviewing concerns undercover interviewing. *Undercover interviewing* is when the interviewers either disguise themselves or their purpose in an effort to trick interviewees into sharing more information than they might have if they knew to whom they were speaking. Many reporters and researchers use this technique to gather information, but it raises ethical questions. Is it right to disguise your motives or identity to gather information? Are there other, more honest, options available to get the information you seek?

Researchers must weigh these questions when thinking about hiding their identity and/or purpose during an interview.

Interviews are not limited to face-to-face interactions, and can take place through e-mail or letters; however these, especially e-mails, must be approached with care. Research indicates e-mails are often read with a negative bias, and that plays a role in how a researcher may interpret information received through e-mail. People also write e-mails in a more informal style than letters, where letters typically follow proper rules of grammar. Some e-mails also contain disclosure notices at the end that may prohibit researchers from using the information contained within the message. It is important when sifting through such messages that you take care to see if this is the case with an e-mail you consider using.

Internet

E-mail occurs on the Internet, but websites are far more commonly used as sources by researchers than e-mail correspondence. Unfortunately, for the many benefits the Internet affords researchers, there are still many pitfalls of which a researcher must be aware. There are different types of websites, each providing information on various subjects with varying degrees of accuracy. Credibility, therefore, is a significant issue when it comes to using the Internet to find information on a topic. Researchers must take care when evaluating information found on websites.

All websites have a form designation at the end of their URL. For example, government produced websites end with .gov, for-profit companies end with .com, educational institutions end with .edu, organizations end with .org, and sites affiliated with a network are labeled .net. International websites use abbreviations to identify their country of origin, as with the United Kingdom which is labeled .uk, or Canada which goes by .ca. The domestic labels each carry different levels of accuracy, bias and credibility.

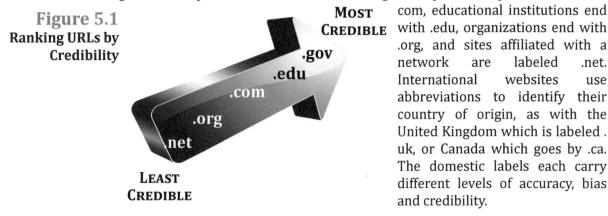

Figure 5.1
Ranking URLs by Credibility

MOST CREDIBLE
.gov
.edu
.com
.org
.net
LEAST CREDIBLE

The most reliable websites are .gov because they are government produced and easily verified. A close second in reliability is .edu because educational institutions have lower levels of bias on a wider range of issues than any other website designation except .gov. Typically placing third in terms of reliability are the .coms which represent the interests and biases of companies. Most financial, historical and organizational information found about the company on these websites is usually accurate; however, other information may not be as reliable. .org is the next on the list, and only slightly more reliable than .net's because both of these URL designations can be obtained by almost any group or individual, making it more likely their biases will bleed through onto their websites. This is not to say all of these URLs are untrustworthy, just that researchers should take care to check the authorship of the website before citing it and using information contained on its pages.

Researchers should also pay attention to the timeliness of the website. Sometimes websites never remove information, and if you are not careful you might use outdated statistics, quotes, or data by citing a website that has not cleaned out old material. This may not always be the way the timeliness problem manifests itself. Consider discussing the historic election of of 2008. Blogs and postings from 2008 would be very relevant; however, those from 2012 would not be. It is important to pay close attention to when the material you found was produced.

Authorship of a website also matters. A few moments ago we discussed websites designated with ".org" and why they can be questionable sources. Most organizations pursue an agenda, and looking at the mission statement of the organization or the biography of the author that produces the website will give you greater insight as to the biases inherent in the information found on that site. The harder authorship is to determine, the less a researcher should use it.

Two popular resources on the web are Wikipedia.com and About.com; however, entries on these websites can be unreliable. Anyone can post, edit, or delete information within entries on these websites, thus causing one to question the veracity of the material found there. A good researcher will not use these as references, rather as initial places to get an idea of potential research questions and direct them toward alternative sources of information.

Table 5.2

Using Wikipedia and Other Online Encyclopedias	
Improper Uses	**Proper Uses**
Citing in paper or speech	Background information that can direct you to other sources
Believing its accuracy is always reliable	Ideas for speech topics

The web provides many benefits in terms of access to information, but it also makes determining the quality of that information ever more important. An information literate individual can both find the appropriate information and determine its quality, especially when it comes from the Internet.

CITING USING APA STYLE

Within the field of communication there are two preferred forms for references, each one slightly different from the other. Most who conduct rhetorical research follow the *Chicago Manual of Style (CMS)*, while those who utilize a social science approach to exploring communication follow the *American Psychological Association (APA)*. You may also encounter a third citation style, that of the *Modern Language Association (MLA)*, when you do research in other fields within the liberal arts and humanities. In addition to formal written bibliographies and in-text citations, students must also verbally attribute their sources when speaking. Because CMM 100 uses APA style as a requirement, in this section, we present a basic overview of APA style.

Chicago Manual of Style (CMS)
preferred reference manual for rhetorical studies

American Psychological Association (APA)
preferred reference manual for social science communication scholars

Modern Language Association (MLA)
a citation style used in disciplines within the liberal arts and humanities

APA uses in-text parenthetical citations in a paper or an outline. These occur at the end of sentences or after an author's name that is referenced in the sentence. In the event the source does not have an identifiable author then it is referenced using a truncated form of the title and the year of publication. In this section we will offer some brief guidance for some common reference types using APA style.

First, let's look at some examples of in-text citations using APA:

- One author, not directly quoted: (Smith, 1990)
- Multiple authors, not directly quoted: (Smith, Jones, & Thompson, 1998)
- One author, directly quoted: (Johnson, 1981, p. 242)
- Multiple authors, directly quoted: (Smith, Jones, & Thompson, 1990, p. 461)
- Website with author, not directly quoted: (Stevens, 2008, December 1)
- Website with no author, not directly quoted: ("The sky is blue," 2003, April 2)
- Website with author, directly quoted: (Morris, 2001, June 1, para. 2)
- Website with no author, directly quoted: ("Great sea," 1991, February 2, para. 1)
- Personal interview: (Peter Hong, personal communication, April 27, 2015).

There are some idiosyncrasies to keep in mind as well. For instance, if a work has more than six authors, you should use the last name of the first author and then the phrase "et al." to refer to the rest of the authors. Additionally, if the author's name is written in the sentence then the parenthetical citation needs only to have the year or the year, and page number if it is directly quoted from the source. Finally, when a work's author is credited as "Anonymous," cite the word "Anonymous" followed by the date in the parenthetical citation.

In addition to the in-text citations, APA calls for a "References" page, which provides a list of all sources that the author has cited in the text of the paper or outline. The References page is organized alphabetically and contains only the sources referenced within the project. Sources not cited in the paper or outline are not included in the References page. If there is no author, the title is treated as author when it comes to placing it in the proper alphabetical spot in the works cited list. Additionally, if the entry runs onto a second line, then that next line, and all subsequent lines for the entry are indented. This is called a hanging indent.

The following are the APA forms for some types of sources commonly included in papers and outlines:

Journal Article in Print:

Author Last Name, First Initial. (Date). Article title. *Journal Title, Volume* (Issue), starting page-ending page.

Smith, J. (1993). Studies show bibliographies are easy to do. *European Journal of Communication, 19*(1), 89–114.

Christians, C. G., & Fortner, R. S. (1981). The media gospel. *Journal of Communication, 31,* 190-199.

- Lead with the last name of the author, followed by first initial and middle initial and then the year of publication in parentheses. If there are multiple authors, list authors' names sequentially in this format, separating the last two authors' names in the list with the "&" symbol, not the word "and."

- Capitalize only the first letter of the first word in the article title, as well as in any subtitle. All other words are not capitalized.

- Proper nouns are an exception. Capitalize them always.

- Capitalize the first letter of all words in the journal title except prepositions (of, in, for) and articles (e.g., a, an, the, that)

- Include the issue number only if the journal is paginated by issue. Otherwise, only include the volume number.

Journal Article from an Online Database with a DOI Assigned:

Author Last Name, First Initial. (Date). Article title. *Journal Title, Volume* (Issue), starting page-ending page. doi:0000000/000000000000 or http://dx.doi.org/10.0000/0000

Brownlie, D. (2007). Toward effective poster presentations: An annotated bibliography. European *Journal of Marketing, 41,* 1245-1283. doi:10.1108/03090560710821161

Wooldridge, M.B., & Shapka, J. (2012). Playing with technology: Mother-toddler interaction scores lower during play with electronic toys. *Journal of Applied Developmental Psychology, 33*(5), 211-218. http://dx.doi.org/10.1016/j.appdev.2012.05.005

- Format the citation for the journal article as you would for the same article in print.

- If a DOI has been assigned to the article that you are referencing, then include it after the page numbers after "doi:" or with the "http://" designation.

Journal Article from an Online Database with No DOI Assigned:

Author Last Name, First Initial. (Date). Article title. *Journal Title, Volume* (Issue), starting page-ending page. Retrieved from http://www.website.com

Smyth, A. M., Parker, A. L., & Pease, D. L. (2002). A study of enjoyment of peas. *Journal of Abnormal Eating, 8*(3), 120-125. Retrieved from http://www.articlehomepage.com/full/url/

- Format the citation for the journal article as you would for the same article in print.

- If you are referencing a journal article that appears online and no DOI has been assigned, then include the URL for the website from which you have retrieved the article. Do not include a period at the end of the URL.

Book:

Author Last Name, First Initial. Middle Initial. (Date). *Book title: Book subtitle.* City, State: Publisher.

Deetz, S. A. (1992). *Democracy in an age of corporate colonization: Developments in communication and the politics of everyday life.* Albany, NY: SUNY Press.

Lead with the author's last name, followed by first and middle initials. If there are multiple authors, separate the authors' names with the "&" symbol, not the word "and."

- Italicize book title and the subtitle, if one is given.
- Capitalize only the first letter of the first word in the book title and the first letter of the first word in the subtitle, if one is given.
- Proper nouns are an exception. Capitalize any proper nouns in the book title.
- Separate title and subtitle with a colon.

Chapter or Essay in an Edited Book or Volume:

Author Last Name, First Initial. Middle Initial. (Date). Chapter or essay title. In Editor First Initial. Middle Initial. Last Name & Second Editor First Initial. Middle Initial. Last Name (Eds.), *Title of edited book or volume* (pp. starting page-ending page). City, State: Publisher.

Whedbee, K. E. (2008). In other's words: Plagiarism as deceptive communication. In R. L. Johannesen, K. S. Valde, & K. E. Whedbee (Eds.), *Ethics in human communication* (6th ed., pp. 283-292). Long Grove, IL: Waveland Press.

- Lead with essay or article author(s)—last name, then first initial and middle initial, if middle initial is given—followed by date.
- Capitalize first letter of first word in chapter or essay title and subtitle, as you do for a journal article.
- After the word "In," give names of editors for the book or volume in which the chapter or essay appears. Unlike you did for the author's name, write the editor's name, beginning with the first initial, then the middle initial (if one is given), and the full last name. Separate the names of multiple editors with the "&" symbol, not the word "and." Afterwards, place the designation "Ed." in parentheses to designate a single editor and "Eds." in parentheses to designate multiple editors.
- Capitalize first letter of first word in edited book or volume title and sub-title.

- Italicize book or volume title.
- If you are citing a specific edition of the book or volume, then include the edition number followed by "ed." in parentheses.
- Include page numbers in parentheses—the same as the edition number, if applicable—after the abbreviation "pp." Use "p." if the essay or chapter spans only one page.

Website:

Author Last Name, First Initial. Middle Initial. (Year Published, Month Date). *Article title.* Retrieved from URL.

Simpson, H. (2007, April 1). *A letter to John Smith.* Retrieved from http://www. xgtsfjmnouiyh.com/jstr/ htm/070908

- Lead with author last name, followed by first initial and middle initial (if given).
- If the website has a corporate author, give the name of the organization in place of the name of individual author(s).
- Give publication date in parentheses, beginning with year published, then the month and day. If no publication date is given, use the abbreviation "n.d." to designate that "no date" was provided.
- Italicize website title.
- Capitalize only first letter of first word in the title and also in subtitle (if present).
- Capitalize all proper nouns, e.g. John Smith in the above example.
- If the website that you are referencing contains more than one web page, use the URL for the homepage or start page. Do not put a period at the end of the URL.

Online Video:

Author Last Name, First Initial. Middle Initial. [Screen name]. (Year, Month Day). *Title of video* [Video file]. Retrieved from http://xxxxx

Apsolon, M. [markapsolon]. (2011, September 9). *Real ghost girl caught on Video Tape 14* [Video file]. Retrieved from http://www.youtube.com/ watch?v=6nyGCbxD848

- Lead with author last name, followed by first initial and middle initial (if given). Then give screen name in brackets.
- Provide title of video in italics. Capitalize only the first letter of the first word in the title – and in the subtitle, if given – with the exception of proper nouns.
- Follow title with the words "Video file" in brackets.

- Give URL after the words "Retrieved from" with no period at the end.

In the case of a Youtube video, sometimes the screen name of the person who posted the video appears without the real name of the person. In this case, use the screen name in the author position without brackets. For instance:

Screen name. (Year, Month Day). *Title of video* [Video file]. Retrieved from http://xxxxx

Bellofolletti. (2009, April 8). *Ghost caught on surveillance camera* [Video file]. Retrieved from http://www.youtube.com/watch?v=Dq1ms2JhYBI&feature=related

- If the poster of the video is an organization, use the organization's name as the screen name.

Newspaper Article Retrieved from an Online Source:

Author, A. A. (Year, Month Day). Title of article. *Title of Newspaper.* Retrieved from http://www.someaddress.com/full/url/

Parker-Pope, T. (2008, May 6). Psychiatry handbook linked to drug industry. *The New York Times.* Retrieved from http://well.blogs.nytimes.com/2008/05/06/psychiatry-handbook-linked-to-drug-industry/?_r=0

- Lead with the full last name of the author of the newspaper article, followed by the first initial and middle initial (if given). If there are multiple authors, separate the last two authors in the list with the "&" symbol, not the word "and."

Data Sets:

Author, First Initial. Middle Initial. (Year). *Title of data set* [Data file]. Retrieved from URL

Corporate author. (Year). *Title of data set* [Data file]. Retrieved from URL

United States Department of Housing and Urban Development. (2008). *Indiana income limits* [Data file]. Retrieved from http://www.huduser.org/Datasets/IL/IL08/in_fy2008.pdf

- Lead with author last name, followed by first initial and middle initial. Then give year in parentheses. If citing a corporate author, then given the name of the organization in place of the names of individual authors.
- Italicize the title of the data set. Capitalize only the first letter of the first word in the title – and in the subtitle (if present). Follow the title with the words "Data file" in brackets.
- Give the URL after the words "Retrieved from" with no period.

Graphic Data:

Name of organization conducting research. (Year). [Explanation of type of data is given and the form in which it has been given]. *Project Name.* Retrieved from URL

Solar Radiation and Climate Experiment. (2007). [Graph illustration the SORCE Spectral Plot May 8, 2008]. *Solar Spectral Data Access from the SIM, SOLSTICE, and XPS Instruments.* Retrieved from http://lasp.colorado.edu/cgi-bin/ion-p?page=input_data_for_ spectra.ion

- Lead with name of the organization conducting the research, followed by the year in parentheses. In the event that individuals have conducted the research, lead with their names in this position, using the format that you have used for the authors of other types of sources.

- In brackets, give a brief description of the type of data that is provided and the form in which it has been given.

- Italicize the name of the project. Capitalize all words in the title except articles or prepositions, as you would capitalize the title of a journal.

- Give the URL after the words "Retrieved from" with no period at the end.

Interviews or E-mails:

Personal interviews or e-mails do not need to appear in APA reference pages, but must be cited in-text by listing the initials and last name of the interviewee and as exact a date as possible for the interview.

Citations allow readers and audience members to know where you found the information you used so they can verify it, or even use it for their own work. It also is designed to give proper credit to the person whose ideas you are using.

If you have questions about citing types of sources other than those that we have listed in this chapter, we recommend that you consult the Style Manual for the American Psychological Association (6th edition). You also can find some information about formatting in-text sources and the references page at the Purdue Online Writing Lab at https://owl.english.purdue.edu/owl/section/2/10/. Many of the examples that we have given here in this chapter appear at that site.

VERBAL ATTRIBUTION

You not only need to cite sources within your manuscript or outline, but you must verbally do so as well. This is much easier than it sounds and helps you build credibility with your audience or conversation partner. Some common ways speakers verbally attribute sources are to preface the information being cited with "according to" or "so-and-so says," but here are a few more examples to use for giving proper credit to source material:

- According to a recent Gallup Poll, Senator John McCain is seen as more knowledgeable on foreign policy than his opponent.

- In his book Perilous Times, Dr. Geoffrey Stone argues that the First Amendment should not be suppressed during wartime.

- Some people, like Dr. Johann Strauss, argue the Motion Picture Association of America should think about the intentions of the moviemaker when rating films for public consumption.

- Many major league baseball players used steroids in the 1990s, according to the Mitchell Report produced by former Senator George Mitchell and his investigative team.

Each of these examples provides verbal attribution to the sources where the information was obtained. It is essential for a researcher to give credit like this when speaking because it helps the audience differentiate between the speaker's ideas and the ideas that came from someone else. The importance of verbal attribution holds true for conversations as well as formal presentations.

SUMMARY

Research and preparation are the most important steps toward developing successful and ethical messages. Proper research skills come from being an information literate person. Information literate people know what they need information for, where to go and find it, how to use it properly, and the ethical implications of information use. It is important to make use of all of the research tools at your disposal, from librarians to the Internet, when seeking different types of sources and information. It is equally important to use a consistent and accepted citation style when referencing material you gathered from other places.

KEY TERMS

accuracy   118

American Psychological Association (APA)   127

background information   122

bias   118

Communication/Mass Media Complete   123

Dewey Decimal Classification System   123

enkyklios paideia   89

evidentiary information   122

formal survey   125

ghostwriting   120

global plagiarism   120

incremental plagiarism   119

informal survey   125

information literacy   118

interviewing   125

JSTOR   123

Lexis-Nexis   123

patchwork plagiarism   120

plagiarism   119

quadrivium   89

research question   115

tangential information   122

trivium   89

undercover interviewing   125

REVIEW QUESTIONS

1. What are the five characteristics of the information literate researcher?
2. What are the three primary forms of information?
3. What are the three main places to find source material?
4. What are the three major citation styles?

THINK ABOUT IT

1. Is it ever ethical to employ undercover interviewing?
2. How do you determine if you need to cite a piece of information?
3. Which reference style is better? Why?

ACTIVITIES FOR ACTION

1. Sit down with a group of friends, classmates, or colleagues and brainstorm topics for speeches. Each time a person introduces a statement about a topic they are interested in reframe it as a research question. By the end of this discussion you should have a list of potential speech topics that are written as research questions rather than topic statements.

2. Find a partner and go on a scavenger hunt for the following items: a magazine article, a newspaper article, a government document, a peer reviewed journal article in communication studies, a documentary film, a news page from microfiche records, a survey result, a blog entry, and an interview transcript. To complicate this activity, give yourself a topic that each item must relate to. For instance, find one of each item related to the topic of the "Beatles musical invasion."

ENDNOTES

1. Edward Alexander Parsons, *The Alexandrian Library* (Barking, Essex, England: Elsevier Publishing, 1952), 83–106.

2. Ibid.

3. Roy MacLeod, "Introduction: Alexandria in History and Myth," in *The Library of Alexandria: Centre of Learning in the Ancient World,* ed. Roy MacLeod (New York, NY: St. Martin's Press, 2000), 4–7.

4. Erin Neff, "Gibbons's Speech Plagiarism: 15 Paragraphs Came from Copyrighted Talk by Alabama Woman," *Las Vegas Review Journal,* March 4, 2005.

5. http://speeches.empireclub.org/61435/data?n=2 (accessed May 28, 2011).

SCENARIOS

Scenario 1

The parts of an oral citation are as follows: name of **publication**, **date** it was published, **name** of author or speaker, and **credentials** of author or speaker.

1.   Create an oral citation from the information given below.

DIRECT QUOTE

Date: April 23, 2012

Publication: Los Angeles Times

What happened?
"It is a tremendous testament to how resourceful California educators can be in the face of really crazy budget cuts. Public education does so much to provide kids with the highest quality education possible but with so much less."

Who is the source? Rebecca Mieliwocki, teacher and winner of The National Teacher of the Year.

PARAPHRASE

Date: April 23, 2012

Publication: Associated Press

What happened?
        The Senate offered a lifeline to the nearly bankrupt U.S. Postal Service on Wednesday, voting to give the struggling agency an $11 billion cash infusion while delaying controversial decisions on closing post offices and ending Saturday delivery.

        By a 62–37 vote, senators approved a measure which had divided mostly along rural-urban lines. Over the past several weeks, the bill was modified more than a dozen times, adding new restrictions on closings and cuts to service that rural-state senators said would hurt their communities the most.

        The issue now goes to the House, which has yet to consider a separate version of the bill. "The Postal Service is an iconic American institution that still delivers 500 million pieces of mail a day and sustains 8 million jobs," said Sen. Joe Lieberman, I-Conn., a bill co-sponsor. "This legislation will change the USPS so it can stay alive throughout the 21st century."

Who is the source? Hope Yen, writer for the Associated Press

WEBSITE DIRECT QUOTE

Last Updated: 2012

Publication: www.diabetes.org

What happened? Type 1 diabetes is usually diagnosed in children and young adults, and was previously known as juvenile diabetes. In type 1 diabetes, the body does not produce insulin.

Who is the source? American Diabetes Association

Scenario 2

1. Create a citation using APA style for this journal publication:

    Article Title: Truly, Madly, Depp-ly
    Author: Frank DeCaro
    Publication: Advocate
    Volume number: 906
    Date: January 20, 2004
    Pages: 76-77
    Source: Gender Studies Database
    Date of access: October 31, 2008
    hyperlink: <http://0-search.ebscohost.com.maurice.bgsu.edu/ login.aspx?direct=true&db=fmh &AN=GSD0048

2. Create a citation using APA style for the following web news publication:

    Article Title: A Civil War Professor Reviews Lincoln
    Author: David Frum
    Publication: The Daily Beast
    Date: November 27, 2012
    Pages: paragraph 5
    Source: Gender Studies Database
    Date of access: January 18, 2014
    hyperlink: http://www.thedailybeast.com/articles/2012/11/27/a-civil-war-professor-reviews-lincoln.html

3. Create a citation using APA style for the following entry on a website:

    Page Title: Type 1 Diabetes
    Author: n/a
    Date: n/a
    Pages: paragraph 2
    Source: American Diabetes Association
    Date of access: January 18, 2014
    Hyperlink: http://www.diabetes.org/diabetes-basics/type-1/

4. Create a citation using APA style for your CMM 100 Textbook.

Scenario 3

Most of us think we know plagiarism when we see it. But is it always as clear-cut as we think? Discuss whether plagiarism or cheating has occurred in the scenarios below. Explain your answers.

1. While working on your term paper, you find a couple of great sources in your research. You use bits and pieces of direct quotes from each source to develop your own ideas, but do not use quotations. Is this plagiarism?

2. You and your friend are excited to have the same class together. You've decided to collaborate on all projects, but will still turn in your own work. Could this be considered cheating?

3. You found a number of excellent sources to help you develop your persuasive speech. While giving your speech, you do not orally cite any sources. Could you be accused of plagiarizing?

4. Your main argument within your speech is based on one theory from a well-respected scholar in your field. You do not directly use any of his/her words and you have plenty of other sources to back up your argument. Are you a plagiarizer?

5. You and your partner have been assigned to work together for the whole quarter. You will be proofreading, floating ideas, practicing, and sharing notes with each other. If you only did these four things, have you cheated?

Scenario 4 (Performance)

Many social commentators today argue that we live in a "post-truth society." On November 16, 2016, *The Washington Post* reported that the Oxford Dictionaries designated "post-truth" as the Word of the Year for 2016. The article cites the *Oxford Dictionary's* definition for "post-truth" as "relating to or denoting circumstances in which objective facts are less influential in shaping public opinion than appeals to emotion and personal belief." Search the Internet for news stories or videos that recount cases in which "emotion and personal belief" seemed to be more influential than "objective facts" for an individual or group of people. Create a short presentation that you can give to the class in which you share three of those stories or videos.

Language

Practically SPEAKING

In the United States, as in many democracies, there is a fundamental right to free speech for every citizen, but even that right is not absolute. For instance, we cannot falsely yell "fire!" in a crowded theater because that speech may result in the creation of a harmful situation. For the longest time, curse words could not be uttered on prime time television, although now that is hardly the case. Language is controversial because it is powerful. It can move people to action, convey a sense of identity for the speaker, or conjure one for the audience. Because language is powerful, even the right to free speech is curtailed. One famous legal case that underscores the power of language and illustrates society's desire to control it in some way involved the late comedian George Carlin.

Around 2:00 p.m. on a Tuesday afternoon in 1973, WBAI (FM), a radio station in New York City, aired a 12-minute segment from a monologue delivered by Carlin. The monologue, entitled "Filthy Words," was initially recorded before a live audience in California and concerned the words a person could not say on public airwaves. Carlin listed the seven words that fit that category and then discussed them in detail. Right before the station broadcasted the words, it warned its audience that the monologue included language that might offend some listeners. Unfortunately for the radio station, not everyone heard the warning. One man complained to the Federal Communications Commission (FCC) and that government agency quickly responded.[1]

The FCC ruled that Carlin's satirical presentation was indecent because it depicted sexual acts and bodily functions, calling his presentation "obnoxious" and stating it reduced humanity to its "bodily functions." It further pointed out that the radio station was at fault because it aired the satire at a time when children would hear it.[2] The case eventually found its way to the U.S. Supreme Court. It ruled that the FCC did not censor the station because it did not edit it in advance or prohibit the broadcast from airing. For the Court, reviewing content after airing is not an issue of censorship.[3]

The Supreme Court's opinion, written by Justice John Paul Stevens, discussed why Carlin's monologue was not subject to the protection of the First Amendment. He wrote that Carlin's monologue was offensive and lacked literary, political, or scientific value and was not related to the marketplace of ideas. Additionally, Stevens claimed that time of day, content of communication, and the medium used are all important considerations when defining obscene and indecent language.[4]

In the case of Pacifica and Carlin, language proved to be inappropriate for some audiences. The words, in effect, endangered the standards and practices of society. Carlin attempted to point out what he saw as the silliness of language choices, but in so doing illustrated the reverence and power we accord language. In this chapter we will explain how you may tap into that power and enhance your speech. First we will discuss the basic building blocks of meaning to illustrate the source of language's power. We will then examine several different types of language strategies that can help you enhance the appeal and effectiveness of your message. Finally, we will offer some concrete guidelines for choosing these words when putting together a speech.

PREP QUESTIONS

1. Discuss how language is arbitrary. If language is arbitrary, how can it be logical?

2. Define how language is ambiguous.

3. Explain whether the linear or transactional model of communication better illustrates how we construct meaning.

4. Discuss the fundamental premise of the narrative paradigm.

5. What is the difference between narrative coherence and narrative fidelity?

6. List the five guidelines for using language.

7. Differentiate between active and passive voice.

8. Differentiate between "I, Me, We" language and "you" language. Based on your understanding of this difference, where do you feel as though the power over your emotions lies when you use "I, Me, We" language? How about when you use "you" language?

9. Give an example of: metaphor, simile, alliteration, and antithesis.

6

MEANING AND SYMBOLS

Meaning, as we have pointed out in earlier chapters, can be expressed both verbally and nonverbally. In both instances we exchange meaning through symbols. In that respect, symbols are the building blocks of how we understand the world. Language is a common way in which we communicate meaning to others, and the symbolic base of language is letters. Letters are, for all intents and purposes, symbols that mean something when connected to form words. Words also are symbols that represent objects, thoughts, values, feelings, and ideas, and they are the foundation of communication. When we share an understanding of what symbols mean we are able to connect with each other in meaningful ways about the world around us. In this section of the chapter we will explore the four characteristics of any language.

Language Characteristics

All languages share four characteristics, regardless of their cultural, ethnic, or regional origins. The first characteristic of a language is that it is *arbitrary*, or that the symbols used to represent things are not intrinsically connected to those things. Since meaning is arbitrary it can change over time as different groups ascribe different definitions and purposes for words. The word "hot," for instance, formerly only meant raised temperature, but now also refers to the attractiveness of something ("she/he is so hot") or the success of an action ("he's a hot hitter right now"). We also develop new words every year to the point where the English language has expanded significantly over the past few hundred years. Words and phrases like "affirmative action," "motherboard," and "airline" did not exist until the last century. The arbitrary nature of language illustrates its flexibility, as language changes according to our need to explain the world around us.

arbitrary
symbols used to represent things that are not intrinsically connected to those things

Because language can change and is dependent on constant use to sustain itself, some languages can disappear. When a language is no longer used by a group we call it a dead language, but this does not mean we do not know how to use it or that we cannot read it. For example, Aramaic is considered to be a dead language and yet there are still people who know how to use it and read it—it just isn't a language you will overhear while waiting in line at the DMV! Some scholars focus their efforts on preserving and understanding language and how it reflects a particular culture. One of the more renowned researchers in this area was Mary

Haas, who worked on American Indian languages and did important work on the Thai language before World War II. In essence, Haas and other scholars like her focus on trying to understand the arbitrary qualities of language.

The fact that language is arbitrary also can be a bit shocking. Why do we call a cat *cat*? It could have very well been labeled "schmoog," but it was not. There was no reason behind the selection of the symbol "cat" to represent those furry little creatures; it just happened and people implicitly agreed to that meaning for the symbol "cat." It was a completely arbitrary creation of a symbol to represent something in our world so we could communicate about it.

ambiguous
language that does not have precise, concrete meanings

Another component of language is that it is ***ambiguous***, or that it's meaning can be interpreted in a variety of ways. When you speak, the language you use doesn't have one precise, concrete or inherent way of being understood by your listener. One name can refer to a plethora of people, one word can mean different things, and without the context in which the word was spoken, there is no way to identify its meaning with any degree of precision.

Cultures imbue words with a variety of meanings, but even within that culture each word has an agreed upon range of potential interpretations and uses. For instance, the term "mean" can refer to the average of a group of numbers or describe a nasty statement or action. Even holidays like Thanksgiving vary in meaning from country to country based on the specific circumstances surrounding that holiday. As a speaker it is always important for you to understand the potential interpretations words can have and use them in the proper context with your conversational partners so that your message is as clear as possible. It is through the ambiguous nature of language that many misunderstandings develop, unless the meaning of the word is made clear.

Movie poster from *Donnie Brasco*

Take, for example, the phrase "friend of mine." For many people this phrase defines a level of association between you and another person; however, different people have different definitions of exactly what a friend is. In the movie *Donnie Brasco*,[5] Al Pacino's character introduces someone he recently met, played by Johnny Depp, to the mobsters for whom he works. On the way over to the introduction he clearly spells out that when he introduces him to his bosses as "friend of mine" it means you are connected but not officially a part of the organization. He further explains that if he said "friend of ours" then Depp's character would have been accorded more respect because it would mean he was a full member of the mob.

This example illustrates how ambiguous language can be, and how important it is to make sure the audience knows the meaning of the words and phrases you use. Not everyone understands the meaning of terms in the same way you do.

Another example of the ambiguity of language can be found in the famous Abbott and Costello skit "Who's on First," where Abbott announces he bought a baseball

6

SPOTLIGHTING THEORISTS: MARY HAAS

Mary Haas (1910–1996)

During the 1930s the most renowned linguist of the era, Edward Sapir of Yale, trained a small number of graduate students. One of those students, Mary Haas, went on to become a renowned linguistic researcher and teacher in her own right.[6] Her dissertation concerned the Tunica Indians, a tribe once located in present-day Louisiana, and she earned her Ph.D. in 1935. She also did linguistic work on several other Southeastern America Native American languages, including the Choctaw, Alabama, and Creek.

Prior to World War II she worked with the Thai language assisting in the preparation of

training materials to be used by the Armed Services. In 1942–1943 she taught Thai at the University of Michigan. In 1943 Haas began teaching Thai in the Army Specialized Training Program at Berkeley. After the war she became a permanent member of the Berkeley faculty.[7]

Haas was a faculty member at that university until 1977. During that time she directed the Survey of California Indian Languages. She is credited with leading students in doing valuable work on languages that have nearly become extinct.[8] Mary Haas died in 1996 at the age of 86.[9] The scholarly journal *Anthropological Linguistics* published a memorial in its 1997 Winter issue.[10]

team and tries to explain his players to his friend, Costello. Comedic encounters like this are not uncommon, and oftentimes comedians will take advantage of the ambiguous nature of language in delivering a punch line to a joke. In Abbott and Costello's case, their sketch has had a long lasting impact on comedy, baseball, and language use. This skit, and indeed the nature of language as ambiguous, underscores the importance of clarifying definitions in conversation. When using a word in a specific way that could be understood differently by the listener it is essential to explain how you are using it. If both you and the other person do not operate with the same definitions for complex or unfamiliar terms understanding becomes impossible. Making sure people understand what words mean is a hallmark of communication in the technical professions, such as engineering.

abstract
words are not tangible items; they are only representations

The third component of language is that it is *abstract*. Abstract means that words are not tangible items; you cannot touch them or feel them as they simply represent something else. Language is removed from the actual objective phenomena it represents, thus making it an abstract construct. Words can vary in their abstractness, according to the degree to which they accurately represent the real thing. The tool for identifying and measuring the degree to which our language is abstract is called the ladder of abstraction, a concept developed by Alfred Korzybski and S. I. Hayakawa in the 1960s.[11]

The ladder of abstraction depicts the most abstract term at the top of the ladder and the closest to the objective phenomenon at the bottom. So, in the following

Who's on First?
by Abbott and Costello

Delivered many times as a comedy skit.

Bud Abbott and Lou Costello were popular on the burlesque comedy stages of America, and joined together to become a popular comedy team in 1936. That year they performed their classic signature skit, "Who's on First," on the Kate Smith Radio Hour and were "hurled to stardom, and to Hollywood."[12] The comedy routine is based on trying to determine the name of the player on first base whose name happens to be *Who*, but due to the ambiguity of language the name causes confusion and consternation for both Abbott and Costello, but lots of laughs for generations of audiences.

Through their routine, Abbott and Costello left an indelible mark and made a lasting impact on comedy and its role in American culture. In fact, their often, imitated and duplicated routine served as a model for many comedians to comment on social and cultural practices through their work. In 1999 *Time* magazine named the *Who's on First* routine the Best Comedy Sketch of the century. This illustrates that civic engagement also takes place through comedy rooted in our cultural practices, norms, and beliefs. Here is an excerpt from their routine:

Costello: Well, then, who's on first?
Abbott: Yes.
Costello: I mean the fellow's name.
Abbott: Who.
Costello: The guy on first.
Abbott: Who.
Costello: The first baseman.
Abbott: Who!
Costello: The guy playing –
Abbott: Who is on first!
Costello: I'm asking YOU who's on first.
Abbott: That's the man's name.
Costello: That's who's name?
Abbott: Yes.
Costello: Well go ahead and tell me.
Abbott: That's it.
Costello: That's who?
Abbott: Yes.

This continues on for several players, all with names that can be confused with days and questions. You can view this video at http://www.americanrhetoric.com and see the frustration the ambiguity of language can cause during dialogue.

example, at the top of the ladder you see "animal." On the level below that, representing a term slightly less removed from the object, is the term "human being." Since there are several billion human beings on the planet we move to the next level and see "musician." Again, even though this term narrows our original term significantly, it is still abstract. The next rung uses the term "pop musician," improving the connection between the term and described object. Finally, on the bottom rung of the ladder of abstraction we see "Taylor Swift," a very specific use of language that is as close to representing the object as possible through words. The more concrete and specific the words we use, the more likely the receiver will accurately interpret our message.

Figure 6.1
Ladder of Abstraction

The ladder of abstraction also is illustrative of the fourth quality of any language. Scholar Kenneth Burke first noted that language, like human beings, is *hierarchical* in nature. That is, it places values of more or less on everything. Think about how we talk about advancing in the workplace. We move *up* from the mailroom when we are promoted. We don't make *lateral* moves. When we go to a hotel we want to stay in the penthouse on the top floor. Language, much like our social lives, reflects a hierarchy in which one thing is more important, or valued more, than another.

hierarchical
language that is structured according to more or less, higher or lower

Math as a Language

Languages come in many forms, and one form not typically thought of as a language is mathematics. Math is a way to transmit meaning between people and fits the definition of language.

First, math is arbitrary. This is not to say that certain numbers can add up to whatever a person wants them to; rather, the symbol of a number has no physical relationship to what it represents. The number one is a symbol, and that symbol can be applied to one hot dog, one dress, or one board game. The symbol "one" only has meaning when used to refer to something else, thus it has no physical connection to what it represents.

Second, math is ambiguous. It is understandable how this might be confusing, but here is an example to illustrate the point. The mathematical equation "x+y" could either be a number itself or a function. Additionally, the more common expression of ambiguity in math is the margin of error, in which a result is plus or minus a certain number, thus giving an ambiguous answer.

Math is also abstract in that it is not concrete or tangible. No one has ever picked up a number and held it. That said, math can be made less abstract when, as we illustrated just a moment ago, it is put in context and related to something else. *Lots of food* is very abstract, whereas *one spear of broccoli* is much more concrete.

Finally, math is hierarchical. This should make sense because numbers are structured to illustrate quantities of something. They illustrate more and less in a hierarchical state so that we all know that one hundred is less than two hundred but more than fifty.

Understanding how math functions as a language helps clarify why there are certain rules to mathematical equations and representations, much like there are rules to the use of other languages in social settings. When someone is not "good at math" it is the same as saying they do not speak Spanish or German very well. Math, however, is the professional language of engineers, financial analysts, and accountants in much the same way English is the professional language for American writers!

Language is arbitrary, ambiguous, abstract, and hierarchical but it is also very useful. Language uses symbols to represent the world around us and serves as the foundation for our ability to connect with each other. In the next part of this chapter we will discuss general forms of language we use in everyday encounters. Understanding what language does for us and how it does it is essential for determining which terms and phrases to incorporate into your messages in order to maximize their effectiveness.

FORMS AND USES OF LANGUAGE

Language can be used in many different ways to send a message. Sometimes, as in casual conversation, single-word strategies are the best way to convey meaning to an audience. In other instances clusters of words form a coherent impression of something for people as well. Luckily, in the United States and many other places around the globe, we are free to employ either, both, or neither of these approaches thanks to freedom of speech. In this part of the chapter we first discuss some single-word strategies that permeate our everyday interactions with others. We then detail a few word cluster strategies that also are common in society. Third, we explain a few creative ways to structure language within messages. Finally, we cover the ethical issues related to word choice and freedom of speech.

Single-Word Approaches

single-word approach
meaning is derived from individual words used in a strategic way

In this part of the chapter we will cover three types of single-word approaches to making language meaningful. A *single-word approach* does not necessarily mean that only one word is required for meaning to be transferred, but rather that meaning is derived from specific individual words used in a strategic way. We are all probably quite familiar in some way with the first two of these strategies. We probably can also recognize words that fit into the third category but are unfamiliar with the formal name of that strategy.

metaphor
comparisons that show how two things are alike in an important way, despite being quite different in most ways

The first single-word approach is a broad category that contains a variety of distinct subsets. *Metaphor* is the broad term used to define comparisons that show how two things are alike in an important way, despite being quite different in most ways. We use metaphors often as they add color, flavor, and vividness to our everyday experiences. Take the following phrase as an example: "I will now shed some light on the issue." Obviously, there is no actual light, but a lack of understanding is compared to darkness, and the speaker's intention to provide knowledge is compared to illuminating that darkness through providing light. Another example involves describing a person who is adept at gardening as having a "green thumb." Again, the person's thumb is not actually green, but the color reminds people of grass and plants, thus making the connection and comparison between the activity and the person who enjoys it.

simile
comparisons between two objects that allow each object in the comparison to retain its unique differences; uses like or as

A second single-word approach is often confused with metaphor, but in fact holds one major distinction that separates it in theory and practice. *Similes*, like metaphors, are comparisons between two objects, but whereas metaphors make both objects appear as if they are equal, similes allow each object in the comparison to retain its unique differences. When you use the word "like" or "as" in comparing two objects you are using a simile because the two objects in the comparison are similar but not equal. Here is an example of a simile: "The quarterback threaded that pass like a needle." The needle and the trajectory of the pass keep their distinctive qualities, but the comparison gives the object a reference to which some aspect, such as difficulty, can be ascribed. Another example: "She is strong as an ox." In this example the two objects in the comparison retain their distinctiveness while sharing a specific characteristic.

Similes sometimes need further explanation so their intended meaning can be properly conveyed. Consider this statement: "Her face was like an autumn sunrise." The intention is to convey a comparison regarding beauty; however, more detail of this simile provides greater and more specific meaning for the object. Just like metaphors, similes are very useful tools for enhancing the vivid nature of a message and allowing an audience to visualize a concept or object you might be discussing.

A third single-word approach to conveying meaning was identified by scholar Michael Calvin McGee in 1980. *Ideographs* are essentially ill-defined politically powerful terms and phrases that can push people to action. Examples of ideographs include terms such as *freedom, terror, rule of law, equality,* and *liberty* just to name a few.[13] Each of these has significant cultural resonance in the United States and has served as justification for a variety of different arguments. As recently as 2001 and 2003 President George W. Bush used the terms "freedom" and "terror" to call for military action against Afghanistan and Iraq, respectively. They also have been used to justify actions such as warrantless wiretapping and indefinite imprisonment at Guantanamo Bay. "Equality" was used during the civil rights era to push for desegregation, and has recently appeared again to justify changes in the tax code and advocate for gay marriage.

ideograph
an ill-defined, politically powerful term or phrase that can push people to action

Ideographs are very powerful because the meaning of the term or phrase is culturally provided, but not everyone in a culture interprets them the same way. Look at the term "fairness," which has been recently applied to tax reform. Liberal politicians argue that higher taxes on those who make more money is only "fair," while conservative advocates argue it is anything but fair because those individuals do not pay the same amount or percentage as others. Regardless of where you sit in this debate, the term "fair" is a perfect example of an ideograph that has an ill-defined but politically powerful meaning within society. You can use such terms like this when you speak, but beware of their ambiguity and potential to activate emotional reactions from others.

Table 6.2

Examples of Ideographs	
Freedom	Terror
Rule of law	Equality
Liberty	Justice

Each single-word approach to conveying meaning we have discussed in this section holds specific power thanks to the arbitrary, ambiguous, and abstract nature of language. You can use them to effectively enhance communication with others by creating more vivid and concrete messages. The more vivid the descriptions you use and the more concrete the detail you provide, the better you will be able to appeal to an audience. Single-word approaches, however, are not the only strategy available to you when making language choices.

Word-Cluster Approaches

word-cluster approach
•••••••••
meaning is conveyed through more complex structures such as stories

Meaning is not only found to be potent in simple words and phrases. In many instances meaning is transmitted through more complex approaches that use language to construct meaning for an event, person, or culture. For the sake of simplicity we will call these *word-cluster approaches* because, unlike single-word approaches, meaning is not contained in individual words used in a strategic way. Rather, meaning is conveyed through more complex structures such as stories. In

SPEAKING of CIVIC ENGAGEMENT

"I Have a Dream" Speech
by Dr. Martin Luther King, Jr.

Delivered August 28, 1963, at the Lincoln Memorial in Washington, D.C.

"I Have a Dream" is one of the most, if not the most, referenced and used speech in public speaking classes and other liberal arts classes. It is worthy of such recognition not only because of its historical significance, but also due to its beautiful tone, structure, and use of metaphor, parallelism, and other language devices.

Dr. King used many metaphors in the speech. One in particular stands out.

"In a sense we've come to our nation's capital to cash a check."[14] This statement implies that a check needs to be cashed to fulfill an obligation. Dr. King extends the metaphor further to make his point: "It is obvious today that America has defaulted on this promissory note, insofar as her citizens of color are concerned. Instead of honoring this sacred obligation, America has given the Negro people a bad check, a check which has come back marked 'insufficient funds.'"

This masterful orator also used a form of repetition to emphasize his points:

"Now is the time to rise from the dark and desolate valley of segregation to the sunlit path of racial justice. Now is the time to lift our nation from the quicksands of racial injustice to the solid rock of brotherhood. Now is the time to make justice a reality for all of God's children."[15]

This speech will go down in the annals of great speeches for centuries to come. Reading the speech is one thing, but actually hearing it and even viewing it brings forth the full power of the day and the man who later lost his life due to his efforts to improve the lives of millions of people.

this section we will explore two different word cluster approaches to conveying meaning: rhetorical history and myth. Any of these tools can be used by you to present information or make an argument in a vivid, creative, and interesting manner.

The first word-cluster approach we will examine involves how we understand and communicate about our past. Think about your past, the country's past, and even world history. Everything you know about these things is only part of the story, but these parts of our past are often used to justify actions in the present. These *arguments from the past* appropriate parts of history to justify present or future actions. Arguments from the past employ stories and explanations to convey meaning. Those stories are interpretations of events that provide the power for arguments from the past.

arguments from the past
....
appropriating historical events, facts, or people to justify present or future actions, or explain events in the here and now

For example, take the events of September 11, 2001, when terrorists attacked the World Trade Center and Pentagon. Immediately following these events people compared the attack to the Japanese sneak attack on Pearl Harbor that precipitated World War II. That comparison imbued 9/11 with certain qualities inherent in Pearl Harbor, thus allowing 9/11 to also become a justification for war against Afghanistan in the same way Pearl Harbor allowed war to be declared against Japan. In this case a past event was used to provide significance to a present situation so future policy could be enacted.

We make arguments from the past in everyday conversations as well. For instance, if you tried to eat sushi once and did not like it but your partner wants to eat sushi for dinner, you need to argue against it. How do you do it? By offering data on the level of mercury in fish? No, you tell the story of your prior experience in an effort to avoid the trip to eat sushi. The story you tell is an argument from the past that may help convince your partner to change his or her mind and go to Skyline Chili instead.

As we have noted, language is imprecise and only somewhat represents an objective reality. History is always incomplete because we were never there and rely instead on the reflections and documents that survive the past. These provide an imprecise understanding of the past because they are incomplete, and because they rely on words—which are ambiguous themselves—to tell the story. Hence it is important to be honest and as accurate as possible when discussing historical events in an effort to explain something or persuade someone. Do not distort the event for your own purposes by leaving something out or embellishing the story; let it speak for itself. Understand, as well, when others use the past to construct an argument that all stories about history are necessarily incomplete.

A second word-cluster approach is even more abstract than incomplete stories about our past because it does not need to rely on actual facts. *Myths* are rhetorical constructions that try to explain natural events or cultural phenomena and are used to identify with a group and justify actions or beliefs. Myths carry similar power to arguments from the past. Speakers often use myths to identify with other people that share the values the myth contains, but myths also can be used as justification to preserve a seemingly sacred event, object or institution.

myth
....
a rhetorical construction that tries to explain natural events or cultural phenomena and is used to identify with a group and justify actions or beliefs

One of the central myths of any culture is the founding or origin myth. Early Mesopotamians portrayed their founding in the story of Gilgamesh, while the Romans looked to the story we now call the *Aeneid* for the myth of their inception. The *Aeneid* allowed Romans to connect their past to the legends of Troy and also served to glorify and legitimize Roman values and practices. Founding myths are useful because when someone tells a version of the myth it allows him or her to connect with others by identifying with their past and the values expressed within the story. The meaning of myths is not inherent in one word or phrase, but is rather a more elaborate and complex use of language.

narrative paradigm
··········
humans are storytelling beings by nature

narrative coherence
··········
the degree to which a story makes sense in the world in which we live

narrative fidelity
··········
the degree to which a story matches our own beliefs and experiences

Myths and arguments from the past are both stories, and as such they need to follow some semblance of a sequence. Psychologist Walter Fisher proposed a reason that explains why such stories are effective at making arguments and explaining the world around us. His *narrative paradigm* argues that humans are storytelling beings by nature, and evaluate all stories according to two elements. First is that the story has *narrative coherence*, or that it makes sense in the world. Myths and appropriations of past events need to make sense in our world for us to believe them when they are told to us. Second, stories must have *narrative fidelity* for us to find them acceptable. This means the story must not only make sense, but it must match our own beliefs and experiences. Stories such as arguments from the past and myths must, in essence, be believable and relate to our own worldview in order for them to be effective.

Simply knowing the characteristics of language and some of the ways in which it can be used to creatively and artfully convey meaning is not enough; in fact, it borders on dangerous. It is also important that you understand the ethical dimensions of using language to convey meaning. In the next part of this chapter we will discuss some of these ethical issues that are only relevant in a society where you have freedom of speech.

Structuring Language

The way you structure your messages can help enhance both your ability to deliver meaning and the audience's ability to understand the meaning. In this section we will cover four specific strategies for creatively structuring language. Strategic use of these structural patterns will greatly enhance your ability to communicate with others, but overuse or inappropriate use will damage your credibility, so be judicious in choosing when to use any of these.

repetition
··········
repeating either the same phrasing pattern for main points, or a phrase you just stated, in order to maximize the audience's ability to receive the information

The simplest structural strategy can often be the most effective at capturing an audience's attention and highlighting an important part of your message for them. *Repetition* occurs in two forms, but both involve repeating the same words or phrases. The first form occurs by using the same pattern of words whenever you introduce a new point. The pattern is not immediately repeated because there is data and evidence between the repeated phrase, but audiences quickly identify the pattern, thus making it easier for them to identify when you introduce another related point. The other version of repetition takes place when you want a specific claim, point, or piece of information to resonate with listeners. Here you simply repeat what you just said. For example: "*Grey's Anatomy* was number one in the ratings last fall. *Number one.*" The number is repeated, emphasizing to the audience that the number was important to know and remember.

A second structural strategy also involves repeating something, but not words or phrases. *Alliteration* repeats the same consonant or vowel sound in subsequent words. Audiences notice this form of speech because it is unique. Phrases like "peace, progress, and prosperity," or "direct, deliberate, and decisive," repeat the same consonant sound at the beginning of three words that follow each other, making it more pleasing to the ear. Additionally, the words build on and relate to one another, thus underscoring your description of an object.

alliteration
repeating the same consonant or vowel sound at the beginning of subsequent words

Repeating patterns of sounds or words is not the only structural way to enhance a speech. We can also use *parallelism*, or the practice of similarly structuring related words, phrases, or clauses. Unlike repetition, parallelism does not require the use of the same words, phrases or clauses, only that the ideas in those clauses are similar. Take for example, the following from a speech by Jesse Jackson at the 1984 Democratic National Convention: "If, in my high moments, I have done some good, offered some service, shed some light, healed some wounds, rekindled some hope, or stirred someone from apathy and indifference, or in any way along the way helped somebody, then this campaign has not been in vain." Here, he uses similar words and phrases like "offered some service," "shed some light," "healed some wounds," and "rekindled some hope" to drive home a point. The ideas of each phrase are the same, and the structure is similar but the words used are different. By structuring different phrases and words in a similar fashion you can emphasize importance and create memorable wording that others are more likely to remember.

parallelism
similarly structuring related words, phrases, or clauses

The fourth and final structural strategy we will cover involves inverting language. *Antithesis* calls for you to take two ideas that sharply contrast with each other and juxtapose them in a parallel grammatical structure. A famous example of antithesis comes from John F. Kennedy's inaugural address: "Ask not what your country can do for you, but what you can do for your country." On the one hand he decries socialism, and on the other he inspires individual effort. These are two ideas that compete with one another but work together to make a point in this statement. This is one of the more difficult structural strategies to employ, but the reward for the effort within the speech is high.

antithesis
two ideas that sharply contrast with each other and are juxtaposed in a parallel grammatical structure

Speech Structure Strategies	
Type	**Example**
Repetition	"The TV show *The Simpsons* has been running since 1989. 1989!"
Alliteration	"I want this report clear, concise, and concrete."
Parallelism	"My hobbies are hiking, boating, and fishing."
Antithesis	"To err is human, to forgive divine."

Table 6.3

Kenneth Burke (1897–1993)

Born in Pittsburgh near the turn of the twentieth century, Kenneth Burke remains one of the most influential American philosophers of all time. Unlike many other twentieth century scholars, Burke never received a college degree. In fact, he dropped out of not one, but two, universities. He preferred to write on his own, rather than pursue a doctorate and a career as a professor. He wrote multiple books and essays that influenced a variety of different disciplines.

Burke graduated from high school in Pittsburgh and then enrolled at The Ohio State University. Soon after attending he dropped out and chose to enroll at Columbia University. That experience also ended in his withdrawal from school. His lack of a college degree or formal higher education did not deter him from entrenching himself in academic life, however.

In 1939 he examined speeches by Adolf Hitler, then the chancellor of Germany. In this essay he eerily predicted the problems Hitler would cause in Germany simply by looking at how he managed to use speech to seize power. The essay entitled "The Rhetoric of Hitler's Battle" proposed a process by which Hitler's speech explained away the troubles of the German people by scapegoating people of Jewish descent and purifying what it meant to be Aryan. This work helped future scholars work to identify the ways in which leaders talk about enemies and war, and even apologize for wrongdoings.

Burke also wrote original poetry, fiction, and a plethora of literary critiques that are still considered essential reading for students in many different fields. His early interests in music and poetry led to his later exploration of language and symbols as explanations of the structure of human action. He eventually theorized that all human action is drama.

Burke's dramatic pentad is still one of the most fascinating ways to understand the relationship between thought, speech, and action. He divided drama, or speech/action, into five component parts: the act, the agent, the agency, the scene, and the purpose.

A message always contains either an explicit or implicit subject performing an action. This subject is the agent, and what the speaker states the subject is doing is the act. For example, when your mother says "take out the garbage" you are the implied agent and taking out the garbage is the act. Agency is how the act is performed by the agent, and the scene is the context within which the act takes place. Looking at the example again, the agency is through manual labor and the scene is a dirty house. The purpose within the message is why the act is to be performed, and in the above example, the reason is to clean the dirty house.

APPLICATION OF KENNETH BURKE'S PENTAD

The following is an excerpt of a speech delivered by Oprah Winfrey on June 15, 2008, to the graduating class of Stanford University:

"The world has so many lessons to teach you. I consider the world, this Earth, to be like a school and our life the classrooms. And sometimes here in this Planet Earth school the lessons often come dressed up as detours or roadblocks, and sometimes as full-blown crises. And the secret I've learned to getting ahead is being open to the lessons, lessons from the grandest universe of all, that is, the universe itself. It's being able to walk through life eager and open to self-improvement and that which is going to best help you evolve, cause that's really why we're here, to evolve as human beings. To grow into being more of ourselves, always moving to the next level of understanding, the next level of compassion and growth."[16]

PENTADIC ELEMENT	APPLYING THE PENTAD
Agent	Graduates
Agency	Openness
Act	Learning
Scene	Life on earth
Purpose	To evolve into better people

According to Burke, all five components of the pentad work together within a message according to a ratio. The ratio helps an analyst understand which parts of the drama are most dominant and important to the message's success. In our "take out the garbage" example, the most important ratio is the scene/purpose ratio. This pentadic approach is emblematic of how complicated Burke understood language to be, and how he believed language related to thought and action.

Although he was influenced somewhat by Marxism, throughout his life Burke never strictly adhered to any ideology or dogma.

He also never held a permanent academic post anywhere, preferring to stay as fluid in his career as he did in his works. He passed away in 1993, having left an indelible mark on communication, philosophy, education, and literature.

So influential was Burke that many master's theses and doctoral dissertations employ and/or analyze Burke's criticism and theories. There also is a scholarly organization called the Kenneth Burke Society, and many different English, philosophy, and communication academic organizations have a Kenneth Burke division dedicated to exploring or employing his work.

GUIDELINES FOR USING LANGUAGE

So far we have covered the characteristics of language, some language strategies that can help you achieve your goals, and two very dangerous pitfalls of language use to avoid. In this part of the chapter we will provide you with five specific guidelines to help you determine the best way to construct and convey messages.

1. **Use Language You Know and Are Comfortable with**: One of the common pressures speakers feel is the misplaced idea that they need to sound smart. Understand that you sound smart by presenting evidence in a logical cogent fashion and making a clear argument, not by filling your speech with big words. In fact, if used too often complex words can lose an audience and also hinder your efforts to identify with them. You need to sound conversational and natural, not formal and forced. This is true in any setting.

2. **Eliminate Wordiness**: Be economical in your choice of words. Just as every speech has a purpose, so too does every word. Be concise and clear rather than overly intricate and elaborate in your description. Try to avoid using words that are unnecessary in helping you make your point. Excess words take attention away from the points within your speech and can confuse the audience. In conversation excessive wordiness can create the impression that you wish to monopolize the conversation. Be direct and clear so that you respect others and their right to speak.

3. **Know When to Use a Thesaurus and When Not to**: An essential tool for any speaker also becomes a threat to a speech's success if used improperly. A thesaurus can help you find synonyms for words you may find yourself using quite a bit. However, when using a thesaurus you must be sure that you know the synonym, are comfortable using it, and use it in the proper context. Varying how you say something is a great way to enhance the appeal of your messages and makes it easier for others to pay attention, but using words just because they are different is a bad idea. Remember the first guideline: use language you know and are comfortable with.

4. **Use Active, Rather than Passive, Voice Whenever Possible**: A simple way to inject excitement into any message is to use active verbs. Active verbs depict movement. Passive voice, on the other hand, is boring and easily identified. Avoid writing or speaking with forms of the verb *to be*, such as the following: *was, being, were, is,* and *are.* These all indicate the passive voice. When you correct these constructions look to craft sentences where there is a subject followed by the action it performs, and then the object upon which it takes the action. Think about the following statements:

   > Passive Voice: *"Harold and Kumar were driving to White Castle so they could buy a snack."*

   > Active Voice: *"Harold and Kumar drove to White Castle to buy a snack."*

Online Help

www.merriam-
webster.com
www.dictionary.com

Which of these sounds more appealing? Which avoids the passive voice? As the example also illustrates, taking care to use active voice sentence construction also eliminates wordiness.

5. **Use "I, Me, We" Language**: This guideline essentially asks that you take ownership of your ideas and statements. Be clear about what is your language and what is attributed to someone else. Words like *we* and *our* also help you connect with others by making it appear as though you speak as a member of a collective group that includes them. This type of language helps you differentiate between your claims and the data that supports the claims, speak more forcefully without being rude, and enhance your relationship with others in a subtle but effective manner. That said, when you believe something, make sure you claim it by using "I" or "my" when you speak. Beware, however, that excessive use of "I" statements that ignore the other people involved in a conversation can create the impression that you are self-absorbed and not interested in other people.

SUMMARY

Without language we would not be able to understand the world around us, let alone communicate with each other. It also is controversial, as we saw with the case of George Carlin and his monologue. Without language, life would be quite dull indeed. In this chapter we discovered that every language, from Cyrillic to Greek to English has four common characteristics. We also explored some word strategies that creatively and effectively help convey messages. Finally, we provided some general guidelines for you when using language to interact with others. Creative and efficient use of words can vastly improve your ability to communicate.

KEY TERMS

abstract 147	myth 153
alliteration 155	narrative coherence 154
ambiguous 146	narrative fidelity 154
antithesis 155	narrative paradigm 154
arbitrary 145	parallelism 155
arguments from the past 153	repetition 154
hierarchical 149	simile 125
ideograph 151	single-word approach 150
metaphor 150	word-cluster approach 152

REVIEW QUESTIONS

1. What are the four characteristics of language?
2. What are the three single-word strategies for enhancing a message?
3. What are the three word-cluster approaches for enhancing a message?
4. What are the four structural strategies for using words to enhance your communication skills?
5. What language tools did Dr. King use in "I Have a Dream"?

THINK ABOUT IT

1. Where did language originate?
2. Are there any other common characteristics of language in addition to the four mentioned in this chapter?
3. Are speech and language different? If so, where is the line between speech and language?
4. How do you see language evolving in the future?

1. Print out the text of Dr. Martin Luther King, Jr.'s "I Have a Dream speech" discussed in this chapter. Go through and highlight as many metaphors as you can find, and then see if you can determine their type. Think about whether or not those specific word choices and metaphor types he employed made the speech as powerful as it was.

2. Sit down and watch (or read) the famous vaudeville skit "Who's on First?" by Abbott and Costello. What characteristics of language discussed in this chapter contribute to the humor of this classic comedy sketch?

3. Print out a famous speech—it does not matter by whom—and count how many versions of the verb form *to be* appear in the text of the speech. The chances are, it will be quite a small number. These forms include *have, has, was, were, be, and being*, to name just a few of the more common forms it takes.

ENDNOTES

1. Kent R. Middleton, William E. Lee, and Bill F. Chamberlin, *The Law of Public Communication* (Boston, MA: Allyn & Bacon, 2005), 405; T. Barton Carter, Marc A. Franklin, and Jay B. Wright, *The First Amendment and the Fourth Estate: The Law of Mass Media*, 9th Ed., (New York, NY: Foundation Press, 2005), 817.

2. Pacifica Foundation Station WBAI(FM), 56 F.C.C.2d 94, 32 P&F Rad. Reg. 2d 1331 (1975).

3. *Federal Communications Commission v. Pacifica Foundation*, 438 U.S. 726, 98 S. Ct. 3026, 57 L.Ed.2d 1073, 43 R.R.2d 493, 3 Med.L.Rptr. 2553.

4. Ibid.

5. *Donnie Brasco*, directed by Mike Newell (Culver City, CA: Tristar Pictures, 1997).

6. Mary Haas: http://www.sealang.net/thai/haas-uc.htm (accessed June 9, 2011).

7. Ibid.

8. www.britannica.com: http://www.britannica.com/EBchecked/topic/250703/Mary-R-Haas (accessed June 9, 2011).

9. Mary Haas: http://www.glottopedia.de/index.php/Mary_R._Haas (accessed June 9, 2011).

10. http://www.indiana.edu/~anthling/v39-4.html (accessed June 9, 2011).

11. S. I. Hayakawa, *Language in Thought and Action*, 3rd ed. (New York, NY: Harcourt, 1972).

12. Abbott and Costello, "Who's on First?" www.americanrhetoric.com. http://americanrhetoric.com/speeches/abbott&costellowhosonfirst.htm (accessed June 21, 2011).

13. Michael C. McGee, "The Ideograph: A Link Between Rhetoric and Ideology," *The Quarterly Journal of Speech 66* (1980), 1–16.

14. "I Have a Dream," by Dr. Martin Luther King, Jr. www.americanrhetoric.com. http://www.americanrhetoric.com/speeches/mlkihaveadream.htm (accessed June 24, 2011).

15. Ibid.

16. Kenneth Burke, "The Rhetoric of Hitler's Battle," *The Philosophy of Literary Form*, 3rd ed. (1941; Berkeley, CA: University of California Press, 1973), 191–220.

SCENARIOS

Scenario 1

Read each of the following headlines. For each, explain how the language in the headline illustrates at least two of the four characteristics of language: abstract, arbitrary, ambiguous, and hierarchical. Then rewrite the headline for greater clarity.

"Miners refuse to work after death"

"Stolen painting found by tree"

"Grandmother of Eight Makes Hole in One"

"Milk Drinkers are turning to Powder"

"Queen Mary has bottom scraped"

"Police Begin Campaign to Run Down Jaywalkers"

"Juvenile Court Tries Shooting Defendant"

"One armed man applauds the kindness of strangers"

Discuss how ambiguous headlines might affect the ethos of the messages' senders.

Scenario 2

Read the following excerpts from Malala Yousafzai's education advocacy speech at the Youth Takeover of the United Nations.

"So here I stand. . . . one girl among many. I speak—not for myself, but for all girls and boys. I raise up my voice—not so that I can shout, but so that those without a voice can be heard.

"On the 9th of October 2012, the Taliban shot me on the left side of my forehead. They shot my friends too. They thought that the bullets would silence us. But they failed. And then, out of that silence came, thousands of voices. The terrorists thought that they would change our aims and stop our ambitions but nothing changed in my life except this: Weakness, fear and hopelessness died. Strength, power and courage was born.

"We realize the importance of light when we see darkness. We realize the importance of our voice when we are silenced. In the same way, when we were in Swat, the north of Pakistan, we realized the importance of pens and books when we saw the guns. The wise saying, 'The pen is mightier than sword' was true. The extremists are afraid of books and pens. The power of education frightens them.

"Honourable Secretary General, peace is necessary for education . . . today I am focusing on women's rights and girls' education because they are suffering the most. There was a time when women social activists asked men to stand up for their rights. But, this time, we will do it by ourselves. I am not telling men to step away from speaking for women's rights rather I am focusing on women to be independent to fight for themselves.

"So today, we call upon the world leaders to change their strategic policies in favor of peace and prosperity . . . let us wage a global struggle against illiteracy, poverty and terrorism and let us pick up our books and pens. They are our most powerful weapons. One child, one teacher, one pen and one book can change the world. Education is the only solution. Education First."

- Identify the metaphors in this excerpt, and state what type of metaphor they are.

- Identify the ideographs in this excerpt.

- Identify the arguments from the past in this excerpt.

- Identify alliteration in this excerpt.

- Identify an example of antithesis in this excerpt.

- Identify repetition in this excerpt.

- Identify parallelism in this excerpt.

Scenario 3

Reread the same excerpts Malala Yousafzai's education advocacy speech at the Youth Takeover of the United Nations. Using Burke's Pentad, analyze how Malala dramatizes in a particular way what happened:

- Who is the agent in Malala's account?

- What act did the agent do?

- By what agency did the agent accomplish this act?

- What was the scene?

- For what purpose did this act occur?

Describe the ratio of these elements in Malala's account.

- Which of the five elements does Malala emphasize most?

- Which of the five elements does she emphasize least?

- How does her dramatization of what happened in this particular way affect how others might understand what happened?

Scenario 4

Think about how "I", "We" and "Me" language allows you to take ownership of your ideas in various ways. The situations below depict common disagreements between roommates. Write an exchange between roommates for each of the disagreements which clearly defines ownership of ideas and supports the roomates' relationship.

Disagreement 1:
John wakes up to discover his roommate Beau is eating the last of John's cereal. John planned to eat this himself and now has to rush to KU for food before class.

Disagreement 2:
A self-proclaimed neat freak, Suzan is dismayed to find that her new roommate Jenni leaves food containers and laundry all over the dorm room.

Disagreement 3:
Used to having his own room, Nick struggles to maintain a level of privacy from his roommate Joe who is always around and frequently interrupts Nick's studying.

Scenario 5

Find the full text of Dr. Martin Luther King, Jr.'s "I Have a Dream speech" online.

1. List at least ten different metaphors that Dr. King uses throughout the speech.

2. For each metaphor, change the wording to reflect a more literal, less figurative way of communicating the same content.

3. Pick three of the metaphors that you identified. For each, explain how Dr. King's use of this metaphor likely evoked a more powerful meaning for his audience than if he would communicated the same content in the more literal, less figurative way that you identified.

Scenario 6 (Performance)

Create a short presentation that you can give to the class regarding social media and language use. In your presentation, make sure that you:

- Explain how social media has changed people's perceptions of communication—including how people use language—and identify which form of social media is most influential for your generation and why.

- Explore how social media have affected how people tell stories and how they evaluate the stories that other people tell.

- Discuss what these changes mean for communication between different generations, especially those who use a different form of communication to interact.

Delivery

7

Practically SPEAKING

In the 1986 movie *Ferris Bueller's Day Off*, the economics teacher, played by Ben Stein, went on a tirade about the economy when his students did not respond to questions.[1] Using a lethargic delivery, Stein woefully made his potentially vibrant points seem irrelevant, boring, and hard to focus upon. Stein used the term "Anyone?" fourteen times during the entire scene. While he was speaking the students in the class predictably fell asleep, put their heads down on desks, and stared off into the distance, daydreaming. Stein's portrayal of the dreadfully boring teacher emphasizes the importance of vocal and physical delivery when addressing an audience.

The combination of word repetition, vocal emphasis, and proper posture and gestures can add force and meaning to words, but when delivered in a monotone with no energy, the rhetorical effect is minimal. In addition to no vocal variety Stein's posture was lethargic, making him appear as bored as his students. He lacked presence, despite having content.

Verbal delivery works in tandem with nonverbal delivery. The verbal content of Stein's message is clear, but the repeated begging for "anyone" to answer did nothing to get the audience's attention. His leaning posture and pleading facial expressions underscored his poor verbal delivery and worsened matters. As illustrated by Stein, verbal and nonverbal delivery can display the speaker's attitude toward themselves and the audience.

Too much focus on delivery, however, can also produce problems. A powerful delivery can detract from content if the audience members focus more on delivery than content. Good delivery comes through practice and balances a desire to gain and maintain attention with the need to keep the audience focused on the message. Audiences do not notice good delivery; rather they remember the content conveyed without saying much about how the speaker conveyed it.

A speaker may have great ideas, a new way to do something, or a way to improve life on campus, but if the speaker mumbles, does not project their voice, fails to make eye contact and does not present themselves well the ideas will likely be lost upon the audience. All of us have seen, or delivered, a message in an awkward manner. This not only makes the speaker feel uncomfortable, but can also cause anxiety and even mental pain in the audience, which makes it doubtful that the audience will believe the information or take the action advocated by the speaker.

This chapter will cover the basics of good delivery, both verbal and nonverbal, discuss how the two work together, and provide some commonsense ways to improve delivery. We will then focus on the public speaking context and discuss the four distinct ways a speaker can deliver a speech to an audience in this format.

PREP QUESTIONS

1. Define the terms pronunciation and articulation. Explain how the two are different.

2. Define dialect. Explain why there is not one correct dialect for any group of speakers.

3. Define slang. Make a list of slang terms you may use with your group of friends or family.

4. Define vocalics. Identify four vocalics that are listed in the textbook.

5. What is tone? Give an example of a time when someone misinterpreted your tone when you said or wrote something to him or her.

6. What are vocalized pauses? Explain how vocalized pauses can affect your credibility if you have too many of them when you deliver your message.

7. What are kinesics? List some nonverbal behaviors that belong to this general category of behavior.

8. List the five functions of effective nonverbal communication. Give an example of a time when your nonverbal behaviors performed each of the five functions.

9. What are conflicting nonverbal cues? Give an example of how two different nonverbal behaviors can conflict with each other.

10. Define each of the three modes of delivery for a speech. Explain which of the three most resembles how people talk in a conversation.

VERBAL ELEMENTS OF DELIVERY

The most obvious component of presenting any message is verbal delivery. Mastering verbal delivery takes lots of practice even when you understand the fundamentals. Those fundamentals include pronunciation and articulation, which contribute to the development and use of different dialects and slang. In this part of the chapter we will cover these aspects of verbal delivery and how to use them when delivering messages to others.

Pronunciation and Articulation

Proper word *pronunciation*, the accepted standard of how the word sounds, is very important to a speaker. In formal presentations, mispronouncing words can hurt your credibility. Would you trust a doctor who couldn't pronounce the name of your illness? You might take this mispronunciation as a sign that your doctor isn't prepared or educated. Even in casual conversation consistently mispronouncing words can create the perception that you do not know what you are talking about. In any situation, this can damage your credibility with others.

pronunciation
the accepted standard of how a word sounds when spoken

We mispronounce words for a variety of reasons. Sometimes we learn how to say a word incorrectly from hearing others say it that way. Other times we try to speak too quickly, resulting in slips of the tongue on more complex words. Sometimes we believe using words with which we are unfamiliar makes us look smarter or more eloquent to others. Whatever the reason, speakers need to correctly pronounce words. Mispronunciation damages credibility, the heart of a speaker's ethos. Mispronunciation of words or names in certain situations can make a difference in getting a job or making a sale.

Table 7.1	Most Commonly Mispronounced Words	
	The website yourdictionary.com lists 100 of the more commonly mispronounced words on its website.[2] Do you make any of these errors? The left column notes how these incorrectly pronounced words would be spelled.	
	Common Mispronunciation	**Correct Pronunciation**
	anartic	Antarctic
	aks	ask
	calvary	cavalry
	fedral	federal
	hiarchy	hierarchy
	irregardless	regardless
	jewlry	jewelry
	libel	liable
	libary	library
	nucular	nuclear
	perogative	prerogative

articulation
· · · · · · · · · · · ·
physically producing the sound needed to convey the word

blending
· · · · · · · · · ·
one of the more common articulation errors, and it occurs when speakers intermingle two words together

Closely related to pronunciation is *articulation*, or physically producing the sound needed to convey the word. In many cases we commit articulation errors by picking up bad habits from others through modeling; in other instances we are just plain lazy. *Blending* is one of the more common articulation errors, and it occurs when speakers intermingle two words together. For example, "I don't know" becomes "I dunno," "give me" is reduced to "gimme," or "would have" transforms into "woulda." There are more egregious articulation errors, such as running three words together like when "I bet you" becomes "Ibetcha." A speaker may get away with sloppy pronunciation and articulation in some casual situations, but professional settings often demand correct speech. It is important to practice good articulation in all interactions, and don't expect to just "turn it on" when it might appear to matter. One suggestion for improving your ability to articulate words is to consciously work to pronounce the final consonant of each word. This practice method has the added benefit of slowing down your rate of speech and making your message more understandable for an audience.

Dialects and Slang

Different people from around the United States sound different when speaking, yet speak the same language and communicate with general success. Anyone who travels to Boston will hear people articulate their "a's" as "ah's," and anyone who goes to states below the Mason-Dixon line find people saying "y'all" rather than "you all." The latter of these two examples is often referred to as southern drawl due to the slower speech pattern. Other recognized variations of Standard English include Ebonics and Gullah, both of which have produced literary products of high regard.

So, what are these differences and how do they occur? They are called *dialects*, or aspects of articulation, grammar, vocabulary, and pronunciation that differ from Standard English. The term *dialect* comes from the Ancient Greek term *dialektos* meaning a tongue, or the language of a particular group of people that makes them distinct. The phrase "speaking in tongues" grew out of this understanding of the word.

dialect
....
aspects of articulation, grammar, vocabulary, and pronunciation that differ from Standard English

A dialect is a sort of subgroup of a language, and can result in some miscommunication between a people when the receiver is either unaware of, or cannot decipher, a speaker's dialect. As Sarah Trenholm notes, "Problems occur when one dialect is defined as the standard and given greater status than other dialects." The important thing to remember is that dialects are regionally accepted forms of articulation and/or pronunciation, and one is not any better or more accurate than another.

Those who speak a particular dialect sometimes develop additions to the general standard vocabulary. In the case of Standard English, certain regions develop words and phrases that are understood by those who reside there, but not by those who hail from elsewhere. Over time these words are appropriated by the general population and become part of mainstream culture. When this happens the terms become *slang*, or words derived from dialects that most people understand, but yet do not use in professional writing or speaking.

slang
......
words derived from dialects that most people understand but do not use in professional writing or speaking

Cultures usually develop their own forms of slang. Watch an old gangster movie and you will hear actors using terms such as *heater, roscoe, piece,* or *rod* when referring to a weapon used to *bump off, ice,* or *whack* an enemy. If caught the shooters might find themselves in "the big house." Each of these terms grew from a small part of society and infiltrated mainstream culture. The terms represented the language used by a subsection of Americans, and eventually they were immortalized in the movies and through other cultural experiences. The words no longer belonged to a particular group, but rather they became part of the general lexicon.

Take the case of the word *ain't*, which until recent versions of the Webster's Dictionary was not considered a word, but rather a slang pronunciation of the term *isn't*. The use of the word *ain't* can even be seen in some landmark speeches in American history, such as the one delivered by Sojourner Truth at the Women's Convention in 1851. When used by Sojourner Truth the word was understood as a form of slang; however, today it is part of the general lexicon.

As such, slang is not cemented in society; that is to say some terms may die over time. Think about the gangster example from the previous paragraph. Do you hear about people being sent to "the big house" for "bumping off someone" at the same level you might have fifty or sixty years ago? No, and the reason is that the usability of the terms as slang is dying out. Now you might hear that someone is "in the can" for "dusting someone off." This phrasing, too, may leave common vernacular if it hasn't already!

Slang, although common, is not recommended for professional settings. Because slang is not common vernacular, and we live and work in a globalized society, the

SPEAKING of CIVIC ENGAGEMENT

Ain't I a Woman?
by Sojourner Truth

Delivered in 1851 at the Women's Convention in Akron, Ohio

Born Isabella Baumfree, Sojourner Truth was raised in slavery. She worked the fields as men did and suffered many physical abuses, including beatings at the hands of more than one slave master.[3] Truth eventually became a free woman and well-known minister. One memorable speech she delivered in this role was entitled "Ain't I a Woman."

The speech was short, especially by the standards of the day, clocking in at only 356 words, but nonetheless compelling. She made use of repetition in her address, specifically a phrase that included grammatical slang. The inclusion and repetition of that slang phrase enhanced the delivery of the speech. Take a look at the following excerpt:

> "And ain't I a woman? Look at me! Look at my arm! I have ploughed and planted, and gathered into barns, and no man could head me! And ain't I a woman? I could work as much and eat as much as a man—when I could get it—and bear the lash as well! And ain't I a woman? I have borne thirteen children, and seen most all sold off to slavery, and when I cried out with my mother's grief, none but Jesus heard me! And ain't I a woman?"[4]

In this speech Truth brought issues such as race and gender to the forefront of her audience's minds. Given that it took place in 1851, these issues would remain important for the American public for years to come. When one considers the lack of rights that all women had at this time and then considers her race, Sojourner Truth's speech was certainly remarkable.

risk of an audience not understanding your use of slang is increased, thus creating problems for communicating ideas to others. It also shows a lack of appreciation for an audience, and so sticking with Standard English is a much better route when speaking in professional settings.

NONVERBAL ELEMENTS OF DELIVERY

In addition to verbal delivery, or the words you use, nonverbal delivery also aids in the transmission of messages and can, in fact, play a much larger role in the success of accurate reception of that message. Nonverbal delivery can be broken down into two distinct areas: nonverbal elements related to voice, and nonverbal characteristics of the body. These aspects of your delivery serve several purposes when it comes to speaking, and a successful communicator incorporates good nonverbal delivery with strong verbal delivery. In this part of the chapter we will discuss the two types of nonverbal delivery and the functions of nonverbal delivery.

Vocalics

When people think of the nonverbal aspects of speech they often focus on the body, but actually most nonverbal behaviors emanate from the voice. When we focus on how loud a person is, whether the speaker's voice is dull or nasally, and how fast or slowly he or she speaks then we are looking at nonverbal actions. Think about it this way: are any of these things associated with pronunciation, articulation, or vocabulary? No, so therefore they are not categorized as elements of verbal delivery. We call these things *vocalics*, or anything that contributes to the creation or maintenance of sound in a person's voice.

vocalics
anything that contributes to the creation or maintenance of sound in a person's voice

One vocalic is the volume of a person's voice. Volume refers to how loud or soft a person's voice is when he or she speaks, and controlling it is trickier than you may realize. Volume can be augmented or reduced based on environmental factors, such as the acoustics of a wall. The distance between the sender and reciever can also influence volume. If a voice is too loud then the audience may leave, too soft and they may not receive the speaker's message. In casual conversation if someone is too loud or too quiet their conversation partner will often let them know. There are also situational expectations for volume, like sitting in a movie theater. Generally, you are asked not to speak during a movie, but if you had to then you should use a lower voice so as not to disturb others. Outside of this context, however, a lower volume may send a different message.

All of us, at one time or another, have been an audience member when someone was speaking and had to strain to hear what the speaker was saying. At its best this is a distraction, but it may also be considered either lazy or rude. Low volume can show shyness, anxiety, a lack of preparation, being unsure, or a speaker's lack of interest in being there. In all of these cases, if an audience cannot hear a speaker then the credibility of that speaker is damaged.

That does not mean that the speaker should shout at the audience. Rather, the speaker should use sufficient volume so that the person farthest away can hear with ease. The size of the room can often influence your decision on how loud you must speak. If you are in a large crowded room it might be necessary to simply ask if the people to whom you are speaking can comfortably hear you. If not, perhaps you speak more loudly or move closer to them to make sure everyone can hear you.

Volume alone does not constitute vocalics. Another element is *tone*, or the syllabic emphasis on a sound that expresses emotion or meaning. Think about our example from the beginning of the chapter. The tone of Ben Stein's character illustrates how speech that has no tonal inflection or variety can quickly lose an audience by conveying a lack of interest in the subject, audience, and occasion. Monotone deliveries can also quickly bore other people and distract them from

tone
the syllabic emphasis on a sound that expresses emotion or meaning

the purpose and goals of the interaction. If you are excited about what you have to say it will be conveyed in your tone and make the message all the more interesting to listen to for the audience.

Tone also expresses different emotions when you adjust it for specific words. Sarcasm is often conveyed through the use of a different tone of voice when making a statement that otherwise might mean something else. Think about the inflection in someone's voice when they respond to the question "How are you doing today?" If they respond "fine" it could mean they are doing ok, but it can also imply that they are not if the word is given a sharper, more cutting edge to it. This is when we might hear someone say that they "heard" some emotion in the person's voice. Tone is a nonverbal vocalic that expresses emotion.

Another aspect of vocalics is the rate at which you speak. The rate, or pace, of your speech can be the result of a variety of things. The average rate of speech in the United States is 150 words per minute. This rate may vary by region. For example, people often observe that individuals from the Northeast speak much faster than people from the rest of the country, so culture can play a role in speech rate. It is also quite normal for a nervous speaker to speak at a more rapid rate than someone who is comfortable. In any communication situation you need to make sure you speak at a pace the other people involved can follow, or else your message will be lost. It is important to note, as well, that when delivering a public presentation your pace will naturally increase over the rate with which you practiced or speak in casual conversation. If you need to time yourself, make sure you prepare for this adjustment.

When speaking publicly, if you are worried about your rate of speech there are a few things you can do. You might want to audio record yourself in a normal situation speaking, or practicing your speech. If you have a concern that you might get caught up in the moment and begin to speak rapidly, you might want to put visual cues in your notes, such as a hand-drawn slow or stop sign on your speaking outline to remind you not to speak too fast. You can also practice formal presentations in front of an audience of friends and colleagues to gather feedback.

In meeting scenarios, your rate of speech increases for potentially different reasons. Sometimes you may feel rushed due to time or the need to get a lot of information out that you have been waiting to say for some time. In these instances, jot down notes before you speak so that you can use them to guide your statements when it is your turn to speak. Also, remember to breathe and give people time to digest what you are saying.

One final element of vocalics is pausing. Pauses are normal and necessary, and in many circumstances are useful tools. Professors use this tactic quite often to quell students talking among themselves in class. Pausing can be effectively used, as when you stop after making a point you want the other person or larger audience to consider. They also can be effective for allowing listeners to catch up, to permit yourself to catch a breath, and even to recognize and subdue an unruly or rude audience. Look at this scenario: some students are chatting among themselves during class, and the professor pauses and looks at the students until they stop.

They stop because the students feel that the whole class's attention is on their conversation, resulting in them ending the rude behavior.

Pauses can also be a powerful tool for any speaker, as they can help emphasize something of importance. After providing a compelling statistic or story, a pause of a few seconds will alert the listener that something dramatic was just said. As with all other vocal qualities the pause must seem natural, and timing them is crucial. Using pauses effectively is a skill you learn with practice, and they can be a distraction if you are not careful. Awkward pauses make speakers look unprepared, unsure, or nervous, but effective pausing can be an equally positive interaction device.

Sometimes speakers feel pressure to speak all the time, and thus do not pause. Instead they fill the perceived void with a noise like *er, um, ah or uh* when they speak. These utterances have a variety of names, but generally they are called *vocalized pauses*. Even polished speakers can fall prey to this speaking irregularity. We have all seen speakers stammer and overuse these annoying pauses and inflections, and we realize how much they hurt delivery. Kept at a bare minimum they may not be much of a problem, but as a speaker you should strive to limit their interfering with your delivery. Vocalized pauses infect everyday interactions as well, and nothing makes a person seem less coherent or intelligent than repeating vocalized pauses like *y'know, like,* and *for sure*. These overused phrases serve no purpose in most messages.

vocalized pauses
utterances that are not words and have no place in a speech, but are done instead of pausing the delivery of the speech

Kinesics

Your voice, although an important element, is not the only nonverbal aspect of your delivery. Your body also conveys information about credibility and emotions to others through facial expressions, gestures, posture, appearance and eye contact, otherwise known as *kinesics*. These nonverbal behaviors are often the hardest to control, but when you learn to do so they can significantly impact your delivery and presence.

kinesics
nonverbal behaviors related to movement

The face is often the first thing people notice about you in any situation, and speaking is no different. Your face expresses emotions and sends messages to the audience in a way that can either aid or damage your ability to get your message across to an audience. If you try to say something you do not believe in, your facial expressions will often give you away, but when you do believe what you are saying then your expressions can illustrate your sincerity to the audience in a way no amount of evidence or list of credentials ever could. How you handle your facial expressions is important, but not nearly as challenging a question to answer as what to do with another part of your body.

One of the things people often struggle with when interacting with others is what to do with their hands. Hands can be effective tools, but they also can become unwanted distractions if not treated properly. Hands are the primary source of *gesture*, or physical movements used to convey a message. Skilled speakers use their hands to complement their messages, pointing to people when they are mentioned, if possible, or making forceful motions to emphasize a point.

gesture
a physical movement used to convey a message

posture
the position of your body

In addition to gestures, your posture is also important when trying to convey a message to others. *Posture* refers to the position of your body, and it means more than simply facing the audience. If you lean toward someone over a table, or slouch in your chair your posture conveys a negative impression to others, just as it does when you stand rigidly and do not move. The key to good posture in delivery is being comfortable, yet confident. See the examples of good and bad posture in Figure 7.1.

Figure 7.1
Examples of Bad Posture (top) and Good Posture (bottom)

Having a comfortable and confident posture is connected with effectively using gestures. To maintain the ability to gesture effectively you should not keep your hands in your pockets, folded in front of you, or even held behind your back. These positions all negatively impact your posture by making you appear uncomfortable. Good posture is relaxed and allows you to make use of your hands when needed.

The next aspect of nonverbal communication we will discuss is appearance. Some professors require students to "dress up" when speaking while some do not. Some high schools also have dress codes for students, borne from the idea that if students dress well they will behave well. Even if you are not expected to wear more formal clothing you should always dress neatly with your hair in place. If you do not respect your own appearance, then people will not respect you and you will never be able to get your message across to them.

Appearance also can boost your self-confidence and help you feel successful even before you say a word. Consider how you feel when you have on your best clothes. We all feel more competent and confident in what we do. Research shows that when you dress professionally for a presentation it often results in better actual and perceived performance. Appearance is especially important for speakers who address an audience who is unfamiliar with them, because the first impression the speaker makes on the audience is based on the speaker's appearance. See Table 7.2 for appearance tips.

Table 7.2

Appearance Tips
• Dress neatly
• No baseball caps
• Hair combed or brushed
• Better to overdress than underdress

The last category of nonverbal action we will discuss is eye contact—perhaps the most feared nonverbal action during a formal presentation. Novice speakers often get nervous when they realize they need to look at the audience during their presentation. This is understandable, but eye contact conveys confidence and interest in the audience, making it an indispensable aspect of any speech. One way to minimize the pressure created by eye contact is to look at a speech as a series of conversations. Instead of a speech being you talking to a group of, for example, 25 people, view it as 25 individual one-on-one conversations. To do this, select one person to look at in the audience and speak directly to them until you reach a new idea or point, then move on to someone else in another part of the room. We typically are not afraid of individual conversations, and yet we make eye contact with the other participant, so taking the same perspective on larger speaking engagements might help. In any event, eye contact, gestures, and posture all play a role in the delivery of a message to an audience.

Functions of Nonverbal Communication in Speech

As individuals we send more nonverbal messages than we do verbal. As such, it is important for communicators to understand the various purposes their gestures, posture, and eye contact can serve with regard to how they present themselves. In this section we will look at the five positive ways nonverbal messages can influence perceptions of your speech, and the one negative role they could play in your delivery if you are not careful.

One way nonverbal actions can influence your message is by allowing you to reiterate your verbal message without saying it. When physical actions restate verbal messages in this manner then nonverbal behaviors *repeat* their verbal counterparts. You can make use of this function by pointing to people in the audience as you reference them, or using your fingers to count along when listing certain items or points.

repeat
when physical actions restate verbal messages

Nonverbal messages can also amplify, or *accent*, your desired message. For example, when you wish to emphasize a point you can pound on the podium or table at the end of stating the point. When you get excited about something you are saying, you can raise a fist in a mock sign of triumph. Not only do these behaviors support your message, but they increase its power and the likelihood the audience understands your point.

accent
nonverbal behaviors that augment a verbal message

Nonverbal actions are most effective, however, when they *complement* the verbal message. This occurs when the nonverbal message is the same as the verbal message. A perfect model of this occurring is when speakers laugh at jokes they make. By laughing, they display the action associated with the verbal content of the joke.

complement
when the action demonstrates the message contained in the verbal content

Facial expressions and body movement also can *substitute* for verbal content on occasion. A person who smiles after being introduced does not necessarily need to state her enjoyment at being there as the smile conveys that message. When asked a question to which you do not know the answer, you may follow with a simple shrug of the shoulder instead of saying "I don't know." Waving to someone you know on the street is another example of a nonverbal behavior substituting for a verbal message.

substitute
physical actions that take the place of verbal messages

One other positive function nonverbal messages perform is *regulating* an interaction. During normal conversations nonverbal actions such as pauses and hand gestures can cue responses and comments from the other person. During speeches they serve much the same purpose—allowing an audience to know when they can ask questions, when they should clap, and when they should cheer. These types of gestures help regulate, or direct, interactions so that receivers know when messages have been completed and it is their turn to speak.

On the downside, *conflicting* nonverbal cues can negatively influence your ability to get your message across. These occur when your message says one thing, but your body sends the opposite message. If you are not pleased to be doing something, but tell people you are, most likely your nonverbal actions tell the truth. It is extremely difficult to hide your true feelings about something because of the prevalence of nonverbal communication in any interaction.

MODES OF DELIVERY

Delivery encompasses more than verbal and nonverbal skills; it also refers to the style speakers use to deliver their messages to their audiences. Different contexts allow speakers the opportunity to bring varying amounts of notes and preparation with them. To quote the Greek philosopher Demosthenes, "The three most important parts of speaking are delivery, delivery, and delivery." You will encounter three primary modes of speech delivery in CMM 100 and your other courses. In this part we will define and discuss each of them.

Manuscript Speeches

Most students welcome the chance to deliver a *manuscript speech*. Manuscript speeches are commonplace today, although they may not seem to be so. Politicians frequently deliver them. When the president gives an address before Congress he speaks directly off of a teleprompter; when he speaks from the Rose Garden he does so with the script right in front of him; and, when the president of the University of Dayton, Dr. Dan Curran, speaks at convocation or graduation he reads from a manuscript. Just because it is acceptable for a variety of occasions, however, does not mean it is the only, or even best, form of delivery.

Speaking off a manuscript carries with it many positives for a speaker, particularly a newcomer to public address. You do not have to fear the freeze as you might with a memorized presentation. Your speech will come off as organized, or at least as organized as you made the manuscript. The opportunity to jump off the manuscript is possible, but it is constrained by the need to stay on message. Finally, manuscript style speaking allows you to note where you need to make gestures and employ different nonverbal actions at moments during your speech. No wonder first-time speakers prefer the manuscript style!

Despite the enormous benefits afforded by manuscript style addresses, the form is not a panacea. Making adjustments to audience feedback, though possible, is extraordinarily difficult without experience. Additionally, there is a temptation to stare directly at the manuscript, reading off of it to the audience, which makes you

SPOTLIGHTING THEORISTS: DEMOSTHENES

Demosthenes (384–322 BC)

Considered one of the greatest of the Attic orators in ancient Greece, Demosthenes reportedly gave his first speech in court arguing to receive what was left of his inheritance. He became a speechwriter and lawyer in Athens, and eventually became one of the leading voices in opposition to Philip II of Macedon and his son Alexander the Great. Demosthenes, like Socrates and Cicero, eventually died in the service of his principles. He took his own life rather than be arrested by Alexander's supporters. Many of his contemporaries lauded him and his contributions to oratory.

Praise for Demosthenes came from many corners of the ancient world. Cicero, the father of the five canons of rhetoric, proclaimed Demosthenes to be the "perfect orator" and Quintilian stated Demosthenes was "by far the most excellent" of the Greek orators.

Like Cicero, Demosthenes believed that speakers should be educated on what they talk about, and therefore often declined to speak on subjects he had not studied before. Additionally, Demosthenes valued delivery (gestures) above rhetorical flourish and style, believing that these elements of a speech contributed more to its success.

To that end, stories tell of Demosthenes practicing his own speeches in unique fashion. One story tells that he practiced his speech in front of a roaring waterfall in order to work on projecting his voice. Another speaks of how he would practice his presentations with pebbles in his mouth to concentrate on improving pronunciation and articulation of words. For Demosthenes, delivery truly represented the most important aspect of any speech.

appear distant and uninterested in the audience—not to mention unable to gauge their reaction to what you say. Manuscript speeches invite speakers to focus on their script, and not the audience or their own gestures and reactions, making it hard to successfully incorporate effective and positive nonverbal communication into the presentation.

The main reason beginning speakers relish manuscript speaking is that it eliminates the freeze factor; however, it can also create a much less energetic speech and ultimately distances the speaker from the audience. There is a middle ground, however, between manuscript and memorized speeches and we will discuss that style next.

Extemporaneous Speeches

Since instructors do not normally expect memorized speeches, and yet typically do not allow students to deliver manuscript speeches, how then are most student speeches delivered? The answer, most student speeches are *extemporaneous speeches*, or speeches delivered with notes in front of the speaker. Extemporaneous speaking requires practice, but also allows for speakers to have organized references in front of them in case they lose their place during the presentation. Extemporaneous speeches much like manuscript speeches, have positive and negative qualities of which every speaker needs to be aware.

The primary benefit of using notes instead of a full manuscript is that you will have a more natural and fluid delivery. You can adapt to audience feedback and expound on or eliminate examples and points based upon the audience's reaction to what you are saying and how you are saying it. Your vocal inflections and physical gestures are not planned, and therefore do not risk coming across as rigid and robotic as in the other styles of delivery. When you stress an inflection of a word or syllable, or gesture in support of a particular statement it comes from your emotions, not your guide, providing your audience with a perception of authenticity.

A secondary benefit of extemporaneous speaking related to the ability to have a natural delivery is improved eye contact. With only notes in front of you it becomes possible to make more eye contact with the audience, increasing your connection and identification with them, thus making you appear more believable. Eye contact is an essential part of any successful speech, and extemporaneous speaking allows you to make eye contact with the audience while also being able to check your notes if you lose your place.

As you can probably imagine, extemporaneous delivery depends on two things: adequate practice and a strong organized set of notes. To deliver a believable address with only notes you must spend a significant amount of time practicing the speech. First you practice with a full text draft, but over time you reduce it to a speaking outline where only direct quotations appear in full text form. This speaking outline comes from paring down a full sentence outline, and still retains the same structural format of the original, just with far fewer words and phrases. The process of drafting, practicing, and then constructing a speaking outline for use during the actual presentation takes a lot of time, but the payoff when you speak more than accounts for that investment.

The most significant obstacles to a successful extemporaneous speech involve creating an effective speaking outline and keeping your notes organized. Some people who deliver speeches off of notes use bulleted lists or even note cards in their speech. Bulleted lists are dangerous because they are not structured, and thus you can easily lose your place when staring back and forth at the list. Note cards can be problematic, especially if they are not numbered, because you might drop them or put them in an incorrect order, causing you to lose your place or get flustered when delivering the speech. But these problems can be minimized and even eliminated through extensive practice and preparation for the presentation. There are, however, some speeches that allow for little to no preparation.

Impromptu Speeches

At one time or another in your life you will need to speak without any preparation, research, or notes. These unplanned unprepared presentations are called *impromptu speeches*, and they can be as short as a minute or as long as ten, depending on the topic, speaker, and situation. These may also be the most nerve-racking of any speech because even the most experienced orator will feel a bit jittery when called on to speak about something without any preparation.

impromptu speech

a presentation done with little or no preparation

When called upon to deliver impromptu remarks it is best to first collect your thoughts and quickly develop a mental outline of what you wish to say. Just because these speeches have no preparation time does not mean they should not be organized or logical. Two topics are always handy when asked to deliver such remarks: the situation and the audience. Connecting your comments to both provides an easy way to focus your remarks.

One of the most common places where you may deliver impromptu remarks is during a celebratory event honoring someone or something. No one will warn you that you might speak, you will not have prepared for the moment, and you might be surprised at the opportunity, but remember to identify with the audience and the event. It may also behoove you to reference the fact that you had no idea you might be speaking, thus acknowledging to the audience the impromptu nature of the address. These are high-stress speeches, but also often are very short. Audiences typically have lower expectations for performance of impromptu speeches than they do for a planned presentation.

SUMMARY

Delivery is a complicated and important element of communication, and it is also the one part that engenders the most fear in people. Delivery is divided into three components, each with equal importance. The first is verbal delivery which focuses on correctly speaking the language. The second part of delivery involves nonverbal actions from vocal variety to physical gestures and posture. Finally, the style of presenting the material in a public speaking setting allows for reading off a manuscript, using limited notes, or delivering unplanned remarks. We must remember that presenting the message is just as important (and complex) as planning it.

KEY TERMS

accent   179

articulation   172

blending   172

complement   179

conflict   180

dialect   173

extemporaneous speech   182

gesture   177

impromptu speech   183

kinesics   177

manuscript speech   180

posture   178

pronunciation   171

regulate   180

repeat   179

slang   173

substitute   179

tone   175

vocalic   175

vocalized pauses   177

REVIEW QUESTIONS

1. What are the two fundamentals of verbal delivery?

2. What is the difference between dialects and slang?

3. What are the two major categories of nonverbal delivery?

4. What are the four functions of nonverbal delivery?

5. What are the three types of speech delivery?

THINK ABOUT IT

1. How would you define great delivery?

2. Which of the nonverbal characteristics of delivery is most important?

3. How do you determine the proper relationship between nonverbal and verbal delivery?

ACTIVITIES FOR ACTION

1. Write down two sentences of average length about any particular topic; the content does not matter for this exercise. Then, take a sheet of paper and cut it into six pieces. On each sheet of paper write one of the following emotions: angry, happy, sad, confused, excited, depressed. Then, on the back of each sheet write a different emotion from the one on the front. Ask a friend to pick a sheet of paper, then give him or her the sentences you wrote and ask your friend to say those sentences using the emotion on the top of the paper selected. Finally, ask him or her to convey the emotion on the other side of the paper without speaking. See if you or others in the audience can accurately identify the emotions.

2. Try saying the following tongue twisters as many times as you can in a row without any errors in pronunciation or articulation: "Sally sells sea shells by the seashore." "How can a clam cram in a clean cream can?" "The thirty-

three thieves thought that they thrilled the throne Thursday." "Picky people pick Peter Pan peanut butter." And, if you really want a challenge: "Out in the pasture the nature watcher watches the catcher, while the catcher watches the pitcher who pitches the balls. Whether the temperature's up or whether the temperature's down, the nature watcher, the catcher, and the pitcher are always around. The pitcher pitches, the catcher catches, and the watcher watches. So whether the temperature rises or the temperature falls the nature watcher just watches the catcher who's watching the pitcher who's watching the balls."

3. We all know the challenge presented by vocalized pauses and the importance of limiting their occurrence. To practice speaking without using a vocalized pause have a friend time you speaking on any given topic as long as you can until you use a vocalized pause. The larger the audience the better for this exercise, as everyone starts listening for the vocalized pauses. The person who goes the longest wins.

ENDNOTES

1. *Ferris Bueller's Day Off,* written and directed by John Hughes (Paramount Pictures, 1986).

2. http://www.yourdictionary.com/library/mispron.html (accessed June 10, 2008).

3. http://www.lkwdpl.org/wihohio/trut-soj.htm

4. http://www.feminist.com/resources/artspeech/genwom/sojour.htm

SCENARIOS

Scenario 1

Take turns with your group members delivering the information in the paragraph below using the different methods of delivery: Manuscript, Extemporaneous, and Impromptu.

Social pressure is another reason people get nervous speaking in front of an audience. There is a certain status quo that we all live up to. If we make a mistake we often believe that it will damage our reputation. We cannot pretend we don't get nervous and we can't avoid the fact that we all get nervous and we cannot allow our nervousness to take us over. So, how can we manage anxiety? Let's break it down. Before we begin, remember this: Accept the fear and make it work for you. Most people cannot see your nervousness, so don't even mention that you are. Use this adrenaline rush of nervous energy by turning it into lots of enthusiasm in your delivery.

1. What are the advantages and disadvantages of each method?

2. Do certain methods work better in particular contexts? Give examples.

Scenario 2

Read each of the following examples and discuss your first impression of the situation. What factors led to your impression? What is the relationship? Occupation? Emotions? Discuss haptics, proxemics, kinesics, chronemics, vocalics etc.

Nancy, a 5'8" 130lb woman, is dressed in a gray business suit with her black hair pulled up in a loose bun. She is wearing black oval reading glasses and is carrying a black brief case and an overcoat. Nancy enters the doctor's office, walks to the check-in window and proceeds to tell the nurse in a low, soft voice: "My name is Nancy Jones. I have an appointment with Dr. Hale."

Sarah is a mother of a 3 year old son and 6 year old daughter. They are crossing the intersection of Fifth and Main Street. They are holding hands and walking quickly as the crosswalk counts backward from 30. Sarah's blond hair is pulled up in a ponytail. She has on yoga pants, a hoodie and gym shoes. The kids have Disney bookbags on their backs. As they reach the other corner, Sarah places her hand on the children's shoulders and guides them down the busy sidewalk.

Chad, 32, and Kate, 30, are sitting at a booth in a low-lit Italian restaurant on a Tuesday night at 9:00. They are sitting on the same side of the booth drinking red wine and whispering to each other. They are both well dressed (Chad in a suit and tie and Kate in a little black dress). They stare in to each other's eyes and touch hands.

Scenario 3

1. Think about a time when you were really nervous or anxious in front of someone (s). Why were you nervous? Did the other person (s) know you were nervous? What did you do to conceal your anxiety? Have you ever seen someone trying to conceal his/her nerves and not be successful? What behaviors gave away their anxiety?

2. What characteristics do you like best in a public speaker? What characteristics do you find annoying? Compare your responses with the members of your group, noting cultural trends.

Scenario 4

Try saying the following tongue twisters as many times as you can in a row without any errors in pronunciation or articulation:

1. Peter Piper picked a peck of pickled peppers.

    Did Peter Piper pick a peck of pickled peppers?

    If Peter Piper Picked a peck of pickled peppers,

    Where's the peck of pickled peppers Peter Piper picked?

2. She sells seashells by the seashore.

    The shells she sells are surely seashells.

    So if she sells shells on the seashore,

    I'm sure she sells seashore shells.

3. Red lorry, yellow lorry.

4. Which wristwatches are Swiss wristwatches?

5. How much wood would a woodchuck chuck
   If a woodchuck could chuck wood?
   He would chuck, he would, as much as he could,
   And chuck as much as a woodchuck would
   If a woodchuck could chuck wood.

6. Unique New York.

7. Many an anemone sees an enemy anemone.

8. Freshly-fried flying fish.

9. She stood on the balcony,
   inexplicably mimicking him hiccoughing,
   and amicably welcoming him home.

10. Imagine an imaginary menagerie manager
    imagining managing an imaginary menagerie.

11. The epitome of femininity.

12. A skunk sat on a stump and thunk the stump stunk,
    but the stump thunk the skunk stunk.

13. Greek grapes.

Scenario 5 (Performance)

This exercise is designed to help members of a group recognize verbal and nonverbal aspects of delivery during a speech. By knowing when and if these aspects occur, group members will get a sense of the important role these elements play in a successful delivery.

Using the paragraph in scenario 1, randomly choose different aspects of delivery that you will or will not apply in your presentation. Choose at least two Verbal Delivery, two Physical Delivery, and two Functions of Physical Delivery (below). Deliver the information in the paragraph purposely focusing on the 6 features of delivery you have chosen. For example, if you choose volume, rate, posture, eye contact, and repeating and accenting, then you could deliver the information in the paragraph very softly, at a very slow pace, hunched over in your chair, looking down at the desk, and performing "air quotes" and pounding your fist on the desk. You can choose to deliver the information in a positive or "dos" manner or a negative or "don'ts" manner. After each student recites their speech, discuss the aspects of delivery that were and were not used, and how these added or took away from the overall success of the speech.

Verbal Delivery:	**Physical Delivery:**	**Functions of Physical Delivery:**
Pronunciation/Articulation	Posture	Repeating
Vocalized Pauses	Facial Expressions	Accenting
Volume	Eye Contact	Complementing
Pitch/Tone	Gestures	Substituting
Rhythm		
Rate		

Types of Persuasion

Practically SPEAKING

On June 12, 1994, police discovered the bodies of Nicole Brown Simpson and Ronald Goldman in the courtyard of Nicole Brown Simpson's Brentwood, California, residence. Simpson and Goldman died from excessive stab wounds, and immediately suspicion fell upon Simpson's ex-husband, former NFL star turned actor O. J. Simpson. On June 13th authorities informed Simpson of the murders while he was on a business trip in Chicago. Upon his return, police took him into custody for questioning and he retained Robert Shapiro as his legal counsel. Within a few weeks a grand jury and judge decided that there was sufficient evidence to prosecute O. J. Simpson for the murders of his ex-wife and Goldman. On July 22, 1994, before presiding judge Lance Ito, O. J. pled not guilty to the crimes, and one of the most famous trials in American history began.

The trial opened on January 24, 1995, after a brief holiday recess. During the trial the defense managed to get admissions of procedural errors from members of the police department regarding the collection of DNA and other evidence. Additionally, detective Mark Fuhrman came under fire for supposedly making racist comments during the investigation. Eventually, after various legal maneuverings by both the prosecution and defense, the trial began to wind down.

On September 26–27, 1995, over a year after the deaths of Nicole Brown Simpson and Ronald Goldman, the prosecution and defense delivered their closing arguments.[1] Deputy District Attorney Marcia Clark and Prosecutor Christopher Darden delivered their closing argument first, making specific mention of the perception that Detective Fuhrman was a racist: "It would be a tragedy if, with such overwhelming evidence, you find the defendant not guilty because of the racist attitudes of one officer." Immediately following their presentation, the defense, represented by Johnny Cochran and Barry Scheck, made its case to the jury, with the former referring to Fuhrman as a "lying, perjuring, genocidal racist," and the latter referring to a "cancer" at the heart of the investigation into the murders.[2] Ultimately, the arguments made by the defense proved to be more persuasive than those offered by the prosecution, and on October 3, 1995, the jury acquitted O. J. Simpson on both counts of murder.

The speeches made by both the prosecution and the defense in the O. J. Simpson trial are examples of one type of persuasive speech but as we will discover in this chapter, there are other categories of persuasion.

PREP QUESTIONS

1. Define the four forms of stasis in Quintilian's stasis theory. Give an example of a dispute that two people might have that illustrates each of the four forms.

2. What are the three types of persuasive questions? Provide an example of each type.

3. Define the two types of persuasive messages that Aristotle recognized.

4. Define the terms kategoria and apologia. When might one find each of these types of speeches today?

5. What is a refutation? How does it differ from a rebuttal?

6. List the four stages of the persuasive process. Explain what happens during each stage.

7. Define the three types of credibility.

8. What are three ways to build credibility during a speech, according to Aristotle?

9. What is dynamism?

10. What are three unethical behaviors that can cause a speaker to lose credibility?

11. Contrast the two types of lying: lying by commission and lying by omission.

12. Why should a speaker not rely only on emotional appeals when attempting to persuade an audience?

FORMS OF PERSUASIVE MESSAGES

In this section of the chapter we will identify the different types of persuasive messages using both classical and contemporary terms. At the heart of any persuasive attempt is what classical philosophers referred to as the issue in dispute, or what contemporary scholars call the question. Quintilian, the Roman philosopher and teacher, wrote extensively about the different ways we dispute a persuasive argument. We will discuss four.

After examining Quintilian's work we will demonstrate the three forms of persuasive messages people use today. We will then define the two types of persuasive messages proposed by Aristotle and how they relate to the issues in dispute. Finally, we will discuss how to use persuasion to respond to arguments made by another person.

Quintilian and Stasis Theory

All persuasive attempts revolve around an issue that is disputed. The speaker thus attempts to persuade listeners that they should agree with the speaker's interpretation of the issue in dispute. This central focus is called *stasis*, the object or idea that people argue over. Quintilian provided four different types of stasis, or disputed issues, that may exist in a persuasive situation. In this section of the chapter we discuss each of them.

stasis
the basic issue in dispute between one or more speaking parties

The first form of stasis is *definitive stasis*, or a dispute over the meaning of a term. When two sides define a term in two different ways, there is definitive stasis. One arena where this occurs is in politics, where terms and phrases are defined differently by each candidate or party. Take, for instance, the issue of marriage. Some define marriage as a contractual agreement only between a man and woman. Others, however, do not define it that way, and interpret it as a contractual bond between any two consenting adults, regardless of sex. When two sides apply different definitions of marriage, then the central issue of their disagreement is an example of definitive stasis.

definitive stasis
when the issue in dispute is the meaning of a term

A second form of stasis is what we saw at play during the O. J. Simpson trial we discussed in the opening of the chapter. *Conjectural stasis* exists when the central issue of disagreement is whether or not something occurred. The issue at stake

conjectural stasis
when the issue in dispute is whether something occurred or not

195

in the Simpson murder case was whether or not O. J. killed Nicole Brown Simpson and Ronald Goldman. All criminal court cases address issues of conjectural stasis.

qualitative stasis
when the issue in dispute involves the morality, ethicality, or value of an action

When the sides in an argument seek to persuade an audience about the moral or ethical nature of an action, the central issue of discussion involves *qualitative stasis*. Debates about issues of qualitative stasis also include those that cover what is best in a given situation. Remember when we mentioned that the district attorney's office decided not to seek the death penalty in the O. J. Simpson case? Arguments for whether or not to seek the death penalty in the Simpson case exemplify an issue where the topic is a matter of qualitative stasis. Would it be right to kill Simpson as punishment for murdering his ex-wife and Ronald Goldman? At the heart of such a question is the morality of capital punishment, thus making the issue of disagreement one of qualitative stasis.

Finally, Quintilian proposed a type of stasis that occurs when both sides debate the competency of the judge in the dispute; in effect, both sides make judgments about the judge. *Translative stasis* involves disputing the competency of the judge or arbiter.

translative stasis
when the issue in dispute is the competency of the judge or arbiter

In 1989 when New York mafia leader John Gotti was on trial, news accounts reported the judge, John Reis Bartels who was 91, and whom President Dwight D. Eisenhower appointed in 1959, fell asleep during the proceedings. Both the judge and the lawyers in the case disputed those stories, arguing that the judge merely closed his eyes during long witness testimonies. The lawyers felt Bartels was competent to serve as judge in the case, while the newspaper reporters questioned his ability to oversee the trial.[4] The debate over the competency of the 91-year-old Bartels was an example of an issue of translative stasis.

Whenever speakers attempt to persuade an audience to change their beliefs or values, or even to act in a particular way, there is a central issue in dispute between the two sides. That disputed issue can be over whether something actually occurred, how to define a specific term, determining if an action is right or wrong, or deciding if a judge is competent to make a decision. These different issues represent what Quintilian referred to as stasis, because the issue the two sides argue over never changes. It is important to you as a speaker and audience member to know which issue is in dispute. This knowledge allows you to maintain your focus and identify the key points to the argument, thereby enabling you to come to a reasoned conclusion. Today we commonly refer to stasis theory in a simpler way, and categorize the central issue in dispute as a *question*.

Contemporary Persuasive Questions

What Quintilian and his Roman colleagues called stasis theory we now refer to as the issue in question. Today, we identify three different types of questions, but each has its roots in stasis theory. These questions, just like stasis, identify the focus for the persuasive appeal, allowing both the speaker and the audience to avoid going off on tangents. The key element of any successful ethical persuasive appeal is that it remains focused on advocating an answer to one of these three persuasive questions.

SPOTLIGHTING THEORISTS: QUINTILIAN

Quintilian (35–99 BC)

Quintilian was the last of the great classical rhetoricians produced by Greece or Rome. He followed in the footsteps of Cicero and Isocrates and attempted to expand Cicero's work by proposing reforms to educational practices throughout the Empire. Quintilian began his career in much the same way as other famous Greeks and Romans—as a lawyer—but did not choose fame and fortune in the political arena.

Quintilian made his mark as a teacher, not a lawyer or politician. He received a grant from the Emperor Vespasian and worked at a school subsidized by Vespasian. Quintilian's resistance to corruption in politics and the prevailing standards of Roman education at the time were not overtly noticeable, but rather emerged through more subtle actions. Unlike people from other schools of his time, Quintilian frowned on physical punishment as a means of teaching his students, instead attempting to foster a family dynamic between himself and his charges.

Like Isocrates, Quintilian felt that students should be well read on a variety of subjects in order to master both concepts and language. His school, therefore, emphasized more reading than repetitive performance exercises. Quintilian famously stated that education should produce "the good man speaking well." This "good man" combined all the positive attributes of a Platonistic speaker who committed himself to seeking the truth, with the Ciceronian and Isocratean emphasis on developing public virtue and character in the service of society.

Quintilian's lone surviving work is the *Institutio Oratorio*, or the *Institutes of Oratory*. This massive project was divided into twelve books, each dealing with a different aspect of the speaking process and education in general. Book One lays out the ideal curriculum and talks about early childhood education; Books Two and Three discuss stasis theory at length; Books Four through Six develop Cicero's concept of invention; Book Seven addresses arrangement; Books Eight and Nine deal with Style; Book Ten identifies the "right" authors a speaker should emulate; Book Eleven covers memory, delivery, and decorum; and Book Twelve covers the character of the perfect orator, or "the good man speaking well."[5]

When speakers seek to persuade people about how to interpret facts they are addressing a *question of fact*. Whenever the reliability, veracity, or interpretation of something is in doubt, a question of fact exists. Questions related to whether or not something exists are questions of fact. A persuasive message about a question of fact is different from an explanation because a speaker seeks to persuade people, not teach them. This type of persuasion is similar to what Quintilian termed conjectural stasis. To explain, let us look again at the O. J. Simpson example. The jury entertained serious doubts about whether O. J. committed the crime or not. The trial and the closing arguments made by the lawyers, attempted to persuade an audience (the jury) that their answer to a question of fact (did O. J. kill his ex-wife and Ronald Goldman?) is correct.

question of fact
when a speaker seeks to persuade people about how to interpret facts

question of value

a persuasive speech about the rightness or wrongness of an idea, action, or issue

The second type of question a persuasive message addresses is similar to what Quintilian referred to as qualitative stasis. Today, this kind of question is referred to as a *question of value*. The focus of a message involves whether something is right or wrong or advocates valuing one thing over another. Questions about value are not limited to moral and ethical questions, but also include disagreements over prioritizing certain items, as one does in a budget. When you prioritize, you are valuing certain items or ideas more than others. This kind of message also might advocate that one thing is better than another, such as when you attempt to persuade a friend to take a particular class because you feel it is a more interesting one than the class selected by your friend.

question of policy

when a speaker takes a position on whether an action should or should not be taken

The third type involves *questions of policy*. With a policy question, speakers take a position on whether an action should or should not be taken. Like questions of value, questions of policy share some characteristics with qualitative stasis, but also contain some qualities not thoroughly explained by Quintilian's definitions of issues in dispute. Questions of policy focus on action, and often disputes over answers to what action to take occur in deliberative bodies such as governments and organizational committees. A union might hold a meeting where members discuss whether or not to go on strike. Legislators may dispute whether or not to vote for a bill that raises taxes to pay for more teachers. This also takes place on campus, when the UD administration recently debated changes to housing policies in the student neighborhood responding to student celebrations during the 2014 Elite Eight run of the Flyer basketball team. When a problem requiring a specific action to solve it exists, there exists a question of policy.

Notice that Quintilian's stasis theory does not really address questions of policy directly, nor does the contemporary approach address definitive or translative stasis directly. Instead, under the contemporary structure definitive and translative stasis are included in questions of fact, as the definition of a term or the competency of a judge can be considered questions of fact. Quintilian would most likely argue that questions of policy address issues of qualitative stasis, or whether taking such action is right or wrong. The important thing, however, is to see that how we talk about persuasion today developed from the classical understanding and approach to persuasion and argument. In the next part of this chapter we will explore the two different situations in which Aristotle noted that persuasion occurs.

ARISTOTLE ON PERSUASIVE SPEAKING

Stasis theory focuses on the issues and central ideas of a persuasive message, but as we hope to illustrate in this chapter and this book, a communication event is more than its subject; it also includes the situation and the purpose. So, in this section we discuss the difference between the two forms of persuasion proposed by Aristotle and where the issues in dispute can be found in each.

Aristotle's Two Types of Persuasion

People sometimes try to persuade others to take action regarding an issue currently in dispute, or as a response to something that might occur in the future.

These types of messages occur most often in decision-making bodies such as the floor of Congress, but also occur when small groups try and determine a way forward to accomplish a task. The speakers deliberate over problems and issues while proposing solutions to them. These messages are what Aristotle referred to as *deliberative messages* and they often attempt to answer questions of policy or questions of value as they try to prioritize problems and propose solutions to those dilemmas.

deliberative messages
one of two forms of persuasive speech proposed by Aristotle; it often takes place in legislative settings and focuses on discussing policies and actions to be taken

One example of deliberative persuasive advocacy occurred during the 2008 financial crisis, when members of the House of Representatives, Senate, and Bush administration spoke about the fiscal emergency and how to properly approach solving it. Some advocated a large federal investment, while others felt the market should be left to correct itself. A third group debated the size of the federal investment that should be made, proposing even more spending than other groups. The messages in support of these various positions were typical of deliberative persuasive appeals. Deliberative, however, is only *one* form of persuasive speech.

forensic messages
an argument where speakers debate the facts of a case and attempt to answer questions of justice

Aristotle recognized that not all persuasion is deliberative, such as in the case of courtroom arguments. Arguments in a courtroom, where speakers debate the facts of a case and attempt to answer questions of justice rather than policy, are examples of what Aristotle called *forensic messages*. Unlike deliberative messages in which the parties advance arguments concerning the most effective way to manage resources and debate action to be taken, forensic messages contain a *kategoria*, or accusation, and an *apologia*, or defense against the accusation. *Forensic oratory focuses on defining the past rather than proposing a path for the future*. In order to craft an effective forensic message, you should be familiar with what your audience values as well as how to wield evidence in the construction of a reasoned argument or position regarding the issue at hand.

kategoria
a forensic speech that makes an accusation

apologia
a forensic speech that makes a defense against an accusation

Forensic messages are most common in courtrooms, but that is not the only place they occur. Any time we take a position or present an argument to interpret something in a specific way, we are making a forensic argument. For instance, in the summer of 2006 actor and director Mel Gibson was arrested for drunk driving and subsequently went on a tirade during which he made anti-Semitic remarks. A short time later he issued a public apology for those remarks and offered an explanation for what he said and why he said it. That explanation was a forensic argument because he presented an interpretation of the events and his feelings afterward to ask for forgiveness. The apology was ultimately accepted by the Anti-Defamation League and Gibson has been able to move on from the incident.

Situation and purpose influence persuasive appeals as much as topics. Certain topics are limited to, or better suited for, certain situations. Both play a role in focusing persuasive messages and are therefore important tools. As a speaker you need to stay focused on the issue in dispute, while providing a reasoned rationale for your argument. As an audience member you need to remain tuned to the issue a speaker presents so you can then follow the argument. In the next section we will discuss one type of persuasive message that does not necessarily address a question per se, but rather seeks to respond to an argument made by someone else. It is also one of the most common forms of advocacy we engage in, as we do so during conversations with friends, family members, faculty, and others.

Refutation

As you know by now, where there is persuasion there is dispute, and where there is a dispute there is a response. In fact, even the Greeks and Romans recognized that often persuasion is not simply advocating for a position in a vacuum, but rather involves responding to the argument of another individual in an attempt to prove their message—or at least a part of what they are saying—wrong or to make their position less appealing. There are two types of persuasive messages that respond to an argument presented by another person. In this section we will detail these two types.

rebuttal
....
a speech that involves overcoming the opposition's argument by introducing other evidence that reduces the appeal of the opposition's claims

The first type of response is a *rebuttal*, which involves overcoming the other person's entire argument by introducing other evidence that reduces the appeal of their claims. In a rebuttal, you use evidence not cited by the other person to illustrate how that argument is incomplete or misleading, thus casting doubt on their entire position. This type of response often takes place in academic and political debates where the person who speaks second seeks to minimize the strength of the arguments made by the person who speaks first. A rebuttal's purpose is always to persuade the audience that the opposition's argument is incomplete and not as strong as it appears. Essentially, a rebuttal does not claim the other person's argument is false, but rather that it is not as strong as they originally made it out to be.

Let's look at an example of a rebuttal. Kane and Jacquelyn were discussing whether Las Vegas should build a new stadium to attract a professional sports team to the city. Kane argued that the city of Las Vegas should use tax revenue to accomplish this goal. He emphasized how much money it would bring to the city in the long run, how many jobs it would create in the short term, and how a sports team would give the city its own image. Jacquelyn did not agree with Kane, and thus issued a rebuttal.

Jacquelyn made several points that did not disprove Kane's argument, but rather made them seem less appealing. She said that yes, there would be short term benefits in terms of jobs created to build the stadium, but to fund such an operation would mean a tax hike on current residents. Further, she said the long range benefits would only be seen if a professional sports team came to the city, and pointed out there was no guarantee that would happen, which might leave the city with a big expensive arena and no team to use it. Finally, she pointed out that Las Vegas already had an image, and that a sports team would not help or change it much. Each of the points in Jacquelyn's rebuttal minimized the effect of Kane's original argument, but did not disprove it entirely. Still, her message was persuasive, as her specific purpose was to illustrate that Kane's argument was not as appealing as he made it sound. As you can see, to issue a clear and effective rebuttal you need to listen closely to the messages of others.

A second kind of response is a *refutation*. A refutation is slightly different from a rebuttal in that it does seek to prove that the opposition's argument is wrong, or false. When refuting an argument you might focus on the faulty reasoning or lack of support provided by the other speaker. The specific purpose, then, for refutation is to persuade the audience that the opposition's argument is wrong or false. Let's look at an example.

refutation
a speech that seeks to prove the opposition's argument is wrong, or false

Caitlin presented an argument to her class that global warming needs to be addressed. She pointed out that temperatures are rising due to increased carbon emissions resulting in the melting of the polar ice caps. She then pressed for increased fuel efficiency standards and called on people to take public transportation whenever possible. Corey responded by refuting Caitlin's claims and citing scientific studies that counter the idea of global warming. He argued that those studies showed the temperature changes Caitlin spoke about are actually cyclical patterns in the Earth's temperature and are not caused by carbon emissions and global warming. Thus, he said people should not feel undue pressure to carpool, ride the bus, or force a change in the way cars are built. In his message, Corey refuted Caitlin's argument by claiming it was false, or erroneous.

Unlike in the case of Jacquelyn and her rebuttal, Corey did not accept certain elements of his opponent's argument, but rather pointed out faulty data by presenting contradictory evidence. The primary difference between a rebuttal and refutation is that a rebuttal takes issue with the conclusions, whereas refutation disputes the entire argument and the evidence presented by the opposition. Like rebuttals, refutation requires careful listening and knowledge of a wide array of topics. You cannot effectively refute an argument with hearsay or innuendo, as you need verifiable data to make others accept your refutation of an original message. It doesn't matter, however, if you are refuting, rebutting or proposing a position; persuasion is a very complex process. To remove some of the mystery surrounding persuasion, we will attempt to "unpack" how that process works in the next section.

Table 8.1

Rebuttals and Refutations	
Rebuttal Characteristics	**Refutation Characteristics**
Introduces evidence that lessens the impact of the evidence presented by the other person	Seeks to prove the opponent's argument is wrong or false
Uses evidence not cited by the other person	Focuses on the opponent's reasoning
Shows that the evidence you are rebutting is incomplete	Points to a lack of supporting material

THE PERSUASIVE PROCESS

Persuasion does not take place simply because there is a topic on which two or more sides disagree. In fact, the persuasive process is much more involved. Additionally, persuasion almost always takes time, and its effectiveness often must be measured in degrees. In this section of the chapter we will discuss the four stages of the persuasive process, the development and importance of credibility in that process, and how to avoid unethical behavior when persuading others.

Stages of Persuasion

Persuasion is a psychological process. When you attempt to persuade someone you are asking for someone to make a decision based on a logical argument

SPEAKING of CIVIC ENGAGEMENT

Television and the Public Interest
by Newton Minow

Delivered May 9, 1961, to the National Association of Broadcasters

In 1961, newly elected President John F. Kennedy selected Newton Minow to be the Chairman of the Federal Communications Commission (FCC), the governmental agency responsible for governing television and radio.[5] Some were surprised at Kennedy's choice of Minow as he had been critical of television and lacked extensive experience with communication law or the media industry.

As FCC chairman, Minow challenged the content on television and asked for reform.[6]

In his speech Minow raised eyebrows, especially with this statement:

> "But when television is bad, nothing is worse. I invite each of you to sit down in front of your television set when your station goes on the air and stay there, for a day, without a book, without a magazine, without a newspaper, without a profit and loss sheet or a rating book to distract you. Keep your eyes glued to that set until the station signs off. I can assure you that what you will observe is a vast wasteland."[7]

These words of Newton Minow became famous, or infamous depending on the audience. In fact, some felt his comments were elitist, and so they even named the S. S. Minnow of Gilligan's Island fame after him as an expression of criticism for his stance on the media industry.

Although Minow never achieved significant broadcast regulation, he did raise awareness of content and the impact of the "vast wasteland." After he retired from the FCC he became a partner in one of America's most powerful communication law firms.[8]

regarding an issue in dispute. Persuasion is different from other less ethical ways to gain agreement from an audience. In this part of the chapter we will discuss the four elements of the persuasive process and then demonstrate why persuasion, when employed correctly, is the most appropriate and ethical means for gaining agreement from an audience.

The persuasive process has four stages, each of which is equally important. The first step in the persuasive process is called *issue awareness*, and we have already begun to discuss it. Issue awareness occurs when you alert other people about the existence of an issue requiring their attention. This stage occurs immediately in the introduction of your message because it is what you use to motivate other people to listen. The issue should be couched in a manner that conveys its importance to the lives of the listeners so that they feel a personal connection with the topic, thus making them more likely to listen. For example, if you are talking to your friends and trying to convince them to eat a gluten-free diet, thus giving up things like pretzels and beer, they likely will not see a reason to do it. However, if you begin by explaining you have a way to increase their energy and help them avoid certain cancer risks, you make the issue that much more relevant to them, thus increasing the likelihood they will listen to you.

issue awareness
the first step in the persuasive process whereby the speaker alerts the audience to the issue requiring its attention

Another concrete example of raising issue awareness in an audience can be found in the case of Newton Minow, who President John F. Kennedy named as chairman of the Federal Communication Commission. Minow made increasing the quality of content on television a priority of his term on the FCC, and when addressing Congress about the lack of good television challenged anyone to watch it for a day and see if they too did not come to see television programming as a "vast wasteland." His comments, and specifically that phrase, made the issue of television content an issue of public concern for decades to come.

Once you engage the attention of your listeners by making them aware of the important issue, you move to the second stage in the persuasive process: *comprehension*. In the comprehension stage, you provide a context for the issue in dispute so the audience understands what you are talking about. Continuing with the gluten-free diet example, this part of the process might involve a discussion of what glutens are and how they impact a person's digestive system in negative ways. The comprehension stage then continues by laying out your position on the issue and why you feel others should share your view. This part of the persuasive process allows you to provide the foundation of your argument and then move to the third stage in the persuasive process.

comprehension
the second step in the persuasive process in which the speaker provides context for the issue in dispute so the audience understands what the speaker is talking about

The third and fourth steps focus less on the speaker and more on the audience. After you establish a context and make your case, it is up to your listeners whether or not they accept your position. *Acceptance* of your message is the third stage in the persuasive process. After carefully considering the facts you presented, the people to whom you are speaking could decide not to agree with you. On the other hand, they may very well be convinced that you are right. Knowing whether or not the audience truly agrees with you after hearing you speak is difficult to determine, but understanding your goals as a speaker enables you to have some

acceptance
the third step in the persuasive process in which the audience decides whether or not to agree with the position for which the speaker advocated

idea as to whether or not your appeal was successful. A little later we will return to this discussion of measuring the effectiveness of your appeal.

integration
the fourth stage in the persuasive process in which the audience makes the speaker's position a part of its own personal philosophy and worldview

If members of the audience ultimately accept your position on the issue in dispute the persuasive process moves to its fourth and final stage: *integration.* Long after the lights have dimmed and your listeners have moved on to other activities, they begin to integrate that position into their daily lives. It becomes a part of their identity and their own personal philosophy. It is easiest to see after a call for immediate action, because people will either do what was proposed, or not. When listeners act in the way suggested by the speaker, they have integrated the speaker's point of view into their own lives.

So, let us summarize the persuasive process. When attempting to persuade an audience you need to make them aware of *what* you are speaking about. Then, you must ensure that they *understand* the issue. This is especially important when speaking about a complex topic. Third, the audience needs to *decide* whether or not they will accept your argument. Finally, if they do accept your ideas, they need to *integrate* them into how they now see things. This process can take place very rapidly, or may take hours, days, weeks, or even years to accomplish. In the next section we will discuss how to determine your expectations for persuasive appeals as a speaker, and how to determine their success after you make them.

Figure 8.1
Stages of the Persuasive Process

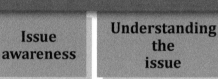

| Issue awareness | Understanding the issue | Acceptance of the issue | Integration into viewpoint |

Credibility and Persuasion

Whether or not we accept a person's argument often depends upon how credible he or she seems to us. Credibility represents a large part of what you will remember Aristotle called ethos, and it is an extremely important element of the persuasive process. As we mentioned earlier, speakers enter a communication situation with a certain level of credibility based on their own background and reputation, their perceived competence or expertise on the topic on which they are speaking, and even their appearance. In this section we revisit how credibility can be maintained and built during any communication event, and we will discuss how your credibility can also be damaged. To effectively persuade other people in any situation you must first establish your credibility, and then build upon it.

Credibility During the Communication Event

initial credibility
the level of believability a speaker has before beginning his or her speech

Initial credibility. You will recall we all bring a certain degree of credibility into any situation, and this is called our initial credibility. In persuasive messages, establishing credibility is just as important, if not more so, than for explanatory messages because you are asking an audience not only to trust what you have to say, but to follow your advice and direction. You are asking them to believe in you and take a leap of faith. You should make every effort to maximize your initial credibility in every persuasive situation. Keep in mind that your initial credibility will vary with different groups for different reasons.

Derived credibility. Credibility can be difficult for any student because the topics discussed in class and researched for term projects in many classes are often not something you have much experience with, and your audiences have no knowledge of any previous work you may have done.

derived credibility
the level of credibility during a speech that comes from what you say and how you say it

Our suggestions for enhancing your credibility during your speech are not new. Aristotle actually laid out three ways to build credibility, and contemporary scholars have given us a fourth way. The first is *good character,* which Aristotle defined as the state of being virtuous. Persons of virtuous character occupy a state of being in which they have learned to have an appropriate emotional response to situations, and they avoid excessive displays that are unsuitable to the moment. Persons of good character tend to have a balanced response to situations and stay "calm under fire." For Aristotle, this ability defines good character. Good character may manifest itself through not attacking another person, yelling, screaming or attempting to inappropriately play upon negative emotions. It is, in short, behaving ethically and civilly by respecting the other people.

Aristotle's second way to derive ethos is through *sagacity*, or the demonstration of reasonableness and sound judgment. Reasonableness and judgment are demonstrated through the proper citation of important and relevant information and evidence. By verbally attributing sources, you not only fulfill your ethical obligations, but also demonstrate that you did research to ensure your competence to speak about the topic. It also means demonstrating a willingness to compromise and recognize strengths in the arguments put forth by others.

Finally, Aristotle proposes that you can derive credibility through demonstrating your *goodwill* toward the audience and the topic. Aristotle defined goodwill as the speaker's unselfish disposition that seeks the good for others regardless of what is good for the speaker. It means placing the good of others above your own desires. Goodwill toward others requires that we not hide our intentions or try to deceive the audience for personal gain. When persuading someone, you derive more ethos by making your motives clear and honestly assessing the benefit of the appeal for the others involved.

Aristotle, however, was not the only one to provide us with ways to enhance our ethos during a speech. Social scientists today have added the concept of dynamism as a way to increase our credibility during a speech. *Dynamism* is a strong, confident delivery that convinces the listeners you are engaged in the topic and in their welfare. The more you speak, the more confident you will get, and that confidence translates into a better performance, thus increasing your credibility.

dynamism
a social science term for strong delivery that creates the impression with the audience that the speaker has practiced and thus cares about what he is talking about

Terminal credibility. By the end of any interaction, you will likely achieve a new level of credibility as a speaker on your topic. The credibility with which you leave the situation is called terminal credibility. Where you end up, however, is largely influenced by how you established and built your credibility throughout your presentation. In any situation we walk away with an impression of the credibility

terminal credibility
the credibility with which you end the speech

of the other person, and sometimes, as in the case with first impressions of roommates, friends, business associates or even romantic interests, this can make or break the development of a relationship. Unfortunately, there are ways you can take steps back, and so we should consider the ways credibility and your reputation could be damaged.

Ways to Lose Credibility

lying by commission
··············
when a speaker willfully makes untrue statements to an audience

There are three unethical behaviors that can irreparably damage your image and credibility with people. The first of these is *lying*. There are several different ways in which you can lie. The first occurs when you willfully present false evidence to another person. Creating new facts out of thin air just to advance your argument is not persuasion, it is *lying by commission. Lying by omission,* on the other hand, occurs when a speaker willfully chooses *not* to acknowledge facts about an argument that might damage its effectiveness. Both of these behaviors are unethical and can destroy a person's credibility.

lying by omission
··············
when a speaker willfully chooses not to acknowledge facts about his or her argument that might damage its effectiveness

Instead of leaving facts out, you should acknowledge them as a rebuttal, as it lets the other people know you did your research and have thought through potential problems with your position. Such a tactic actually tends to increase your credibility with an audience. Ignoring these problems, or trying to hide them, makes it appear you are serving a selfish interest and are not out for the good of the community.

manipulation
··············
the deliberate misrepresentation of facts and evidence to an audience

A second behavior that can cause significant harm to your credibility is *manipulation*. Manipulation is the deliberate misrepresentation of facts and evidence so that listeners will see what you want them to see, rather than presenting them with a reasoned argument and trusting their ability to come to a careful conclusion. An example of the use of manipulation by a speaker involved former President Bill Clinton when he made statements regarding his relationship with an intern, Monica Lewinsky. President Clinton misrepresented the nature of his association with Lewinsky by stating that he did not have "sexual relations" with her, when, in fact, he did have sexual contact with her. The term Clinton used misled the audience by inferring he had no sexual relationship with Lewinsky. In this example he did not, strictly speaking, lie to the American people in that he did not have intercourse with Lewinsky, but he did mislead them as to the nature of their association.

coercion
··············
the use of force or threats to make someone do something against his or her will

Finally, you can damage your credibility by using the *threat of force* instead of reason to obtain agreement from your audience. *Coercion* is the use of threats or pressure to get listeners to do something against their will, and it can manifest itself in both physical and psychological ways. The least likely is physical, in that no one expects you to put a proverbial gun to the heads of your listeners to make them agree with you. It is possible, though, that you could coerce your listeners by threatening them with negative consequences if they do not agree with you. For instance, you might be coerced into taking an extra shift at work by a boss who threatens to fire you if you do not comply. A more common version of coercion is the "guilt trip" in which someone tries to elicit a feeling of guilt in you in order to get you to do something, thus expunging the guilt. Psychological coercion involves making others unduly afraid of what will happen if they do not agree with you. Using such tactics will damage your credibility by making you appear to be selfish or a fear-monger, rather than someone who can construct a rational plan to which people might agree.

Your credibility, or ethos, is an essential part of every message you deliver. If your listeners think you will tell the truth, then they are more likely to pay attention to your argument and give you a fair hearing. The trust others have in you is something you should protect by trying not to lie, manipulate, or coerce them into agreeing with your position. If your position is right, and you present a well-reasoned argument, your listeners should come to the same conclusions you do about the issue in dispute. If they do not, then at least you allowed them to make the choice on their own while making the best case you could. It also bears noting that a rejection of your appeal does not mean a rejection of you as a person, because if you handled yourself civilly and ethically then there will be another opportunity in the future to engage in persuasion with the same individuals. If, however, you did not, then you may not be able to discuss matters with them in the future. Always remember that true persuasion leaves a choice for the audience.

Developing Emotion in Persuasive Appeals

Ethos and logos, otherwise called credibility and logic, are two of the three dimensions of persuasion and speech identified by Aristotle. The third, pathos, also must be addressed because it complements both ethos and logos in the persuasive process. It is important to remember that employing pathos alone in a persuasive appeal distracts listeners from the issue at hand in an effort to have them make a decision based purely on emotions and not evidence or information. Such a message design is unethical, even if the goal is ethical. So, let's take a moment and discuss the proper place for pathos in advocacy.

Pathos is concerned with the audience's emotions, sympathies, and imagination and is used to connect those feelings and images to the topic of the message in a way that increases the likelihood of achieving your purpose. Pathos can help make abstract concepts and statistical data more palpable and real for an audience. Ultimately, however, proper use of pathos depends on knowledge of to whom you are speaking.

Pathos is primarily accomplished in four different steps. The first step is to determine the emotion that you want to produce in your audience. Do you want to make your listeners angry? Excited? Do you want them to feel pity? Compassion? The emotion you want to create is the goal of the particular pathos appeal, and therefore what tools you choose to use to achieve that goal must have the emotion at the core.

Once you determine the emotion you wish to create in the audience, you need to connect it to an object. That object can be a person, place, or thing, but it must be real and recognizable to the audience. It is the thing for which you want the other people to feel the emotion and to which you want them to connect. As a general rule, people connect better to singular specific objects than large masses of things. Thus, people feel pity when the advertisements of the American Society for the Prevention of Cruelty to Animals (ASPCA) depicts one dog that has been injured or abandoned, but they would not feel that way if the pictures were of multiple dogs at once. The same principle applies for advocacy messages: connect the emotion to a concrete singular object to which the person or people to whom you are speaking can relate.

Step three is the use of language or images that evoke the specific emotion you wish to encourage the audience to feel. Pictures and strategic language choices help to accomplish this, and this stage is where you make the decisions about when and how to describe the object and the emotion. Different words can convey different emotions, and can elicit different responses as well. For instance, when describing a policy you could choose to label it "moronic" or "ill-advised." What emotions does each trigger? How does that emotional reaction enhance or damage the perception those listening may have of you? These are important considerations for you when crafting your message. You need to make sure your emotional language choices are not the primary driver for persuasion, but rather that they complement the evidence you use and reinforce your goodwill and virtuous character to the audience.

In today's mediated environment, we can also use visual imagery to capitalize on pathos in our persuasive appeals. A moment ago we talked about the ASPCA advertisements, and the pictures of dogs to help give an audience an object with which they can connect. Visual images in this respect can be powerful vehicles for pathos appeals because they provide the audience with a specific object on which to focus their attention, while the narrator provides the verbal message containing the emotional dimension sought by the use of the image.

The final step of incorporating pathos into persuasive messages involves the story, or narrative, you provide about the object. The story uses the vivid language in stage three while also connecting the emotion to the overall logic of the persuasive appeal. The story needs to be connected in some way not just to the emotion, but to the overall topic. If you are seeking to help the ASPCA, for example, you might tell a vivid story about a golden retriever who was abandoned and found half-starved walking the street in front of your home sniffing around garbage bags for food. This quick anecdote used vivid language in telling a story related to your purpose in a way that was designed to create a feeling of pity for the dog. That dog then becomes an analogy for all dogs helped by the ASPCA, thus helping to provide people with both a logical and an emotional reason for acting on your message.

Pathos is a powerful persuasive tool when used appropriately. It can enhance your credibility as a speaker as well as augment the power of the logic behind your appeal. It involves four important steps, beginning with determining what type of emotion you want to have your audience feel. You should then connect that emotion to a singular object, and use vivid language to tell the story about that object in a way that connects it with the larger purpose of your message.

SUMMARY

Persuasion takes place when there is an issue in dispute, or as Quintilian called it, an issue of stasis. Over the years stasis theory developed into what we now call persuasive questions. These issues in dispute are part of larger categories of persuasive appeals, identified by Aristotle as deliberative or forensic in nature. Regardless of the issue in dispute, or the form of persuasion you undertake, it always follows the same process: issue awareness, comprehension, acceptance, and integration. In order to successfully implement the persuasive process you need to come across as credible on the topic which you speak about, logically craft your speech, and construct appropriate emotional connections between the audience and your speech topic.

KEY TERMS

acceptance   203
apologia   199
coercion   206
comprehension   203
conjectural stasis   195
definitive stasis   195
deliberative messsages   199
derived credibility   205
dynamism   205
forensic messages   199
integration   204
initial credibility   204
issue awareness   203

kategoria   199
lying by commission   206
lying by omission   206
manipulation   206
qualitative stasis   196
question of fact   197
question of policy   198
question of value   198
rebuttal   200
refutation   201
stasis   195
terminal credibility   205
translative stasis   196

REVIEW QUESTIONS

1. What are the four types of stasis proposed by Quintilian?
2. What are the three forms of questions that a persuasive message could address?
3. What are the two types of persuasive messages proposed by Aristotle?
4. What are the three types of credibility a speaker has or can have?
5. What are the three ways you can irreparably harm your own credibility?
6. What does dynamism add to our understanding of credibility?

THINK ABOUT IT

1. Are there any types of issues in dispute not covered by the four forms of stasis proposed by Quintilian?

2. Are there any other ways you can damage your credibility? Enhance it?

3. If it is so unethical, why do people often manipulate data or lie to audiences to achieve their goals?

4. Could dynamism not be a factor in credibility?

ACTIVITIES FOR ACTION

1. Look at the stages of the persuasive process in this chapter. Think about how you have had your mind changed in the past, and identify how that process unfolded for you. Then, if there are differences, devise an alternative method for explaining how the persuasive process worked in your example. Are there different stages? Fewer? More?

2. Imagine a politician who has been caught cheating on his spouse, has been arrested for drunk driving, and has a tax lien on his property. If you were his political consultant, what would you suggest he do to increase his credibility? What might he do to re-establish his credibility?

ENDNOTES

1. The timeline of events can be found at: http://www.law.umkc.edu/faculty/projects/ftrials/Simpson/Simpsonchron.html (accessed October 16, 2008).

2. CNN, "OJ Simpson Trial: Marcia Clark, Johnny Cochrane Deliver Closings," http://www.cnn.com/2007/US/law/12/11/court.archive.simpson11/index.html (accessed October 16, 2008).

3. Thomas Morgan, "Competency of Judge, 91, in Gotti Case Questioned," *The New York Times* (April 20, 1989). Available: http://query.nytimes.com/gst/fullpage.html?res=950DEFDC173CF933A15757C0A96F948260 (accessed October 17, 2008).

4. Patricia Bizzell and Bruce Herzberg, *The Rhetorical Tradition: Readings From Classical Times to the Present,* 2nd Ed. (Boston, MA: Bedford St. Martin's, 2001), 38–39.

5. http://www.museum.tv/eotvsection.php?entrycode=minownewton (accessed June 1, 2011).

6. Ibid (accessed June 1, 2011).

7. http://www.americanrhetoric.com/speeches/newtonminow.htm (accessed June 1, 2011).

8. http://www.museum.tv/eotvsection.php?entrycode=minownewton (accessed June 1, 2011).

SCENARIOS

Scenario 1

Consider the following broad topics. For each, create a question of fact, a question of value, and a question of policy. Discuss whether or not each of these questions would be appropriate for a persuasive speech and what a persuasive speech that answers that question might be like.

1. **The death penalty**

   Question of fact:

   Question of value:

   Question of policy:

   Which of these questions would be an appropriate focus for a persuasive speech? Explain.

   What would a persuasive speech that answers each of these questions be like?

2. **Legalization of marijuana**

   Question of fact:

   Question of value:

   Question of policy:

   Which of these questions would be an appropriate focus for a persuasive speech? Explain.

   What would a persuasive speech that answers each of these questions be like?

3. **Paying college athletes**

   Question of fact:

   Question of value:

   Question of policy:

   Which of these questions would be an appropriate focus for a persuasive speech? Explain.

   What would a persuasive speech that answers each of these questions be like?

Scenario 2

Identify a topic currently discussed in today's popular media that illustrates each type of stasis. Explain how people in today's society disagree or otherwise have divergent views on this topic that reflect that type of stasis. Describe how a persuasive speech could be created by taking a position within that disagreement and making an argument.

1. **Definitive stasis**

   Topic in today's popular media that illustrates this type of stasis:

   Different sides or positions that people take with regard to this topic:

   How a persuasive speech could be created to make an argument relative to these positions:

2. **Conjectural stasis**

   Topic in today's popular media that illustrates this type of stasis:

Different sides or positions that people take with regard to this topic:

How a persuasive speech could be created to make an argument relative to these positions:

3. **Qualitative stasis**

Topic in today's popular media that illustrates this type of stasis:

Different sides or positions that people take with regard to this topic:

How a persuasive speech could be created to make an argument relative to these positions:

4. **Translative stasis**

Topic in today's popular media that illustrates this type of stasis:

Different sides or positions that people take with regard to this topic:

How a persuasive speech could be created to make an argument relative to these positions:

Scenario 3 (Performance)

Choose a character from a favorite movie, TV show, graphic novel, comic, or book. Outline a persuasive speech that accuses, blames, or otherwise holds that character responsible for something in the story: what in forensic persuasion is called the kategoria. Make sure that the outcome or event for which you are holding the character responsible is clear. List several reasons why you believe that character is responsible for this outcome in the story. Be prepared to share with the class what you outlined.

Now, outline a persuasive speech that defends that character by absolving him or her of responsibility for that same outcome in the story or making a case for why his or her behavior is excusable: what in forensic persuasion is called the apologia. Make sure that the outcome or event for which you are absolving the character of responsibility or regarding which you are excusing his or her behavior is clear. List several reasons why you believe that character is not responsible for the outcome in the story. Be prepared to share with the class what you outlined.

Scenario 4

Suppose that you are wanting to study overseas in a study abroad programs administered through the Center for International Programs here at the University. You are worried that you will not be able to pay for the cost of the trip, so you have decided to talk with your parents and ask them for assistance. As you prepare for this conversation, you are thinking about how you can convince your parents to believe in you, regardless of what they might think about the topic: what Aristotle called ethos. Identify one way that you might convince your parents to believe in you for each of the four ways of building ethos, identified in the chapter.

Sagacity:

Good character:

Goodwill:

Dynamism:

Scenario 5

Television commercials typically do not present an argument that is strong in logic and evidence: what Aristotle calls logos. However, they often excel in creating emotional appeals: what Aristotle called pathos. Search the internet for the Chrysler commercial featuring Eminem that was first aired during the 2009 Super Bowl. As you watch the commercial, consider how the commercial creates an emotional appeal by reflecting on the four-step method identified in the chapter.

Step 1: Determine the emotion you want to produce in your audience.

What specific emotion are the makers of the commercial trying to evoke in viewers? Justify your answer.

Step 2: Connect that emotion to an object.

To what object are the makers of the commercial trying to connect that emotion for viewers? Justify your answer.

Step 3: Use language and/or images that evoke that emotion for your audience.

List specific words or phrases has the maker of the commercial has used to evoke the desired emotion.

Describe some of the images that the maker of the commercial has used to evoke the desired emotion.

Step 4: Tell a story about the object that uses the language and/or images in Step 3 to evoke the desired emotion.

What story does the commercial tell about the object?

How does this story relate to the viewer?

Scenario 6

Reflect upon a time when someone convinced you to do something that you had not previously done. Tell your groupmates the story of what happened. After you have shared your stories, analyze how the process of persuasion unfolded over time in each of your experiences by examining what happened at each stage in that process.

Stage 1: Issue Awareness. How did you first become aware of the topic or issue in question? What did the other person do that impacted how you first experienced this topic or issue?

Stage 2: Comprehension. What did the other person do or say that helped you to understand the topic or issue in question? What did she or he do or say to help you to understand what you could do with regard to that topic or issue?

Stage 3: Acceptance. What motivated you to do what you ultimately did? What did the other person do or say that was especially convincing to you?

Stage 4: Integration. Have you continued to do this behavior or action? If so, why? If not, why not? What did the other person say or do that has motivated you to keep doing what you initially did—or not to continue doing it, if that is what happened?

Analyzing Persuasion

Practically SPEAKING

For the last 50 years the Harvard Law School Forum has invited domestic and international celebrities to speak to the campus on a host of different issues. Included among the speakers who have come to the Forum in the past are Fidel Castro, Gerald Ford, and even sex therapist Dr. Ruth. No speaker in recent years, however, caused more of a stir than former head of the National Rifle Association (NRA) and Oscar-winning actor, the late Charlton Heston.[3]

On February 16, 1999, Heston addressed a crowd of about 200 people, consisting of students, faculty, conservatives, and liberals. The speech, entitled "Winning the Cultural War," inspired much debate around the campus for about a month after he delivered it, and if it wasn't for one event it probably would have faded into obscurity (For a transcript of Heston's speech, see: http://www.americanrhetoric.com/speeches/charltonhestonculturalwar.htm). On March 15, 1999, almost a month to the day after he gave the speech, popular conservative talk show host Rush Limbaugh read Heston's speech word for word on the air. After his rendition, thousands of people sought copies of the speech transcript, flooding both the Harvard Law School Forum and Limbaugh's radio station with requests.[4] The now immensely popular speech had only one problem: its argument.

Within the speech itself Heston attempted to make a logical argument; however, he was not very successful, despite the fact people loved the speech. He employed many of the logical fallacies later explained in this chapter to make his case. The unfortunate outcome of this was the wide support for his point of view coming from an audience that did not critically examine the message itself. In this chapter we will discuss models of reasoning and constructing an argument, which Heston did not use. Finally, we will use examples from his "Winning the Cultural War" speech as well as other texts to illustrate the different types of logical fallacies employed by speakers. By the end of this chapter the differences between correct and proper logic and improper appeals will be clear and easy to identify.

PREP QUESTIONS

1. Define syllogism. List its three component parts.

2. Define categorical syllogism, disjunctive syllogism, and conditional syllogism.

3. Provide an example of a syllogism that is structured correctly but is invalid.

4. Define enthymeme and its relationship to a syllogism. Do messages contain more syllogisms or enthymemes?

5. Compare and contrast an inductive and a deductive argument.

6. Discuss whether making an argument is better illustrated by the linear or transactional model of communication.

7. Define reasoning by example and explain how it is different from reasoning by analogy.

8. Define reasoning by cause.

9. Compare and contrast a necessary and a sufficient cause.

10. Define kairos, and explain how it might influence a persuasive message.

11. Discuss the relationship between kairos and civility.

12. List and define each of the ten common fallacies in reasoning that violate logic.

9

CLASSICAL MODEL OF REASONING

We construct ethical and effective arguments by providing clear evidence that supports our claims. When we demonstrate the connection of the evidence we provide to the claims we make, we demonstrate reasoning skills. Aristotle proposed two different basic forms of reasoning: deductive and inductive. In this section we will detail the elements of both. We also will explore several different forms of reasoning that can help you make an argument stronger.

Syllogisms and Enthymemes

Building an argument is much like building a house. A house is not just simply placed into existence; it is built, brick by brick, around a structure. The bricks in an argument are the evidence you present, but they are useless without placing them in and around a structure that makes sense. That basic structure for an argument is called a *syllogism*. A syllogism is a form of deductive reasoning, or an argument that reasons from known premises to an inevitable conclusion. A *deductive argument*, is based on generally accepted principles or known facts which are then applied to a particular or specific situation. The conclusion of a syllogism is inevitable because the conclusion is contained within the premises of the argument. For this reason, conclusions of syllogisms have a strong degree of certainty.

Syllogisms always contain three different parts. The first is called the *major premise*, which is a general statement on the subject about which you construct your argument. This statement is taken to be completely accurate, and not a statement about something that is probable or possible. The second part of a syllogism is called the *minor premise*, which is a statement about a specific case related to the general characteristics of the major premise. The final part of a syllogism is the conclusion drawn from the components of both the major and minor premises. Essentially, the conclusion is the claim made by the speaker, the minor premise is the specific application of the principle, and the major premise represents the principle or "truth" that links them both.

The conclusion in a syllogism is true when the major and minor premises are true. The classic example of a syllogism told in classrooms for years looks like this:

syllogism
the basic structure of a deductive argument that comes to an absolute conclusion

deductive argument
an argument that reasons from known premises to an inevitable conclusion

major premise
the first part of a syllogism, consisting of a general statement about the subject of your argument

minor premise
a statement about a specific case related to the general characteristics of the major premise

221

Major premise:	All men are mortal. [General principle]
Minor premise:	Socrates is a man. [Specific application of the principle]
Conclusion:	Therefore, Socrates is mortal.

As you can see, the major premise is true, as all men are mortal. If, however, we found a man who was immortal then the major premise would be false and the argument would fall apart. If the major premise that you use for an argument is not accepted as fact by your listeners, it will be necessary for you to supply evidence to support it. Once the major premise is accepted by your listeners, the rest of the argument becomes a challenge for others to refute.

The fact about the specific case in the minor premise is also true, as Socrates is a man. If, though, Socrates was a dog or a plant, then the minor premise becomes untenable. The conclusion flows from the facts in both the major and minor premises, and since those facts were true then the conclusion is also true. It is important to remember, though, that despite the simplicity of this example there are a variety of different syllogisms.

inductive argument
· · · · · · · · · · · · ·
reasoning from individual observations or events to conclude a general principle

If you turn a syllogism "upside down," you can begin to see the structure of an *inductive argument.* An inductive argument begins with observations of specific instances, and the recognition or identification of a pattern in those individual observations results in a general principle. The strength of an inductive argument lies in the number and representativeness of the observations. Therefore, if the number is low, or if the observations do not represent enough or all the possibilities, the inductive argument can be weakened. For this reason, the conclusions of an inductive argument are generally less certain than the conclusions reached in a syllogism.

For example, Joe likes to fly his kite in a large field just south of town. Nearly every time he visits the field, he notices that large numbers of ducks land there to look for food. After several trips to the field, he began to notice a pattern: all of the ducks were brown. After several weeks of watching very carefully, he always saw brown ducks. His conclusion, based on his observations, is that "all ducks are brown." Joe derived a general principle by seeing a pattern in his observations of a particular situation. The weakness, as you probably gathered, is that ducks come in more than one color. How do you know that? Observations! More extensive observation over a much wider territory would strengthen (and likely change) Joe's conclusion.

categorical syllogism
· · · · · · · · · · · ·
a syllogism in which the argument is based on membership in a group

We define syllogisms by their component parts. For example, the argument in the first type of syllogism we will discuss, *categorical syllogism*, is based on membership in a category. Within a categorical syllogism, the major premise establishes the groups in which the evidence should fit. Like all other syllogisms, categorical syllogisms' major premises state universal generalities. Here is an example:

| Major premise: | All students in CMM 100 are in their first or second year at the University of Dayton. |
| Minor premise: | Alvin is in CMM 100. |

| Conclusion: | Therefore, Alvin in his first or second year at the University of Dayton. |

In categorical syllogisms such as the one involving Alvin, there are certain requirements. First, all categorical syllogisms contain only three items to make the case. Secondly, each of the three terms must be used in the syllogism twice. Each term can only be used once in each premise. Items may only appear in a conclusion if they originally appeared in either the major or minor premise. Finally, in terms of tone, one premise must be stated in a positive way, but if one premise is negative then the conclusion must be negative. Let's look at one more example:

Major premise:	All students cannot pass if they do not deliver all their presentations.
Minor premise:	Amber is a student.
Conclusion:	Therefore, Amber will not pass if she does not deliver all her presentations.

Notice the negative conclusion due to the negative major premise. Notice also that all the items in the syllogism appear twice.

A second form, the ***disjunctive syllogism***, contains two or more mutually exclusive alternatives. This means that only one of the alternatives may be true, not both. In order for this line of reasoning in an argument to work, the minor premise must either accept only one alternative or exclude all alternatives but one. Let's look at this example:

disjunctive syllogism
a syllogism in which the major premise includes two or more mutually exclusive alternatives

Major premise:	Either COM 100 is in Miriam 205 or it is in Zehler 101.
Minor premise:	COM 100 is not in Miriam 205.
Conclusion:	Therefore, COM 100 is in Zehler 101.

Because the minor premise rejected one of the two alternatives the other logically became true. Unfortunately, most disjunctive syllogisms are not this simple and involve more than two alternatives.

In life, we often present and are presented with situations where it appears as though there are only two alternatives, but that is not always the case. So, in order for a disjunctive syllogism to be sound, the major premise must consist of all the possible alternatives. Here is an example of a disjunctive syllogism with multiple alternatives:

Major premise:	I must take math, English, or an elective course this semester.
Minor premise:	I will take an elective course this semester.
Conclusion:	Therefore, I will not take English or math this semester.

In this example, one issue separated the three different options, making the choice obvious. The two main requirements for a valid disjunctive syllogism are that the alternatives must be mutually exclusive and that all the alternatives are presented.

conditional syllogism
a syllogism in which the major premise contains a hypothetical condition and its outcome

consequent
the outcome of the hypothetical condition in the major premise of a conditional syllogism

antecedent
the hypothetical condition in the major premise of a conditional syllogism

The third and final type of syllogism we will discuss is called a *conditional syllogism*. Here, the major premise contains a hypothetical condition and its outcome. These are more commonly referred to as "if-then" statements. The "if" portion of the major premise is called the *antecedent*, while the "then" statement is labeled the *consequent* because it is a direct result of the occurrence of the "if." Just like every other syllogism, this form also depends on the universality of the major premise. In other words, the "if-then" must be true in all cases. Look at this example of a conditional syllogism:

Major premise:	If we increase revenue then we will not need to downsize the workforce.
Minor premise:	We increased revenue.
Conclusion:	Therefore, we do not need to downsize the workforce.

Conditional syllogisms require that the antecedent and consequent both be accepted and explain only what you know. That would not have been the case had there been the following slight change to the minor premise and conclusion:

Major premise:	If we increase revenue then we will not need to downsize the workforce.
Minor premise:	We did not downsize the workforce.
Conclusion:	Therefore, we increased revenue.

The argument is *invalid* because there could be other explanations for the conclusion than the one offered. Something else could have contributed to not downsizing the workforce given the structure of the syllogism. An easy way to understand this is to see the statement as "if-then" and not "then-if."

Syllogisms are logical ways to lay out a claim and its support in a way that allows you to see if your argument is valid and makes logical sense. When we speak, we rarely include the major premise, minor premise and conclusion in our verbal explanation to an audience. Rather, we delete one or two of the three elements of the syllogism and allow the audience to reason them out on their own. When a syllogism misses one or two of its parts it is called an *enthymeme*.

enthymeme
a syllogism missing one or two of its parts

Enthymemes are truncated syllogisms. Look at each of the three forms of syllogisms we discussed and eliminate the minor premise. Do they still make sense? Of course, because the supporting evidence offered by the minor premise is common knowledge that does not bear repeating to an audience. In the example of Socrates we could just as soon of said "Socrates is mortal" and you would have been able to internalize the major and minor premises.

The fact of the matter is we speak using enthymemes more often than syllogisms. This is because we can assume the audience does not need to hear certain parts of the syllogism to understand the message. When Hillary Clinton, then First Lady, took to the podium in Beijing during the United Nation's 4th World Conference on Women trying to shed light on women's issues in the mid-1990s, she did not need to lay out her logic step by step. She could assume the audience could fill in certain elements for themselves. In essence, the speech serves as a great example of how people speak enthymematically, not syllogistically.

You can also construct visual enthymemes. Visual enthymemes make a case without using words. Rather, they show images that make an argument. Advertisements frequently do this. Take a video that begins with people looking unhappy on the couch. Then a product, let's say a soft drink, is introduced and everyone then becomes happy. The syllogism inherent in these images is:

Major premise:	People are happy when they have something to drink.
Minor premise:	Fizzy-Bubbler is a drink.
Conclusion:	People with Fizzy-Bubbler are happy.

There are no words used to describe this argument, only images, but the case is effective. In marketing, conversation, and even music videos, visual enthymemes are commonly used to make arguments without saying a word.

Syllogisms and enthymemes are the foundation of any argument within a persuasive attempt. They are used to connect evidence to your claims, and when used effectively they strengthen your case. In the next section we expand our discussion of reasoning to include several different ways you can connect different types of evidence to support specific claims you make.

Types of Reasoning

Syllogisms and enthymemes are the forms we use to make arguments, but different types of evidence dictate the types of reasoning we use to make our case. Good persuasive messages wield several different types of evidence when presenting a reasoned argument to an audience. As Aristotle noted, reasoning can be either deductive or inductive, depending on whether you seek to apply general principles to specific events in order to demonstrate certainty, or to make more general claims based upon limited evidence. In this section of the chapter we will cover three different types of reasoning, each using different forms of evidence.

The most common form of reasoning involves taking specific cases and making general conclusions based on their characteristics. The process of inferring general conclusions and making general claims from specific cases is called *reasoning by example* and it is a form of inductive reasoning. On rare occasions only one case or example allows you to make a generalization, but more often than not you will need to use multiple cases to strengthen your ability to make a general claim. Additionally, there are several important elements you must pay attention to when choosing the examples that support your claim.

reasoning by example
the process of inferring general conclusions and making general claims from specific cases

First, the examples must be relevant to the case you make. The more closely you can tie the examples to the claim the stronger your claim. You also must provide a reasonable number of examples to support your case. Relying on just one may make it appear that there is not enough evidence to support your argument. The examples you use must also be typical and represent that larger population of which they serve as a sample. Finally, you must be sure that the examples you choose do not contradict your argument.

Women's Rights Are Human Rights
by Hillary Clinton

Delivered September 5, 1995, at the United Nations 4th World Conference on Women in Beijing, China

First Lady Hillary Clinton advocated for the rights of both children and women during her husband's time in office. In 1995 she traveled to the 4th United Nations Conference on Women in China. It is also a nation that allows little political dissent.

As First Lady she had significant prior ethos and initial credibility, and she derived more by noting her involvement on the issue of women's rights:

"Over the past 25 years, I have worked persistently on issues relating to women, children, and families. Over the past two-and-a-half years, I've had the opportunity to learn more about the challenges facing women in my own country and around the world."[5]

Mrs. Clinton made her case often through the use of enthymemes, or syllogisms missing one or more parts. Take the following passage as an example: "What we are learning around the world is that if women are healthy and educated, their families will flourish. If women are free from violence, their families will flourish. If women have a chance to work and earn as full and equal partners in society, their families will flourish. And when families flourish, communities and nations do as well."[6]

Mrs. Clinton uses this parallel structure to enthymematically argue for better treatment of women around the world. It is an enthymeme because it is a syllogism missing a part. If it were a syllogism it would look more like this: Communities and nations wish for their members to flourish. Women are members of communities and nations. Therefore, communities and nations wish for women to flourish. The enthymematic argument sounded a lot easier on the ears than the syllogism and also got the point across more creatively and effectively.

Table 9.1

Tips for Reasoning by Example
• Ensure the example is relevant.
• It is wise to have more than one example.
• Make sure the examples are typical of the issue.
• The example should not contradict the point you are making.

A second form of inductive reasoning you may use when speaking to other people involves making a comparison. *Reasoning by analogy* is when you compare two similar cases in order to argue that what is true in one case is also true in the other. Analogies can be constructed in two ways. A *literal analogy* occurs when the two cases being compared are classified the same way. For instance, if you argued that a certain crime prevention program would work in Los Angeles because it also worked in Houston, you are making a literal analogy between two real cities. The other form of analogy, a *figurative analogy*, occurs when the items are from completely different classifications. These analogies employ similies, such as this example: *The art of compromise is a lot like modern art.* Compromise and modern art are not in the same classification; however, the analogy allows you to take characteristics of one and ascribe them to the other.

reasoning by analogy
when you compare two similar cases in order to argue that what is true in one case is also true in the other

literal analogy
when the two cases being compared are classified the same way

When reasoning by analogy you must be aware of several things. First, the items in the comparison must have significant points of similarity, and those points must be crucial to the association you are making. You may need to explain those connections, but as long as you can in a cogent manner then you should be fine. You also need to recognize that all analogies have points of difference, but so long as these points of difference are not critical or important to your comparison then the analogy should hold. Also, you must remember that as effective as figurative analogies are, they cannot be used for making a logical proof for your argument; rather they are best suited for explanations. To employ an analogy for a logical proof you must instead rely on literal analogies. Analogical reasoning is an effective way to make a point because it allows you to use more concrete language and make your point using items with which your audience may be more familiar.

figurative analogy
when the two cases being compared are from completely different classifications

Tips for Reasoning by Analogy
• Points must be similar.
• Points need to be crucial to the case.
• Be prepared to explain connections.
• Be aware that all analogies have differences.
• Figurative analogies cannot be used for proof.
• Figurative analogies can be used for explanation.

Table 9.2

The third and final form of reasoning is called *reasoning by cause*, and it refers to arguments that claim one event or factor produces an effect. Almost all causal reasoning is based on probabilities. Here is an example of one such case: *Obtaining a college education will allow students to get better paying jobs when they graduate.* The cause is a college education and the effect is a better paying job; however, we all know it is not a guarantee that a college degree will get you a better paying job. It merely increases the probability that such an effect will come to pass. Causal reasoning can be very persuasive with an audience, but it must be carefully constructed.

reasoning by cause
arguments that claim one event or factor produces an effect

Much like the other forms of reasoning we have discussed so far, causal reasoning also must be conducted with several things in mind. First, the cause you discuss must be relevant to the effect you describe. For example, you could claim that chewing a new piece of gum during every inning of a baseball game caused your team to win. These two events are completely unrelated, and the gum chewing almost certainly does not have any bearing on the result of a baseball game. A second aspect of the relationship you must be aware of is whether the cause you discuss is the only possible cause for the effect in your argument. Almost always more than one cause contributes to an effect, and recognizing this in your argument is important. Also at issue is whether the cause is actually capable of producing the effect you discuss. For instance, generally people believe that receiving a college degree will cause them to get a job when they graduate. Although the idea of college degrees helping students get jobs upon graduation has some merit, other factors are also at play, such as how well the applicant interviews, how the student performed while in school, and a whole host of other variables.

Table 9.3

Tips for Reasoning by Cause
• Cause must be relevant to the effect.
• Are there other possible causes?
• Is the cause really capable of producing the effect?

necessary cause
a condition that must be present for the effect to occur

sufficient cause
a condition that automatically produces the effect in question

Finally, and most importantly, you must determine if the cause you present is necessary and sufficient. A *necessary cause* is a condition that must be present for the effect to occur. A temperature of less than 32 degrees Fahrenheit must be present for freezing to occur. A *sufficient cause* is a condition that automatically produces the effect in question. For example, a broken spine is a sufficient condition for paralysis. Academically, plagiarism is a sufficient cause for failing a class, but it is not a necessary cause for failure as other things can also cause someone to fail a course. The necessary cause for failing a course is not completing the work assigned in an acceptable manner. When sufficient conditions are known, they can be brought together to ensure an event's occurrence. See Figure 9.1 for additional examples.

Figure 9.1
Examples of Necessary Cause and Sufficient Cause

Necessary Cause Examples

- People need water to live.
- Oxygen must be present for fire to burn.
- Metal will expand when the temperature becomes hot enough.

Sufficient Cause Examples

- A gunshot wound to the head is sufficient to cause death.
- Stealing at work is a sufficient cause to be fired.
- Lack of fertilizer is a sufficient cause for a plant to die.

Enthymemes often employ each of these three forms of reasoning to make a case for a speaker. Knowing how to carefully craft arguments using each of these reasoning processes will help make your speech that much more effective. One key to constructing the most persuasive argument possible in any given context, be it a conversation with a boss or friend, or a sales presentation to a larger

SPOTLIGHTING THEORISTS: ISOCRATES

Isocrates (436–338 BC)

As one of the ten greatest orators of Ancient Greece, otherwise called the Attic Orators, Isocrates taught rhetoric to many Greeks and influenced the work of Cicero, Quintilian and many other Roman rhetoricians. He was born into a wealthy family that provided him with an opportunity to receive a good education. Unfortunately, following the Peloponnesian War his family was stripped of its money, forcing Isocrates to find gainful employment.

His early efforts to make a living involved work as a logographer, or courtroom speechwriter. Later, around 392 BC, he opened his own school to teach rhetoric where he charged a much higher fee than most schools at the time. He still amassed many students and eventually reconstituted his family's fortune.

Isocrates focused on practical speaking in situations where finding absolute truth was not possible. He believed that the ideal orator was someone who not only possessed talent in delivery, but also was well learned in a variety of different areas. Additionally, he felt they needed to be virtuous in intent, value freedom—or at least the Greek notion of it—and practice self-control. A good Isocratean speaker, therefore, could knowledgeably speak on a variety of different topics, in a variety of different situations, and do so in an ethically sound manner.

One of the most influential concepts in rhetoric most linked to Isocrates is that of kairos. Kairos is the notion of timing, so it was said "Kairos is all," or as we now say it, "Timing is everything." Kairos is the speaker's ability to adapt to any occasion and deliver a speech fit for that moment. This is relevant to all speaking situations, including those for which epideictic address is necessary.

A good ceremonial speaker can adapt to the audience, the moment, and the topic to deliver a knowledgeable, ethical, and practical speech that balances the importance of the moment with the emotion of the audience. Proper attention to kairos enables someone to speak well at any event. Kairos is all.

audience, is appreciating the context in which you find yourself. Your ability to find examples or choose analogies that resonate with a given listener, and the careful timing of delivering those reasons may determine success or failure in your effort. For example, approaching a friend to ask a favor may not work when he or she just received a bad grade on an exam, no matter how strong your case may be. Waiting until the most opportune time is essential for maximizing your potential for successful persuasion. This idea of timing was first discussed at length by the Greek philosopher Isocrates, who proposed that "kairos is all." *Kairos*, or a person's ability to adapt to any occasion and deliver a message fit for

kairos
a person's ability to adapt to any occasion and deliver a message fit for that moment

that moment, is best understood as timing. Today, we paraphrase this important principle taught by Isocrates as "Timing is everything."

It is important to understand that the classical models as well as more contemporary approaches can be very effective at making a successful persuasive appeal. You don't have to limit yourself to the classics if you find other methods and styles that work well for you. As the Greeks, Romans, and many others have noted, creating a reasoned argument is not easy. In fact, the "easy road" to argument often involves using improper modes of argument known as logical, or reasoning, fallacies. In the next section we will discuss ways in which the reasoning process we have discussed so far can be damaged or perverted through the use of such fallacies.

REASONING FALLACIES

Making a reasoned argument may seem like a simple task, and we all may believe that we use reason properly all the time, but in fact many times we use fallacious, or erroneous, reasoning. There are ten common fallacies that distort the reasoning process by only *appearing* logical when, in actuality, they are not. In this section we will discuss these ten different reasoning fallacies and illustrate how they damage your ability to make an ethical and effective persuasive claim.

Types of Fallacies

begging-the-question fallacy
when a speaker presumes certain things are facts when they have not yet been proven to be truthful

The first of the reasoning fallacies is dangerous because it presumes truth without proof. The *begging-the-question fallacy* occurs when someone presumes that certain things are facts when they have not yet been proven to be truthful. This fallacy is easy to identify as it involves making statements that begin with things like "Everyone knows that" and "It should go without saying." These phrases assume that the statement that follows is an absolute indisputable truth, even though that is almost always not the case. When seen as a truth, the information then becomes false grounds upon which the remainder of the argument rests.

At the beginning of the chapter we told the story of a speech given by Charlton Heston at Harvard in 1999. We mentioned that the speech included quite a few logical fallacies, and the begging-the-question fallacy was one of them. At one point Heston stated:

> "Americans know something without a name is undermining the nation."[7]

This statement presumes that every American believes there is something wrong with the country, while he provides no evidence to back up this likely erroneous statement. Accepting the implicit argument in this statement, however, is the foundation of the speech and without analyzing it for what it is, the audience simply accepts it and moves closer to agreeing with Heston. Begging-the-question is faulty logic that depends on audiences accepting broad assumptions with no support.

A second form of reasoning not based on logic is the non sequitur, from the Latin phrase for "does not follow." A *non sequitur fallacy* occurs when you make an unwarranted move from one idea to the next. Often this happens because you do not provide evidence or fail to clearly connect your evidence to your claim. The evidence you provided does not relate to the claim you made. If the relationship between the evidence and your argument remains unclear and you still move to the next point, you have committed a non sequitur.

Heston also included non sequiturs in his speech. Take this passage, for example:

> "As I have stood in the crosshairs of those who target Second Amendment freedoms, I've realized that firearms are not the only issue. No, it's much, much bigger than that. I've come to understand that a cultural war is raging across our land, in which, with Orwellian fervor, certain acceptable thoughts and speech are mandated."[8]

example: non sequitur fallacy

The passage starts with a discussion of firearms and the Second Amendment, but then suddenly moves to freedom of speech, which involves the First Amendment. He provides no evidence for the move from one issue to the next, except to say it involves a larger problem.

Non sequiturs can sometimes be confused with a third type of logical fallacy. The *slippery slope fallacy* is a logical fallacy that assumes once an action begins it will follow, undeterred, to an eventual and inevitable conclusion. Whereas the non sequitur makes leaps from claim to claim without evidence, the slippery slope assumes a predetermined path for events simply because the first stage occurred. Again, Heston's speech at Harvard provides us with a perfect example:

> "What does all of this mean? It means that telling us what to think has evolved into telling us what to say, so telling us what to do can't be far behind."[9]

example: slippery slope fallacy

Here, Heston assumes that people are being told what to think and say. Additionally, since that is happening, people will inevitably be told what to do. There is no evidence for any of these stages; there is a presupposition they are true, and more importantly, he assumes a direct causal connection between each that eliminates the possibility of other contributing factors or the occurrence of a change in the process he outlined. In other words, he presents the appearance of an inevitable series of events, thus fitting the description of a slippery slope fallacy.

A fourth logical fallacy also involves erroneously assuming causal connection between two events. The *post hoc, ergo propter hoc fallacy* comes from the Latin for "after this, therefore because of this" and assumes that because one event happened after another, then the preceding event caused the event that followed. Many superstitions grew from this fallacy, like the black cat walking across your path brings bad luck. As if the color of the cat that walks in front of you causes bad things to happen to you! In persuasive arguments such as the one presented by Heston at Harvard, however, it is much more seductive.

In the final segment of his speech Heston attempted to demonstrate a point regarding the power of social activism. He described his attendance at a stockholder meeting for Time/Warner, which at the time produced an album by rapper Ice-T entitled "Cop-Killer." At the meeting he read the lyrics of two songs, one depicting acts of violence against police and another about sodomizing two 12-year-old nieces of Al and Tipper Gore. After these renditions, he claimed:

> "Two months later Time/Warner terminated Ice-T's contract."[10]

This statement assumes that his actions caused the termination of Ice-T's contract, yet that most likely is not the case. It may have contributed to it, but it is very doubtful, without specific statements corroborating the claim, that Heston's speech at the stockholder meeting caused the ensuing termination. He erroneously assumed that since Ice-T was fired after his speech, then his speech must have been the cause.

either-or fallacy
....
an argument in which you present two options and declare that one of them must be correct while the other must be incorrect

Another common logical fallacy involves options and ultimatums. Speakers often present their audiences with only two alternatives, as if there were no other options. This type of argument is indicative of the *either-or fallacy*, where you present two options and declare that one of them must be correct while the other must be incorrect. Many candidates in elections operate with this faulty reasoning, declaring that "you will vote Republican, or you will vote Democrat." Such reasoning presents a false image of the political landscape and the choices every voter has. There are multiple parties they can vote for, and they can also choose not to vote.

red herring fallacy
....
when a speaker introduces an irrelevant issue or piece of evidence to divert attention from the subject of the speech

A sixth fallacy of reasoning attempts not to present an image of fewer alternatives than actually exist, but rather to divert attention from the issues and arguments at stake. The *red herring fallacy* exists when a speaker introduces an irrelevant issue or piece of evidence to divert attention from subject of the speech. Red herrings begin with a topic under discussion, then introduce something else as if it is relevant to the original topic, and ultimately they disregard the initial topic altogether. Here is an example of a red herring at work:

> "I believe we need to increase enrollment requirements for undergraduate education. With fewer students, we can help solve the budget crisis we face today."

The budget crisis, although seemingly related to increased admission standards, is actually not related to the requirements for entry into college, and thus serves as a red herring. To avoid this fallacy it is important to make sure your evidence directly supports your claims.

The next reasoning fallacy we will discuss is also concerned with the evidence you provide for claims within your speech. Sometimes individuals feel that they should do something because everyone else does it, but as speakers we must avoid using this type of reasoning as a justification for agreeing with our argument. When we attempt to persuade people by arguing that our position is reasonable because so many other people are doing it, or agree with it, we are employing the bandwagon, or *ad populum fallacy*. Many magazine advertisements, beer commercials, and speeches employ this fallacy by trying to convince you of the popularity of an item, event, or idea. Many messages fall victim to this fallacy by relying on too much qualitative evidence and peer testimonials and not enough hard data to support claims and conclusions.

Appeals to the masses are not the only types of appeals that are illegitimate and invalid. Sometimes the reason people provide for their argument relies entirely on their ethos or the credibility or venerability of a tradition because it has significant authority. An appeal for persuasion based on higher authority or tradition is emblematic of the *ad verecundium fallacy*. Again we return to the Charlton Heston speech at Harvard for an example of this fallacy at work.

One of the main claims advanced by Heston was a call for his audience to:

> "disobey social protocol that stifles and stigmatizes personal freedom."[11]

He explained that disobedience is justified and honorable because of the fact people like:

> "Gandhi, Thoreau, and Jesus and every other great man who led those in the right against those with the might" did it before. He went on to say that "disobedience is in our DNA."[12]

Such appeals justify disobedience based on the authority and tradition of the action, not for any other reason. Other more common examples of the ad verecundium fallacy include when your parents told you to do something "because I am your mother/father." There is no logical connection between the action advocated and the reason provided for you to act.

When logic fails them, individuals sometimes revert to attacking their opponent in a debate instead of criticizing their ideas in a reasonable manner. When speakers attack the person making the argument, and not the argument itself, it is representative of the *ad hominem fallacy*. Ad hominem attacks often exist under the guise of attacks on a speaker's credibility, but in truth they are irrelevant to the argument and do not justify claims about the topic of debate. For instance, when an attorney in a court case argues that a prostitute's testimony should not be admitted because prostitutes are not trustworthy or reliable sources, it is an example of an ad hominem attack. In this case, the credibility of the individual making the claim is not in question, nor is the content of her testimony; instead, the prosecutor makes her seem unreliable by attacking her profession through stereotypes. An interesting thing to keep in mind about ad hominem attacks is that the more frustrated or angry we get in a conversation with those who do not agree with us, the more likely we are to devolve into using these types of claims. It is thus important to keep a cool head and focus on the issue, even when we are upset.

We can look to references made by Heston for examples as well. In his speech he claimed that as a result of his support for the NRA the public attacked him. At one point he said:

ad populum fallacy
when we attempt to persuade people by arguing our position is reasonable because so many other people are doing it or agree with it

ad verecundium fallacy
an appeal for persuasion based on higher authority or tradition

example:
ad verecundium
fallacy

ad hominem fallacy
when speakers attack the person making the argument and not the argument itself

example:
ad hominem
fallacy

"I ran for office, I was elected, and now I serve . . . I serve as a moving target for the media who have called me everything from 'ridiculous' and 'duped' to a 'brain-injured, senile, crazy old man.'"[13]

Now, Heston himself did not use an ad hominem, but he pointed out that others used that line of reasoning against him by attacking him and not his position on guns.

straw man fallacy
when a speaker ignores the actual position of an opponent and substitutes it with a distorted and exaggerated position

The tenth and final common reasoning fallacy we will discuss most often occurs in the rebuttal section of a speech. The *straw man fallacy* occurs when a speaker ignores the actual position of an opponent and substitutes it with a distorted and exaggerated position. He or she then proceeds to attack the incorrect position because it is easier to defeat, although the process itself is illogical because it does not accurately respond to the original position.

Think about a political debate over funding the defense department, specifically the development of a missile defense shield in Europe. Candidate X wants to cease funding the research behind this project, and Candidate Y responds by saying "I cannot believe you do not support protecting the American people." First, the original position specifically called to question one program, not the entire goal of defense. Second, Candidate Y substituted that one program with a more exaggerated position that was easier to use as an attack. The equation of opposing a missile defense shield with not protecting the American people is illogical and erroneous based on the statements made here, and are thus illustrative of the straw man fallacy.

The sheer fact that there are ten common logical fallacies should serve as a reminder to you to be careful when you construct messages. Your claims must be well supported and the evidence you use must relate to those claims. These ten fallacies are seductive in their simplicity, but destructive in their effects. They damage your credibility as a speaker and also potentially take advantage of your audience. Although it involves more effort and work, the payoff of taking the time to construct a proper speech that avoids these fallacies far outweighs the consequences of using them. Conversely, being able to identify them when used by others also makes us better critical consumers of messages. See Table 9.4 for a summary and additional examples of these ten fallacies.

Table 9.4

Chart of Fallacies and Examples		
Fallacy	**The Error in Reasoning**	**Example**
Begging-the-question	When a speaker presumes certain things are facts when they have not yet been proven to be truthful	"Oh, everyone knows that we are all Christians."
Non sequitur	When you make an unwarranted move from one idea to the next	"Well, look at the size of this administration building; it is obvious this university does not need more funding."

Slippery slope	Assumes that once an action begins it will follow, undeterred, to an eventual and inevitable conclusion	"If we let the government dictate where we can pray, soon the government will tell us we cannot pray."
Post hoc, ergo propter hoc	Assumes that because one event happened after another, then the preceding event caused the event that followed	"Every time Sheila goes to a game with us, our team loses. She is bad luck."
Either-or	Presents two options and declares that one of them must be correct while the other must be incorrect	"We either raise tuition or massively increase class size."
Red herring	When a speaker introduces an irrelevant issue or piece of evidence to divert attention from the subject of the speech	"Why do you question my private issues, when we have social problems with which to deal?"
Ad populum	When we attempt to persuade people by arguing our position is reasonable because so many other people are doing it or agree with it	"Why shouldn't I cheat on this exam? Everyone else cheats."
Ad verecundium	An appeal to persuasion based on higher authority or tradition	"If the president of Harvard says it is a good idea, then we should follow suit." Or, "That is how we have always done it."
Ad hominem	When speakers attack the person making the argument and not the argument itself	"We can't believe anything he says; he is a convicted felon."
Straw man	When a speaker ignores the actual position of an opponent and substitutes it with a distorted and exaggerated position	"Oh, you think we should agree to a cut in our salaries. Why do you want to bleed us dry?"

SUMMARY

This chapter provided you with various ways to construct a well-reasoned, ethical, and effective argument. Whether you choose to employ the classical mode of argument or a more contemporary model, you now have a blueprint for crafting a solid persuasive message. It is also important to remember that any one message can use different types of reasoning to accomplish its goals. The classical approach includes three different ways to reason involving different types of evidence. Some other models that you learn may be, at times, more flexible, but they all stress the importance of connecting evidence to your arguments. Whichever route you take, you must take good care to avoid logical fallacies, no matter how attractive it may seem to use them.

KEY TERMS

ad hominem fallacy   233

ad populum fallacy   233

ad verecundium fallacy   233

antecedent   224

begging-the-question fallacy   230

categorical syllogism   222

conditional syllogism   224

consequent   224

deductive argument   221

disjunctive syllogism   223

either-or fallacy   232

enthymeme   224

figurative analogy   227

inductive argument   218

kairos   225

literal analogy   227

major premise   221

minor premise   221

necessary cause   228

non sequitur fallacy   231

post hoc, ergo propter hoc fallacy   231

reasoning by analogy   227

reasoning by cause   227

reasoning by example   225

red herring fallacy   232

slippery slope fallacy   231

straw man fallacy   234

sufficient cause   228

syllogism   221

REVIEW QUESTIONS

1.   What are the three types of syllogisms proposed by Aristotle?
2.   What is the difference between an enthymeme and a syllogism?
3.   What are the three different types of reasoning from evidence?
4.   What are the ten logical fallacies?

THINK ABOUT IT

1. Are there any circumstances under which ad hominem attacks are acceptable? When?

2. What are some enthymemes you are exposed to every day through advertising?

3. How ethical are the persuasive appeals in advertising and political campaigns today? Do they employ logical fallacies? If so, which ones?

4. How can you as avoid argument fallacies?

5. As an audience member do you have an obligation to voice concern about a speaker's fallacies?

ACTIVITIES FOR ACTION

1. Find a copy of the text for the "Winning the Cultural War" speech by Charlton Heston mentioned in the opening of this chapter. Look through the text closely and see how many logical fallacies you can identify. Then, have a friend read the speech and see what his or her initial impression is. After your friend tells you, point out all the logical fallacies in the speech to him or her and see if your friend changes his or her mind.

2. One evening, while watching television, pay close attention to the commercials. As you watch, refer to the reasoning fallacies described in this chapter, and see how many you find. As you note them, think about whether the advertisements that used the fallacies were interesting or effective. Did the fallacies have anything to do with the success of the ad?

ENDNOTES

1. Harvard University, "The Early History of Harvard University," http://www.hno.harvard.edu/guide/intro/index.html (accessed November 7, 2008).

2. Harvard Law School, "Alumni News and Publications," http://www.law.harvard.edu/alumni/news/index.html (accessed November 7, 2008).

3. "Winning the Cultural War" (February 16, 1999), http://isocracytx.net/hp-org/hestonlaw.html (accessed November 7, 2008).

4. Ibid.

5. http://www.americanrhetoric.com/speeches/hillaryclintonbeijingspeech.htm (last accessed: June 6, 2011).

6. Ibid.

7. Ibid. para. #6.

8. Ibid. para. #4.

9. Ibid. para. #11-12.

10. Ibid. para. #23-27.

11. Ibid. para. #19.

12. Ibid.

13. Ibid. para. #3.

SCENARIOS

Scenario 1

Read each of the following excerpt from a speech made by Presidential candidate HillaryClinton.[1] Explore the inductive reasoning that she uses in the excerpt by identifying the claim that she is making and listing the specific examples that she uses to illustrate that claim:

Hillary Clinton: *"It's clear that Donald Trump doesn't believe we are stronger together. He has abused his primary opponents and their families, attacked the press for asking tough questions, denigrated Muslims and immigrants."*

1. What overarching claim is the speaker making?

2. List the specific examples that she gives to illustrate what he is claiming.

3. If you wanted to challenge the logic in this argument, how could you do so?

---

1 "Read Hillary Clinton's Historic Victory Speech as Presumptive Democratic Nominee," last modified June 8, 2016, http://time.com/4361099/hillary-clinton-nominee-speech-transcript/.

Scenario 2

Read the following excerpt from a speech made by Donald Trump during the 2016 election.[2] Explore the deductive reasoning that he uses in each excerpt by outlining the core elements of the argument: major premise, the minor premise, and the conclusion. Note that one or more of these elements might be left unsaid in any given case, in which case the argument is an enthymeme. You as an audience member in such cases would be expected to supply the missing element. Note also that the elements of a deductive argument do not need to appear in any particular order.

Donald Trump: *"President Obama has not been a friend to Israel. He has treated Iran with tender love and care and made it a great power. Iran has, indeed, become a great, great power in just a very short period of time, because of what we've done."*

1. What conclusion is the speaker trying to persuade the audience to accept?

2. Major premise: What is the general principle that the speaker is invoking to reach this conclusion?

3. Minor premise: What is the specific case that the speaker invokes, to which if the major premise is applied, the conclusion logically follows?

4. Is the argument an enthymeme? Has the speaker left any of the elements unsaid?

5. Which of the three types of syllogism does this argument exemplify?

2 "Transcript: Donald Trump's Foreign Policy Speech," last modified April 27, 2016, http://www.nytimes. com/2016/04/28/us/politics/transcript-trump-foreign-policy.html?_r=1.

Scenario 3

Read the following excerpts from the same speeches. Explore the analogical reasoning that the speaker uses in each excerpt by identifying the two cases that the speaker is assuming to be similar and explaining how the speaker is drawing a conclusion about one of the cases based on that similarity. Note that some elements of an analogical argument might remain unsaid or might be implied by the speaker.

Donald Trump: *"We're getting out of the nation-building business and instead focusing on creating stability in the world. Our moments of greatest strength came when politics ended at the water's edge. We need a new rational American foreign policy, informed by the best minds and supported by both parties, and it will be by both parties—Democrats, Republicans, independents, everybody, as well as by our close allies. This is how we won the Cold War and it's how we will win our new future struggles, which may be many, which may be complex, but we will win if I become president."*

1. What two cases is the speaker assuming to be similar?

2. What does the speaker suggest to be true about one of the cases?

3. Because of the similarity between the two cases, the speaker is suggesting what is true about the other case?

4. If you wanted to challenge the logic in this argument, how could you do so?

Scenario 4

Read these excerpts from the same speeches. Explore the causal reasoning that the speaker in each excerpt uses by identifying the outcome that she or he identifies, the event(s) or condition(s) that she or he identifies as the cause of that outcome, and the nature of the causal relationship between the two.

Hillary Clinton: *"...we've reached a milestone – the first time in our nation's history that a woman will be a major party's nominee for president of the United States. Tonight's victory is not about one person. It belongs to generations of women and men who struggled and sacrificed and made this moment possible. In our country, it started right here in New York, a place called Seneca Falls, in 1848. When a small but determined group of women, and men, came together with the idea that women deserved equal rights, and they set it forth in something called the Declaration of Sentiments, and it was the first time in human history that that kind of declaration occurred. So we all owe so much to those who came before...."*

1. On what outcome is the speaker focusing the audience's attention?

2. What event or condition does the speaker identify as the cause of this outcome?

3. Does the speaker present this event or condition as a necessary cause? A sufficient cause? Both? Explain.

4. Look at Table 9.3. If you wanted to challenge the logic in this argument, how could you do so?

Scenario 5 (Performance)

Suppose that you and your partners as a team have been hired by the University to create a promotional video that can be shown to high school students by campus recruiters to persuade them to apply to UD. Outline how you might use inductive reasoning in the video to convince the students to accept some claim that your video will make about the University. Be prepared to share with the class what you created.

1. What is one claim that you will try to get the students to accept?

2. List at least four specific examples that you can describe, show, or otherwise present to the students to illustrate this claim.

Now, outline how you might use deductive reasoning in the video to convince the students to accept some conclusion that your video will make about the University.

3. What is one conclusion that you will try to get the students to draw about the University?

4. What is a general principle, not necessarily relating directly to UD, that you can invoke that either the students are likely to believe already or can be convinced to accept relatively easily? (major premise)

5. What is a specific case relating to UD that you can invoke to which this general principle can be applied? (minor premise)

6. Explain briefly how the conclusion that you want the audience to accept follows logically from the application of the general principle to the specific case.

Scenario 6

Read the following statements. Identify which logical fallacy it illustrates. Explain briefly how the statement illustrates that particular fallacy.

1. "The majority of Americans favor legalizing marijuana, so it must be good for our country. After all, why would so many people support something that isn't good for them?"

2. "We never had any problems with crime in this city until those people moved into the area. They must be the cause of all of the crime that has been occurring lately."

3. "You are either with us or against us. You need to decide which side you are on."

4. "People who do not support same-sex marriage must be homophobic."

5. "All of us want a society in which people can have a higher standard of living. Who wouldn't want that?"

6. "How can you believe her argument? She's a liar and a cheat."

7. "Of course, I'd make a great mayor. Look at how successful I have been in the world of business."

8. "If we don't change our policies regarding immigration, then in five years, this country's economy is going to be a wreck. America will become truly a second-class society."

Scenario 7 (Performance)

Choose a product. Suppose that you and your partners work for an advertising firm that has been asked to design a television commercial for this product. Your team is not particularly interested in creating quality logical appeals, so you do not have any qualms about using logical fallacies in your ad. Create two logical fallacies that you might include in your ad. Identify each of the logical fallacies below and describe how you would incorporate it into the ad, including the specific wording that you would use. Be prepared to share with the class what you created.

Logical Fallacy 1:

Logical Fallacy 2:

Is it ethical to use logical fallacies in persuasion? Explain your position.

Analyzing Persuasion   245

Crafting a Persuasive Message

CHAPTER OVERVIEW

- Explains how to combine classical and contemporary approaches to developing introductions and conclusions for persuasive messages
- Describes the organizational patterns for persuasive messages

Practically SPEAKING

In 1924 at a small YMCA in Santa Ana, California, a small group of people met to help each other become better public speakers and have a little bit of fun in the process. Over the years, that small group expanded and became a group called Toastmasters International, a nonacademic leader in helping people develop oral communication skills. This nonprofit organization now boasts nearly 235,000 members at over 11,700 clubs in 92 different countries.[1]

Thousands of corporations, companies, and civic organizations encourage their employees and affiliates to participate in Toastmasters because of the practical benefits gained from the group. Toastmasters use a manual to help members develop certain speaking skills. It focuses on the use of humor, gestures, and eye contact. Upon completion of the manual, members progress to more advanced instruction.

Toastmasters International also contributes much in the way of community service. They promote youth programs designed around developing oral communication and leadership skills. They support "Gavel Clubs" where they bring speech training inside prison walls. They work with community organizations and businesses to help them tell their stories to their communities. Additionally, they offer short courses on crafting effective messages.[2]

A central focus of the Toastmasters International programs is organization. In fact, they make it a point to tell people that one of the ten most common errors in public speaking is lack of preparation and organization. When you do not organize your thoughts in a logical manner, and then try to present them to an audience, it makes it very challenging for your listeners to follow what you are saying and ultimately get anything out of your presentation.

Persuasive messages must be carefully structured to ensure that the speaker achieves the specific purpose. In fact, persuasive speeches were the foremost concern of the Greeks and Romans. This chapter will briefly highlight the methods classical Greeks and Romans taught students to construct persuasive messages. Finally, we will offer organizational patterns you can use for crafting effective persuasive messages.

PREP QUESTIONS

1. List the four strategies for creating a strong persuasive speech introduction.

2. Name the six strategies/guidelines for creating a strong persuasive conclusion.

3. Typically, how long (how much of the speech) should the introduction, body and conclusion be?

4. Compare and contrast problem-solution organization with problem-cause-solution.

5. Define the comparative advantages organizational pattern.

6. List the five steps to Monroe's Motivated Sequence.

7. How could you use the Monroe's Motivated Sequence in everyday language?

8. Discuss whether it is necessary to use the word "please" when asserting a call to action in a persuasive message.

9. Explain whether persuasion is best illustrated by the linear or transactional model of communication.

10. Is it ethical to induce emotion in the conclusion of the speech? Why?

11. Think of a disagreement you had with another person. What method of persuasion did you use to persuade this individual?

Constructing Persuasive Introductions and Conclusions

It is often said that you do not have a second chance to make a first impression. This is true, and particularly important when trying to persuade someone. Additionally, it is equally important to leave them with a lasting positive impression of your argument in the hope they will accept it. In this section we will provide you with some strategies for developing effective introductions and conclusions. We will then explore different organizational strategies for the body of a persuasive message. Keep in mind that these categories of introduction, body, and conclusion apply to a variety of communicative formats, and not just public speaking. They are also ways to think about how to structure a conversation, commercial, or any other type of interaction.

Strategies for Persuasive Introductions

The Greeks and Romans noted the uniqueness of introductions and provided several different options for developing them. These observations also illustrate the differences that exist between persuasive and explanatory introductions. That said, there are similarities between the two types. This section will note the similarities while also providing you with ways to effectively construct an introduction appropriate for a persuasive message.

Cicero and Quintilian suggested that the introduction be the last part that you write, and this advice holds with persuasive as well as explanatory prepared presentations. You should not set up the introduction until you know what you are going to say, as well as have an idea of the knowledge level and disposition of your audience. This information is essential to making sure you effectively capture the audience's interest, establish credibility, and focus the audience's attention. When entering a meeting or making a statement to someone, you should also take care to think through the best way to accomplish these tasks, even though you often do not have time to prepare this in advance.

Those three goals of an introduction are the same for when you explain something as well as when you try and convince someone of something. You need to get an audience's attention, but as Cicero and Quintilian noted, be sure to do so without offending the people to whom you are speaking. You must be attuned to the audience's feelings about the topic or the occasion and determine how best to introduce yourself and your argument. You also need to establish your credibility almost immediately by stating why an audience should listen to you on a particular subject. To this end, it is important to develop your skills of observation to quickly identify things in your surroundings that can help you choose the most effective introduction in a given situation. Finally, you need to preview the main points in much the same way you would for an explanation.

Table 10.1

Tips for an Effective Persuasive Introduction
• Develop the introduction last.
• Capture the attention of the audience.
• Establish your credibility.
• Focus the audience's attention.

Strategies for Persuasive Conclusions

Just as with introductions, there are elements common to both explanatory and persuasive conclusions, as well as parts that are different. That said, introductions and conclusions do mirror each other in certain ways. For example, while introductions end with transitions, conclusions start with one. In this section of the chapter we will discuss those similarities and differences while also providing tips on how you can create a strong conclusion when advocating for something.

One of the aspects of conclusions shared by both explanations and persuasive messages is the need for a signpost at the opening of the conclusion. Signposts serve the same function for persuasive message conclusions that they do for explanations: they let the audience know the speech or conversation is almost complete.

Similarly, both types of conclusions should summarize the main points and demonstrate how they connect to and support your argument. You should never introduce new evidence or ideas in a conclusion, but rather re-emphasize the fundamental points of your message. This allows the audience to walk away from your presentation understanding your central point and how you got there. Rarely will listeners recall all the specific evidence you lay out, but they will remember main points. With regard to persuasive messages, this summary also enables you to build up your clincher, which can be a much more powerful statement than those used to end an explanation. A key to any good interaction is adequately summarizing key points so that everyone leaves with an understanding of what was said and what is expected or encouraged.

Although both explanations and persuasive messages have clinchers, persuasive messages allow for much more creativity and direct calls to action with their clinchers. The reason for this is simple: the general purpose of a persuasive message is to persuade, which involves some sort of willing change made by the audience.

The success of your effort at advocacy often depends on your ability to channel and incite the proper pathos through this clincher. The clincher should not take long to state, and there are a variety of ways to construct an effective one for a persuasive message. Most importantly, however, it is essential for you to find a way to reiterate what you want from the audience.

A common error that novice speakers make in conclusions is reserving the persuasive effort for the clincher. Do not wait until the last few moments of your time with the audience to persuade them! The clincher should be the last push and should be a logical next step based on the case you laid out throughout the message. In short, the conclusion should feed off of the rest of the message to accentuate your case and its significance for the audience.

One final note about conclusions bears mentioning. Conclusions should not be very long. In fact, in a formal presentation they should take about as long as your introduction, and thus typically account for no more than 20% of the message. If your conclusion rambles on, it loses its effectiveness and you lose your audience. In a conversation if you do not end the interaction after signaling a conclusion the other party may get irritated and impatient and even lose the point of the conversation. If conclusions are too short, your audience may never truly understand the point of your message. Remember that your conclusion is the last chance you have to underscore your case and its importance for your listeners.

Conclusions are essential elements of any good persuasive message. They involve letting the audience know you are almost finished, restating your argument and main points, and clinching your appeal with a call to action. They share some similarities with conclusions for explanations, but there are key differences you must be aware of when approaching the end of a conversation or preparing the end of a speech. The development of strong introductions and conclusions is only part of the process of crafting a successful persuasive appeal. In the next section we will explore methods that you might use to properly organize the bulk of the content to develop your persuasive message.

Table 10.2

Tips for a Persuasive Speech Conclusion
• Provide a signpost at the beginning of the conclusion.
• Summarize the main points.
• Do not present new evidence.
• Emphasize the fundamental points.
• Build up the clincher.
• Do not wait until the conclusion to present persuasive appeals.
• Accentuate the points in the body and case.
• Make it approximately the same length as the introduction.

Persuasive Organizational Patterns

The general and specific purposes of a persuasive message differ from those of an informative address, but they too help you determine how to arrange your points. A closing argument in a courtroom is a persuasive message in which the general purpose is to persuade and the specific purpose is tied to the facts of the case. For example, the lawyer for Kelly, who was accused of stealing money from a CVS pharmacy, gave a closing argument where the specific purpose was "to persuade  the jury that Kelly did not steal the money because she had no motive or opportunity to commit the crime." This specific purpose statement encouraged the lawyer to use a particular organizational pattern to accomplish the speaking goals. In this section of the chapter we will detail common organizational strategies that you can effectively employ when advocating for a position to other people. Although these may seem only appropriate for speeches, they still apply to other contexts in which you are trying to convince someone to agree with you. By keeping your purpose in mind when dealing with others in any context, your goals will help tell you which pattern would be most effective.

Persuasive messages have very different general and specific purposes than explanations, but in both cases the specific purpose typically dictates what organizational pattern should be used. Persuasive messages can be directed at a specific problem or the problem's fundamental cause. They also can focus on stating that one option is better than another. Finally, there are persuasive messages that attempt to move people to immediate action. Depending on which of these is your goal, you may choose any one of four potential organizational patterns.

Problem-Solution Order

problem-solution order
......
a means of organizing a persuasive speech in which the discussion of the problem is followed by the preferred solution

If you seek to convince an audience that a specific policy or action will solve an existing problem, the *problem-solution order* might be best. In this arrangement you first must convince the audience that there is a problem, and then make the case that the solution you propose will alleviate that problem. To effectively arrange this message you must first establish a clear specific purpose that states exactly what you want your audience to do. Then you must consider several important questions to evaluate the merits of your case as you develop it and prepare to present it to your audience.

The first question deals with the definition and scope of the problem. You should establish how you see the problem at hand and convince your audience to see it that way as well. If your listeners disagree with your definition of the problem, then you can never get the them to accept your solution because you will be stuck arguing what you will recall Quintilian called definitive stasis. In short, make sure all parties agree on the definition of the problem. So, before even offering a solution, you need to clearly establish the scope of the problem you plan to address.

In explaining the scope of the predicament, you may wish to discuss whether any parties are harmed by the problem and explain how they are damaged. This can help create an emotional connection between the audience and the issue, thus enabling you to add some pathos to your appeal.

Once the dilemma that faces the audience is established, you move on to the solution. The initial part of this portion of your message should answer the question of evaluative criteria. You should clearly establish for your listeners, or with your conversational partners, the particular criteria by which a potential solution to the problem should be judged. When constructing this list of criteria, you should check your proposed solution against it to ensure that what you propose actually resolves the problem you described. If it does not, then your solution will likely not be adopted by the audience.

Finally, you need to explain to the others how your solution can be put into effect. The "how" element is important because it is the prescription for action that you want them to follow. It should contain practical and specific steps for the other party to take that will actually enact the solution and solve the problem facing the community.

Let's look at the hypothetical case of Lionel to illustrate how a simple problem-solution message might be approached. Lionel is tired of the potholes in the road in front of his house, so he attends the City Council meeting and addresses the members. First he explains that the road in front of his house contains ten potholes in a three block span, and then informs the council that they have caused several thousand dollars in damage to the cars that drive that road in the last month alone. He then proposes to them that they use city funds to fill the potholes with macadam (a mixture of broken stone) to avoid further damage.

Here Lionel detailed the problem and proposed a solution once the problem became clear to everyone. Using the problem-solution order this message would roughly look like the following:

> Body
> I. Main point: State of the road in front of the house *(problem)*
> II. Main point: Funding road repairs *(solution)*

This can be an effective way of convincing an audience to support your plan; however, it is not always the most compelling way to propose a solution. Sometimes, you need to do more.

Problem-Cause-Solution

Problems, public or personal, always have a root cause. To effectively resolve the problem you need to address that root cause; otherwise, the symptoms will recur. To this end you must look at the situation and ask what are the causes of the problem, and whether or not those causes can actually be addressed. If they can, then the message needs to recognize the problems faced by the community, but also add a discussion of why the problem exists—its cause. In short, you must convince the others not just of the existence of a problem, but also of why the problem is there in the first place. Addressing that root cause is the most effective way to handle the situation. Let's return to Lionel and see how this works.

Would it make even better sense not to just fix the potholes, but to make sure they don't happen again? This would involve changing the specific purpose and, as a result, the organization of the main points. Lionel's specific purpose would change to reflect his new goal, and it would be something like this: "to persuade the audience to redesign the street where potholes have damaged cars so that they will not occur again."

Blood, Toil, Tears and Sweat
by newly elected Prime Minister Winston Churchill

Delivered May 13, 1940, to the British House of Commons

Prime Minister Winston Churchill delivered a terse yet powerful call to action shortly after becoming prime minister of Great Britain in May 1940. As if the war was not a large enough complication for the new leader, outgoing Prime Minister Neville Chamberlain received a boisterous round of applause, while Churchill was greeted with a subdued reaction from members of the House of Commons, thus illustrating the fragile coalition supporting Churchill and his government.[5]

At the time of the address Adolf Hitler's Nazi war machine was crushing opposition everywhere it went. Britons were concerned that their country's safety, freedom, and sovereignty were at risk. Churchill rose to the task of inspiring confidence in both his leadership and the country itself with this brief (only 688 words) address to Parliament.

In his statement of facts, Churchill noted he selected a five-person war cabinet that represented diverse political views. He pointed out that Britain was already fighting in Norway and Holland, that the Mediterranean was a concern, and that the air battle over the remainder of Europe was "continuous." He argued that these facts required that "many preparations have to be made here at home."

Churchill proclaimed the famous line: "I have nothing to offer but blood, toil, tears and sweat"[6] as part of his rebuttal, and aimed it at those who might criticize the swift creation of the cabinet without "ceremony." In fact, his phrase made it seem like he pled with them to accept it because he was essentially trying his best.

In his peroration the prime minister closed with a clarion call to action after admitting the country faced "many, many long months of struggle and suffering." These words, his declaration of a policy of victory, and his concluding statement of, "Come then, let us go forward together with our united strength"[7] all created emotional connections between the initially divided audience, himself, and his policies.

The goal for Lionel now is to address the problem (potholes) by providing a solution to it and its cause (poor design of the street).

Body

I. Main point: The state of the road in front of the house *(problem)*

II. Main point: The poor street design *(cause)*

III. Main point: Funding for proper road repairs *(solution)*

His arrangement now is ***problem-cause-solution order***, where he first discusses the immediate problem, then explains what caused it, and finally provides a solution that addresses both the potholes and the poor street design.

problem-cause-solution order
a means of organizing a persuasive speech in which you discuss the problem first, then its root cause, and then your preferred solution that addresses both the problem and its inherent cause

Comparative Advantages

More often than not, you will not be the only one offering solutions to a problem. In fact, having multiple ideas about how to fix something or address an issue is commonplace. The important thing to remember is to research and evaluate all the other potential solutions that might be offered to solve the problem. After doing so, if you believe yours is the best, then it might be helpful to recognize the fact you are aware of other potential solutions, but that they would not be the best option. This approach looks at the strengths and weaknesses of other solutions and compares them with your own. Such an approach can help increase your ethos with the audience and make your case even stronger.

Continuing with the example of Lionel and the dangerous potholes, perhaps he is not the only one who has brought this issue to the attention of the city council. In fact, the council already knows about and agrees there is a problem and that its cause is poor street design. Let's say that the day before Lionel presents his message, the council comes out in favor of a plan to fill the potholes, but not redesign the street because it would be cost prohibitive to do so. Lionel, aware of this alternate plan, needs a different specific purpose and organizational pattern than in either of the two previous scenarios. Now his specific purpose is "to persuade his audience that paying the money to fix the street now is a better solution than simply fixing the potholes."

He then structures the body of this message by using the *comparative advantage* organizational pattern, in which every main point in the argument explains why redesigning the street is better than just fixing the potholes and not addressing their root cause.

comparative advantage
an organizational pattern that uses each main point to explain why the speaker's solution is better than another proposed solution

Body

I. Main point: Fixing potholes is temporary; a proper repair job will be permanent

II. Main point: Fixing the road will create a smoother surface

III. Main point: Fixing the road correctly will be less expensive in the long run

The case of Lionel and his topic illustrates several different ways of organizing persuasive messages. Each one helps to establish a strong case for adopting a particular policy.

Comparative advantage is also a very good way to argue for a position in a conversation in which multiple parties suggest alternative solutions. You can listen to the solutions of others and recognize their strong points, but then argue for why your position is better (if in fact it is, after listening to the other solutions with an open mind). If you pay attention to the statements of others, evaluate their evidence, and think critically about your own ideas, it will allow you to make a good case for an effective solution to the issue under discussion. There is, however, one more organizational pattern we need to discuss which is particularly useful when seeking immediate action from an audience.

Monroe's Motivated Sequence

Monroe's Motivated Sequence
a five-step organizational pattern that combines psychological elements with speech persuasion to move an audience to action

The fourth organizational pattern for main points we will discuss provides a way to effectively arrange a message designed to incite immediate action from an audience. Alan Monroe, a professor at Purdue University, developed *Monroe's Motivated Sequence* in the 1930s. The five-step sequence combines psychological elements with persuasive structure in an effort to move an audience to action. First, Monroe advocated something the Greeks, Romans, and we have emphasized: getting the *attention* of your audience. Then he argued that a speaker should clearly lay out the *need* for change. Once you clearly establish the problem, you propose a solution to the problem to *satisfy* the need. Fourth, Monroe's sequence calls for you to intensify the audience's desire for your solution to the problem by *visualizing* its success. This involves the use of imagery, and asks the people listening to actually see themselves doing what you call for—at least to see it in their mind's eye. Finally, once you state your case and have gotten the people to visualize what life would be when it was successful, using emotionally stirring language you tell them *how to act*.[8]

As an example: A student participating in the School of Business's Business Plan Competition, in which students compete for over $175,000 in prizes each year by developing their own business plans and elevator pitches, needs to find a way to get the judges to select his plan. He composes the following order for his points using Monroe's Motivated Sequence:

Attention: "Do you have a yard where you have to both mow and edge your grass? Would you love to be able to do both with the same machine, rather than use a lawn mower and edger separately?"

Need: "Most houses have grass that lawn mowers cannot get to, requiring you to finish mowing most of the lawn before going and getting an edger to complete the job. This takes valuable time, and you need to buy multiple tools to get the job done, increasing the costs." (Pictures would be a good visual aid at this juncture.)

SPOTLIGHTING THEORISTS: ALAN H. MONROE

Alan H. Monroe

Alan H. Monroe served as a member of the faculty at Purdue University in Indiana beginning in 1924. He was initially hired as an instructor in English to teach basic courses in the English Department. He quickly infused the English curriculum with classes such as Principles of Speech and Debating in English. Today, we recognize these topics as communication rather than English courses. Through Monroe's efforts Purdue University established a strong Communication department known for teaching and research.[9]

In 1927 Monroe became the head of the Speech faculty in the English Department at Purdue, but he was not formally recognized in that role until 1941. Along with other members of the then English Department at Purdue, Monroe led efforts during the 1930s to expand the curriculum, specifically adding courses in oral interpretation, public address, and debate. In 1935 Monroe published the first edition of his book *Principles and Types of Speech*, which is now in its 16th edition, a testament to the ingenuity and importance of what Monroe accomplished while at Purdue.

In 1948 Purdue inaugurated its own Ph.D. program in Speech Communication, largely through Monroe's efforts. Monroe worked using relationships he had developed in the Purdue Department of Psychology to help push the Speech Communication Department toward a Ph.D. program. He resigned as head of the department in 1963, after successfully creating an independent Communication Department, separate from English, with its own robust undergraduate and graduate curriculum.

As a researcher, Monroe is best remembered for the development of the Monroe's Motivated Sequence model for persuasive speeches that seek immediate action. This model is still taught today, and if you look closely you can see it at play in things as varied as commercials and political speeches. Alan Monroe truly made a mark on the campus of Purdue University as well as the discipline of communication and public speaking education.

Satisfaction: "Thankfully I have a product that would enable you to do both tasks without having to buy both tools, saving you time and money."

Visualization: "This piece of equipment looks like a combination of a lawn mower and a dyson vacuum, in that it is more flexible, with a side compartment of blades to get those hard-to-reach stretches of lawn up against your house." (Visuals of the piece of equipment would be effective here.)

Action:	"All we need is some start-up funds to perfect the prototype and market the LawnWhacker to Lowes, Home Depot, and Menards. So, join with me, and invest in the future of lawn maintenance."

Let's take a moment and look at each one of these elements.

The first step, gaining the audience's attention, is nothing new. It simply employs a rhetorical question to raise awareness of the topic. Any form of attention-getter we covered earlier in the book would be acceptable for this stage of the Motivated Sequence. The second step of establishing need is a way of presenting a problem to the audience, but it differs slightly from the way we discussed it when we explained the problem-solution order.

Of course, the need for the audience can be to solve a problem. In fact, solving a problem is a terrific motivator when the listeners recognize there is a dilemma that affects them which needs to be resolved. That said, establishing a need can also include constructing or illuminating a need of which the audience may not be aware. For instance, in the above example, investors may not have experience with lawn care, either because they live in an apartment or hire a private company to take care of their property. Not all problems that exist are obvious to an audience, and so sometimes speakers need to work extra hard to establish a need before persuading an audience to act. In short, the Motivated Sequence recognizes that a speaker needs to both raise awareness of a problem and create a need to address it.

Once the need is established, you next must produce a way to satisfy the need. It would be tremendously awkward, if not unethical, to tell people there is a problem but not give them a way to solve it! Monroe labels this step "satisfaction" because it is the point in the message where the solution is provided and couched in a way that it firmly satisfies the need. This can be accomplished by proposing a change to a specific policy or through encouraging an audience to take a particular course of action. Here is where you must offer solid reasoning and evidence that illustrates how your proposed solution satisfies the need and is an appropriate and effective remedy for the problem facing the community. We must be mindful, however, that we do not fall into the trap of using reasoning fallacies in an effort to achieve our goal. The means of satisfying the need, and the tools we use to tell the audience about those means, are just as important as the end goal of attaining audience support and action. So, let us look at how we might go about accomplishing the satisfaction step in Monroe's Motivated Sequence.

In the example regarding the new lawn care product, satisfaction is achieved through providing a product that does the work of two items at a lower cost. In this case, the speaker needs to show how the product fulfills the personal need or desire for the audience. If, for example, you tell an audience that bad breath is both unhealthy and unattractive and thus they need to keep it from occurring, then you need to tell them that the path to satisfying that need to avoid bad breath can be fulfilled by purchasing and using Colgate toothpaste, for example.

Monroe's Motivated Sequence does not stop at satisfaction, however, as the next step is getting the audience to visualize fulfilling the need. Visualization uses concrete language and calls upon listeners to actually see themselves as the instruments of satisfying the established need. It helps the speaker further connect listeners with the issue, its solution, and the speaker by getting them to picture a future where the need has been fulfilled. Such efforts employ both emotional and logical appeals to the audience. Ultimately, when listeners can see themselves taking part in an action that effectively satisfies a need for either themselves or the community, it becomes a simple task to call them to action—the final step of Monroe's Motivated Sequence.

All told, Monroe's Motivated Sequence represents a modernized pattern of organization for a balanced persuasive appeal to an audience. It is also more common in everyday experience than you might think. Commercials employ it to craft quick and effective persuasive appeals for products. We also use it when trying to persuade friends and families to do something or go somewhere. Its five steps are easy to follow as both a speaker and an audience. This strategy is also most effective when immediate action is sought.

STRUCTURING YOUR MESSAGE

Outlines are one of the most crucial components of a properly organized speech, and they are not simple things. In fact, most speeches and situations you will encounter call for two outlines. First, you develop a full sentence preparation outline which essentially works as your speech draft. Then, after practicing with this outline until you are comfortable with it, you will reduce it to a much shorter speaking outline. This appendix first provides the principles that guide the creation of an effective outline. It then gives you directions and models for how to format a full sentence outline. Finally, it explains why outlines are much more useful than drafts, and ultimately how you may change full sentence outlines into speaking outlines so you do not read off your materials during your speech. Keep in mind, though, no matter how good your outline, if you do not practice with it your speech will not be as successful as you want it to be.

Outlining Principles

Much like the other aspects of public speaking, the process of outlining is grounded in theory. Many people believe that simply establishing bullet points or jotting down some notes is enough to call something an outline, but that is not the case. Outlines, in fact, are formal structures that organize content, but it is important to remember that the elements of an outline are not a part of the content of a speech. There are three tenets of outlining theory that are important to keep in mind when crafting an outline for a speech: subordination, coordination, and division.. In this section we will discuss each of the three principles relevant to developing outlines for speeches, but first detail the symbolization technique to be followed in an effective outline.

Outlines are formal constructs that help organize the elements of a speech through the use of consistent symbolization. The symbols refer to things like main points and sub-points within the three main parts of the speech. As such, those three parts—the introduction, body, and conclusion—are not indicated by symbols. The first level within each part of the speech consists of main points, and these main points are indicated by Roman numerals. The second level, consisting of those sub-points related to the main points on the first level, are indicated by capital letters. A third level might also become necessary if you have a sub-sub-point, or an item that relates to the sub-point designated by a capital letter. Items on this level are indicated by Arabic numerals. Here is a sketch of how the symbol system for an outline works:

Body (denotes the part of the speech)
  I. Main point
    A. Subpoint (related to main point above)
      1. Sub-subpoint (related to sub-point A above)
      2. Sub-subpoint (related to sub-point A above)
    B. Subpoint (related to main point above)
      1. Sub-subpoint (related to sub-point B above)
      2. Sub-subpoint (related to sub-point B above)
  II. Main point

In this sketch you see how each symbol designates something else, but is related to the level above it. The basics of symbolization also illustrate one of the principles of outlining effectively.

The idea that what appears on one level is more general than the information appearing in levels under it is called subordination. *Subordination* is essentially the organization of a hierarchy of ideas where the most general appear first, followed by subsequently more specific ideas. In the example above you can clearly see how the sub-points each relate to the main point, and that they each have sub-sub-points that are subordinate to specific sub-points. Subordinating ideas allows for a more clear articulation of logic, as well as a more thorough articulation of the relationship between statements. Additionally, subordination is also indicated by the fact that each time you move from main point to main point, or between parts of the speech, the symbols reset. This is demonstrated in the example above as the sub-sub-points for each different sub-point begin with the number one, and do not go 1-2-3-4, as such an order of numbering would indicate they all were related. The use of ranked symbols allows subordination to occur within an outline, and it also allows you to put into practice another principle of effective outlining.

Using symbols to rank items in an outline also allows for coordination of ideas and concepts. *Coordination* refers to the notion that all information on the same level should have the same significance. So, looking at the template from a few moments ago, all Roman numerals indicate main points, while all capital letters are sub-points. Even though these items will be different in content, their meaning and significance is the same as indicated by their appearance on the same level of an outline. Subordination and coordination are the first two principles of effective outlining, and now we will cover the final principle.

Consider that each time you provide sub-points related to a main point, or even main points to a specific purpose of a speech, you are dividing the information into its component parts. This is important because when you divide something you must have more than one piece after the division occurs. If you divide a dollar between two or three people, all three do not end up with one dollar, right? *Division* is the third principle of outlining, and it states that in order to divide a point you need to end up with two or more items. So, in terms of symbols within an outline, there can never be a Roman numeral "I" without there being at least a Roman numeral "II"; there can never be an "A" without at least a "B"; and, there can never be a "1" without at least a "2."

Now that we have covered the three basic principles of outlining and detailed the symbolization system used within an outline, we can discuss more specifically the components of a full sentence preparation outline and a speaking outline.

Preparation Outline Components

After you conduct research on your topic, identify the types of information you found, and formulate your specific purpose and thesis statement (or argument) you begin constructing your speech. The natural temptation for anyone is to sit down and write a draft in essay format first; however, this is a dangerous proposition. Instead you should outline your speech structure using traditional formatting. The outline you create after gathering and organizing information for your speech is called a preparation outline. A *preparation outline* is essentially detailed outline that uses full sentences next to symbols in an effort to help you organize the speech. They identify all the main components of an outline discussed in this textbook. They clearly separate the three main parts of the speech: introduction, body and conclusion. In this section of the appendix we will discuss and illustrate how outlines work to organize the components of your speech.

Introductions need to accomplish five main goals, and outlines help ensure you do just that. First, introductions need to get the attention of the audience. They then need to state your thesis or argument, which simultaneously introduces the topic of your speech and makes it relevant your audience. Third, the introduction needs to establish your credibility on the topic. Then the introduction needs to preview the main body of the speech. Finally, you need to finish the introduction by transitioning to the body of your speech. Let's look at how an outline organizes information and helps you accomplish these goals.

Introduction
   I.   Attention-getter
   II. Introduce topic
   III. Thesis statement [introduces topic/relates to audience]
   IV. Credibility statement
   V.   Preview statement
        A. Preview first main point
        B. Preview second main point
[Transition to body]

It is important to note that if it takes more than one sentence to accomplish the attention-getter, thesis statement, or credibility statement then according to the outlining principles we discussed earlier you drop down and use capital letters to continue that segment of your speech. Doing that allows you to subordinate your ideas and more clearly demonstrate an organized and logical speech.

Also notice that the transition does not receive a symbol designation. This is because the outline must follow the principle of coordination, whereby each symbol designates items of the same level of significance. Transitions are not main points of an introduction or any part of the speech for that matter. They also are not sub-points or subordinate ideas to other elements of the section of the speech. For that reason they are "set aside" in their own place in an outline.

The body of a speech follows the same principles that the introduction does, but contains different elements. The body, for instance, does not contain attention-getters and credibility statements; rather, it includes main points and sub-points. Like introductions, however, it does make use of transitions between main points. Additionally, you may again recall from Chapter Ten that the body of a speech makes use of internal previews and internal summaries. These are similar to the preview at the end of the introduction, but tend to more condensed and work to keep the audience connected with the speech's thesis or argument. Let's look at how the body of a speech is structured within an outline.

Body
    I. Main point #1
      [Internal Preview]
      A. Subpoint
      B. Subpoint
         1. Sub-subpoint
         2. Sub-subpoint
      C. Subpoint
  [Transition]
    II. Main point #2
      A. Subpoint
         1. Sub-subpoint
         2. Sub-subpoint
      B. Subpoint
      [Internal Summary]
  [Transition]
    III. Main point #3
      A. Subpoint
         1. Sub-subpoint
         2. Sub-subpoint
      B. Subpoint
      C. Subpoint
  [Transition]

There are several things to notice in this example. First, you see where internal previews and internal summaries are typically inserted. Internal previews fit at the start of a main point as a way to orient listeners to what they should listen to in the immediate future. Internal summaries work best after at least the second main point as a means to recap what you have already covered. It is also important to note that internal previews and internal summaries are placed in brackets the same way transitions are for the same reason: they are not main points, sub-points or sub-sub-points.

One final aspect of constructing the body of a speech that outlines can help with is determining the number of main points. Most speeches that you will encounter should include 2-4 main points within the body. This is due to two factors: time and focus. The shorter the speech the fewer main points you can have because they take time to develop and explain. Also, the more main points you have the harder it is for you and your audience to focus on what is important.

Conclusions are essential when it comes to making sure your audience understands the important concepts within your speech, and outlines help here as well. Just like the main components of an introduction, the central tenets of a conclusion can be laid out properly in an outline. Conclusions contain three main elements. First, you need a signpost to indicate you are beginning to wrap up the speech. Some instructors place the signpost at the end of the body with the transition from the final main point, but we have put it in the conclusion; the important thing to remember is that it indicates the end of the speech is about to begin. Additionally, you should be aware that many instructors have a pet peeve about hearing "in conclusion," so it is best to consider avoiding using that phrase as your signpost. After signaling the end of the speech, conclusions need to restate the thesis and summarize the main points of the speech. Finally, conclusions need to contain a clincher. Let's look at how conclusions are structured within an outline:

> **Conclusion**
> I. Signpost
> II. Summary [restate thesis]
>   A. Restate main point
>   B. Restate main point
>   C. Restate main point
> III. Clincher

In this example you begin with the signpost that indicates the speech has arrived at a conclusion. Then, the summary begins with a brief restatement of the thesis or argument and continues with restating the main points. This illustrates the principles of subordination and division in that restating the main points relates to the summary and thesis statement, while also showing how there was more than one main point that needed to be restated. Finally, the clincher statement finishes the conclusion.

So, outlines are formal structures that allow you to organize the content of your speech in a logical fashion. In this part of the appendix we looked at how the structure of an outline allows you to ensure that you incorporate all the elements of an effective speech in an appropriate and logical way. In the next section we will move from the form of outlines to a brief discussion of the linguistic content and why outlines are more useful than drafts.

Speaking Outline

After practicing with your full sentence outline you will become more conversational in your delivery and will not need to look at your outline as much. Additionally, you will begin to remember the information in the full-sentence outline rather than needing to read it. So, to help you deliver your speech in a more natural and conversational style you use a *speaking outline*, or a truncated form of your full sentence preparation outline that does not include complete sentences unless you are using direct quotations from another source. Speaking outlines are easy to develop from a completed full sentence outline.

The same format you used to create your full-sentence preparation outline applies to a speaking outline. When you create your speaking outline you still retain all the formatting elements of the full sentence preparation outline in terms of Roman numerals, capital letters and numbers, and you still follow the principles of outlining we discussed earlier. The only things that do not appear on a speaking outline but appear in a full-sentence preparation outline are in-text citations, your stated general purpose, and your stated specific purpose.

The core fundamental difference between the two outlines is that a speaking outline does not include sentences unless you use a direct quotation, in which case getting the quote correct is of paramount importance. There are many words in every sentence you write that you do not need to see so that you remember to say them. Let's look at this brief full-sentence example and see if we can identify unnecessary words:

> **Introduction**
>
> I. Attention-getter: Imagine yourself stranded, along with about 50 other people, on a desert island after a plane crash.
>
> A. Well, that is the premise of the critically acclaimed television show *Lost*.

When looking to cut, look specifically at the full sentences. Obviously, the terms "with," "on," "that," "is," "the," "of," and "a" do not need to appear on a speaking outline because you could easily insert them when speaking without a prompt. But what else could go after practicing? What about the entire sub-point? It would make sense to delete the sub-point w-because it should flow naturally after the attention-getter. In fact, you might be able to deliver this attention-getter from a mere handful of words, such as this:

> **Introduction**
>
>   I. Imagine/stranded/50 people/island /plane crash. *Lost*

This is what a speaking outline contains: words and phrases from the original prose in the full-sentence outline separated by backslashes.

Even though we believe we have made a case for the use of outlines in this manner, we feel it necessary to answer some questions you might have regarding format. First we will counter those who might suggest bullet-points instead of outlines. Bullet-points do not visually display the logical hierarchy behind the speech and also create the danger of going off on tangents and not making your case to the audience as clear as possible. Bullet-points are, for all intents and purposes, a list of items with no clear connection. Outlines provide that connection for the speaker and, consequently, the audience.

Others also might agree to an outline, but instead of indenting the tiers of information appropriately believe that it wastes space and the outlines would make as much sense all starting at one side of the page. This, although better than bullet-points, still does not clearly differentiate each level of information and its connection to the rest of the material in the speech for either the speaker or the audience. In short, it fails to properly employ the principle of subordination. So, the proper indentation of each level is essential for the speaker and the audience.

Outlining your speech begins early in the speaking process and continues until you deliver the presentation. It allows you to organize your thoughts and information into a coherent order. It provides you with something to practice from and thereby develop your speaking voice and rhythm, something altogether different from your written voice and rhythm. Most importantly, outlining is the manner by which a speaker arranges his speech from beginning to end.

Whether you are debating policy positions, factual accuracies, or the value of one solution over another, or are calling an audience to act, you can use a wide variety of organizational patterns in a persuasive message. Just like explanations, the arrangement of persuasive messages largely depends on the formulation of your specific purpose. Once that is identified, however, the message can quickly take shape. Knowing the main parts of a message and how you can organize your main points will help you to prepare your presentation. The most crucial step in message creation is organizing the product of your research into a cogent, coherent, and persuasive message.

For a summary of the organizational patterns for persuasive speeches covered in this chapter, see Table 10.3.

Table 10.3	Organizational Patterns for Persuasive Speeches
	• Problem-solution
	• Problem-cause-solution
	• Comparative advantage
	• Monroe's Motivated Sequence

SUMMARY

In this chapter we discussed the components of introductions and conclusions for advocacy messages. Most notably we identified the similarities and differences between constructing the parts of a persuasive message and those of an explanation. We also provided some suggestions for effective organizational patterns for persuasive appeals. Finally, we encourage you to look at the chapter on outlining to help provide the structure and coherence that you need to develop your persuasive message.

KEY TERMS

comparative advantage   257

Monroe's Motivated Sequence   258

problem-cause-solution order   257

problem-solution order   254

THINK ABOUT IT

1. What are the four ways you can organize the main points in a persuasive message?
2. What are the five parts of Monroe's Motivated Sequence?

REVIEW QUESTIONS

1. Is there ever a good time to present your strongest argument first?
2. How could you determine whether your credibility increases or decreases during a persuasive message?
3. Is it ethical to induce emotions in a conclusion, or in any part of the speech? Why or why not?
4. How could you use the Motivated Sequence in everyday language?

1. Working in a group of three members, develop several different ways to get an audience's attention. Then, state several ways you could establish credibility. Finally, figure out a way that statements could both get the attention of the audience and establish credibility, thereby killing two birds with one stone.

2. In this chapter we discussed Monroe's Motivated Sequence. Divide into groups of three and assign each group a product on the market right now. Give each group 10 minutes to create a "commercial" in which Monroe's Motivated Sequence is used to sell the assigned product. Every person in each group must have a speaking role in the skit.

ENDNOTES

1. Toastmasters International, "What Is Toastmasters?" http://www.toastmasters.org/MainMenuCategories/WhatisToastmasters.aspx (accessed September 19, 2008).

2. Toastmasters International, "Community Service," http://www.toastmasters.org/MainMenuCategories/WhatisToastmasters/CommunityService.aspx (accessed September 19, 2008).

3. Quintilian, *The Institutes of Oratory,* translated by H. E. Butler, Loeb Classical Library (Cambridge, MA: Harvard University Press, 1980), IV, i, 5.

4. Raymie E. McKerrow, Bruce E. Gronbeck, Douglas Ehninger, and Alan H. Monroe, Principles and Types of Speech Communication, 15th Ed. (New York: Longman: 2003).

5. Winston Churchill, "Blood, Toil, Tears and Sweat," Speech to the British House of Commons, http://www.historyplace.com/speeches/churchill.htm (accessed June 13, 3011).

6. Ibid.

7. Ibid.

8. Raymie E. McKerrow, Bruce E. Gronbeck, Douglas Ehninger, and Alan H. Monroe, *Principles and Types of Speech Communication,* 15th Ed. (New York: Longman: 2003).

9. W. Charles Redding "An Informal History of Communication at Purdue," http://www.cla.purdue.edu/communication/graduate/informalhistory.pdf.

SCENARIOS

Scenario 1

The UD administration has announced an initiative to develop Saturday classes as part of the regular schedule. The reasoning behind the initiative is that it will alleviate the current problem with classroom space shortages, reduce University operating costs, allow more access to heavily scheduled facilities, and enable students to plan their class work and study time more effectively.

It's your job to persuade a group of students to support this initiative.

1. Choose either the Problem-Solution Order or the Problem-Cause-Solution organizational pattern and construct a brief outline of a persuasive message to accomplish the goal.

2. What are your reasons for selecting the organizational pattern that you used? How is it more appropriate for this application than the one you did not select?

3. How would your approach to the message change if you were trying to persuade members of the University faculty that the Saturday classes proposal was a good idea? Consider that, if adopted, the proposal would add one work day each week for faculty members.

4. How would your approach to organizing this message change if you were arguing against the proposal to an audience of students? Would you consider one of the organization structures listed above, or would you consider one of the other two discussed in the textbook (Monroe's Motivated Sequence or Comparative Advantages)? Explain your selection.

5. Briefly outline a conclusion for the message crafted in Scenario 1 without committing any of the common conclusion errors as described in the textbook.

6. Would the inclusion of a joke in the introduction of this persuasive message be a good idea or a bad idea? How would you capture the attention of the intended audience in an introduction?

Scenario 2 (Performance)

Your group has been tasked with creating a brief one minute advertisement for the University of Dayton. The goal of this segment is to recruit prospective students to the University of Dayton. The message will be broadcast online as well as shown to families and students when they visit UD. It will also air periodically on campus television. Use Monroe's Motivated Sequence to create this advertisement, and make sure you use all elements of the sequence in your advertisement. Write out a script for the advertisement and make sure everyone in the group has a speaking role. Be prepared to perform your advertisement for the class.

Scenario 3

Construct a brief outline for an argument in support or against one of the following claims. Be sure to use proper outlining techniques and also identify which organizational structure you will use to make your argument. Include and highlight the following: a rebuttal or refutation, two main points, introduction, conclusion, transitions and an emotional appeal.

1. UD should institute a policy prohibiting alcohol on campus.

2. There should be a minimum age requirement for Facebook users.

3. College athletes should be paid.

Scenario 4

Work with your group to generate ideas for the topic "stopping air pollution." Have each person in the group take one step of Monroe's Motivated Sequence and then put your ideas together to create an outline.

Civility

PracticallySPEAKING

In the Spring of 2010, the University of Mount Union's Regula Center for Public Service, the University of Akron's Ray C. Bliss Institute, and Cleveland State University's Levin College of Urban Affairs collaborated on an investigation of the quality of public discourse in Ohio. This Ohio Civility Project brought together a retired political reporter for the *Columbus Dispatch*, a former Lieutenant Governor, columnist for the *Cleveland Plain Dealer* and a former Minority Leader in the State Senate in a panel to discuss the state of civility in Ohio politics. This group agreed that incivility is a major problem in Ohio politics, and this position was supported by a summer 2011 poll that found almost three quarters of Ohioans felt incivility was either a "very serious problem," or "a somewhat serious problem."

The Ohio Civility Project issued a white paper on the subject that pointed to four primary causes of incivility in Ohio politics. Three of these they called "initiators," or groups that instigate uncivil discourse because of the benefits they gain from behaving badly. These three drivers were career-minded politicians, the dictate to win campaigns, and financial windfall provided to media by controversy and conflict. The public, though, did not drive incivility, but rather responded to to it based on the emotional power in the message itself.

In addition to the causes of uncivil behavior, the Ohio Civility Project also identified some causes of this misbehavior. These include self-interest by politicians, disagreement over issues and policies, the advent of the Internet, and general poor manners by individual people. All of these, they argue, work together to intensify and augment the quantity and quality of uncivil behavior and communication in Ohio today.

Sadly, this trend is not restricted to Ohio. Just look at cable news programs that deliberately pit people of differing position in a contest of who can yell the loudest on their shows; or look at people who use cell phones in movie theatres, smoke inside restaurants, fail to do the dishes in a shared dorm room, and who do not engage their neighbors in friendly conversation. In fact, the lack of civility in our culture has become so pervasive that college campus, like the University of Dayton, are expanding their training and focus for students to help instill civility in tomorrow's leaders. Others are joining the cause too, like Johns Hopkins University which now has the Civility Project, Project Civility that now runs at Rutgers University, and the consortium behind the Ohio Civility Project consists of colleges in that state[1].

In this chapter we will explore civility and how it can enhance our ability to communicate with one another and succeed in our professions. First, we will attempt to reconnect you with what exactly civility means and how it relates to ourselves. We will also identify some basic components to civil behavior. Second, we will explore how civility functions in society today. Finally, we will briefly analyze some areas of contemporary life where we could and should more effectively incorporate civility.

---

1 See: The Ohio Civility Project: Report and Recommendations, http://www.uakron.edu/bliss/about-us/ohio-civility-project. dot?newsId=2328165, Last accessed April 28, 2014.

PREP QUESTIONS

1. Describe the five concepts that contribute to the definition of civility.

2. Describe the relationship between self-esteem, self-control, and restraint as it relates to being assertive.

3. Define facework and face threats.

4. Describe the three faces we seek to present to others.

5. Explain what it means to say that image management is a process.

6. Define self-monitoring and how it is done. Compare and contrast between high and low self-monitors.

7. Provide two examples of how silence can be interpreted.

8. List the three foundational behaviors of civility. Discuss whether civility always means agreement.

9. Explain whether it is possible to multitask.

10. Explain what it is we disagree with when we disagree. Discuss whether disagreement means rejection of the entire message or just parts.

11. List the eight behaviors for a civil interaction.

12. Consider the impact social media has had on civility in society. Are the expectations for civility the same for online media versus face-to-face interactions?

13. Explain whether or not civility in oral communication requires every participant to play the role of sender and receiver simultaneously. Why?

DEFINING CIVILITY

Many people today confuse the notion of civility with a form of fakery, where people hide their own feelings about something or someone to avoid conflict. Others view civility and politeness as a form of weakness that invites bullying and leads to sacrificing personal positions, goals, and feelings for no good reason. These misconceptions make the idea of civil behavior appear useless and ineffective in society. Unfortunately, by abandoning the practice of civility we create a society that is closer to Thomas Hobbes' pessimistic notion of the natural state of man, which is to say it is "nasty, brutish, and short." [3]

Instead, it is useful to conceive of civility in relation to "civilization" and "being civilized." *Civility* in these contexts does not mean fakery. Rather, it means the ability to have lasting, stable, and peaceful interactions with others. If we consider the world we live in today as civilized, it is because we practice civility, and without treating such practices as sincere we risk degrading the civilization in which we live. In this part of the chapter we will explore some of the components that serve as the foundation of civility. Understand that each of these is a component of civility, but on their own they are not synonymous with it. We will begin with some definitional terms, and then discuss how civility functions with regard to the way we present ourselves. We will conclude this section with an overview of some civil behaviors in different contexts.

civility
the use of tact when dealing with others; a genuine and reciprocal expression of respect for ourselves and other people through our actions and statements

Components of Civility

"Civility" is a broad term that encompasses parts of several other concepts in its application. Any one of these behaviors on its own does not constitute civility, but rather their combination helps lead us to an understanding of what it means to actually be civil. In this section of the chapter we will discuss five different concepts that when taken together create a more substantial definition of civility.

Politeness

We mentioned a moment ago that civility is often confused with politeness. This is understandable because politeness is a component of civility; however, the two are not the same thing because civility encompasses more than simply being polite. The term *polite* refers to showing consideration for others in accordance

polite
showing consideration for others in accordance with social decorum

with social decorum. At times it can mean being polished or elegant, but on a basic level politeness is the use of tact in dealings with others. Politeness, therefore, may be best understood in contrast to rudeness, which is acting in a way that violates social decency or demonstrates a lack of social skills and appreciation for others. On the one hand, people who are deemed polite have made some effort to consider other people and how they feel. On the other hand, we sometimes view politeness in others not as a nicety, but as a tool to manipulate and deceive us or as a condescending form of communication. [4]

To understand this odd approach to politeness, let's look at how the term is used. If we attend a concert or a comedy club act and the performance is not very good we still feel the need to give "polite applause" to those on stage. If we cannot, or do not, want to go to a reception or other event we issue a "polite reply" telling the host we will not attend. Then there are times where we feel that the truth may hurt someone's feelings, so we deliver a "polite lie." Each of these instances makes it appear as though we are hiding our feelings, or protecting the feelings of others at the expense of honesty. Politeness is also seen as indirect communication, but one can be direct and polite at the same time. We often conflate directness in communication with rudeness, by being short and not respecting the other person. Envision a scenario in which a person in your class whom you do not know invites you to join a study group, but you prefer studying alone. You could tell very bluntly, "I'm not interested," or you could send the same message by saying, "Thanks for the invitation but I prefer to study on my own." The latter is polite, the former rude.

As you can see, politeness can mask our own feelings, but being civil requires us to assert our feelings in a respectful manner. A civil person is honest, but not in a way that offends the other party. Civil politeness requires that we not be polite just to help spare others the truth, but to make both them and us feel good about

our deeds and actions through an honest and respectful delivery of information. For instance, there should not be a need to issue a polite lie, because it comes across as disingenuous and simply plays upon the perception most people have today when someone is "just being polite." Rather, polite civility issues the truth in a way that does not intentionally hurt anyone involved. This is, as you can imagine, a challenging task to accomplish. Politeness, though, is only one part of the civility equation.

Good Manners

The second component of civility might remind you of children because they are constantly reminded to say "please," and "thank you" as an element of good manners. *Good manners* refers

good manners
behaviors that societies deem as appropriate and positive ways of interacting with others

to behaviors that societies deem as appropriate and positive ways of interacting with others. As you can imagine, when understood this way good manners are not restricted to children, nor are they as simple as just saying "please" and "thank you." In fact, we have even gone so far as a society to police certain types of manners to ensure they are practiced.[5]

There are policies in place in a variety of contexts by both companies and government entities designed to promote the practice of good manners. When we go to the movies we are asked to silence cell phones before the start of the film because holding a conversation and texting during a show distract others from enjoying the movie. Additionally, one of the reasons behind the Federal Aviation Administration's regulations regarding cell phone usage during a flight is, to be sure, safety; however, it is also meant to keep people from having phone conversations in crowded areas. After all, you do not want others to know your personal business, and they do not want to be disturbed by your conversation. These are just two examples of public efforts to maintain good manners.

Despite policies and rules regarding certain behaviors, not all good manners can and should be legislated. In fact, there are other good manners people should practice simply because they demonstrate an appreciation for other people. Here are a few behaviors that are usually considered good manners in American culture with which you may or may not be familiar:

1. Be on time for meetings and appointments.
2. Don't gloat when you win, or sulk when you lose.
3. Don't talk with your mouth full.
4. Patiently wait in line.
5. Don't ask intimate or sensitive questions—even if you ask permission first.
6. Don't make rude or sarcastic comments that devalue the work of others.

These are just a few good manners that respect the other person in an interaction. Such behaviors are a core element of civility and represent practicing politeness. Civility is, however, even more than being genuinely polite and practicing good manners.

Courteousness

A third component of civility is *courteousness*, which refers to showing consideration and attention to others. The term itself derives from "court," but not in the legal sense—rather the courts of kings where people who sought to speak with the monarch displayed an elegance and deference to those of higher stature. Today, courtesy is not as formal, nor does it involve status; rather we talk about certain behaviors as being "common courtesy." Such behaviors are often understood as polite, good manners, and civil, as well.[6]

courtesy
showing consideration and attention to others

We often refer to courtesy as *common* because it is generally expected that everyone exhibit these basic behaviors. Common courtesies include things like holding a door open for the next person to come through, standing up to greet someone when they enter your room or office, and acknowledging drivers who allow you into traffic in front of them. These are the small gestures we can do in a day that cost nothing but generate good feeling by letting others know we value and pay attention to them. At their heart, common courtesies involve an understanding of one's surroundings and respect for others, which brings us to our next component of civility.

Respect for Others

respect
....
an acknowledgement of the inherent humanity and existence of other people

Civility requires that we be polite, practice good manners, and extend courtesy to others because it is fundamentally about respecting other people. By *respect* we mean to say an acknowledgement of the inherent humanity and dignity of other people. Respect does not require deference to others, but rather an acknowledgement of them and an attempt to understand how they may feel about a statement, action, or event. One of the worst things we can do to other people is ignore them or behave as though their thoughts, feelings, and opinions do not matter. When such things are done to us we get upset and feel like we do not belong. There is no situation where behaving in such a way toward another person is acceptable.

Respect can come in different levels. It can mean we place individuals or their opinions in high esteem and value them more than others because of an existing relationship or some type of expertise they bring to the table. It can also mean an appreciation for an honor or even the position a person holds. At a minimum, however, we should respect everyone as individuals and acknowledge their feelings and thoughts. Doing so will encourage reciprocity where they return that respect in their interactions with you. This is the road to creating a culture of civility. There is, however, one more dimension of civility we must discuss.

Assertiveness

assertive
....
the ability to clearly and confidently state our positions

After detailing the first four elements of civility, it may seem as though it largely asks us to suppress our own ideas and thoughts in deference to others, but nothing could be further from the truth. In fact, civility demands honesty and the ability to clearly and confidently state our positions. This is what it means to be *assertive*, but it is essential we assert ourselves respectfully and not in an effort to dominate or devalue other people and their ideas. Assertiveness is a vital part of being happy and creating a civil society.

It may seem easier to simply try to please others by allowing them to state their positions while we keep ours to ourselves, but such actions actually do not demonstrate a respect for ourselves. One of the hardest things to assert is also the first word many children learn: the ability to say "no." As P. M. Forni, a noted Italian professor who teaches and writes about civility at Johns Hopkins University, notes, "'No' to others is nothing but a 'yes' to ourselves," and in doing so we aren't "taking something that belongs to others; we are simply keeping something that is rightfully ours."[7] Simply put, when people ask something of us, we are not required to give it, nor are we required to explain why to them though we may feel it right and necessary to do so in some situations. The ability to say "no" to others and "yes" to ourselves is a key element of civility.

We may believe that saying "no" will injure, or perhaps even destroy, our relationship with the other person, but in not protecting our own interests and time we might be doing that anyway.[8] In freely giving our time, treasure and talents to others, even when we do not want to, we may create an unbalanced relationship with the other person. By this, we mean the other person may come to expect us to always give of ourselves and may not reciprocate. It also can engender our quiet and unexpressed resentment of the other and consistent devaluing of our own ideas, time, and feelings. This is not healthy, nor is it civil. Being assertive simply means we respect ourselves just as much as we respect others. Without this final piece, civility is nothing more than sacrificing oneself to the interests of the other. To that end, we define civility as a genuine and reciprocal expression of respect for ourselves and other people through our actions and statements.

Now that we have explained the characteristics of civility, we will turn our attention to how we practice civility. In the next section we will discuss some communicative dimensions of civility as it relates to how we present ourselves. We will then follow that with covering some basic principles of civil behavior.

Civility and Self-Expression

Creating a civil society naturally involves the way we communicate with each other. This occurs in many different contexts and requires a specific set of abilities for us to effectively, respectfully, and civilly interact with each other. In this part of the chapter we will discuss this set of skills and how they relate to civility.

Facework

Everyone desires others to see them in the best possible light, and so we present our face in a manner that we believe creates that type of impression. The behaviors we employ to maintain this positive image with others are called *facework*. There are three faces we seek to present to others, and each occurs within a different context. These faces also are sometimes threatened by the actions of others or external events we cannot control.

facework
the behaviors we exhibit to maintain a positive impression of ourselves by other people

We all have a desire to be liked and appreciated. In fact, social relationships and our own psychological and physical health depend on such connections with others. The need to have others like and respect us is fulfilled through the expression of our *fellowship face*. We want others to perceive us as approachable, likeable, and friendly, so we try to create that impression through the way we interact with others. This type of behavior can especially be seen in our initial interactions with new people we meet.

fellowship face
an effort to fulfill the need to have others like and respect us

Take, for example, the case of Lynn who has just moved into her dormitory room. During the move-in process she meets her new roommate, Olivia, who is still unloading her belongings from her car. After introducing herself to Olivia, Lynn offers to help unload Olivia's car and move her into the room. This behavior is a manifestation of civility, and also creates a positive fellowship face for Lynn with Olivia.

The second face we seek to create is less about developing friendships and more about engendering respect from others. When we want others to listen to what we have to say on a topic, we both need and want them to see us as competent, and so the *competence face* refers to efforts to promote our expertise on subjects to others. We all are good at something, and we like it when others recognize our talents, so the competence face is how we want others to see us when it comes to those things we know or are good at doing. This is especially important when we are asked to explain material to non-experts, because we want them to respect what we have to say.

competence face
our efforts to promote our expertise on subjects to others so they respect us

The third, and final, face we seek to maintain with others is related to assertiveness. We all want to be seen as capable individuals in our own right who can make decisions and take action on our own without the assistance of others. This is the expression of our *autonomy face*, which refers to when we seek to avoid others' making decisions and doing things for us by being seen as capable in our own right. When we are assertive and respect ourselves, we demonstrate this autonomy, and when we do not we are seen by others as more dependent. As with anything, we are not entirely autonomous or dependent, but we do need to maintain the perception we can do some things on our own.

autonomy face
the perception that we can do things on our own and our desire to avoid others making decisions for us

Sometimes we encounter things that threaten to damage the image we work to present to others. These *face threats* can come from both internal and external causes. For instance, we may feel like we did not do enough research, practice our presentation enough, or even study enough for an exam. These internal feelings turn into threats to our competence face as the effects of those beliefs may make us appear as less of an expert to others. On the other hand, we may also be in a situation where others around us make jokes at our expense, and we feel the need to respond because these jokes damage our ability for others to like or respect us. How we manage threats to our face is just as important as the face itself. Facework is directly tied to civility, because when people are rude, lack good manners or are not courteous we perceive it as a threat to our face and thus conflict can ensue.

face threats
things that threaten to damage the image we work to present to others

Image Management

We have no single image that we present to all parties. For instance, we seek to have our parents perceive us one way, our friends another, and our colleagues at work yet another way. We also try to maintain consistency with the images each group has of us. You may be familiar with the term "two-faced", which is what we sometimes call people who present two different and conflicting images of themselves in different sorts of situations. Managing multiple images with various groups is both collaborative and complex, but effective management of our situations is a hallmark of being civil.

image management
the constant attempt to control the presentation of ourselves to others

When we say that *image management* is collaborative, we mean it is a constant result of the interaction between ourselves and others. We seek to present

SPOTLIGHTING THEORISTS: P. M. FORNI

P. M. Forni

Pier Massimo Forni is an award-winning Italian literature professor at Johns Hopkins University, where he has taught for the majority of his career. Forni graduated from the University of Pavia in 1974, and received his doctorate in Italian Literature in 1981 from UCLA, where he studied the works of Italian Renaissance author Giovannie Boccaccio. Over his career his work moved toward a discussion of ethics and a commentary on civility in society, particularly the United States, his adoptive home.

In 1997 Forni cofounded the Johns Hopkins Civility Project, which brought together academics and community outreach programs in an effort to assess "the significance of civility, manners, and politeness in contemporary society." He also co-directed an international symposium in 1998 entitled "Reassessing Civility: Forms and Values at the End of the Century." He has delivered numerous workshops and written several books, including *Choosing Civility: Twenty-Five Rules of Considerate Conduct, The Thinking Life*, and *The Civility Solution: What to Do When People are Rude.*

Dr. Forni's work on civility has appeared in a number of press outlets, and he himself has made appearances on numerous television programs to discuss civility in contemporary society. He currently teaches at Johns Hopkins University, where he is also director of the Civility Initiative. His work has inspired similar efforts at a number of other institutions.[9]

ourselves in a specific manner, and other people either accept or do not accept that presentation. In the event they accept our image, we continue to behave in ways that reinforce that image with that particular group. If, however, our image does not seem to be accepted by others, we may adjust and adapt our own understanding of ourselves. This is a way of managing behavior and personal interactions with both ourselves and others in mind.

Image management is also complex because of the multiple audiences with whom we seek to cultivate relationships. To say we present ourselves one way to our friends is even a bit too broad, because we all have different groups of friends with whom we associate and each sees us differently. For instance, a college athlete may have friends on a sports team, in the dormitory, in classes, and from high school who attend different institutions. Each of these groups knows different versions of the student, but the student seeks to maintain an image with each group. We also present different images to our family. This gets even more complex and difficult to manage when different groups are in the same situation. Just think about the first time you and a significant other had dinner with your parents. Which image did you seek to present? This is the challenge of image management, but when we adhere to the principles of civility it lessens the burden of such complicated interactions.

Self-Monitoring

self-monitoring
....
the ability to be aware
of your own behaviors
and statements and
how they affect other
people; can be either
high or low

To effectively manage our image and present faces the way we want we must be good communicators, and a major aspect of competent communication is *self-monitoring*. This skill refers to the ability to be aware of your own behaviors and statements and how they affect other people. To identify your ability level when it comes to self-monitoring, think about it as a line, somewhere upon which you fall. At one end of the line there are low self-monitors, and at the other end are high self-monitors.

Low self-monitors speak and act without thinking of what the effect on others will be. In short, they do not pay attention to what they are saying and doing beyond the immediate moment. This can often cause hurt feelings, emotional outbursts, and misunderstandings and it cultivates the image of a selfish individual. Being civil requires that we think before we speak and act, thus making it necessary for people who tend to act and speak impulsively to become better self-monitors.

High self-monitors, on the other hand, are aware of their behaviors and statements, as well as how they will potentially affect and influence those around them. As we have discussed, being civil requires a genuine respect for others and yourself, and so high self-monitoring is a necessary skill set for a civil society. It allows us to think through what we want to say, and then say it in a manner that respects the other party while still maintaining our own ability to assert our position. It may sound easy enough, but monitoring and thinking about our behavior and statements before we do or say something is a very challenging task.

Self-Restraint

self-restraint
....
the ability to refrain
from comments until
the time and tone are
appropriate to do so

It might seem a bit odd to include *self-restraint* as a principle of civil communication when we already said you must be able to assert yourself and your ideas, but it is important to remember to be balanced. Just because you have an idea or a thought does not mean it must be stated or asserted. In fact, learning *when* to assert yourself is an important situational skill in any profession. To borrow from country singer Kenny Rogers, you have to know when to hold them and know when to fold them.

It is not always imperative that you respond, let alone respond immediately, to comments from others. In fact, often it is best if you wait to do so, especially in emotionally charged situations. If you are upset over something, a grade for example, wait a day before contacting your professor to discuss it so that you can have a calmer and more rational conversation. If someone says something to you that you disagree with, consider what your goal is in responding. The chances of changing the other person's mind may be very small, in which case you may not even want to say something. P. M. Forni, the Italian civility scholar we mentioned a little while ago, notes that silence is not a failure to communicate, but rather an informed choice to process and reflect upon information. Shooting from the hip in response to something often creates a more combative and negative environment that invites uncivil behavior.

Self-restraint does not imply you deny your own right and ability to assert yourself; instead, it calls for us to concentrate on the best possible way to assert our opinions and positions. Timing and tone are everything. Remember that people will respond to the tone of your voice first, even before they think about what you said. The tone with which you speak can go a long way toward creating a supportive climate for conversation and preserving civility in an interaction. The same words said with a different tone can convey completely opposite things to another person, so measuring your tone of voice and paying attention to the emotions you try and convey when speaking is vital for having productive interactions with others, especially when the topics of discussion are sensitive or controversial. Keep this in mind before you choose to respond and take a minute to process what the other party said.

In today's fast paced society we often feel the need to immediately respond, since everyone seems to be available at almost any time thanks to e-mail and cell phones. Just because you receive an e-mail that demands a reply, it does not require that you reply as soon as you are done reading it. Also, just because someone calls in while you are speaking to someone on the other line does not mean you need to answer it. Self-restraint means we must try to control our inclination to "run after something shiny as soon as we see it" and concentrate on the moment in which we currently reside. It is, simply, thinking before acting.

Foundational Civil Behaviors

We could spend an entire book explaining and discussing specific behaviors that are civil, but that is not the aim of the book or this chapter. Instead, we wish to acquaint you with some foundational concepts that inform civil behavior so that they help you understand how to engage in an effective dialogue with other people. To that end, we have covered the root terms of civility and how it relates to the presentation of ourselves to others. The final component of explaining what civility is, however, is a discussion of three foundational behaviors that all civil communication has in common: mutual respect, listening, and disagreeing without being disagreeable.

Mutual Respect

A civil culture depends on its members valuing mutual respect. That is to say, members of society must respect all other members as well as themselves and must be willing to develop and engage in the skills we have discussed in the chapter. Each individual must value the ideas and opinions of others and begin with the precept that everyone seeks the good of the community as whole, until such time as someone demonstrates he or she is not out for that goal. In short, believe in the best that people can be, and respect their values, experiences, and expertise in the same way you wish them to do for you.

Mutual respect is not driven by a person's achievement, position, or title, but rather by his or her inherent humanity and value as a person. All people bring something to the table that we can learn and we must respect that for them to respect what we have to offer. Without genuine mutual respect, we cannot have a

First Inaugural Address
by President John F. Kennedy

Delivered January 20, 1960

John F. Kennedy, a senator from Massachusetts, was elected president in November 1960 and took the oath of office on Friday January 20, 1961. The Democrat, Kennedy, defeated Republican candidate Richard Nixon and took over as the youngest president in U.S. history for the man who was then the oldest ever to hold that office, Dwight Eisenhower. In his narrow victory, Kennedy also became the first Roman Catholic president in American history. At the time the United States was deeply ensconced in the Cold War with the communist Soviet Union, during which both countries aggressively pursued nuclear weapons and fought for influence over smaller states around the globe.

Kennedy wrote the speech along with his close advisor, Ted Sorenson, over the course of three months. At 1,364 words the speech took only 13:59 to deliver, making it the fourth shortest inaugural in presidential history. In the address, which presidents use for many purposes including laying out the broad principles of how they plan to govern, Kennedy sought a more collaborative relationship with countries around the globe, including the Soviet Union. His desire for this was embedded in this call: "So, let us begin anew—remembering on both sides that civility is not a sign of weakness, and sincerity is always subject to proof. Let us never negotiate out of fear, but let us never fear to negotiate. Let both sides explore what problems unite us instead of belaboring those problems which divide us."[11] This quotation illustrates a civil approach to public discussion and debate and shows that even when two sides appear to be at such starkly different positions, there is always an opportunity for engagement.

civil society. This is not to say that everyone must behave this way for it to work; in fact, that is not the case even today. It is, however, an invitation to begin the effort of making society more civil by respecting those with whom we come into contact.

Even at the height of the Cold War our leaders were able to, at times, express mutual respect and a desire for civil interaction. In one of the more famous speeches in the twentieth century, then newly elected President John F. Kennedy used his inaugural address to both assert American ideals and extend an invitation for dialogue and negotiation with the Soviet Union. He actually even mentioned civility specifically in an effort to tone down tensions and begin more collaborative communication with the Soviet Union—a communist country at that time understood as a superpower and chief rival to the United States in international affairs.

Listening

Earlier in this book we discussed listening and how it related to public speaking, but its importance is much broader than simply attending to messages in formal situations. To be civil we must listen to what the other party is saying, in effect giving them our undivided attention. We may believe we can multitask and pay attention to multiple things at once, but this is a myth. In his book *Brain Rules*, John Medina explains that it is actually physically impossible for our brains to focus on two things at once,[10] making paying attention to more than one person impractical in addition to uncivil.

We owe it to others to give them our attention when we expect the same in return when we speak. The idea of listening transcends conversations and speaking situations, to include e-mails, text messages, and phone conversations. We all have had situations in which we tried to do something else while on the phone with a friend, but when we do that we are not truly listening. It would be much better to actually say we needed to do something else and arrange another time to talk, or to even have a shorter more focused conversation in which we actually listen to the other party. Genuine listening is the manifestation of respecting other people and being there with them.

Listening also entails the ability to come to an understanding of what the other person is saying. This may require asking clarifying questions, paraphrasing messages, or other forms of perception checking. Remember that making sure you understand the other person is a hallmark of genuine listening, and not a rude behavior. It does not mean, however, that you agree with the other person, just that you understand them. In fact, the third and final civil behavior we will discuss in this section involves the ability to assert disagreement.

Disagree without Being Disagreeable

As we mentioned earlier, civility requires us to express ourselves and assert our positions. This does not limit itself to moments of agreement. We also must be able to express ourselves when we disagree. Unfortunately, people tend to view agreement and disagreement as the only two options available, when in fact they are not absolutes. More often than not we find ourselves wanting to agree with parts of a person's argument while disagreeing with other aspects of it.

To express such complicated positions in which we both agree and disagree with another person at the same time calls for specific and delicate skills. In order to do this, it is important to first stress areas of agreement with the other party. This establishes a more comfortable climate for the interaction and enables both parties to see the exchange in a positive and constructive light. When focusing on areas of agreement, be as detailed as you would be with those things with which you disagree. Then, after expressing agreement, detail those things with which you disagree and explain why. The explanation is important because it shows you listened to the other party, but have information of your own to offer to the discussion. In more tense situations it may also be necessary to conclude with a statement reinforcing that just because you disagree with all or parts of the other person's argument it does not mean you do not like or appreciate that person. The position is not the person.

Agreement and disagreement are not "all or nothing" propositions. In fact, things are always more complicated than they appear and we must be able to articulate that complexity when we explain how we agree and disagree with someone. By detailing both agreement and disagreement we can preserve aspects of the person's argument without seeming to devalue everything he or she had to say. This respects other people's willingness to express themselves while also explaining yourself appropriately as well.

Now that we have established the basics of civility, we will explore how it has functioned in human history. The idea of respect for other people and ourselves is nothing new, and has played a role throughout human history. In the next part of this chapter we will briefly explore the practice of civility today.

Table 11.1

Behaviors for a Civil Interaction
1. Describe instead of evaluate
2. Focus on the problem, not controlling the outcome
3. Acknowledge the feelings of others
4. Be provisional instead of certain
5. Control your own facial expressions
6. Do not interrupt someone when they are speaking
7. Do not disparage others when they are not present
8. When disagreeing, describe the points with which you disagree and agree

CIVILITY TODAY

The fact of the matter is that civil behavior affects our quality of life in myriad settings, and all it takes is a small effort to take the feelings of others into consideration before acting or speaking. To be sure, every area of our lives is complicated, from the boardroom to the dining room table. But in today's technologically advanced world where we are all so closely and quickly connected, taking a moment to think before we speak and incorporating civility into our approach is more necessary than ever. In this part of the chapter we will discuss some foundational dimensions and variables of every interpersonal interaction, and then briefly explore how we can recognize these aspects of a situation and become more civil in our dealings with others.

Foundational Dimensions of Interpersonal Interactions

In every relationship, from the business world to the classroom to the home, multiple variables influence the way we interact with each other. All of these things are also aspects we must be attuned to in order to effectively incorporate civility into our approach to others. The first of these involves what we will broadly call cultural values, the second involves the power one wields, and the third relates to gender.

Cultural Values

Not every culture, country, or society holds the same values as do Americans. In fact, not all Americans hold the same values to the same degree. If we were to conceptualize measuring cultural values, we would recommend thinking about it as a linear continuum. On one end of the continuum are collectivistic societies, and the other individualistic. Any culture can be placed at some point along that continuum. In this section we will examine what each of those categories means and how they might affect our ability to be civil.

A *collectivistic culture* is one that values harmony in group and societal relationships. Collectivistic cultures tend to have very strong family units, strong ties within their communities and high levels of loyalty to employers. These cultures also do not value conflict and direct communication the way most Americans do. In fact, they handle conflict in a much more indirect fashion, because it helps maintain social harmony. On the other hand, in *individualistic cultures* people feel the strongest loyalties lie with themselves and not their social groups. It should come as no surprise that the United States today falls much closer to individualistic than collectivistic on this scale.

collectivistic culture
values harmony in group and societal relationships

individualistic culture
people feel the strongest loyalties lie with themselves and not their social groups

This has not always been the case, however. Given our definition of civility, a healthy society depends upon a balance between collectivistic and individualistic values. In the mid-twentieth century some of the most popular groups were the Kiwanis, Knights of Columbus, and other such social and service clubs. Additionally, communities worked together to maintain their neighborhoods and raise families, and often went bowling together. Today, in places like Las Vegas, homes are built with large stone walls blocking homes from neighbors, and, more significantly, as author Robert Putnam notes in his book *Bowling Alone*, membership in social groups has drastically dropped off from just a few decades ago. People today just do not interact with each other the way they used to, and this lack of connection contributes to both an exaggerated individualistic society and a culture where civility is less prevalent than in prior times.

Power Distance

No matter how hard we may try, there is always a power dynamic in any relationship. Just think of some of the clichés bandied about in the world today, like "the customer is always right." Power exists in any relationship, and it can and does affect our ability to be civil with each other. Sometimes we speak respectfully because of someone's title or ability to reward or punish us, but this is not, by our definition, civil. Rather, it is being polite or courteous based on the other person's power or position, not because of the respect he or she should be accorded as a human being.

low power-distance cultures
members value equality and believe no one person should dominate

high power-distance cultures
where there is an uneven distribution of power and one person or a specific group of people dominate

Power, much like culture, can be thought of on a linear scale based upon how a particular group or society understands it. On the one end of this scale are *low power-distance cultures* where members value equality and believe no one person or group should dominate. These groups are indicative of democracies like the United States. On the other end of the spectrum are *high power-distance cultures* where there is an uneven distribution of power and one person or a specific group of people dominate. These cultures often are reflective of monarchies and dictatorships. Interestingly, if you think back to the origins of the term "courtesy" from earlier in the chapter, you will see it has its roots in the latter of these two types, which is yet another reason it is not synonymous with our definition of civility.

Power influences our communication with each other in many ways, and we can often "feel" its presence. Some people, like bosses, have power based on their positions; others have power thanks to their knowledge about certain things. Some jobs come with the power to reward or punish others as well. The fundamental thing to take away from all this, however, is that power is not static; rather it is fluid. One person wields power in one area of his or her life, but not others. If we think about that for a moment, we realize then that being civil in all situations and not abusing power when we do have it can increase our ability to create a culture of civility.

Gender Gaps

gender
. . . .
the socially constructed expectations and roles that accompany a particular sex, and these vary between cultures

sex
. . . . .
a biological distinction between men and women

In addition to culture and power, gender also plays a role in our interactions. It is also important to note that gender and sex are two different things. *Gender* refers to the socially constructed expectations and roles that accompany a particular sex, which vary between cultures. *Sex*, on the other hand, is a biological distinction between men and women. In fact, men and women communicate in significantly different ways. In order to be civil and respect others, then, it is important that you understand the differences between the genders and how they approach communication. In short, you should not expect everyone to communicate the way you do, and appreciating that fact can lead to more civil relationships with those around us. Let's take a moment and briefly discuss some of these differences.

One of the key differences between how men and women communicate involves what role they attribute to communication in relationships. Women tend to view communication as the primary vehicle for expressions of intimacy and the maintenance of close bonds between partners. Men, on the other hand, view communication more as a tool used to accomplish tasks and complete projects. In short, women use communication to express feelings; men use it to accomplish tasks.

This difference can often lead to problems in relationships, for when men listen to women express feelings and discuss problems and challenges they respond by offering solutions. On the surface this can seem like a supportive gesture, but it is not always what women wish from the interaction. In these situations, men should listen carefully before jumping to the conclusion that there is a problem to be solved, so they can understand what their conversational partner wants from the interaction. This does cut both ways, though, in that women, or men who exhibit this behavior, should to appreciate the fact that when men offer solutions it's a way of expressing support. Here we see the importance of listening attentively in an effort to have a more civil interaction.

There are other differences in how men and women construct messages that are worth noting. Women tend to ask more questions in a conversation and more openly discuss emotions than men. Men in turn tend to use more self-references and judgmental adjectives when describing things to others. To be civil you must understand these gender distinctions in behaviors so that you do not get frustrated by expecting others to conform to your way of interacting.

Now that we have covered some of the basic dimensions of interpersonal interactions and cultural influences on how people relate to one another, let's examine some contemporary environments where we can use this information to enhance civility in our own communities.

Contemporary Contexts for Civility

In this section of the chapter we will briefly discuss five settings in which we can apply civil communication to improve understanding and general wellness in our social relationships. We begin with those in your own immediate context: the classroom. We then will discuss how civility can operate and improve our interpersonal relationships with friends and significant others. Third, we will look at the professional world which you will enter in just a few short years. Next, we will examine the general lack of civility in news media, before we conclude with a discussion of civility in social media.

Civility in the Classroom and on Campus

Learning for every student in a classroom depends upon a civil atmosphere, and the responsibility for creating this falls on both instructors and students. In fact, every student at UD has seen and recited the pledge in UD's Commitment to Community (see Table 11.2). This document represents a collective promise to engage in behaviors that create a civil, responsible, and connected community at UD. That promise manifests itself in dormitories, the Student Neighborhood, and even the classroom. Additionally, both the faculty and students have responsibilities to uphold this commitment. On the one hand, instructors should allow students to express their questions, comments, and thoughts about course content without fear of reprimand or mockery. They also should listen when students have questions regarding grades or requests for accommodations. Finally, instructors should welcome student visits during office hours to discuss course material and academic progress.

Students also bear a significant portion of the burden for creating a civil classroom climate. Students should not argue with instructors for the sake of arguing, nor equate instructor experience and knowledge with opinion. Students should also begin e-mails and visits to the office with cordial introductions and conclude them with a genuine note of gratitude. They also should treat each other with respect and listen to peers when they offer questions and commentary and rather than judge them for their ideas, engage them to understand the thinking behind the statements their peers make. Finally, students should follow course rules and policies as outlined in the syllabus, particularly those regarding laptop and cell phone use. Being on the Internet or texting a friend during class is very rude to the instructor and your fellow classmates.

Table 11.2

Civility is important to develop and uphold community. Here at the University of Dayton, we express the Catholic and Marianist values of the community in our own Commitment to Community, C2C. You might say C2C is our articulation of the values of civility and respect. C2C highlights three Catholic and Marianist principles for learning and living in community and seven key habits for living that are derived from them. C2C shapes the spirit of campus hospitality, calls us to academic rigor integrated with faith and life, and challenges each community member to take up the hard work necessary to build the intellectual, spiritual, religious, moral, physical, and social dimensions of community.

Every student at the University of Dayton takes the Commitment to Community pledge at New Student Orientation. As members of the UD community, all students are called to understand these principles and develop the habits in daily life. Doing so strengthens our educational community and prepares you to live as a mature member of society. Here is the pledge:

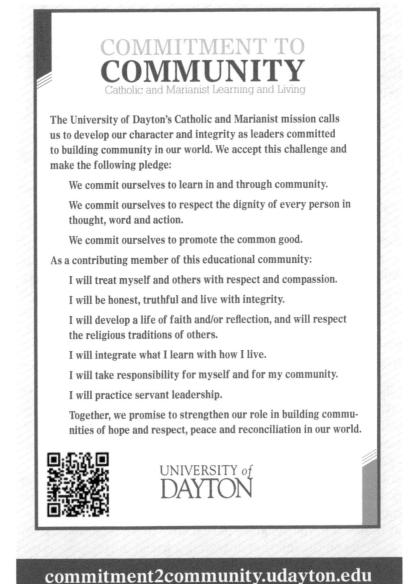

COMMITMENT TO
COMMUNITY
Catholic and Marianist Learning and Living

The University of Dayton's Catholic and Marianist mission calls us to develop our character and integrity as leaders committed to building community in our world. We accept this challenge and make the following pledge:

We commit ourselves to learn in and through community.

We commit ourselves to respect the dignity of every person in thought, word and action.

We commit ourselves to promote the common good.

As a contributing member of this educational community:

I will treat myself and others with respect and compassion.

I will be honest, truthful and live with integrity.

I will develop a life of faith and/or reflection, and will respect the religious traditions of others.

I will integrate what I learn with how I live.

I will take responsibility for myself and for my community.

I will practice servant leadership.

Together, we promise to strengthen our role in building communities of hope and respect, peace and reconciliation in our world.

UNIVERSITY of
DAYTON

commitment2community.udayton.edu

Simple behaviors like this by both instructors and students will create an environment in the classroom more conducive to learning.

Civility in Relationships

As we briefly covered earlier, you maintain multiple relationships in your life. These include those with friends, family, co-workers, and even the barista at your local Starbucks. Each of these relationships is an opportunity to connect with a larger, more robust community and a chance to learn about different people, cultures, and experiences. The trouble is that we all know how difficult these relationships are to maintain and develop over time, especially when we have disagreements with members of each group. That said, practicing civility can help enhance these relationships in every situation.

At home, you naturally behave with respect toward your parents, brothers, sisters, and significant others, but conflicts often do arise. With your friends you also practice a degree of civility, but sometimes you may say something to which they might take offense. It is ironic, but people generally are accepting of genuine apologies, but these apologies are also simultaneously the hardest thing for us to issue. We do not like admitting when we are wrong, and even when we do admit it we often qualify the apology with some explanation. If you are going to apologize, do so earnestly and without a qualification. This civil practice can go a long way toward maintaining healthy relationships with those closest to you.

Civility, however, also extends to those you encounter elsewhere but with whom you may not be close. Salespeople, hotel front desk agents, and even the person who makes your morning coffee all deserve the same type of respect and civility you accord to family and friends. Sometimes, simply having a brief conversation in which you ask about their day or just say "good morning" can go a long way toward improving their life in that moment. It is also important to recognize that people in these roles have lives you do not know, and they are people too. So, if someone in one of these roles says something or behaves in a way that frustrates or upsets you, concentrate your disapproval on the behavior or statement and not the person. If you do this, you will more likely come to a quicker and more acceptable resolution, while not unnecessarily upsetting or ruining someone else's day. This is an example of being able to disagree without being disagreeable.

Civility in Business

To conduct business effectively requires civil conduct by people in various positions. These behaviors can be as simple as respecting the time of others by not being late to scheduled meetings, or calling well in advance to reschedule them if necessary. It also includes things like knocking before entering offices, not taking calls in the middle of meetings, and learning the names of those present at a meeting. Business relationships occur between two or more people, and the emphasis should be on the fact they are people first. People are very quick to change providers or go with a different company if they feel they are treated as numbers instead of valued clients.

In an increasingly global environment, successful business relationships also require that people learn and value the cultural background of all parties. This means adhering to cultural expectations of host countries, but also understanding how other people operate. In some Asian cultures, for example, direct discussion of business only comes after a lengthy socializing process so all involved get to know each other. In fact, people often make business deals with others with whom they feel the most comfortable, not necessarily those who submit the best offer. It is important to know that up-front blunt communication may not always be the best route to go.

When negotiating for a new position, there are also certain behaviors to keep in mind. First, do not mention or discuss salary until an offer has been made or the company brings it up. Additionally, begin all interactions with greetings and conclude them with gratitude. Finally, be prepared with questions when you interview, as this reciprocity is expected. There are multiple other elements to successful interviewing, and other courses will provide you with that type of instruction, but for the purposes of our discussion here just know civility can go a long way in the interviewing process.

Civility in News Media

Unfortunately, today we need look no further than the news media and talk radio for examples of incivility and disrespectful communication. In spring 2012 talk show host Rush Limbaugh called a female Georgetown law student a "whore" for testimony she issued to Congress regarding the cost of contraception for women. In April 2007, morning talk show host Don Imus referred to the Rutgers University women's basketball team as "nappy headed hoes." Finally, just look at all of the news programs and talk shows that pit members of opposite sides of an argument against each other. These shows devolve quickly into, at best, a recitation of talking points, or, at worst, a shouting match. In both instances nothing of substance is ever truly discussed, and emotions overshadow content.

Rutgers University women's basketball team

These are the models of civility people are exposed to every day. As we have discussed, civility demands that we assert our own ideas, and these shows definitely allow for this to take place; however, it also calls for respect and understanding, which many of these shows do not demonstrate for the public. If these programs are an example of civil society, then civility is most definitely on the wane today.

That said, there are examples of dialogue and civility in the news media. Sunday morning talk shows often bring in diverse viewpoints and rarely culminate in shouting matches. Instead, ample time is afforded to participants to express their views, explain their data, and listen to counterarguments. This type of exchange, although ineffective at changing minds of those on the show, at least disseminates information for people in a way that does not encourage emotional outbursts. Alas, these shows are often broadcast at times when people generally do not watch television.

Civility and Social Media

More and more people today use social media to stay in touch with friends and family, conduct business, and promote themselves and their products. Facebook,  Twitter, and LinkedIn are just a few of the social media tools employed to accomplish these tasks. Even though these resources do not allow for face-to-face communication, they do not reduce or eliminate the need for civil communication. Civility is more than just behaving well to others when they are in front of you; it is a lifestyle where we always genuinely think about how what we say and do can affect other people.

To this end, it is instructive to think before posting status updates to Facebook, issuing a tweet about how you feel regarding an event or issue, or even uploading your resume to LinkedIn. Remember that you need not share everything on Facebook, and that what you choose to share is now on the Internet. The Internet is like plastic—it never goes away—so you should make sure that what you post will be acceptable later as well as now. Take care when issuing comments to others as well, and even if you disagree, do so with respect and make sure it's the position and not the person with which you disagree. There are people who have lost their jobs over what they posted to Facebook, after all.

Bill Maher
(left) comedian

Tim Tebow
(right) football player

Twitter presents just as many issues for expression and it is, like Facebook, a place where self-restraint could come in handy. In late 2011, comedian Bill Maher issued a tweet mocking the religious beliefs of then-Denver Broncos quarterback, Tim Tebow. Others have issued similarly scathing tweets that have caused more problems than the expression was probably worth. In fact, in response to a negative *New York Times* review of his movie *The Avengers* in May 2012, actor Samuel L. Jackson castigated the writer in a tweet that was then met with harsh criticism across the country. Just because you may feel a certain way and can post it through social media does not necessarily mean you should. Additionally, we communicate more and more through e-mail, but that medium is not always used in a way that promotes civil correspondence between people. Make no mistake e-mail is an extraordinary tool for communication, but it is also rife with potential pitfalls. Table 11.3 shows some guidelines for e-mail use that will help ensure you use it to maximum effect while also remaining civil in the tone of what you write.

Table 11.3

Some Things to Consider When Writing an E-mail
In General
1. Use e-mail to request or provide succinct pieces of objective information 2. Avoid discussing sensitive issues through e-mail 3. Use e-mail to publicly praise, but not to blame employees 4. Use e-mail to share insights, not to instigate confrontation 5. Judiciously use blind copy function
As Sender
1. Give e-mail a clear and direct subject heading 2. Get to the point 3. Avoid hedgers and qualifiers as phrases 4. If asking a question, be sure to ask the question (don't issue evaluation) 5. Specify who should respond 6. Be clear about when you need a response 7. Provide relevant context 8. One message, one topic 9. Provide brief summary when sending an "FYI" or forward e-mail 10. Don't use sarcasm
As Receiver
1. Don't make assumptions about sender's emotional state 2. Don't escalate by sending an emotionally charged response (sleep on it; perhaps don't reply by e-mail) 3. Don't respond right away 4. Be careful quoting e-mails out of context in a reply

SUMMARY

Communication is a unique and powerful characteristic of being human. It allows us to connect with others and express our own ideas and feelings, but how we choose to do it matters as much as having the ability to express ourselves. Civility in our communication and actions allows for greater understanding and healthier society. In this chapter we defined what civility means and how it relates to other terms such as politeness, courtesy, respect, and good manners. We then explored how civility has been practiced during different periods of history, before concluding with a discussion of five areas in which civil communication could improve life today.

KEY TERMS

assertive   282

autonomy face   284

civility   283

collectivistic cultures   291

competence face   284

courtesy 275

face threats   284

facework   283

fellowship face   283

gender   292

good manners   280

high power distance cultures   291

image management   276

individualistic cultures   291

low power distance cultures   291

polite   279

respect   282

self-monitoring   286

self-restraint   278

sex   292

REVIEW QUESTIONS

1. What are the five defining characteristics of civility?
2. What are the four ways civility influences how we present ourselves to others?
3. What are the three fundamental components of any civil behavior?
4. What are the three foundational dimensions of interpersonal interactions?
5. What are five contemporary arenas in which civility can improve our quality of life?

THINK ABOUT IT

1. Are people naturally civil, or is this a psychological restraint put on our natural state of being?
2. Have you ever been uncivil in your dealings with an instructor or friend? How so?
3. Does today's mediated environment make it less or more difficult for us to be civil toward one another? Why?

ACTIVITIES FOR ACTION

1. Watch a series of political advertisements or a listen to an airing of a political talk show. Write down what you believe the central message to be, and also the ways the person makes the case. Were they civil in their approach? Did the host or the guest try to understand the views of the other side? What behaviors encouraged or discouraged dialogue and understanding? What behaviors could have been employed to encourage understanding?

2. Write down a list of simple kind behaviors you could do in any given day. Include things like opening a door for a stranger, helping someone carry groceries, and engaging in a simple discussion with a barista or salesperson you come into contact with. Then, the next day, see how many of these behaviors you can accomplish. Also, pay attention to how many times someone else does these things with you. At the end of the day, compare the two lists.

ENDNOTES

1. For a complete account of "Miss Manners" visit her website at: http://www.missmanners.com/home/about-miss-manners.html (accessed June 6, 2012).

2. Ibid.

3. Thomas Hobbes, *Leviathan,* Part I, Chapter 13.

4. P.M. Forni, *Choosing Civility: The Twenty-Five Rules of Considerate Conduct*, (New York, NY: St. Martin's Press, 2002), 10.

5. Ibid. 11.

6. Ibid. 10.

7. Forni, 112.

8. Ibid.

9. For more information on Dr. Forni, visit his website at: http://krieger.jhu.edu/civility/background.html.

10. John Medina, *Brain Rules: 12 Principles for Surviving and Thriving at Work, Home and School* (Seattle, WA: Pear Press, 2008).

11. For a complete transcript of the address, see: http://www.americanrhetoric.com/speeches/jfkinaugural.htm.

12. Rod L. Troester & Cathy Sargent Mester, *Civility in Business and Professional Communication,=* (New York, NY: Peter Lang Publishers, 2007), 30.

13. Ibid. 33.

14. Ibid.

15. Jon Meacham, *American Lion: Andrew Jackson in the White House,* (New York, NY: Random House, 2008).

SCENARIOS

Scenario 1

Many fictional stories have used the premise of the end of the world, depicting a post-apocalyptic landscape where there are no laws, no governments, and no social structures. Such shows and movies include *The Walking Dead, World War Z,* and even *The Leftovers.* In effect, these situations depict what producers envision would be the natural state of man—human nature. Discuss with your group whether you agree with Thomas Hobbes that the natural state of mankind is "nasty, brutish, and short" or if you believe we are inherently civil people.

1. What does your position mean for civilization?

2. If we are not inherently civil, how and why do we become so?

3. Is, or should, civility be legislated? If so, what behaviors should be outlawed to ensure civility?

Scenario 2

At the 2009 Video Music Awards (VMAs), Taylor Swift received the Best Female Video award for the music video for her hit song You Belong With Me. When Swift got up to the stage to accept her award, Kanye West ran up to the stage, took the mic from Swift, and said "I'm sorry, but Beyonce had one of the best videos of all time."

1. How might Kanye's behaviors be perceived as face threats by Taylor Swift?

2. Which of her faces were potentially threatened, and how?

3. Would you consider Kanye West a high self-monitor or low self-monitor? Why?

4. How should occurrences like this be handled?

Scenario 3

You are applying to be an assistant manager upon graduating from the University of Dayton. As a group, generate a list of five qualities you want in your supervisor and rank them in order of importance.

Take a look at the list you created and see if any of the leadership qualities relate to civility. Specifically, do they relate to any of the behaviors named in Table 11.1?

Next, tell your group about the worst boss or teacher that you've ever had. How do you think civility played a role in why this particular person was an ineffective leader? How did it impact your performance as their employee or student? Be specific.

Scenario 4 (Performance)

At the conclusion of class, the professor returns your latest examination. You discover that you earned a grade lower than you expected on it and are quite disappointed. In fact, it puts you at risk of failing the class entirely. You disagree with the grade and want to bring it up with the professor.

1. How do you go about approaching the instructor? When, where, how and using what language do you initiate contact.

2. Consider using email to make contact. Write the email to the faculty member.

3. Consider an in-person meeting. Detail how you would go about doing this and provide a script of what you would say. Be prepared to role-play your skit for the class.

Scenario 5

Look at the list of questions below. As a group, decide which answer is appropriate for each question.

1. The word "businessman" IS NORMALLY USED to mean women as well as men.

   Agree strongly   Agree Neutral   Disagree   Disagree strongly

2. The word "businessman" SHOULD BE USED to refer to both men and women.

   Agree strongly   Agree Neutral   Disagree   Disagree strongly

3. The word "salesman" IS USED to mean women as well as men.

   Agree strongly   Agree Neutral   Disagree   Disagree strongly

4. The word "salesman" SHOULD BE USED to refer to both men and women.

   Agree strongly   Agree Neutral   Disagree   Disagree strongly

5. The statement "All men are created equal" includes women.

   Agree strongly   Agree Neutral   Disagree   Disagree strongly

6. The terms "businessperson", "chairperson" and "salesperson" are ugly.

   Agree strongly   Agree Neutral   Disagree   Disagree strongly

7. People SHOULD USE terms like "fire-fighter", "business executive" and "camera operator" to refer to both men and women.

   Agree strongly   Agree Neutral   Disagree   Disagree strongly

8. It's awkward to have to write "he" or "she" all the time in essays.

   Agree strongly   Agree Neutral   Disagree   Disagree strongly

9. "They" is NORMALLY USED to refer to one person of unknown sex (e.g. "If anyone wants me they'll have to wait.")

Agree strongly   Agree Neutral   Disagree   Disagree strongly

10. You SHOULD USE "they" when referring to a person of unknown sex.

Agree strongly   Agree Neutral   Disagree   Disagree strongly

11. "Girl" SHOULD NOT BE used to refer to an adult woman.

Agree strongly   Agree Neutral   Disagree   Disagree strongly

12. "Waiter" should be USED for women as well as men.

Agree strongly   Agree Neutral   Disagree   Disagree strongly

13. "Actor" SHOULD BE USED for women as well as men.

Agree strongly   Agree Neutral   Disagree   Disagree strongly

- What do your answers say about gender and communication in your lives? Were your deliberations over each civil?

- What do the language terms and issues illustrated by these statements say about communication and gender? For instance, should we eliminate gendered nouns and pronouns in language?

Scenario 6

You are finishing up a course in which the textbook and classroom discussions have questioned some of your most closely-held beliefs and values. In general and even though you put in the time and energy needed to learn the course material, you feel as though you did not get as much out of the class as you had hoped. It is now time to complete the anonymous Student Evaluation of Teaching (SET) for this class, and you want to make sure someone hears about your experience.

1. Does the expectation of civility in the classroom extend to SET? If so, in what ways? If not, why not?

2. What is your obligation to the instructor in terms of UD's Commitment to Community and other values?

3. How do you believe your comments in SET impact faculty teaching and the classroom experiences of future students?

4. How might you express your concerns within the framework of civility?

5. How do you believe department chairs (who see all SET results for faculty in their departments) respond to student comments within SET that are not civil?

Scenario 7

Joseph Grenny, author of Crucial Conversations, conducted an online survey regarding hostility and social networking. Eighty percent of those surveyed believed incivility in social media was on the rise, 75% admitted to having witnessed an argument over social media, while nearly 50% admitted to having unfriended or blocked family members or close friends due to hostile posts or emails. Additionally, 81% said emotionally charged conversations they have had via electronic media remained unresolved.

1. Does social media make expressing things like mutual equality difficult? Why or why not?

2. Consider the difference between assertiveness and aggressiveness. Do you think social media makes people behave more aggressively or assertively? Why do you think so?

3. How do you think social media might affect self-esteem?

4. What are five behaviors on social media that you think we can engage in that would reduce Grenny's unfortunate findings?

Dialogue

12

- Explains what dialogue is, and how it contrasts with other forms of communication
- Provides behaviors and attitudes necessary to engage in dialogue
- Discusses appropriate use of dialogue and application at UD

Practically SPEAKING

Kerry Patterson is an award-winning consultant and corporate trainer. While studying for his Ph.D., Patterson began doing research on how to develop healthy organizations. In his book *Crucial Conversations*,[1] Patterson and his coauthors tell a story about a startling discovery in a study of what made certain people successful and influential corporate leaders. In an effort to find out why some people are more effective than others, Patterson and his colleagues wanted to develop a detailed understanding of how the most effective leaders did their jobs. To do so, they widely surveyed within companies to learn which people were regarded as highly influential. They wanted to find only those people with widespread reputations for truly remarkable effectiveness.

Upon identifying an extraordinarily effective person, the researchers trailed this person at the job to see what he or she did that worked so well. One person they studied was a man named Kevin, who was one of eight vice presidents in his company. After following Kevin for nearly a week, the researchers had seen nothing out of the ordinary and began to wonder why he received such high recognition from so many people in his company. Then they sat in an important meeting in which the CEO was to make a decision about moving the company offices. Two vice presidents presented their plans, and both faced intense scrutiny. Next, the CEO presented his proposal, which the researchers observed "was both unpopular and potentially disastrous."[2] Efforts from several vice presidents to question this plan were met with defensive responses and they backed off. Then Kevin calmly spoke up, skillfully questioning the CEO and ultimately even suggesting that the CEO was going against his own principles in making this decision. Surprisingly, the CEO thoughtfully accepted Kevin's critique and admitted that he needed to rethink. In the end, a decision was reached that was better for the company.

After the meeting, one of the others said to the researchers, "Did you see how he did that? If you want to know how he gets things done, figure out what he just did."[3] How was Kevin able to question, and even critique, his superior in an environment where others had been intimidated into backing down? In their ensuing 25 years of research on effective employees, Patterson and his colleagues found time and again that the common element was that these extraordinary people were masters of dialogue. Their ability to use dialogue in crucial conversations gave them an ability to succeed where others less skilled at dialogue could not.

We share this story to show how powerful dialogue can be. But what is truly impressive is that the story only begins to illustrate the importance of dialogue. Yes, dialogue will enable you to make some amazing accomplishments at work. It is also central to the ability to maintain healthy and satisfying social relationships, such as friendship, marriage, and family. But, even more important, dialogue is an essential tool for engaging in the Marianist *Commitment to Community* (C2C) principles for living in a community, as well as for developing relationships with people who are different from you. And, it is a necessity for communicating ethically in some situations. While dialogue is a powerful tool in oral communication, its greatest importance lies not in what it can do for you, but in what it allows you to do for others.

Now look around you. Watch how people treat each other on reality TV. You won't find much dialogue there. Dialogue has been largely absent from political communication as well,[4] both among politicians and among the media (think Rush Limbaugh or Keith Olbermann). Jerry Springer, a former mayor of Cincinnati, has made millions from a show featuring people doing the exact opposite of dialogue.

Dialogue requires considerable effort, humility, ability to suspend judgment, and willingness to listen carefully to someone with qualities or views we initially dislike. These skills require strength of character many people have not developed. But those who can master dialogue discover its value in helping them achieve success at the workplace and in their personal lives. They discover how much richer it makes the quality of their lives and those around them.

PREP QUESTIONS

1. Discuss the relationships between ethics and dialogue.

2. Explain the two types of monologues people can deliver.

3. Explain the relationship between dialogue and civility.

4. Compare and contrast debate, dialogue, and monologue.

5. Detail the four skills you must master to engage in dialogue effectively.

6. Explain the relationship between presentness and listening.

7. Define what it means to allow the other person to speak fully.

8. Define what it means to suspend judgment.

9. Explain the primary goal of a clarifying question.

10. Define unconditional positive regard.

11. Define Gibb's six supportive and defensive communication climates.

12. Differentiate between judgments and facts.

13. Define the term genuineness.

14. Describe the five general situations when dialogue would be helpful.

12

A Brief History of Dialogue in Our Society

Although principles of dialogue have existed as long as people have had a spoken language, dialogue drew widespread attention both in our society and in communication research and theory in the 1960s. As Americans struggled with difficult questions about social and political issues (such as equal rights regardless of race or gender), people started to see dialogue as an important means of nonviolent response to differences. They looked at the writings of influential scholars like Carl Rogers and Martin Buber, and they began to see dialogue as a means by which we should communicate with each other in a wide variety of situations.[5] Dialogue wasn't just seen as a technique for communication; it was seen as an ethical requirement.[6]

This identification of dialogue as an ethic instead of a technique has had important implications for its history. The movements of the 1960s left a lasting impact on American culture. Martin Luther King, Jr. became a national hero, and the decade's social movements had a permanent impact on race relations, women's rights, and other social issues. However, while some enduring ideas were carried forward, certain fads were left behind. Most would agree that some of the fashion statements of the 1960s and 1970s are best left as historic relics. By the late 1970s, many people saw an excessive emphasis on dialogue as one of the fads of the 1960s, and the teaching and study of dialogue diminished greatly.

In the mid-1990s, however, an interesting change took place. Scholars started to realize that they made a mistake in abandoning dialogue, and they began once again to write and theorize about it. However, their theoretical approach changed. Instead of thinking about dialogue as part of the social movements of the 1960s, they began to think about dialogue from different theoretical perspectives. Dialogue was no longer seen as an ethical requirement for all interpersonal communication, but instead as a way to develop better understanding and build relationships in situations where those were important goals. Despite this change, the ethical elements of dialogue have never been completely forgotten. After all, the interactions in which we use dialogue require that we make moral choices. So, rather than being seen as an ethical obligation for how people must communicate, dialogue now tends to be seen as a form of communication in which ethics are one essential element. As we introduce you to dialogue, pay attention to how much of a role ethics play in our discussion of the topic. And notice how

311

Air Conditioning

On a muggy Saturday in August, when the temperature reached almost 100 degrees, the air conditioning in one of the authors' homes failed. With an 8-month-old baby in the house who couldn't tolerate heat the way an adult would, he called a repair company right away. A wire attached to the compressor had broken, so the repair worker simply fixed that wire. The entire job took about 15 minutes and involved no parts. The customer was astonished to see he had been charged $225.

Unhappy at what seemed like unreasonable pricing, he called the company. He told the customer service agent that he wasn't calling to make a threat or ask for anything, but he simply wanted to let them know his reaction as a customer to his experience. He mentioned that while he knew it was their right to set pricing as they wanted, he wouldn't be using their services again because of the cost. He also mentioned that he was pleased with the work itself. The customer service agent looked into how the bill had been calculated. Although a standard service call was $75, the company had to pay employees time-and-a-half for weekend work. And they had to pay the employee's time not only for the service call itself, but also for the trip to and from the customer's house. But the major factor affecting the bill was that any job involving the compressor was classified as a major repair and a large surcharge was applied for that. The customer acknowledged these factors and noted that even though the compressor was involved, no work was done on it, and so in his opinion this didn't meet their definition of a major repair. No changes resulted from the conversation. The customer ended the call by thanking the representative for helping him better understand the process, but noted that he still disagreed with how the bill had been calculated.

About an hour later, the customer's phone rang. It was the customer service representative. "I've been thinking," she said, "Our policy guarantees satisfaction or the job is free. Since you weren't satisfied, we'd like to offer that we make this job free." The customer thought for a moment, then said, "That isn't right. I needed the work done, and your technician did a great job. Taking that work for free would be ripping you off, and my ripping you off is no better than you ripping me off." There was a surprised silence at the other end of the line for a moment, then the agent asked, "Well, what price do you think would be appropriate?" The customer thought for a minute. "I originally thought $75 would be appropriate, since it was a quick job involving no cost in parts. But, I didn't know that you had to pay driving time and overtime for weekend work. That makes me think that $125 would cover your costs and give you an appropriate profit as well. That is about what it would have been if it wasn't classified as a major repair." The customer service agent agreed, and the bill was adjusted.

The customer's goal was never to get the price changed. He merely wanted the company to understand how customers felt about what seemed like unfair pricing. In the process he learned more about why the price had been set, and learned of some shortcomings in his expectations.

It is possible that an angry threatening call might have also resulted in a price adjustment or a free repair, but that would certainly have led to resentment on the part of at least one party. Dialogue met its goal of mutual understanding, and it also led to relationship building. The mutually satisfactory pricing was merely an unanticipated side effect. And as is always the case when dialogue happens, ethics played a vital role in this exchange.

important *integrity* and ethical character are to those who wish to use dialogue in their daily and workplace lives. A person with no moral compass cannot fully understand and employ dialogue.

integrity
a quality of discerning and acting on one's ethical principles

Dialogue: What It Is, and What It Is Not

Dialogue is a communicative event in which people with different perspectives seek to understand each other's views. Dialogue is, essentially, speaking so that others want to listen and listening so that others want to speak. Dialogue neither demands nor expects that people adopt each other's views or even come to agreement. If different perspectives are in conflict, dialogue often leads to an effective and satisfying resolution to the problem—typically much more satisfying than any other means of interaction can produce. However, those outcomes are a byproduct of the process, not the goal of it. To see how that can happen, take the case of one of the authors of this book, who encountered a challenging situation at home when the bill for fixing a broken air conditioner arrived and it was well above the expected cost. Many experts will tell you that engaging in dialogue changes you and leads to growth in understanding and character. One writer so strongly considers growth to be part of the nature of dialogue that he defines the concept as "a process of *inter*action through which human beings listen to each other deeply enough to be changed by what they learn."[7]

dialogue
an interaction in which people with different perspectives seek to understand each others views; speaking so that others want to listen and listening so that others want to speak

Dialogue can be contrasted with monologue.[8] *Monologue* is a communicative event in which only one voice is present. Commonly, monologue refers to one person speaking without really listening. This may happen when someone is either oblivious to the importance of listening to the other, or if a person feels that the other's voice just isn't important. For example, a supervisor who has made a decision at work might simply tell workers what they must do without inviting their input. While this form of monologue can sometimes reduce the quality of work that gets done, it might also be appropriate in cases where there is no need for the supervisor to listen or where listening could even be problematic. Certainly, the military uses monologue to great advantage in many operations. An army could not function effectively if everyone were to share an opinion with the general over how and when each operation should be conducted.

monologue
an interaction in which only one voice is present.

However, monologue can be much more aggressive when it consists of a speaker shutting down or oppressing the voice of another. This can happen when someone knows the audience may disagree with a message or the message might even be detrimental to the audience. In these cases, monologue has sometimes been used as a form of violence against another.[9] For example, when powerful people mistreat those with less power and unjustly try to keep them from telling anyone about it, then monologue is a means of oppression and it is an unethical weapon used to maintain control. Organizations and individuals who take away the opportunity for individuals or groups to speak on topics important to them exert a damaging form of monologue. Propaganda, brainwashing, and other manipulative tactics are other forms of monologue that have done great harm to humanity over the centuries.

Dialogue can also be contrasted with various forms of persuasive speech such as *debate*, a practice where people listen to each other from a critical perspective with the goal of defeating the other's arguments and triumphing through reasons and evidence. The rules of debate provide all parties an equal opportunity to make their case and attempt to resolve a controversy through good reasons and evidence. As such, debate is an admirable way to address positions of difference when compared to monologue. Both dialogue and debate provide voice for all parties, and both demand an interaction governed by reasons and evidence.

However, debate differs from dialogue in important ways. Whereas debate is a forum designed to produce a winning and a losing argument, dialogue imposes no such expectations. Dialogue seeks understanding and allows for examination of reasons and evidence, but it makes no attempt to produce a winner and a loser. Both people are working together toward common understanding and a shared goal. In the example of Kevin from the beginning of the chapter, the dialogue centered on understanding the CEO's reasons, with a shared goal of making a good move for the company. So, rather than a competitive activity, dialogue is collaborative.

Furthermore, debaters doggedly defend their position while attacking the opponent. Debate does not foster creative new solutions, since the goal is for one of the two fixed positions to win. And, it is not conducive to either of the parties admitting that their initial position is flawed. In contrast, people engaged in dialogue are free to consider new ideas, admit that some of their ideas or their partner's ideas might have problems, and rethink anything they desire. People in dialogue are not constrained to a predetermined position, and they have total freedom in how they think about a topic. Whereas debaters function as lawyers defending or prosecuting a case, people in dialogue are adventurers, exploring uncharted territory and drawing their own conclusions based on whatever they discover.

Think about your interactions with others on a daily basis. How many times do you get into an argument or debate with a friend, classmate, or colleague over something because you wanted to "win" the discussion instead of reach a mutually agreeable solution? Or how often do you approach it as an effort of learning about the other person and what is important to him or her? We too often use debate tactics in dialogic situations, which is counterproductive and creates unnecessary discomfort for you and the other person. In the next section we will explore some attitudes and behaviors that can help create a healthy dialogue in such situations.

ATTITUDES AND BEHAVIORS FOR DIALOGUE

Dialogue is a complex activity. Entire volumes have been written about what it is and how to do it well. This chapter can only give the briefest overview, so consider it a starting point in your understanding of dialogue, rather than a complete description. We encourage you to continue exploring dialogue throughout your time at UD through reading more about the topic, through practice and application in other classes that discuss difficult and controversial topics, and through your interactions with other members of the university community.

To explain how to engage in dialogue effectively, we address four areas that you must master: listening, developing attitudes that foster dialogue, creating a supportive climate, and appropriately shaping your messages.

Listening in Dialogue

Listening is the most prominent element of dialogic communication. Although there are vital qualities in sending messages that are essential, good dialogue begins with the way a person listens. If communicators do not listen effectively, dialogue cannot take place.

You will recall from an earlier chapter that *listening* is the cognitive processing of what is heard, and that people routinely hear without listening. Dialogue requires that participants make a commitment to listen fully and completely to the other party. In order to make this happen, people need to do a variety of actions. Although this list is not complete, a person who does all the behaviors below is likely to be a highly effective listener in a dialogue.

listening
the mental processing of what a person has heard

Give complete attention

Giving complete attention, often referred to as being "fully present" in the interaction, means that people focus all of their attention on the interaction and the people to whom they are listening. As a first step, this means eliminating elements of the environment that could be distracting. Putting away communication devices (phone, laptop, etc.) is an essential start. Turning off other devices that could be a distraction (e.g., television or radio talk show) might also be necessary in some settings. It may even be useful to move to a location where other people or activities won't disrupt the conversation. Being physically capable to participate is also necessary to be a fully present participant in any interaction, so obviously it is hard to give full attention to someone when you are intoxicated or sleep deprived.

A difficult part of *presentness* can be setting aside mental distractions. Notice how hard it is to pay attention in class just after you got really good or bad news, or when you are nervous about an event right after class? It's difficult not to think about those topics and to direct your full attention to the class. Being fully present in dialogue requires the ability to tune out mental distractions. If you cannot do that, then rescheduling the conversation may be the best option.

presentness
giving full attention to someone in dialogue

One widely shared misconception people have is thinking that they can multitask while listening. While it is possible to multitask in certain ways, such as listening while walking, the research is conclusive with regard to one aspect of multitasking: *For cognitive functions that require you to pay attention (such as listening, reading, driving, or texting), **it is impossible to multitask**.*[10] This limitation is not something you can overcome with practice or experience, such as having texted all your life. Rather, this is a physical limitation. As molecular biologist John Medina notes, "We are biologically incapable of processing attention-rich inputs simultaneously."[11] Just as your physiology makes it impossible for you to jump 50 feet in the air, the physical design of your brain makes it just as impossible for you to pay attention to two different mental inputs at once. Instead, you shift rapidly between the two objects of attention, and in so doing, you not only miss one when paying attention to the other, you also miss out on *both* as you transition between the two.

So, if you believe you are good enough at texting that you can do it while paying attention to something else, you are mistaken. There can be no argument: In order to listen effectively in dialogue, you cannot multitask with another activity that requires mental attention.

Notice that being present—like all the listening skills we discuss as part of dialogue—will have a significant impact on your success as a student. If you spend time in class texting or checking social media online, or if you come to class hung over or too tired to pay attention, your listening will be diminished, and that will hurt your ability to do your best in class. And here is the payoff: Depending on your listening habits at present, you may be able to improve your grades at UD without any additional study time simply by applying the listening skills of dialogue in your classes.

It is also important to know that multitasking is regarded as rude in many settings. While workplace norms are still developing to accommodate today's rapidly changing communication technology, checking your messages or texting in a business meeting is likely to be viewed as offensive to others in the meeting, and may reduce others' respect for you. In class, almost all professors consider it rude when students engage in activities unrelated to class on phones or laptops. Just think: If you have to hide doing something so the other person will not notice it, then it is not an ethical approach to dialogue or civil behavior. So, realize that multitasking in this manner likely has a negative effect on your relationships with others who may be important to you and your success.

Allow the other to speak fully

One of the most common mistakes people make in conversation is failing to let the other party complete what they want to say. This can be caused by a variety of reasons, from the seemingly positive (e.g., the listener got so excited about the point that he or she couldn't wait to jump in) to the seemingly negative (e.g., the listener wanted to keep someone from making his or her points). But regardless of the reason, interruptions keep the listener from getting all the information the speaker wanted to share. And that information may include not just the content of the message, but also the other information that is inherent in communication, such as information about the speaker's emotional state or about the speaker and listener's relationship. In some cases, speakers may be happy enough with the outcome that they might not mind never having a chance to finish, but in most cases people feel frustrated when the listener doesn't even give them a chance to say what they wanted to say.

To allow the other to speak fully, you must put aside your desire to respond and instead focus on your role as a listener. It is helpful to think of yourself as a detective who is seeking all the clues. If you make an agreement with yourself that you won't speak until you have a full understanding of the other, you'll be more effective as a listener.

Ask clarifying questions

Once a person has spoken fully—or during the course of their speaking turn if appropriate—ask the speaker any questions needed for you to have complete understanding. Since asking a question is an an act of speech, it may seem unusual that we consider it as an important component of listening. However, asking clarifying questions demonstrates that you were listening closely enough to identify the areas of the message you didn't fully understand. These questions allow you to fill in information that was missing from the message. You may wish to ask about relevant facts; about a person's reasons, assumptions, feelings; or about anything else that will fill in missing pieces. But wait until they are done to respond; otherwise, you disrespect the other person by rudely interrupting him or her.

The most important point about follow-up questions is that they must be intended and worded to obtain information. Many people ask questions that are intended to criticize or attack, rather than to solicit information. Such questions are destructive to dialogue. "Why would you do something so stupid?!" is a criticism phrased as a question, rather than a true attempt to better understand. Consider the case in which an international student speaks in class about foods his family eats that most Americans would not. Other students ask the following questions:

"How do you make that food?"

"Do you eat that as an everyday staple, or just on certain occasions?"

"How desperate would you have to be to eat that stuff?"

"Now that you're used to good food here, could you ever go back to eating that?"

It is easy to see that the first two questions help the listener better understand the food and its social context, whereas the latter two questions reveal prejudice and might even be intended to demean the people and cultures under discussion.

Make sure your questions function only to solicit information, not share your own opinions. A clarifying question should result in a flow of information from the speaker to the listener, not the other way around.

Suspend your judgment

One of the more difficult skills essential for many dialogic encounters is the ability to suspend your judgment during a conversation when a person seems wrong, unlikeable, or even unethical. Listening in dialogue must happen with an open mind. This is not to say that you should not interpret, or even state, moral judgments where yours are different from a dialogic partner's. But if a listener cannot seek understanding without conveying judgmental messages against the partner, dialogue will not take place. You may wish to make judgments after a dialogue, but only do so after you have collected all relevant information.

What may surprise you is that getting to understand other people often reduces negative judgments. Once you understand their situation, their reasons, and their perceptions you often find that they are people like you, who have feelings and values you understand, external pressures they navigate every day, and commitments they seek to keep. That is not always the case, of course, and the opposite can even happen—you might like and respect a person even less when you get to know him or her better. But the only way to know what the outcome will be is to withhold judgment about other people until you have gotten to know their perspective with an open mind.

Suspending judgment requires you to be honest with yourself. It is possible to pretend to be open minded and even to fool others into believing you are open minded when in fact you are not. But if you go into a dialogue with judgments about the other person already set, you will reduce the effectiveness of the dialogue and deny yourself the opportunity to find out what you might have thought. At the outset of this chapter, we noted that dialogue requires strength of character that can be difficult for many people. The ability to suspend judgment while you listen to someone who has positions you find offensive or that you disagree with is hard to do, and may take years of practice to do well.

Plan your responses later

Another of the more common deficiencies in listening is being focused more on your response than on what the other person is saying. This happens often because it is a natural reaction to statements we disagree with. It differs from the problem of not letting speakers finish because when people do this they often let the speaker finish. But in this case, it doesn't matter what the speaker is saying because the listener isn't paying attention. The listener is preoccupied by formulating the perfect comeback.

Like suspending judgment, there isn't an easy technique that will prevent this problem. It just takes mental discipline. If you find yourself thinking of a great response to something that was said, consider jotting a keyword down so you won't forget that topic, and then put the issue out of your mind.

Practice accurate empathetic understanding

The goal of listening to another is to develop a complete understanding of that person's position, experience, attitudes, or ideas. Although it might be sufficient to list this only as a cognitive goal to understand the content of the message, you need to know the importance of the emotional side of human behavior. Nobody functions in a solely rational manner like the fictional Vulcan Mr. Spock, on *Star Trek*. Instead, all of our work and social interaction involves elements of both reason and emotion (logos and pathos). Scholars explain how our brains work using the metaphor of a rider on an elephant.[12] The rider (the rational, cognitive functions) tells the elephant (the emotional part of the brain) what to do, and the elephant provides the motivation and force to make actions happen.

Often, both reason and emotion work together seamlessly, but sometimes they conflict. When they do, it can be difficult for reason to triumph over emotion. This is the challenge with losing weight. No matter how much the rational side of the brain says "Don't have a second piece of cake," it can be difficult to exert that control. The same is true of social interaction. Often we say and do things we know we shouldn't, because our emotions get the better of us. In contrast, when our emotions are taking us in a direction that our rational side supports, we can be highly effective. And in other cases, emotions don't really seem to have any bearing on the outcome of a situation. You just have to assess it. Regardless of what, if any, role emotions play in a situation, it is essential as a listener to pay attention to a person's feelings if they seem to be showing through in a conversation, and consider how that person might feel given a particular piece of information, phrase, or vocal inflection. To that end, it is important to also listen for clues as to what triggered an emotional response from the other person. Often a person's past experiences or current circumstances may help explain their emotional state and reaction. When engaging in dialogue, heeding these clues can help you avoid getting sidetracked while also respecting the other person and where they are at emotionally and mentally in a given moment.

The importance of understanding another person's feelings does not mean that you should necessarily ask about them. Doing so might make you seem like an aspiring therapist. A person who tells her boss, "Before you made that decision yesterday, I had information I wanted to share," probably doesn't want a response of "How did my not asking about that information make you feel?" So, the message about accurate empathetic understanding isn't that you must explore the inner landscape of a person's feelings in every dialogue. Instead, you should be aware of the importance of emotions, be attentive to that information, and understand it to the degree it is relevant to the situation. In many situations it is not relevant at all. But in cases where emotional information seems to be coming through in the dialogue, pay attention to it (see Table 12.1).

Table 12.1

Listening Behaviors That Build Dialogue	
Dos	**Don'ts**
• Take notes when someone is speaking • Let the other person speak fully • Ask questions to clarify what was said • Bring appropriate materials to a meeting • Arrange appointments in advance • Use a person's preferred name or title (and if you don't know it, ask them what they prefer to be called)	• Play on your cell phone or iPad • Interrupt other speakers • Assume you know what a person means • Show up without appropriate materials • Barge into a person's office • Use abbreviated names/ nicknames without permission

Attitudes Necessary for Dialogue

Dialogue is a meeting of *people*, not just an exchange of information. The character that each person has shapes the nature of the interaction. Every conversation is different because of the personalities of the people in it. Two different sets of people talking about an event they both just experienced may have very different interactions, just as two sets of people negotiating for the same goal may have conversations that sound quite different.

You have already seen some important attitudes reflected in the guidelines for listening (such as the value of presentness). But there are several attitudes that writers identified as being essential for dialogue that need to be considered here, because they influence every facet of the interaction. Two that we will discuss are unconditional positive regard and a spirit of mutual equality.

Unconditional positive regard

The term unconditional positive regard was coined by psychologist Carl Rogers, as a central tenet in his person-centered therapy. Rogers believed that therapists needed to create a nonjudgmental environment in which patients saw that therapists showed an acceptance of, and positive attitude toward, clients as human beings. This attitude suggested that the therapist wished them well, regardless of what they thought or said. To Rogers, unconditional positive regard was essential for therapists because it made clients comfortable speaking about whatever issues were troubling them. It is important to note that this positive regard did not mean that the therapist approved of a client's destructive behaviors, only that the therapist wanted the best for that person regardless of what the client said or did.

Unconditional positive regard is helpful for dialogue because it establishes good will even when people have goals that seem to conflict. An attitude of unconditional positive regard tells the other person, "We may or may not agree, but I value you as a person and will treat you with respect and dignity." This message can have a powerful impact on making dialogue possible, even in cases where differing positions could cause antagonism in the conversation. Consider again the story of Kevin, from the beginning of this chapter. It is reasonable to assume that Kevin showed positive regard for his boss, even though he had concerns about the soundness of his plan. It seems likely that had Kevin not shown unconditional positive regard, that conversation would not have turned out the way that it did.

This example helps show that dialogue cannot just be reduced to a set of techniques but rather, it also depends on the character of the people involved. Unconditional positive regard can seem difficult to enact at times when you encounter someone hard to like. Even when you disagree with a person's beliefs, attitudes, or actions, the ability to respect another person's humanity and desire the best for her or him is a powerful force in enabling dialogue to take place. Showing goodwill may open communication options you thought were impossible. One of the most common ways we can express unconditional positive regard is through "agreeing to disagree." When we do this you allow for the other party to hold their position, while you hold yours, and the relationship is not damaged. You accept the fact you disagree and harbor no ill will toward the person for their beliefs. The practice of unconditional positive regard involves separating the areas of disagreement and "annoying behaviors" a person exhibits from your relationship because those things do not cause you serious distress or harm.

Think about a case where your roommate has left dirty dishes in the sink. Rather than getting upset with the person for this annoying behavior, you could engage them in a a conversation about it. You might find out your roommate had a bad day or emergency to attend to that caused them to not do the dishes. Just because the dishes were not done does not make your roommate a bad or lazy person.

Spirit of mutual equality

Having a spirit of mutual equality means that participants in dialogue consider each other equal as human beings, even if they have differences in social esteem or organizational authority. Thus, parents and children or bosses and subordinates see each other not as different in authority or rank, but equal as two people. This equality does not eliminate the fact that one party has greater power than the other, but it means that their communication treats each person as equal in value as a person rather than treating one person as superior to the other. Communication scholar Richard Johannesen describes the spirit of mutual equality this way: "Although society may rank participants in dialogue as of unequal status or accomplishment, the participants themselves view each other as persons, not as objects to be manipulated or exploited. The exercise of power or superiority is to be avoided. Participants do not impose their opinion, cause, or will."[13] For a list of behaviors that do not exhibit a spirit of mutual equality, and try instead to exercise power and superiority in an interaction, see Table 12.2 below.

Table 12.2

Behaviors that Encourage and Discourage a Spirit of Mutual Equality	
Encourage	**Discourage**
• Paraphrase what was just said • Encourage others to speak • Allow others to speak • Let conversation develop • Collaborate on solutions • Treat conversation as an unfolding process	• Seek to comment on every comment • Work to achieve your own goals • Compete for attention • Try to control conversation's direction • Desire final say on decision • Treat conversation as a game to be won

Maintaining a spirit of mutual equality is important in dialogue. If it is clear to a lower-ranked participant that the higher-ranked person does not treat his or her perspective as equally worthy, there is little reason to engage in conversation. Think of someone who seems to look down on you as being of lesser intelligence or experience. How much do you disclose to that person? Probably not as much as with someone who values your perspectives. Or consider a boss who treats you as less capable than him- or herself. How willing are you to offer your thoughts about improving the workplace? On the other hand, consider a teacher you have had who truly valued and respected your ideas in class. You are likely much more willing to share your thoughts with that teacher than with the others, despite your large deficit in education and experience on the class topic, because that person treats you with a spirit of mutual equality. You may have less education or fewer credentials on the topic, but if the teacher acknowledges that you might have interesting ideas that he or she never thought about, it invites you to participate fully in the conversation.

As the preceding examples make clear, a spirit of mutual equality does not eliminate status or power differences. What it does is remove them from the effort to gain mutual understanding. Once that process has taken place, the party with authority needs to make an appropriate decision. Remember, dialogue means a free exchange of ideas with a goal toward understanding, not agreement.

Creating a Supportive Climate for Conversation

supportive climate
. . . .
a communication situation in which a person feels he or she can speak freely without risk of harm

defensive climate
. . . .
a communication situation in which a person feels threatened

chilling effect
. . . .
an action that discourages others from speaking their mind

A necessary condition for dialogue to take place is the creation of a *supportive climate*. Supportiveness is the opposite of defensiveness. A *defensive climate* exists when people feel threatened or attacked, and believes that messages they send may be used against them. Johannesen notes that a person who creates a supportive climate "allows free expression, seeks understanding, and avoids value judgments that stifle. [That person] shows desire and capacity to listen without anticipating, interfering, competing, refuting, or warping meanings into preconceived interpretations."[14] People feel much more comfortable sharing ideas, brainstorming, and self-disclosing in supportive environments. That is not the case when they feel the need to defend themselves. Consider a time when you felt threatened by another person, and knew that anything you said would potentially be used against you. How likely were you to open up and share honestly with that person? Probably not at all. This is why defensive climates eliminate the possibility of dialogue. Attention to creating a supportive climate is important for everyone, but it is especially important for those who hold greater social or organizational power than the person with whom they are speaking. The *chilling effect* of defensiveness is amplified when combined with power. As an example of the chilling effect at work, let's consider a conversation with a parent about the classes you are considering taking. The student wants input and advice, and is ultimately responsible for choosing their classes, while their parents pay their tuition. The student's father makes it clear that he feels the student should take Economics, the class that is the least interesting to the child. Rather than explaining why, the father states, "It's foolish and stupid to take the history class because you can always read about it later from a book at Barnes and Noble, so you should learn economics from an expert." The student feels like further conversation will not be helpful because of the way their father conveyed his opinion and thoughts, and also worries that if they do not take Economics they will lose their parent's support for their school bills. No threat was made in this example, but the way the subject was addressed by the one party did not create a climate in which conversation about all the options could be explored. The dialogue was chilled.

How can you create a supportive climate? Communication scholar Jack Gibb wrote an article in 1961 that is still used today to guide behavior in creating supportive climates.[15] Gibb provided six contrasting behaviors that promote either supportive or defensive communication:

Supportive behaviors		Defensive behaviors		Table 12.3
Description	Non-judgmental statement or account	*Evaluation*	Statement that passes judgment in some way	
Problem orientation	Seeks to find a good solution to a problem	*Control*	Seeks to impose a specific solution	
Spontaneity	Thought up at the moment	*Strategy*	Preplanned approach designed to manipulate a person or situation	
Empathy	Cares about the other person's feelings	*Neutrality*	Doesn't care about others' feelings	
Equality	Two people are equal as humans	*Superiority*	One person is greater than the other on some characteristic (e.g., power, wealth, intellect)	
Provisionalism	An idea seems promising, pending further consideration	*Certainty*	An answer is final and requires no further consideration	

Consider how these behaviors work to create supportiveness or defensiveness with the following example. A doctoral student, Reyna, was having difficulties completing her dissertation because her adviser was not reading drafts of her work and giving her feedback within a reasonable time. Reyna needed the professor's feedback and his eventual approval in order to take her dissertation to the committee that would judge whether her research passed or failed. She contacted the department's Director of Graduate Studies (DGS) to see if he could help. The DGS wanted to resolve the issue but he had no authority over the adviser, who was a faculty peer. Stop and think for a moment about how the DGS could use the strategies above to address the issue and help Reyna while minimizing the adviser's defensiveness.

In this case, the DGS stopped by the adviser's office so they could talk in person. He told the adviser that the student felt she wasn't getting feedback in a timely manner, and said that he wanted to learn more about the situation. He indicated that he hadn't formed any conclusions about what was happening because he hadn't yet listened to the adviser. As the conversation unfolded, the adviser provided some information that seemed contradictory to what the student said, but also some information consistent with the student's claims. The DGS expressed sympathy at one point for the adviser's busy schedule. The two explored some ideas together for resolving the issue, and eventually they worked out a plan that seemed like it would suit everyone's interests. The DGS relayed this information to the student, and within a month the dissertation was done.

How did the DGS create a supportive environment? First, the conversation began with a description ("Here is what the student said") rather than an evaluation ("I've heard that you're not doing your job well enough"). He showed empathy by noting the adviser's busy schedule. He treated the adviser with equality, and allowed both of them to work out a solution together. The collaboration on solutions resulted from a problem orientation, and also allowed room for discussion instead of certainty in their conversation. Together, these behaviors created a supportive climate for the conversation, rather than making the adviser defensive.

It is important to note that dialogue won't always result in a positive outcome. The adviser could have reacted negatively to any suggestion that he was negligent, he could have promised actions that he didn't follow through with, or he could have become angry at the student's allegations and become a harsher critic of her work. We don't suggest that dialogue is a magic potion that makes all problems end well. But we can say this: if the DGS had created defensiveness in this initial conversation, it's a pretty safe bet that a problem which proved to have an easy solution wouldn't have worked out so well. What this example illustrates is not that dialogue solves all problems, but that it opens possibilities that non-dialogic approaches preclude. And even if a non-dialogic solution could have helped the student complete her dissertation, it is a reasonable to assume that the DGS and adviser's relationship would have been lower in quality going forward than it was a result of the dialogic approach.

Principles of Speaking in Dialogue

We have saved principles of speaking for last in our discussion of how to promote dialogue for two reasons. First, we wish to emphasize that your attention in dialogue should foremost be on listening and maintaining the requisite attitudes. Although dialogue is a two-way interaction, it works best when both parties are more concerned with listening than with getting their message across. Second, the attitudes and guidelines for creating a supportive climate provide considerable guidance for how to frame your messages in a dialogic encounter. We could almost have left speaking out of our discussion of how to engage in dialogue without hurting your ability to do it well. But, there are a few specifics beyond what we have mentioned that are worth noting.

Don't confuse judgments and facts

When sharing your views, there are many types of information you might share—facts, your feelings, opinions, positions you take, judgments you make, preferences, and much more. When talking with someone whose perspectives are different from yours, it is important that your claims be appropriate to the type of information in question. If facts are called for, then it is important not to mix in opinions and present them as fact. If your attitudes or feelings are relevant, then talking about them as such is perfectly appropriate.

"I received the paper at 8:58" is a fact, whereas "The paper was late because she has time management problems" mixes fact with assumption. Confounding those two can create problems in dialogue if you are just trying to sort out the facts. On the other hand, sticking with the facts alone might not be helpful in a dialogue if someone really wants to understand your opinion about the situation. It is important, though, to always own your own feelings and beliefs when you present them as such. When we blame others for how we feel we actually diminish respect for ourselves and make it appear others can control our emotions and beliefs. For examples of how to change common "you" statements to respectful "I" statements see Table 12.4.

Table 12.4

Phrases for Owning Your Feelings and Opinions
"I feel upset by this" INSTEAD of "You don't care about my feelings"
"I believe I have not explained myself yet " INSTEAD OF "You never let me tell my side of the story"
"I don't believe you are being honest" INSTEAD OF "You don't keep your word"
"I am not enjoying myself" INSTEAD OF "You are no fun"
"I do not believe that is true" INSTEAD OF "You don't know what you are talking about"
"Please give me a moment, I feel a little frazzled" INSTEAD OF "You're driving me crazy"

Genuineness

Genuineness refers to being "direct, honest, and straightforward."[16] When acting in a genuine manner, you are not being strategic or manipulative, but instead speaking openly and honestly with the other person. This authenticity is important in dialogue, because it promotes trust and allows for a true flow of information. People who hide behind a façade or communicate in a tactical manner designed to create a strategic advantage eliminate the possibility of mutual understanding, which is the very purpose of dialogue. Furthermore, when people suspect that their conversational partners are not being genuine, an environment is created in which wariness and distrust dominate and lead to further degeneration of dialogue. Communication scholars Charles Brown and Paul Keller noted, "The reason truth . . . is important is that people cannot build bridges between them that crumble when tested."[17]

However, the importance of being genuine raises one of the great dangers of dialogue. In being genuine, you expose yourself to *risk*. Any behavior that can have either good or bad consequences is risky. If there is no element of danger, then the action is a safe bet, not a risk. When one person is genuine and the partner is not, the person being genuine can easily be taken advantage of.

risk
an action with either positive or negative outcomes

This risk creates a circular dilemma. If a person is untrustworthy, then it is not likely a good idea to be genuine. Yet without genuineness, it is hard to build trust. So, what can you do? Strategy and manipulation are wrong in dialogue, so engaging with someone who is untrustworthy means you will need to be guarded. Being honest and direct, but being careful about what and how much you disclose, is probably the best approach. That allows as much genuineness as possible without exposing yourself in ways that could ultimately be harmful. In this process we encourage you to be realistic about your assessment of how trustworthy others are. People who are distrustful of *everyone* often become reclusive and withdrawn. On the other hand, people who are too trusting often get hurt.

There is a great paradox about risk. Taking risk means you will get hurt some of the time, but never taking risks doesn't assure positive outcomes; in fact, it ultimately leads to negative outcomes. In the long run, playing it safe can be the most dangerous course of action. People who fear rejection and thus never show their feelings or ask out people they are attracted to avoid the pain of rejection—but they may also never find love. So, the unwillingness to take a risk does not necessarily keep a person from ever failing; instead it often keeps a person from ever succeeding. By definition, risk requires the possibility of failing and getting hurt. But never taking risk almost assures it.

Life is not safe, so you will have to take chances some of the time. Just don't be reckless about them. In the movie *Batman Begins* a young Bruce Wayne falls down into a cavern and when his father comes to get him Bruce is upset at falling. His father asks him, "Why do we fall?" to which the child responds, "So we can learn to get back up again." Risk involves being willing to fall, because only when we stumble can we grow and learn. Experience, even setbacks, can be the greatest teacher.

Disagree with respect

In 2010, Holocaust survivor and Nobel Prize winner Elie Wiesel spoke at the Schuster Center as part of UD's speaker series. One of the subjects of his address was dialogue. In his speech, Wiesel told the university community that dialogue is vital to us because of the "need to disagree with elegance and respect." As follows from being genuine, it is essential to note that dialogue requires that people be honest with each other. Dialogue does not ask us to withhold our true feelings in an effort to be nice to others. Instead it asks us to be honest and disagree as appropriate—but to do so in a manner that shows caring and respect. Just because we disagree with an idea someone has, or a position they hold, does not make them a bad person, poor thinker or not worth our time; we can, should, and need to be able to have disagreements and live together knowing we hold different opinions. It is essential for a civilized open society to express and accept disagreement in a respectful manner.

DIALOGUE AND COMMUNICATION CONTEXT

dyadic
an interaction between two people

Throughout the discussion of dialogue, we avoid limiting the context in which it may take place. Many dialogues happen in *dyadic* settings, such as when romantic partners discuss their relationship, when a professor and student talk about problems the student is having in class, or when coworkers discuss workplace issues. But dialogue can take place in any setting. In the workplace,

---

SPOTLIGHTING THEORISTS: RONALD ARNETT

Ronald Arnett

One of the most influential contemporary scholars on the subject of dialogue is Ronald Arnett, currently a professor at Duquesne University. Arnett received his graduate education in the early 1970s, and read widely from the writings on dialogue of the 1960s. He was interested in helping people better understand and practice dialogue in everyday life. Some of his early books, such as *Dwell in Peace* and *Communication and Community* offered insights into the philosophy underlying dialogue and issues people needed to be aware of to better understand and apply it. Other books considered dialogue in certain settings, such as *Dialogic Education*, which gave teachers ideas of how dialogue could lead to better educational outcomes.

As well-versed as any scholar at the philosophical foundations of dialogue from the 1960s, Arnett began to see shortcomings of some of the ideas from that era. At the same time, he also saw the value that dialogue had for society. Arnett began to think and write about some limitations of older conceptions of dialogue and to present alternative philosophical perspectives.

Arnett's books have so much depth that beginners cannot always appreciate all the ideas in them, but they have helped reshape the way contemporary scholars think about dialogue. Newer books such as *Dialogic Civility in a Cynical Age* or *Dialogic Confession: Bonhoeffer's Rhetoric of Responsibility* explored not only dialogue, but also the intersection between dialogue and larger societal issues.

If you are interested in dialogue, try reading one of Arnett's books now, then reread it ten years later. You'll find a whole new layer of wisdom that eluded you when you first read it.

dialogue is often very helpful when used in business meetings. Kevin's example from the beginning of this chapter is a good case where dialogue was used in a group setting. And dialogue is especially important at a societal level. We have noted earlier the deficit of dialogue in our political system. If all politicians worked with each other dialogically the positive impact on society would be spectacular. There are a number of organizations that exist whose mission includes fostering greater public dialogue about important social and political issues. Two of these include the Kettering Foundation, based here in Dayton, and the Center for Public Deliberation, which is housed in the Communication Studies Department at Colorado State University.

Your classes at UD provide a rich environment where dialogue can take place, especially when you discuss controversial topics. Each student has a lot to contribute to his or her classes. The University of Dayton is especially interested in students tackling difficult issues of social and personal importance. Sharing your perspective and respectfully listening to others is an essential activity in getting the most out of class. Classes may push you to confront ideas you haven't thought about or encounter others whose viewpoints conflict strongly with your own. Use the principles you have learned in CMM 100 to engage these differences in a dialogic manner and you may be impressed with the way it expands your understanding and builds connections with other students. Dialogue will open a bigger world for you than you would otherwise have known.

CRITICISMS OF DIALOGUE

When dialogue began to fall out of favor in the 1970s, critics raised a number of concerns about the merits of dialogue. Several of their points raise issues you should consider. One person who helped respond to these criticisms is Ronald C. Arnett, a professor at Duquesne University. He recognized some of the limitations of dialogue as it was practiced and discussed in the 1960s, but also saw its potential if used appropriately. This section details some of the criticisms of dialogue that manifested in the 1970s and also responses to those criticisms that were informed, at least in part, by the important work of Ronald C. Arnett.

Dialogue Is Not Always Possible

The criticism

In order for dialogue to work, all parties must follow the principles of dialogue. If one person refuses to listen, acts in a manner that creates defensiveness, or fails to be genuine, then dialogue cannot happen.

A response to the criticism

It is true that dialogue is not always possible. And not only is it impossible when some people aren't cooperative; people with abusive personalities or people with psychological disorders might not even be capable of interacting dialogically. Dietrich Bonhoeffer, a famous theologian who favored pacifism, was involved in a plot to assassinate Adolf Hitler because he felt that was the only way to effectively oppose the evil of Hitler's regime. Bonhoeffer had concluded that dialogue with the Nazi party was impossible.

So, the charges are true. This criticism, however, can sometimes be taken too far. While there are cases in which dialogue is neither possible nor ideal (see the next three criticisms for cases where it is not ideal), there is a large set of circumstances in which dialogue would be possible for people skilled enough at making it happen, and where it would be beneficial if only people made an honest attempt. Assess for yourself when dialogue is possible, but be careful not to rule it out too swiftly. It will work more often than most people think. Take a case that occurs for most students at least once during their academic career. If you have a large paper due and feel that you cannot complete it by the instructor's deadline you have several choices:

1) Miss the deadline, and appeal after the fact;

2) Hand in what you have finished;

3) Speak with the teacher in advance.

Of these, the most frightening and least employed by students is the third—but it is also the most effective. By engaging with your instructor beforehand and having a dialogue about your situation and the assignment's due date you will probably be able to generate some acceptable positive outcomes. Making the assumption that the instructor will not speak with you leaves you no viable options, so take the leap and try speaking with the instructor in advance of the deadline and see what happens.

In relationships you choose to form, you and your partner mutually create the rules of interaction. Romantic relationships are very important to many people and to society. Realize that you have total control over the way that you and a partner respond to differences. We encourage you to practice dialogue in romantic relationships. Doing so will set you up to beat the societal statistics on failure of long-term relationships. And if you find that a person you are dating is unwilling to meet differences dialogically, you might ask whether this is someone you want to commit to long term. You are going to encounter a *lot* of difficult issues to resolve over a lifetime together.

Dialogue Makes You Vulnerable

The criticism

Being genuine and open when others are being manipulative makes it easy for others to take advantage of you—and some will.

A response to the criticism

Like the first charge, this one is true as well. We have already discussed this issue when we talked about risks of being genuine. We revisit this criticism in this context as a reminder that dialogue requires some risk, but that you should be intelligent in judging risk. We also offer a suggestion on managing these encounters: Be careful how much information you share. In most situations you can establish a supportive climate, maintain your integrity, and listen dialogically without putting yourself in any jeopardy, and that alone can do quite a lot to reap the benefits of dialogue even in the presence of someone who is not to be trusted.

Dialogue Requires Too Much Effort

The criticism

Dialogue takes a lot of time and effort. In cases in which a person has the authority to make a decision, all the effort of dialogue may not be worth it. That time and energy come at the expense of something else, and for busy people (like business leaders) the time and effort spent on dialogue may require that time and effort be taken away from other areas.

A response to the criticism

Like the previous critiques, we include this because it contains an element of truth. Dialogue does take more time and effort than a command decision. The question to consider is what consequences you are seeking. If the decision is simple and no one is highly invested in any particular outcome, then the effort of dialogue might offer no gain—and it will certainly cause negative outcomes if people feel frustrated with dragging the process out. In these cases, dialogue is not the best choice.

But, in cases where the decision is important and there are significant differences, then dialogue is likely to build greater support for a decision and better relationships among the people affected by it. Furthermore, if a decision is unpopular, there may be appeals or resistance to it, and in the long run those consequences may require more time and effort than the initial dialogue would have taken. Keep in mind, though, that engaging in dialogue doesn't assure that people will be satisfied with a course of action. It only increases the odds in the immediate situation, and encourages engagement and respect in future endeavors. Human behavior is so complex that we can rarely make perfect predictions about outcomes.

This criticism raises important questions you should consider when deciding how to act in the face of difference:

- How large are people's differences, and how strongly do they feel about their positions?
- How important is it that people understand each other or support a decision?
- What consequences are likely to follow from this situation?

Use that information to decide whether dialogue is worthwhile. Don't use dialogue when it is an unnecessary waste of time and energy.

Dialogue Is Not Appropriate for Every Relationship and Situation

The criticism

Dialogue is great for building relationships, but no one needs to have a meaningful dialogue with the plumber, tax accountant, or grocery clerk. And you definitely don't want to settle in for a long dialogue about the best way to get out of a burning building.

A response to the criticism

True again, and this was one of the reasons why dialogue initially fell out of favor. In the 1960s dialogue was sometimes seen as a cure-all, and some people advocated using it too widely. You *don't* need to engage in dialogue while paying for your groceries or getting your drain unclogged. And if the building is burning, efficiency in communication definitely trumps the relationship-building capacity of dialogue.

Dialogue, in its fullest sense, is not necessary in any situation in which you interact with someone as a role rather than as an individual. In a brief service encounter, your concern is largely that the person in uniform is capable of doing a job well, not in building a meaningful and lasting personal relationship with that individual. In those situations, a simple businesslike transaction will usually suffice. That being said, there are still many elements of dialogue that can be implemented with no more effort than not doing them. For instance, treating the plumber as an equally worthy human being (showing *equality* instead of *superiority*) doesn't take any more effort than being condescending, and it's likely to have a positive effect. So, even though it's probably a bad idea to ask probing follow-up questions to the plumber about how the stubborn clog in your drain makes them feel, treating them with some respect is likely to be a good idea. You shouldn't implement every aspect of dialogue in every situation, but using a few simple and appropriate elements is a good idea even when dialogue is not necessary.

DIALOGUE VERSUS DEBATE

Two of the goals of CMM 100 are to teach you how to use dialogue and how to wield persuasive arguments. You may have realized by now that these two approaches are not completely separate. In a dialogue you will often examine the quality of arguments, and in a debate you can use some of dialogue's listening skills to be more effective. That said, the two approaches of dialogue and debate are fundamentally different in their goals and many of their methods. Debate seeks to win a contest or propel action through superior reason and evidence. Dialogue, on the other hand, seeks to build mutual understanding, and that understanding may not even offer a solution to a disagreement or problem.

Both dialogue and debate are powerful forms of communication for those who have mastered them. A strong debater can stand up in a corporate board room, make a case for a business plan, and defend it from ill-conceived attacks or counterarguments. A lawyer who can skillfully defend an innocent client, a corporate leader who can advocate a sound business plan, and a lab worker who can persuade coworkers to adopt a better procedure are going to be highly successful in their professions. UD's graduates should *Learn, Lead, and Serve*. Leading effectively requires the ability to persuade others to make good choices, and making good choices requires a strong grounding in ethics and an understanding of social justice. Leadership also requires knowing how to build respect from those around you. Dialogue helps you do this.

While society is quick to recognize the power of persuasion, fewer people are as aware of the power of dialogue. Kevin's example showed just what dialogue can do in the workplace. Dialogue is also essential in personal and family relationships. A skilled debater who doesn't know when to stop arguing and just listen will alienate loved ones and coworkers alike. Understanding others not only builds relationships; it also allows a person to act in a manner that will gain support. And certainly, the trust that can be built through dialogue can be an important factor in working together.

When to Use Dialogue

The question of when to use dialogue is complex and cannot be answered in a paragraph. Developing judgment of when dialogue is appropriate takes years of experience to assess many elements of a situation. We offer just a couple major factors you might think about, but we encourage you to consider discussing this further in class and paying attention to it in your own life. Here are a few suggestions to get you started in your thinking. Dialogue is useful in situations in which:

- You are trying to understand a complex problem.
- People have strong interests and widely divergent views.
- Seeking new ideas and a better understanding is essential.
- You have to make a decision that has a significant impact on someone else.
- The relationship among the people is as important as the process and its outcomes.

What other criteria can you think of for judging when to use dialogue?

TAKING NOTES DURING A DIALOGUE

Dialogues take place in a variety of situations, from a lunch conversation with friends, to family dinners, to meetings with colleagues and co-workers. Not all of these situations call for taking notes, but when the issue is important, the topic controversial or complex, or when a record of what was said might be useful in the future, it is important to take notes during the discussion.

When discussing something important, like the family budget, plans for an upcoming event, or a potential job opportunity, taking notes is not only useful, but necessary. It allows you to track what is said and determine what things you might misunderstand and thus ask a question about. Notes keep you from interrupting by recording the question you want to ask so you do not forget, while not having to cut someone off mid-statement.

The same holds true for dialogues about controversial or complex topics. These situations might arise in classrooms during discussions, visits with doctors or lawyers, applying for a mortgage, or during business meetings. When topics are controversial our passions might get the better of us and result in interrupting others, shouting, making impulsive assumptions about the other party, and getting argumentative. Note-taking allows us to slow down our emotional reactions, clarify what we want to know, and ask it at the appropriate time. This allows the other person to speak fully and ensures we learn what we need to properly understand the other person's position.

There are also dialogues when the notes we take serve as records of the conversation. Whenever you have a meeting with someone, be it a job interview or discussion with a faculty member about a class, taking notes can be very helpful for having an accurate record of what was said. Going in with prepared questions, taking notes about the answers provided to those questions, and jotting down other things that came up also helps you have a clear understanding of what transpired. Without notes, you rely entirely on memory which is actually not very accurate—in fact, the further you get from the conversation the less you recall accurately. Notes help fill that gap. They help you remember what tasks you were told to complete, how to improve your grade, and even what salary and compensation was offered. Notes help us keep important information straight, and are thus an essential tool for success in dialogues.

You might be wondering, "What should these notes look like?" That answer varies with each person and situation. When preparing notes before the dialogue, such as walking into a meeting with a professor about a grade or entering a job interview, they should contain the key points you want to make clear as well as the questions you feel you need to ask. When your comments express disagreement, make sure you clearly lay out the other person's original position as well as where and why you disagree in your notes. They should have proper references to resources that support your position, especially in case someone asks for that information. They also should not be so burdensome to make it seem like you are reading off your notes—in other words, not a manuscript. Generally, you just want to write key words and phrases.

It is also important in taking notes to be able to discern which information is more important and what is less important, so you can focus your note-taking on the important information. In high school, teachers often give handouts for class notes that tell the students what the most important ideas are. But in college—and in life—you rarely have someone else do the thinking for you. If your boss is explaining a project you need to do or giving you feedback on your work, she or he will not usually begin by giving you a handout telling you what to listen for. You need to develop this skill yourself. So, begin by asking yourself what makes some information in any type of communicative situation (class lecture, group meeting, conflict, etc.) more important.

When taking notes during the dialogue, everyone develops their own version of shorthand. It is not important that you write down everything that is said—if you did this you would not be listening and thinking about the other person's comments. What is important is that you record who said the piece of information you feel is important to recall, and if that statement prompted you to think of a question, write the question down so you don't forget it or who it is directed towards. These notes can also contain "notes to self" that remind you to examine something prompted by the dialogue at a later point. These notes help you keep up with the conversation and identify places where you can or need to contribute with added information or questions for clarification.

Throughout your undergraduate career every class you take at UD provides an opportunity to hone your dialogue skills, specifically those related to note taking. We too often believe that note-taking is something done during lecture, but it is a tool with much wider implications than recalling classroom content for a test. It enhances our ability understand complicated subjects, engage people on controversial topics without jumping to conclusions, and perhaps most importantly, it provides us with a clear and accurate record of important conversations. Table 12.5 provides some tips for good note-taking behaviors during a dialogue.

Table 12.5

Good Note-taking Behaviors during a Dialogue	
Dos	**Don'ts**
• Prepare questions in advance when possible • Paraphrase position of other person with whom you disagree • Identify the most important points from what is said • Identify who said something that sparked a response from you • Keep notes in a place you will remember	• Write down everything said • Issue judgments of others • Forget references • Cut someone off • Write unrelated information

DIALOGUE AT THE UNIVERSITY OF DAYTON

Because dialogue is essential for building community, the Marianists are strong advocates of mastering and using dialogue. Dialogue is specifically mentioned in *Commitment to Community* when talking about treating others with respect: "Learn to handle conflict with respect, dialogue, understanding, and forgiveness." However, dialogue is much more widely infused through *C2C* than in just that phrase. Taking responsibility for yourself and your community means you will need to "be aware of the weakest and most vulnerable around you and seek to serve them." Developing your faith life means you'll need to "learn about and show respect for the religious traditions of others." And being honest, truthful, and living with integrity requires that you "practice behavior that is not insulting, demeaning, destructive, or harmful to you or others" and "respond truthfully and respectfully when your behavior is questioned by another." These actions can only be fully accomplished through dialogue.

Dialogue is an essential means of communication in many of your classes. The Common Academic Program asks you to engage in ideas that may be different from what you learned growing up. It asks you to understand a diversity of perspectives, and to wrestle with complex issues that even great thinkers have struggled with. You will need to engage in dialogue with your professors, with students, and with other members of the university community in order to get the most out of your college education and experience. And don't hesitate to challenge your professors in a dialogic manner. The key is that you challenge yourself and others with the respectful approach to dialogue we have discussed in this chapter.

Dialogue is essential at UD outside of class as well. Using dialogue to address conflicts in your residence hall or in the ghetto can help develop better community. Off-campus service learning projects or other interactions with the broader Dayton community can benefit from dialogue as well. As UD diversifies its student body, the opportunity to understand those who are different from you can truly enhance your education. With over 1,000 international students, there is a great opportunity for all UD students to learn from cultural similarities and differences.

We encourage you, regardless of your background, to step out of your comfort zone and dialogue with those of different cultural experiences. Invite each other to events or just to have dinner together and talk about your life history and how you ended up at UD. You'll be amazed what you learn and how that can enrich you and our community.

SUMMARY

We conclude by repeating a point we have made several times before: Dialogue is not a magical cure-all that makes all things good. All it does is offer an opportunity for understanding. Beyond that, the outcomes of an interaction are a result of what you choose to do. If you can master dialogue, it won't solve all problems or make your life perfect, but it will offer possibilities that are unimaginable for those who cannot use it effectively.

KEY TERMS

chilling effect 322	listening 315
debate 314	monologue 313
defensive climate 322	presentness 315
dialogue 313	risk 325
dyadic 326	supportive climate 322
integrity 313	

REVIEW QUESTIONS

1. How has our thinking about dialogue changed and stayed the same over the years?
2. What is dialogue, and how does it compare and contrast with other modes of communication?
3. What behaviors are essential for dialogic listening?
4. What attitudes and speaking behaviors are necessary for dialogue?
5. Why is character important to dialogue?
6. What are four criticisms of dialogue, and how should we respond to them?
7. How should you apply dialogue at UD?

THINK ABOUT IT

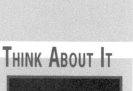

1. In what ways do people most commonly deviate from dialogue when communicating about difference?
2. If everyone mastered dialogue in high school, what impact would it have on our lives and society?
3. How have digital communication technologies affected the use of dialogue in everyday life?
4. How can you use dialogue to make UD a better community?

ACTIVITIES FOR ACTION

1. Watch some government action on C-SPAN. In what ways do the representatives engage in or violate dialogue? What aspects of dialogue could be employed to offer outcomes better for the people of the local, state, or federal government? Now, watch a reality TV show in which contestants have significant interaction. How do they model or violate dialogue? Considering that they are competing against each other, are there ways they could use elements of dialogue without hurting their chances in the game? Then compare and contrast what you observed between the contexts of government and entertainment.

2. Choose one element of dialogue you think you could use more effectively. Apply that element in class and in your personal life for a week. Do you observe any positive impact on account of using just that one element of dialogue? What do you take away from this experience?

ENDNOTES

1. Kerry Patterson, Joseph Grenny, Ron McMillan, & Al Switzler, *Crucial conversations: Tools for Talking When Stakes Are High* (New York: McGraw-Hill, 2002).

2. Ibid. 19.

3. Ibid. 19.

4. Jon A. Hess, & Joy Piazza, "Public and Relational Communication Ethics in Political Communication: Integrity, Secrecy, and Dialogue in *The Contender*," In P. Japp, M. Meister, & D. Japp (Eds.), *Communication Ethics, Media, and Popular Culture* (New York: Peter Lang Publishers, 2005), 137–160.

5. For example, see: Ronald C. Arnett, *Communication and community: Implications of Martin Buber's Dialogue*, (Carbondale, IL: Southern Illinois University Press, 1986).

6. Paul W. Keller & Charles T. Brown, "An Interpersonal Ethic for Communication," *Journal of Communication, 18*(1), 1968, 73–81; Paul W. Keller, "Interpersonal Dissent and the Ethics of Dialogue," *Communication, 6*, 1981, 287–303.

7. Harold H. Saunders, *A Public Peace Process: Sustained Dialogue to Transform Racial and Ethnic Conflicts*, (New York: St. Martin's Press, 1999).

8. David S. Young, *The Gift of Dialogue*, (Westfield, IN: The Greenleaf Center for Servant Leadership, 2012).

9. Keller & Brown, 1968.

10. John Medina, *Brain Rules: 12 Principles for Surviving and Thriving at Work, Home, and School.* (Seattle, WA: Pear Press, 2008).

11. Ibid. 85.

12. Jonathan Haidt, *The Happiness Hypothesis: Finding Modern Truth in Ancient Wisdom*, (New York: Basic Books, 2008).

13. Richard L. Johannesen, "The Emerging Concept of Communication as Dialogue," *Quarterly Journal of Speech, 57*, 1971, 376.

14. Ibid.

15. Jack R. Gibb, "Defensive Communication," *Journal of Communication, 11*(3), 1961, p. 141–148.

16. Johannesen, 376.

17. Charles T. Brown & Paul W. Keller, *Monologue to Dialogue: An Exploration of Interpersonal Communication*, (Englewood Cliffs, NJ: Prentice-Hall, 1973).

18. Stephen L. Carter, *Integrity* (New York: Harper Perennial, 1996), 7.

SCENARIOS

Scenario 1

Construct statements indicative of each of the defensive climates identified by the book, then reformat those statements so that a supportive climate is created.

Scenario 2

Look at each of the following statements. Identify which ones are judgments and which ones are facts. For those that are judgments, turn them into statements of fact.

These pants are size 8.

Your lateness just shows you are irresponsible.

I never got a response to my email, so they must not be interested in hiring me.

Only lazy people skip workouts.

My husband didn't tell me I looked pretty.

I must not be very smart because I got a C on the exam.

I did not practice my speech.

Diet soda contains less sugar than regular soda.

Rice bread tastes like cardboard compared to wheat bread.

The new student housing building is a waste of money.

Scenario 3

Look at the following excerpts taken from recent statements on current events published on the web and in newspaper columns, and imagine these are being said by someone to you over lunch. What are some properly worded clarifying questions you might ask the person who said these statements? Also, how might you paraphrase each of these excerpts into two sentences or less?

"Exciting new research conducted at the Creighton University School of Medicine in Nebraska has revealed that supplementing with vitamin D and calcium can reduce your risk of cancer by an astonishing 77 percent. This includes breast cancer, colon cancer, skin cancer and other forms of cancer. This research provides strong new evidence that vitamin D is the single most effective medicine against cancer, far outpacing the benefits of any cancer drug known to modern science. This research on vitamin D is such good news that the American Cancer Society, of course, had to say something against it. An ACS spokesperson, Marji McCullough, strategic director of nutritional epidemiology for the American Cancer Society, flatly stated that nobody should take supplements to prevent cancer."

QUESTIONS:

PARAPHRASE:

"Like health care, prices are rising rapidly for higher education because of the predominant role of thirdparty payments—federal student loans and grants, state government support for institutions and students, private philanthropic gifts and endowment income. College seniors who borrow to finance their education now graduate with an average of $24,000 in debt, and student loan debt now tops credit card debt among Americans. When some else is paying a lot of the bills, students are less sensitive to the price, thus allowing the colleges to care less about keeping prices under control. And the nonprofit nature of institutions reduces incentives for colleges and universities to be efficient. The key to getting costs under control is contained in three words that begin with the letter "I"—information, incentives and innovation."

QUESTIONS:

PARAPHRASE:

"According to the court, diversity, while a permissible and laudable goal, can no longer be a code word or substitute for the idea of achieving only racial or ethnic heterogeneity. The court suggests that if a university is to pursue preferential admissions in the name of diversity, then the concept must entail many forms of social diversity, not just or even primarily the applicant's race. Also, the absence of a fixed quota for a racial group or the absence of awarding of points for admission based on race does not give a university's affirmative action program constitutional approval. If race is a "meaningful factor" in the admissions process in any way, then the program is constitutionally suspect! And finally, the court declares in no uncertain terms that a preferential admissions program with race as a component is not to be justified on the basis of redressing past discrimination, since the business of redressing past wrongs is the province of courts and legislatures, not universities and their faculties."

QUESTIONS:

PARAPHRASE:

Scenario 4 (Performance)

Read the following statement and it to develop a mini-dialogue. First, each group member will deliver a brief statement outlining their response to it. Then, use each other's responses to generate a larger discussion that lasts about five minutes about the topics each person perceives as important.

In Summer 2012 Dan Cathy, president of the private family-owned national fast food chain Chik-Fil-A, ignited a controversy overran interview he conducted with Baptist Press, where he said the company was "guilty as charged" for endorsing the Biblical view of traditional marriage. He furthered the controversy a few days later when he said "I think we are inviting God's judgment on our nation when we shake a fist at him and say 'we know better than you as to what constitutes a marriage', and I pray God's mercy on our generation that has such a prideful, arrogant attitude to think we have the audacity to define what marriage is about." It later became known that Cathy and Chik-Fil-A oversee a charitable organization called the Winshape Organization that provides financial support for organizations like Focus on the Family and Exodus International. What followed included a proposed national boycott of Chik-Fil-A by supporters of same-sex marriage and a countermovement entitled "Chik-Fil-A Appreciation Day" by those that opposed same-sex marriage. The boycott cost Chik-Fil-A revenue, and also created a negative perception of the company and its employees.

After each group member delivers their responses and the group has a brief dialogue regarding the issue, reflect on the following questions.

Finally, answer the following questions about your group's dialogue experience:

1. Did any group member take notes during the comments others made?

2. Did any group member interrupt another when they spoke? What did this do to the climate?

3. How did each person perform when it came to suspending judgment?

4. Were there any statements that contributed to a defensive climate? A supportive climate? What were they?

5. Would you characterize the discussion your group had as a debate, monologue or dialogue? Why?

6. Did anyone ask any clarifying questions? What were they?

7. How did group members perform when it came to expressing unconditional positive regard for the opinions and reactions of others in the group?

8. Were responses by group members genuine? If so, how could you tell?

SAMPLE OUTLINES

Sample Explanatory Speaking Notes

Purpose: To explain to my listener the concept of ideology in the field of organizational communication.

Thesis: Ideology is a concept that scholars in the field of organizational communication use to explain why social change does not occur in some cases, even when change might be in people's best interests.

Introduction

Greeting and expression of gratitude

Question: one social problem that you would like to be overcome?

Link to ideology. Taken any courses on it?

Degree in org comm – a central concept.

Can help you to understand why X problem has not yet been solved.

Thesis: Ideology = a concept that scholars in organizational communication | explain why social change does not occur in some cases, even when might be in people's best interests.

Body

Point 1

State the Point: One function of ideology = disposes people to see the way things are as they way that they should be or even must be.

Present Material Using the Principles and Tools from Chapter 4
- *Information*: Giddens (1979), professor at Cambridge University and director of the London School of Economics, ideology = "naturalizes the present."
- *Metaphor*: A veil. Can see through but not fully. Distorted.
- *Story:* Plato's (2009) allegory of the cave. [Video 0:56-1:51]

Make the Connection between Supporting Material and the Point: Naturalization = traps a person in a particular way of seeing.

Point 2

State the Point: Another function of ideology = disposes people to see what is in interests of few as being in everyone's interest

Present Material Using the Principles and Tools from Chapter 4

- _Information:_ Giddens (1979), "sectional interests" and "universal interests"
- _Definitions:_ Sectional interests = what only benefits certain people; universal interests = what benefits all people
- _Narrative:_ Hunger Games? Convince that system benefits all, while only the Capitol. [Video]
- _Information:_ Dennis Mumby (1987), Professor of Communication at University of North Carolina, ideology as a mechanism of control.

Make the Connection between Supporting Material and the Point: Said to benefit all, but really benefits the few.

Point 3

State the Point: A third function of ideology = resist that which challenges the system

Present Material Using the Principles and Tools from Chapter 4

- _Information:_ Giddens (1979) "the denial or transmutation of contradictions"
- _Definition:_ "contradiction" = anything that could lead people to question the status quo, an anomaly. "deny" or "transmute" = explain it away, make it less a threat
- _Narrative:_ Stick to the Status Quo [Video from _High School Musical_]

Make the Connection between Supporting Material and the Point: Teaches people how to defend the ideology so that the system can continue

Summary Question

Ask listener to review points

Conclusion

Summary of Main Ideas

- **Thesis:** Ideology = a concept that scholars in organizational communication | explain why social change does not occur in some cases, even when might be in people's best interests.
- **Main Points:** Review three functions of ideology

Thanks for time, more info = can recommend readings

References

Giddens, A. (1979). *Central problems in social theory: Action, structure and contradiction in social analysis.* Berkeley: University of California.

Mumby, D. K. (1987). The political function of narrative in organizations. *Communication Monographs, 54,* 113-127.

Plato (2009). *The republic* (B. Jowett, Trans., chap. 7). Retrieved from http://classics.mit.edu/Plato/republic.8.vii.html

Persuasive Speech Outline

Thesis: Universities and colleges should eliminate honors designations for college and university graduates because they do not mean much anymore.

Introduction

I. Attention Getter: Ask yourselves this question: "When everyone is an honors student, where is the honor in your achievement?"

> **A.** Across the country students in colleges and universities all feel like a disappointment when they do not graduate with honors.

> **B.** So, they pressure faculty to give them better grades in classes so they can graduate with honors.

II. Introduce Topic: The fact is, honors designations seem to mean a lot to students, but when they are over-awarded, then the honors distinctions means very little to anyone else.

III. Thesis/Argument: In order to stop this nonsense and allow grades to mean what they indicate for a student, universities and colleges should eliminate the honors graduation designation.

IV. Establish Credibility: As a student myself who values my degree I looked into this issue over the past few weeks and discovered I am not alone in wanting to eliminate honors designations.

V. Preview: Today I want to provide you with the reasons why I believe there is no honor in the honors system.

> **A.** To make my case I will first show you two of the popular models colleges use to determine who will graduate with honors.

B. Next, I will explain how these approaches damage the idea of graduating with honors and do a disservice to the students.

C. Finally, I will explain how eliminating the honors designation for graduates is the solution to this problem.

[Transition: The problem with honors is a function of the way in which universities choose to bestow it, as we will now see.]

Body

I. Main Point #1: Universities and colleges in the United States typically use one of two models for determining which graduates will receive honors when graduating.

> **A. Subpoint:** Most higher education institutions award the best students the designation "summa cum laude," the next tier of students "magna cum laude," and a final group of students "cum laude" to differentiate them from the rest of the students.
>
> > **1. Sub-subpoint:** Each of those three titles comes from Latin, meaning "with the highest praise," "with much praise," and "with praise."
> >
> > **2. Sub-subpoint:** The use of these titles has been practiced in academia for centuries.
>
> **B. Subpoint:** Many institutions today set GPA standards for each honors category, and students must graduate with a cumulative GPA that meets the threshold of that category to receive the honor.
>
> > **1. Sub-subpoint:** For example, on a 4.0 scale, if a student achieves between a 3.9–4.0 as a cumulative GPA then at schools like the University of Alabama, University of New Mexico, and George Mason University the student will receive summa cum laude on their diploma.[1]
> >
> > **2. Sub-subpoint:** On the same scale at the same schools, if a student achieves between a 3.7–3.89 cumulative GPA then they will receive magna cum laude on their diploma.[2]
> >
> > **3. Sub-subpoint:** Finally, students who finish with between a 3.5–3.69 will be designated cum laude.[3]

[Transition: The GPA standard is not the only manner in categorizing student graduation honors used by schools today.]

---

1 Adam Sikula, "Faculty Senate Proposal," UNLV, Spring 2006.
2 Ibid.
3 Ibid.

II. Main Point #2: Some schools choose to award honors only to the top 10% of their students, regardless of their GPA.

> **A. Subpoint:** In this selection method, students receive honors regardless of their GPA, but instead the focus is on their standing at the completion of their career—a percentage of their class rank, in other words.

> **B. Subpoint:** This method allows for only a fixed number of students to receive honors, but the top performer, regardless of their GPA is guaranteed to receive the distinction of summa cum laude.

>> **1. Sub-subpoint:** The University of Nevada Las Vegas uses a variation of such a method whereby the top 1% of graduates receive summa cum laude, the next 4% receive magna cum laude and the final 5% of the top 10% of the class receive cum laude.[4]

>> **2. Sub-subpoint:** New Mexico State uses a different version of this method by giving only one person summa cum laude a year, then the top 1.5% of the class receives magna cum laude and the top 15% receive cum laude.[5]

[Transition: Regardless of whether this method or the GPA threshold method is used, these categories for graduates do not accurately recognize student achievement and thus do more harm than good to the students.]

III. Main Point #3: If honors truly showed the best and brightest students, they would mean something, but unfortunately, as I will now show you, they do not do that.

> **A. Subpoint:** The first criticism I will make addresses the GPA threshold method, which essentially says if you meet a certain GPA you receive that category's honors designation.

>> **1. Sub-subpoint:** The problem here is related to grade inflation and the fact too many students reach the honors threshold.

>> **2. Sub-subpoint:** For example, in 2001 half of the grades received by Harvard University students were in the A- to A range.[6]

>> **3. Sub-subpoint:** At Princeton between 2004 and 2007, 47% of grades received by undergraduates were some form of A.[7]

---

4 Patricia Velasco, "Grad Status Under Debate," *The Rebel Yell,* (April 27, 2006), available at: http://archive. unlvrebelyell.com/print_article.php?ID=9279 (last accessed: January 14, 2009).
5 Sikula.
6 "Grade Inflation Scrutinized at Harvard and Elsewhere," *Academe Online,* http://www.aaup.org/AAUP/ pubsres/academe/2002/MA/NB/Grade.htm?PF=1, (last accessed: January 14, 2009)
7 Thomas Bartlett and Paula Wasley, "Just Say 'A': Grade Inflation Undergoes Reality Check," *The Chronicle of Higher Education,* vol. 55, issue 2, September 5, 2008, A1-A12.

4. Sub-subpoint: This problem isn't recent either; in 1997 the City University of New York awarded almost 50% A's and B's to students.[8]

B. Subpoint: When 50% of the students are A students, what, then, is average and how can you adequately and fairly determine who deserves to graduate with honors?

[Transition: Even though the GPA threshold method is problematic, the percentage of class rank method is not much better at finding out who deserves honors.]

IV. Main Point #4: Using the percentage of class rank to determine who deserves honors is not much better than using GPA thresholds because it only identifies who was best in a group, not who excelled.

A. Subpoint: When you take GPA out of the mix and go with class rank it is possible that a student with a low GPA could end up receiving summa cum laude.

1. Sub-subpoint: Take this case for example: Students who finish #1 in their class with a 3.45 GPA would, according to the class rank system, receive summa cum laude.

2. Sub-subpoint: This designation does not accurately represent the student's achievement.

B. Subpoint: Even if you don't think that is likely, what about a situation where many students finish with a 4.0, how do you differentiate who should receive summa cum laude from who should receive magna cum laude?

1. Sub-subpoint: For example, at UNLV in 2005 78% of the grades given to students in the College of Education were A's, and the average GPA of students was 3.6.[9]

2. Sub-subpoint: When everyone is getting A's then everyone is worthy of honors.

C. Subpoint: The third and final point I want to make here, is that students in this system do not receive a comparable degree to someone at another institution.

1. Sub-subpoint: By this, I mean that students from two universities, each using a different system for marking honors, who receive the same grades would not receive the same honor upon graduation thus making one degree appear better than another's.

2. Sub-subpoint: This does not allow for any type of reasonable comparison between honors at two different institutions.

---

8   Karen W. Arenson, "At CUNY, a Debate on Grade Inflation," *The New York Times,* July 28, 1997, B3.
9   April Corbin, "Standardizing Honors Status," *The Rebel Yell* (August 6, 2007), available at: http://archive.unlvrebelyell.com/print_article.php?ID=10881, (last accessed: January 14, 2009).

[**Transition:** With such an unfair system for bestowing honors upon graduates, the best solution is to just eliminate the system altogether.]

V. Main Point #5: Eliminating honors designations for graduates at the university level will help reduce grade inflation and equalize the worth of degrees from different schools.

    A. Subpoint: The elimination of honors will help reduce grade inflation by reducing the pressure on students to make honor rolls.

        1. Sub-subpoint: Students will not feel like outcasts or underachievers when they do not hit a specific grade level.

        2. Sub-subpoint: Additionally, when students are close to the level for a type of honors they beg for grade changes, resulting in inflation; if honors are eliminated then this practice will be minimized at least, stopped at best.

    B. Subpoint: Eliminating honors is also better than the class rank percentage model because the GPA will stand for itself.

        1. Sub-subpoint: Whereas in the class rank method of honors selection a student with a 3.8 could possibly graduate without honors, when you eliminate honors altogether that 3.8 shows that the student did very well.

        2. Sub-subpoint: Students with high GPAs that miss honors are cheated out of the distinction their GPA should have, so by eliminating honors for all the GPA becomes the distinguishing feature for everyone.

    C. Subpoint: Most importantly, eliminating honors designations at all universities and colleges equalizes the playing field for all graduates.

        1. Sub-subpoint: When all employers have to go on is GPA, instead of an honors label that was determined differently for each graduate, then all students are on a more level playing field in the application process.

        2. Sub-subpoint: Graduates will be evaluated by performance and not an inconsistent designation of honor.

[**Transition:** Put succinctly, eliminating honors designations for graduates is the fairest and most equitable way to distinguish one student's performance at one school from another student's performance at a different college.]
Conclusion

I. Signpost: In conclusion, honors designations for college graduates are a terrific idea, but terrible in execution and thus should be eliminated.

II. Summary: Honors designations based on GPA thresholds contribute to grade inflation and thus make the honors label worth less than it should be.

    A. Using a system based on percentages of the rank in the graduating class also is unfair because it may leave students who achieve high marks out of the honors category altogether.

    B. Most problematic, however, is that both methods are used by various institutions across the country, making the meaning of honors inconsistent for all graduates.

    C. To solve the problem of inconsistent and unfair honors labels we must abolish honors designations altogether and let the GPA stand as the distinguishing criteria for determining student achievement.

IV. Restate Thesis/Argument: Only when our true performance, illustrated by our GPA, is the measure of our honor and abilities will the gamesmanship and pressure for higher grades so students can receive honors designations stop.

III. Clincher: The honor in student achievement should come from performance, not some watered-down label.

Bibliography

Arenson, Karen W. "At CUNY, a Debate on Grade Inflation." *The New York Times* (July 28, 1997): B3.

Bartlett, Thomas and Paula Wasley. "Just Say 'A': Grade Inflation Undergoes Reality Check." *The Chronicle of Higher Education* vol. 55, issue 2, (September 5, 2008): A1-A12.

Corbin, April. "Standardizing Honors Status." *The Rebel Yell* (August 6, 2007). http://archive.unlvrebelyell.com/print_article.php?ID=10881. Last accessed: January 14, 2009.

"Grade Inflation Scrutinized at Harvard and Elsewhere." *Academe Online* (nd). http://www.aaup.org/AAUP/pubsres/academe/2002/MA/NB/Grade.htm?PF=1. Last accessed: January 14, 2009.

Sikula, Adam. "Faculty Senate Proposal." University of Nevada Las Vegas, Spring 2006.

Velasco, Patricia. "Grad Status Under Debate." *The Rebel Yell* (April 27, 2006). http://archive.unlvrebelyell.com/print_article.php?ID=9279. Last accessed: January 14, 2009.

KEY TERMS

A

abstract	words are not concrete or tangible items; they are only representations
accent	nonverbal behaviors that augment a verbal message
acceptance	the third step in the persuasive process in which the audience decides whether or not to agree with the position for which the speaker advocated
accuracy	the truthfulness or correctness of a source
active listening	listening to understand a message by processing, storing and potentially evaluating a message. It also involves reactions by the listener in some form
ad hominen fallacy	when speakers attack the person making the argument and not the argument itself
ad populum fallacy	when we attempt to persuade people by arguing our position is reasonable because so many other people are doing it or agree with it
ad verecundium fallacy	an appeal for persuasion based on higher authority or tradition
alliteration	repeating the same consonant or vowel sound at the beginning of subsequent words
ambiguous	language does not have precise, concrete meanings
ambushing	selective listening where the audience ignores the strengths of a message and hears only the weaknesses
American Psychological Association Manual	preferred reference manual for social science communication scholars
antecedent	the hypothetical condition in the major premise of a conditional syllogism
antithesis	two ideas that sharply contrast with each other and are juxtaposed in a parallell grammatical structure
anxiety disorder	abnormal mental outlook in which individuals experience high levels of apprehensiveness that keep them from living life
apologia	a forensic speech that makes a defense against an accusation
arbitrary	symbols used to represent things are not intrinsically connected to those things
arguments from the past	appropriating historical events, facts, or people to justify present or future actions, or explain events in the here and now
arrangement	the second canon of rhetoric in which you determine the most effective way to organize your case for the topic and the audience

articulation	physically producing the sound needed to convey the word
artistic proof	constructed by the speaker for the occasion; concerns ethos, pathos and logos
assertive	the ability to clearly and confidently state our positions
asymmetrical balance	emphasizes imbalance thus creating an impression of stress, energy and excitement
attention getter	a devise that immediately attracts the audience's interest to the subject which the speaker plans to discuss
autonomy face	the perception that we can do things on our own and our desire to avoid others making decisions for us
axial balance	formal balance that strives for equal distribution of the elements of a visual so they do not appear tilted on one side of the image

B

background information	material that provides context for a topic
balance	the positioning of elements within the image
begging-the-question fallacy	when a speaker presumes that certain things are facts when they have not yet been proven to be truthful
bias	presenting information in a way that unfairly influences the perception of something or someone
blending	one of the more common articulation errors, and it occurs when speakers intermingle two words together

C

categorical syllogism	a syllogism in which the argument is based on membership in a group
cause and effect arrangement	orders main points first by discussing the cause of something that occurred and then moving to an explanation of the impact of its occurrence
channel	the mode through which the message is conveyed to another party
chart	a visual device that helps you summarize or list blocks of information
Chicago Manual of Style	preferred reference manual for rhetorical studies
chilling effect	an action that discourages other from speaking their mind
chronological order	arranging points in the order in which they occur, or occurred, from start to finish
civic engagement	acting upon a sharp awareness of one's own sense of responsibility to their community
civility	the use of tact when dealing with others; a genuine and reciprocal expression of respect for ourselves and other people through our actions and statements
clarity	the ability of a speaker to clearly articulate what they wish to say
classroom response systems	devices that allow students to answer questions posed during a lecture and provide tabulated results of the poll for everyone in the room in a timely manner
clincher	the final statement in a speech

coercion	the use of the threat of force to make someone do something against his or her will
collectivistic culture	values harmony in group and societal relationships
color pattern	collection of hues in your presentation aids
communication apprehension	the fear or anxiety associated with real or anticipated communication with another or others
Communication/Mass Media Complete	an electronic database for academic journals and popular sources related to communication and journalism
comparative advantage	an organizational pattern that uses each main point to explain why the speaker's solution to a problem is better than another proposed solution
comparison	connecting new information with something a person already knows
competence face	our efforts to promote our expertise on subjects to others so they respect us
complement	when the action demonstrates the message contained in the verbal content
comprehension	the second step in the persuasive process in which the speaker provides context for the issue in dispute so the audience understands what the speaker is talking about
conditional syllogism	a syllogism in which the major premise contains hypothetical condition and its outcome
conflicting	kinds of nonverbal cues that covey a message that contradicts the verbal statements of the speaker
conjectural stasis	when the issue in dispute is whether something occurred or not
consequent	the outcome of the hypothetical condition in the major premise of a conditional syllogism
context	the circumstances in which an event occurs that influence the meaning of the moment and the message
contrast	how objects and letters stick our from the background
coordination	all information on the same level has the same significance
correctness	the accuracy of information presented and the honest representation of the speaker
courtesy	showing consideration and attention to others
crescendo	an organizational pattern in which the strongest point is placed at the end and is built up to by smaller main points

D

debate	a competitive interaction in which people attempt to make a case through reason and evidence, while showing weakness in the other's arguments
decoding	the process of taking a message that has been sent and using one's own experiences and knowledge to give it meaning
deductive argument	an argument that reasons from known premises to an inevitable conclusion
defensive climate	a communication situation in which a person feels threatened
definitive stasis	when the issue in dispute is the meaning of a term

dehumanization	making people seem less than human in order to more easily motivate action against them
deliberative message	one of two forms of persuasive messages proposed by Aristotle; it often takes place in legislative settings and focuses on discussing policies and actions to be taken
delivery	the fourth canon of rhetoric; the manner in which you physically and vocally present your message
demagoguery	speech that attempts to win over an audience through appealing to their prejudices and emotions, particularly those of fear, anger, and frustration
demographic	groups determined by select population characteristics
depth	the graphic nature of an item; involves both level of detail and the amount of background provided to the image
derived credibility	the level of credibility during a speech that comes from what you say and how you say it
Dewey Decimal Classification System	the coding system for books, magazines, and journals used in libraries
dialects	aspects of in articulation, grammar, vocabulary, and pronunciation that differ from Standard English
dialogue	an interaction in which people with different perspectives seek to understand each other's views; speaking so that others want to listen and listening so that others want to speak
discourse	communication of thought by words; talk; conversation
disjunctive syllogism	a syllogism in which the major premise includes two or more mutually exclusive alternatives
division	in order to divide a point you need to end up with two or more items
dyadic	an interaction between two people
dynamism	a social science term for strong delivery that creates the impression with the audience that the speaker has practiced and thus cares about what he is talking about

E

either-or fallacy	an argument in which you present two options and declare that one of them must be correct while the other must be incorrect
Elaboration Likelihood Model (ELM)	a theory that proposes two primary cognitive processing paths we use to make decisions
encoding	the process of attaching symbols to ideas and feelings so that others may understand them
enkyklios paideia	rounded education spread under the reign of Alexander the Great
enthymeme	a syllogism missing one or two of its parts
episteme	universal knowledge, or understanding about the common characteristics of like materials
ethos	the credibility of the speaker

evidentiary information	information that supports main points within a speech and is directly related to the topic
exigence	a decisive point at which a response is invited or required
explanation	a process of making information clear to a person who previously did not understand it
extemporaneous speech	a speech delivered with notes but not the entire speech in front of the speaker

F

face threats	things that threaten to damage the image we work to present to others
facework	the behaviors we exhibit to maintain a positive impression of ourselves by other people
famous quotation	an actual statement closely related to the topic of the speech made by individuals that the audience will easily recognize
feedback	the responses and reactions to the messages transmitted by the sender and is itself a new message sent back to the original sender
fellowship face	an effort to fulfill the need to have others like and respect us
figurative analogy	when the two cases being compared are from completely different classifications
fixed-response questions	items on a survey that allow only for prescribed answers
forensic message	an argument in which speakers debate the facts of a case and attempt to answer questions of justice
form	how items appear in terms of their representation, size and texture
formal survey	a time consuming way of gathering data on a population which employs randomized sampling to ensure reliability and validity
frame of reference	our own singular perspective on the world around us

G

gender	the socially constructed expectations and roles that accompany a particular sex, and these vary between cultures
general purpose statement	a brief statement representing what you intend to do in the speech
gesture	a physical movement used to convey a message
ghostwriting	to write for and in the name of another person
glazing over	daydreaming instead of hearing the message
global plagiarism	taking an entire speech from a single source and pawning it off as your own
good manners	handling our relationships with others in a positive way
graph	a presentation device that indicates relationships found in numerical data

H

harmony	when all parts and aspects of the presentation aid complement one another within the aid's framework

hate speech	rude and crude speech that attacks or demeans a particular social or ethnic group many times with the intent of inciting action against that group
hearing	the physiological action of processing sounds, conducted by one's ears and brain
hierarchical	language is structured according to more or less, higher or lower
high power-distance cultures	where there is an uneven distribution of power and one person or a specific group of people dominate

I

ideograph	an ill-defined, politically powerful term or phrase that can push people to action
image management	the constant attempt to control the presentation of ourselves to others
impromptu speech	a presentation done with little or no preparation
inartistic proof	all the evidence, data, and documents that exist outside of the speaker and the audience but nevertheless can aid in persuasion
incremental plagiarism	failure to give proper credit for parts of a speech that are borrowed from others
individualistic culture	people feel the strongest loyalties lie with themselves and not their social groups
inductive argument	reasoning from individual observations or events to conclude a general principle
informal survey	polling a few people based on convenience
information literacy	the ability to figure out the type of information you need, find that information, evaluate it and properly use it
initial credibility	the level of credibility a speaker has before they begin their speech
integration	the fourth stage in the persuasive process where the audience makes the speaker's position a part of their own personal philosophy and worldview
integrity	a quality of discerning and acting on one's ethical principles
intermediate knowledge	knowing what does not reflect an excess or a defect but instead what is intuitively correct to the person
internal preview	serves as an outline of what is to come next in a speech and is often combined with transition statements
internal summary	a statement that summarizes what you already covered, precedes transitions
interviewing	a direct method of gathering information from a human source that allows for questions to adapt to responses
invention	the first canon of rhetoric in which you choose the best possible arguments for your case
issue awareness	the first step in the persuasive process whereby the speaker alerts the audience to the issue requiring its attention

J

Jargon	terminology that relates to a specific activity
JSTOR	an electronic database for political journals

K

kairos	a person's ability to adapt to any occasion and deliver a message fit for that moment
kategoria	a forensic speech that makes an accusation
kinesics	nonverbal behaviors related to movement

L

Lexis-Nexis	an electronic database for newspapers and magazines
linear model of communication	communication process that involves a sender who encodes a message and sends it through a channel where it competes with distracting forces called noise while on its way to a receiver who then decodes the message
listening	the psychological process of making sense out of sounds
listening for appreciation	listening for enjoyment; not high in cognitive commitment
listening to comprehend	listening to understand a concept or message
listening to criticize	listening to make a judgment about a message; involves a high level of cognitive commitment on the part of the audience
literal analogy	when the two cases being compared are classified the same way
logos	the logical dimension of the appeal
low power-distance cultures	members value equality and believe no one person should dominate
lying by commission	when a speaker willfully makes untrue statements to an audience
lying by omission	when a speaker willfully chooses not to acknowledge facts about an argument that might damage its effectiveness

M

major premise	the first part of a syllogism, consisting of a general statement about the subject of your argument
manipulation	the deliberate misrepresentation of facts and evidence to an audience
manuscript speeches	when a speaker has his or her entire speech written out word for word in front of them as they speak
memory	the fifth canon of rhetoric; refers to one's ability to recall names and important information in the middle of a speech as well as to deliver a cogent speech without notes
message	the actual content you send to an audience, both intentional and unintentional
message of self preservation	message where the speaker''s topic is introducing himself or herself to the audience
metaphor	comparisons that show how two things are alike in an important way, despite being quite different in most ways
minor premise	a statement about a specific case related to the general characteristics of the major premise
models	to-scale devices that depict an actual object

Modern Language Association Manual of Style	a citation style used in disciplines within the liberal arts and humanities
monologue	an interaction in which only one voice is present
Monroe's Motivated Sequence	a five-step organizational pattern that combines psychological elements with persuasion to move an audience to action
movement	the appearance of or actual activity depicted with an image
multimedia presentation	a presentation aid that combines and integrates video, audio, pictures and notes into one medium
myth	a rhetorical construction that tries to explain natural events or cultural phenomena and is used to identify with a group and justify actions or beliefs

N

narrative coherence	the degree to which a story makes sense in the world in which we live
narrative fidelity	the degree to which a story matches our own beliefs and experiences
narrative paradigm	humans are storytelling beings by nature
necessary cause	a condition that must be present for the effect to occur
noise	anything that interferes with the encoding, transmission, and reception of a message
non sequitur fallacy	when you make an unwarranted move from one idea to the next
nonlistening	providing the appearance of listening without actually paying complete attention to the message

O

object	a tangible item used in conjunction with a speech
Occam's Razor	one should not increase, beyond what is necessary, the number of entities required to explain anything
one-to-one conversation	a talk in which participants share responsibility and ownership for the interaction in a manner that is more equal than in a speech
open-ended questions	items on a survey that allow room for the person taking the survey to answer in his or her own words

P

parallelism	similarly structuring related words, phrases, or clauses
passive listening	listening without reacting
patchwork plagiarism	stealing ideas from two or three sources without referencing them
pathos	the emotional dimensions of the appeal that can influence an audience's disposition toward the topic, speaker, or occasion
plagiarism	to present another person's work or ideas as your own
polite	showing consideration for others in accordance with social decorum
post hoc, ergo propter hoc fallacy	from the Latin for "after this, therefore because of this;" assumes that because one event happened after another, then the preceding event caused the event that followed

posture	the position of your body
practicality	the proper places within the speech, the where, when, and how
prejudging	entering into a presentation with a judgment already formed about the message being delivered
preparation outlines	detailed outlines that use full sentences next to symbols in an effort to help you organize the speech
presentation aids	visual devices used to assist a speaker in communicating ideas to the audience
presentness	giving full attention to someone in dialogue
problem-cause-solution order	a means of organizing a persuasive speech in which where you discuss the problem first, then its root cause, and your preferred solution that addresses both the problem and its inherent cause
problem-solution arrangment	orders points by first discussing a problem and then how it was addressed; a subset of chronological order
problem-solution order	a means of organizing a persuasive speech in which the discussion of the problem is followed by the preferred solution
profanity	coarse and irreverent language
pronunciation	the accepted standard of how a word sounds when spoken
propriety	good behavior and faithfulness to what one considers moral and just
pseudolistening	when people attempt to hide their inattention to the speaker's message
public speaking	speaking where communication moves typically from one speaker to an audience of many

Q

quadrivium	arithmetic, geometry, music, and astronomy
qualitative stasis	when the issue in dispute involves the morality, ethicality, or value of an action
question of fact	when a speaker seeks to persuade people about how to interpret facts
question of policy	when a speaker takes a position on whether an action should or should not be taken
question of value	a persuasive speech about the rightness or wrongness of an idea, action, or issue

R

reasoning by analogy	when you compare two similar cases in order to argue that what is true in one case is also true in the other
reasoning by cause	arguments that claim that one event or factor produces an effect
reasoning by example	the process of inferring general conclusions and making general claims from specific cases
rebuttal	a message that involves overcoming the opponent's argument by introducing other evidence that reduces the appeal of the opponent's claims
receiver	the person or persons who receive the encoded message sent by the sender

red herring fallacy	when a speaker introduces an irrelevant issue or piece of evidence to divert attention from subject of the speech
refutation	a speech that seeks to prove the opposition''s argument is wrong, or false
regulating	using nonverbal actions to help govern the course of a speech or interaction
repeating	when physical actions restate verbal messages
repetition	repeating either the same phrasing pattern for main points, or a phrase you just stated in order to maximize the audience's ability to receive the information
research question	the question about your topic you seek to answer
respect	an acknowledgement of the inherent humanity and existence of other people
rhetoric	the ability to speak well and persuade audiences
rhetorical question	asking the audience a question related to the subject that does not require an answer from them
rhetorical situations	moments that call for a rhetorical response
rhetors	speakers
risk	an action with either positive or negative outcomes

S

schema	a mental representation that organizes information about a subject
script	when a schema includes a sequence of behaviors
seductive details	bits of interesting information associated with your topic, but not part of it
self-fulfilling prophecy	believing that something will happen before it actually does, and then when it does come true it reinforces the original expectation
self-monitoring	the ability to be aware of your own behaviors and statements and how they affect other people; can be either high or low
self-presentation	a message used to introduce a speaker to listeners
self-restraint	the ability to refrain from comments until the time and tone are appropriate to do so
sender	the person who desires to deliver a message to another person or group of people
sex	a biological distinction between men and women
shorthand	the process of shortening words, or eliminating word clutter in the transcription process
signpost	a connective that lets the audience know what is next; most effective form of connective for moving from the last main point to the conclusion
simile	comparisons between two objects that allow each object in the comparison to retain their unique differences
single word approach	meaning is derived from individual words used in a strategic way
slang	words derived from dialects that most people understand but yet do not use in professional writing or speaking

slippery slope fallacy	a logical fallacy that assumes once an action begins it will follow, undeterred, to an eventual and inevitable conclusion
sociophobia	the fear of social situations and/or people
socratic questioning	the process of asking questions of a speaker focused on their responses to previous questions; its ultimate goal is to uncover the truth
sophists	itinerant teachers who travelled from city-state to city-state in Classical Greece, training people in public speaking
spare brain time	the time available for your mind to wander due to your ability to process messages faster than it takes to construct them
spatial order	arranges points according to geography or logical movement through an area
speaking outline	a truncated form of your full sentence preparation outline that does not include complete sentences
specific purpose statement	a narrower version of the general purpose statement that identifies what you will talk about, what you will say about it, and what you hope the audience will come away from the speech with
speech of refutation	a speech that seeks to prove the opposition's argument is wrong, or false
spotlight syndrome	the belief encouraged by the room set up that all eyes are focused on you as the speaker
stasis	the basic issue in dispute between speaking parties
straw man fallacy	when a speaker ignores the actual position of an opponent and substitutes it with a distorted and exaggerated position
style	the third canon; involves word choice, phrasing and the level of formality in the language you use to present your case to the audience
subordination	the organization of a hierarchy of ideas where the most general appear first, followed by subsequently more specific ideas
substituting	physical actions that take the place of verbal messages
sufficient cause	a condition that automatically produces the effect in question
summary	the central part of the conclusion; it is where you reiterate the speech's thesis statement and recap the main points you addressed throughout the body
supportive climate	a communication situation in which a person feels he or she can speak freely without risk of harm
syllogism	basic structure of a deductive argument that comes to an absolute conclusion

T

tangential information	evidence used to provide color and capture an audience's interest
techne	experiential knowledge; knowledge of particular events in the world around us; the least reliable form of knowledge
terminal credibility	the level of credibility attained at the end of the speaking event

thesis statement	the verbalized foundation of your entire speech in a single sentence which presents your topic, main points and goal to the audience in an explicit and understandable way
tone	the syllabic emphasis on a sound that expresses emotion or meaning
topical arrangement	the arrangement of main points by sub-points that do not naturally fit together in another way
traditional aids	aids that do not apply electronic means to communicate ideas to the audience
transactional model of communication	recognizes that we simultaneously send and receive messages; a cyclical model of the communication process
transitions	signal you are done with one point, and that you are moving on to another
translative stasis	the issue in dispute is the competency of the judge or arbiter
transparencies	transparent sheets containing information illuminated by a projector
trivium	grammar, rhetoric and logic

U

undercover interviewing	the interviewer disguises either themselves or their purpose in an effort to trick someone into sharing more information than they may have if the interviewee knew to whom they were speaking

V

virtues	personal qualities that manifest moral excellence and make one capable of performing noble deeds
vocalics	anything that contributes to the creation or maintenance of sound in a person's voice
vocalized pauses	utterances that are not words and have no place in a speech, but are done instead of pausing the delivery of the speech

W

word cluster approaches	meaning is conveyed through more complex structures such as stories

Index

literal analogy 227
logos 10, 207
low power-distance cultures 291
lying by commission 206
lying by omission 206

M

Maher, Bill 297
major premise 221
Malaysia Airline Flight 370 86
manipulation 206
manuscript speech 180
McCain, John 56
McGee, Michael Calvin 151
McLuhan, Marshall 63, 68
Medina, John 66, 289, 315
memory 9
metaphor 101, 150
minor premise 221
Minow, Newton 202, 203
monologue 313
Monroe, Alan H. 259
Monroe's Motivated Sequence 258
myth 153

N

narrative coherence 154
narrative fidelity 154
narrative paradigm 154
necessary cause 228
Nichols, Marie Hochmuth 37–39
non sequitur fallacy 231

O

Obama, Michelle 16–18
Ohio Civility Project 276
Olivier, Sir Laurence 30
one-to-one conversation 15
open-ended questions 66

P

Pacino, Al 146
parallelism 155
patchwork plagiarism 120
pathos 10, 207
Patterson, Kerry 308
Petty, Richard E. 90
Philip of Macedon 2
plagiarism 119
polite 279
post hoc, ergo propter hoc fallacy 231

posture 178
PowerPoint 95
presentation aids 95
presentness 315
Prezi 95
problem-cause-solution order 257
problem-solution order 254
profanity 23
pronunciation 171
propriety 11
Ptolemy I 112
public speaking 14

Q

quadrivium 112
qualitative stasis 196
question of fact 197
question of policy 198
question of value 198
Quintilian 74, 195, 197, 198, 251

R

Ranganathan, S.R. 121
reasoning by analogy 227
reasoning by cause 227
reasoning by example 225
rebuttal speech 200
red herring fallacy 232
regulate 180
repeat 179
repetition 154
research question 115
respect 282
rhetoric 5
rhetorical situations 69
rhetors 10
risk 325
Rogers, Carl 311, 320
Roosevelt, Eleanor 18
Royal Aeronautical Society 86
Rutgers University 296

S

schema 90
script 91
seductive details 94
self-monitoring 286
sender 33
September 11, 2001 153
sex 292
similes 150

interchange

English for international communication

Jack C. Richards

with Jonathan Hull
and Susan Proctor

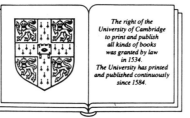

The right of the
University of Cambridge
to print and publish
all kinds of books
was granted by law
in 1534.
The University has printed
and published continuously
since 1584.

1

Student's Book

Cambridge University Press

Cambridge • New York • Port Chester • Melbourne • Sydney

Published by the Press Syndicate of the University of Cambridge
The Pitt Building, Trumpington Street, Cambridge CB2 1RP
40 West 20th Street, New York, NY 10011, USA
10 Stamford Road, Oakleigh, Melbourne 3166, Australia

First published 1990

Third printing 1991

Printed in the United States of America

Library of Congress Cataloging-in-Publication Data
Richards, Jack C.
Interchange: English for international communication: student's book
one/Jack C. Richards with Jonathan Hull and Susan Proctor.
p.   cm.
Summary: Textbook for studying English as a foreign language
providing activities and exercises to develop the skills of listening,
speaking, reading, and writing.
ISBN 0-521-35988-0
1. English language–Textbooks for foreign speakers. [1. English
language—Textbooks for foreign speakers.] I. Hull, Jonathan. II.
Proctor, Susan. III. Title.
PE1128.R457 1990
428.2′4-dc20   89-22101
                                                                      CIP
                                                                       AC

British Library Cataloging in Publication Data
Richards, Jack C.
Interchange: English for international communication.
Student's book 1.
1. English language. Usage
I. Title   II. Hull, Jonathan   III. Proctor, Susan
428
ISBN 0-521-35988-0

ISBN 0 521 35988 0 Student's Book One
ISBN 0 521 35989 9 Teacher's Manual One
ISBN 0 521 35990 2 Workbook One
ISBN 0 521 35203 7 Class Cassette Set One
ISBN 0 521 35204 5 Student Cassette One

Book design: Peter Ducker
Layouts: Circa 86, Inc.
Cover design: Tom Wharton

Illustrators
Kevin Callahan
Bill Thomson
Sam Viviano

Contents

Plan of Book 1

	Topics	Functions	Grammar/Pronunciation
UNIT 1	**Topics** Greetings; names; occupations; countries; nationalities; spelling	**Functions** Introducing oneself; asking for personal information; greeting people; saying goodbye	**Grammar** Present tense statements with *be*; Wh- and Yes/No questions with *be*
UNIT 2	**Topics** Greetings; occupations and workplaces; numbers; names; addresses	**Functions** Greeting people; describing occupations; describing work	**Grammar** Wh-questions with *do*; prepositions: *for, at, in, to*; present tense statements **Pronunciation** Word stress
UNIT 3	**Topics** Money; prices; expenses; shopping	**Functions** Asking about prices; selling and buying things	**Grammar** Possessive pronouns; demonstrative adjectives and pronouns (singular, plural); Wh-questions with *be* **Pronunciation** Plural *s*

Review of Units 1–3

UNIT 4	**Topics** Music, movies, and TV programs; entertainers; invitations; dates and times	**Functions** Describing likes and dislikes; making invitations	**Grammar** Object pronouns; Yes/No questions with *do*; *there is*; prepositions: *at, on* **Pronunciation** Question intonation
UNIT 5	**Topics** Families; interesting people	**Functions** Asking about and describing families; describing people; making small talk; ending a conversation	**Grammar** Wh- and Yes/No questions with *do/does* (3rd person) **Pronunciation** Third-person *s*
UNIT 6	**Topics** Leisure and recreation; sports and exercise	**Functions** Describing routines and activities; talking about frequency; asking about and describing exercises	**Grammar** Adverbs of frequency **Pronunciation** Reduced form of *do*

Review of Units 4–6

UNIT 7	**Topics** Greetings; weekend activities; vacations	**Functions** Talking about past events; asking for information; narrating	**Grammar** Past tense; Wh- and Yes/No questions in past tense **Pronunciation** Past tense *-ed*
UNIT 8	**Topics** Cities and places; neighborhoods; houses and apartments	**Functions** Asking about and describing locations of places; asking about and describing a neighborhood	**Grammar** *There is, there are; one, any, some* **Pronunciation** Vowel contrast /ey/ and /ɛ/

Topics	Functions	Grammar/Pronunciation

UNIT 9

Topics People; dress and appearances; clothes; colors

Functions Describing people's dress and appearance; describing what people are doing

Grammar Present continuous

Pronunciation Sentence stress

Review of Units 7–9

UNIT 10

Topics Past experiences; unusual events

Functions Asking about and describing past experiences; describing events; telling a story

Grammar Present perfect; past participles; connecting words: *first, after that, next, then, finally*

Pronunciation Linking sounds

UNIT 11

Topics Cities; hometowns; countries

Functions Asking about and describing a city and country; giving suggestions; describing vacations

Grammar Adjectives and adverbs; modal *should*

UNIT 12

Topics Parts of the body; health; illnesses; medications; remedies

Functions Describing minor illness; advising someone about a health problem; buying things in a drugstore

Grammar Imperatives; modal verbs: *can, could, may, would*

Pronunciation Consonant contrast /ө/ and /t/

Review of Units 10–12

UNIT 13

Topics Food and restaurants

Functions Making restaurant reservations; ordering a meal; expressing thanks; saying goodbye

Grammar Countable and uncountable nouns; modal verbs *would, will*

Pronunciation Reduced forms of *would* and *will*

UNIT 14

Topics Comparing cities and places; world geography

Functions Describing similarities and differences; describing cities and countries

Grammar Comparisons with adjectives

Pronunciation Intonation: questions of choice

UNIT 15

Topics Messages; invitations; leisure activities; excuses

Functions Giving and receiving messages; inviting someone out; accepting and declining invitations

Grammar Requests with *tell, ask*; present continuous with future meaning

Pronunciation Reduced forms of *could you* and *would you*

Review of Units 13–15

Interchange Activities

Listening	Reading/Writing	Interchange Activity	
Listening Listening to sounds and identifying what people are doing; listening to a description of a missing person	**Writing** Writing a description of someone **Reading** Fashion firsts; dating customs	**Interchange** Describing people in a picture	UNIT **9**
		Review of Units 7–9	
Listening Listening to descriptions of events; listening for order of events	**Writing** Writing a story in the past tense **Reading** Car facts; article about catching a thief	**Interchange** Narrating a story based on pictures	UNIT **10**
Listening Listening to descriptions of hometowns; listening for correct and incorrect information	**Writing** Describing a country **Reading** City living; famous cities	**Interchange** Planning a "perfect" vacation	UNIT **11**
Listening Listening to complaints and advice; listening to questions	**Writing** Writing about a home remedy **Reading** Facts about colds; home remedies	**Interchange** Taking an exercise class in English	UNIT **12**
		Review of Units 10–12	
Listening Listening to someone making restaurant reservations; listening to restaurant orders	**Writing** Writing a restaurant review **Reading** Food facts; when and how much to tip	**Interchange** Ordering a meal in a restaurant	UNIT **13**
Listening Listening to a radio quiz show; listening for correct and incorrect information about places	**Writing** Writing a comparison of two cities **Reading** World geography; nations of the world	**Interchange** A quiz that tests general knowledge	UNIT **14**
Listening Listening to and receiving telephone messages; identifying invitations	**Writing** Writing invitations and excuses **Reading** Free time; how to make an invitation	**Interchange** Giving and receiving phone messages	UNIT **15**
		Review of Units 13–15	
		Interchange Activities	

Acknowledgments

Illustrators

Kevin Callahan 36; 41; 42; 58; 60 *(top);* 66 *(center);* 68 *(bottom);* 77 *(bottom);* 78 *(top);* 83; 84 *(top)*

Bill Thomson 2 *(top);* 6 *(bottom);* 7; 8; 12; 18; 20; 25; 29; 30; 33; 37; 52; 54; 56; 60 *(bottom);* 62 *(bottom);* 66 *(top);* 74; 77 *(top);* 84 *(bottom);* 86; 87; 91; 92; 94; 96; 98; 101; 118

Sam Viviano 3; 10; 15; 27; 34; 38; 40; 50; 57; 63; 65; 67; 75 *(top and bottom);* 79; 80; 90; 99; 102; 104; 115; 117

Kam Yu/Reno Art Works 16 *(bottom);* 17

Drawing G on page 37 by Steven Petruccio

Photographic Credits

The authors and publishers are grateful for permission to reproduce the following photographs. Every endeavor has been made to contact copyright owners, and apologies are expressed for omissions.

4 *(center, clockwise from upper left)* Courtesy of the Boston Symphony Orchestra, Inc.; John Chiasson/ Gamma Liaison; source unknown; Ralph Dominguez/Globe Photos; *(bottom, left to right)* source unknown; Snowdon/Gamma Liaison; Frances Kelly/Gamma Liaison; Globe Photos; Steve Schapiro/Gamma Liaison

9 *(center, above)* Dahlgren © 87/Stock Market: *(center, below)* Dick Luria/FPG

10 *(left to right)* P. Markow/FPG; Richard Alcorn/FPG; T. Tracy/FPG; Courtesy of Mac Campbell/Reprinted from the July/August 1989 issue of *Fine Woodworking Magazine.* Copyright 1989 from the Taunton Press. Not for resale; © 1989 Bill Losh/FPG; Courtesy Swiss Air Transport Co. Ltd.

11 *(left to right)* Scott Dornblaser (Biomedical Photography TAH-LVHC)/Allentown Hospital, Allentown, Pa.; Jeff Greenberg, Teaneck, N.J.; Dick Luria/FPG

16 *(both)* © Fredric Petters, New York. All rights reserved.

17 © Fredric Petters, New York. All rights reserved.

20 *(upper left)* Patrick Piel/Gamma Liaison; *(right and lower left)* source unknown

23 Courtesy Island Records, New York

24 *(clockwise from upper right)* Globe Photos; Globe Photos; © Adam Scull, Rangefinders/Globe Photos

25 Courtesy The Blue Note, New York

26 *(center, left to right)* Courtesy Columbia Pictures; © 1939 Selznick International Pictures, Inc. Ren. 1967 Metro-Goldwyn-Mayer Inc./Turner Entertainment Co.; source unknown; *(bottom)* Courtesy New Yorker Films, New York

28 Frederic Lewis, Inc.

35 *(top to bottom)* © Fredric Petters, New York. All rights reserved; © 1988 Lol, Inc.; courtesy Club Med Sales, Inc.

41 Joe Baker/FPG

43 *(top to bottom)* © 1976, United Artists Corporation, all rights reserved/The Museum of Modern Art Film Stills Archive/ Turner Entertainment Co.; Peter Gridley/FPG; © Michael A. Keller 1986/FPG

45 *(top)* © Joe Carini/The Image Works; *(middle, left to right)* Amos Kotomori; Luis Villota/The Stock Market; © Rudi Von Briel, New York; *(bottom)* Courtesy Québec Tourism, Québec Government House, New York *(both)*

46 Travelpix/FPG

48 © 1989 Roger Mastroianni, Cleveland, Ohio

51 *(all)* Jeff Greenberg, Teaneck, N.J.

52 *(top to bottom)* Roger Miller Photo, Ltd., Baltimore; Harold M. Lambert Studios/Frederic Lewis; © Paul Steel/The Stock Market

58 Mark Baratta, New York

64 © Corkery/News/Globe Photos

69 *(clockwise from upper left)* © 1988 Tibor Bognár/The Stock Market; © 1986 Gordon R. Gainer/The Stock Market; © 1988 Tibor Bognár/The Stock Market; © Luis Villota/The Stock Market

70 *(top)* © 1986 Mark E. Gibson/The Stock Market *(above);* © 1988 Tibor Bognár/The Stock Market *(below); (bottom)* Mark Nohl/New Mexico Economic Development and Tourism Department

71 *(above, clockwise from upper left)* Travelpix © 1989/FPG; © Dennis Hallinan, Acapulco/FPG; © Secretaria de Turismo de Mexico; *(below, top to bottom)* © James Blank; © Four by Five; Bob Couey/© 1989 Sea World, Inc. All rights reserved. Reproduced by permission.

72 *(top, left to right)* Roger Miller Photo, Ltd., Baltimore; © Joe Viesti, Viesti Associates; © Robert Frerok/The Stock Market; *(center)* © Tourespaña, Madrid *(left and middle);* Eberhard E. Otto/FPG *(right); (bottom)* Travelpix/FPG

73 *(top to bottom)* Italian Government Travel Office, New York; © D. J. Maenza; Harold M. Lambert Studios/Frederic Lewis, Inc.

74 © William Hubbell 1989, Greenwich, Conn.

81 *(all)* © Fredric Petters, New York. All rights reserved.

86 © Jeff Zaruba/The Stock Market

88 *(left to right)* © Stan Ries/International Stock Photo; © Tom McHugh/Photo Researchers, Inc.

89 *(top to bottom)* Courtesy Canadian Tourist Office, New York; © Aust. Picture Library. All rights reserved./WESTlight; Courtesy Hong Kong Tourist Association, New York; © Jeff Hunter LXXXVIII/The Image Bank

90 *(both)* Japan National Tourist Organization, New York

92 *(above)* © 1989 John M. Roberts. All rights reserved/The Stock Market; *(below)* © George Y. F. Chan/Shostal Associates

101 © 1989 San Francisco Examiner. Used with permission.

105 Jeffrey Sylvester/FPG

109 *(all)* Sandra Graham

110 *(upper left)* © Pedro Coll/The Stock Market; *(upper right)* © Richard Lacey/Frederic Lewis; *(center)* © Tourespaña, Madrid; *(lower left)* © 1987 J. Messerschmidt/The Stock Market; *(lower right)* © Tourespaña, Madrid

114 and **116** Courtesy USA for Africa

Introduction

Interchange is a three-level course in English as a second or foreign language for young adults and adults. The course covers the skills of listening, speaking, reading, and writing, with particular emphasis on listening and speaking. The primary goal of the course is to teach communicative competence – that is, the ability to communicate in English according to the situation, purpose, and roles of the participants. The language used in *Interchange* is American English; however, *Interchange* reflects the fact that English is the world's major language of international communication and is not limited to any one country, region, or culture. Level One is for beginners and takes students from beginner or false beginner to low-intermediate level.

COURSE LENGTH

Interchange is a self-contained course covering all four language skills. Each level covers between 60 and 90 hours of class instruction time. Depending on how the book is used, however, more or less time may be utilized. The Teacher's Manual gives detailed suggestions for optional activities to extend each unit. Where less time is available, the course can be taught in approximately 60 hours by reducing the amount of time spent on Interchange Activities, reading, writing, optional activities, and the Workbook.

COURSE COMPONENTS

Student's Book   The Student's Book contains fifteen units, with a review unit after every three units. There are five review units in all. Following Unit 15 is a set of communication activities called Interchange Activities, one for each unit of the book. Unit Summaries, at the end of the Student's Book, contain lists of the key vocabulary and expressions used in each unit as well as grammar summaries.

Teacher's Manual   A separate Teacher's Manual contains detailed suggestions on how to teach the course, lesson-by-lesson notes, an extensive set of optional follow-up activities, complete answer keys to the Student's Book and Workbook exercises, tests for use in class and test answer keys, and transcripts of those listening activities not printed in the Student's Book and in the five tests. The tests can be photocopied and distributed to students after each review unit is completed.

Workbook   The Workbook contains stimulating and varied exercises that provide additional practice on the teaching points presented in the Student's Book. A variety of exercise types is used to develop students' skills in grammar, reading, writing, spelling, vocabulary, and pronunciation. The Workbook can be used both for classwork and for homework.

Class Cassettes   A set of two cassettes for class use accompanies the Student's Book. The cassettes contain recordings of the conversations, grammar focus summaries, pronunciation exercises, and listening activities, as well as recordings of the listening exercises used in the tests. A variety of native-speaker voices and accents is used, as well as some nonnative speakers of English. Exercises that are recorded on the cassettes are indicated with the symbol ▭.

Student Cassette   A cassette is also available for students to use for self-study. The Student Cassette contains selected recordings of conversations, grammar, and pronunciation exercises from the Student's Book.

APPROACH AND METHODOLOGY

Interchange teaches students to use English for everyday situations and purposes related to work, school, social life, and leisure. The underlying philosophy of the course is that learning a second language is more rewarding, meaningful, and effective when the language is used for authentic communication. Information-sharing activities provide a maximum amount of student-generated communication. Throughout *Interchange*, students have the opportunity to personalize the language they learn and make use of their own life experiences and world knowledge.

The course has the following key features:

Integrated Syllabus   *Interchange* has an integrated, multi-skills syllabus that links grammar and communicative functions. The course recognizes grammar as an essential component of second language proficiency. However, it presents grammar communicatively, with controlled accuracy-based activities leading to fluency-based communicative practice. The syllabus also contains the four skills of listening, speaking, reading, and writing, as well as pronunciation and vocabulary.

Adult and International Content *Interchange* deals with contemporary topics that are of high interest and relevance to both students and teachers. Each unit includes real-world information on a variety of topics.

Enjoyable and Useful Learning Activities A wide variety of interesting and enjoyable activities forms the basis for each unit. The course makes extensive use of pair work, small group activities, role plays, and information-sharing activities. Practice exercises allow for a maximum amount of individual student practice and enable learners to personalize and apply the language they learn. Throughout the course, natural and useful language is presented that can be used in real-life situations.

WHAT EACH UNIT CONTAINS

Each unit in *Interchange* contains the following kinds of exercises:

Snapshot The Snapshots contain interesting information about the world, introduce the topic of the unit or part of the unit, and also develop vocabulary. Either the teacher can present these exercises in class as reading or discussion activities, or students can read them by themselves in class or for homework, using their dictionaries if necessary.

Conversation The Conversations introduce the new grammar of each unit in a communicative context and also present functions and conversational expressions. The teacher can either present the conversations with the Class Cassettes or read the dialogs aloud.

Pronunciation These exercises focus on important features of spoken English, including stress, rhythm, intonation, reductions, and sound contrasts.

Grammar Focus The new grammar of each unit is presented in color panels and is followed by practice activities that move from controlled to freer practice. These activities always give students a chance to use the grammar they have learned for real communication.

Listening The listening activities develop a wide variety of listening skills, including listening for gist, listening for details, and inferring meaning from context. These exercises often require completing an authentic task while listening, such as taking telephone messages. The recordings on the Class Cassettes contain both scripted and unscripted conversations with natural pauses, hesitations, and interruptions that occur in real speech.

Word Power The Word Power activities develop students' vocabulary through a variety of interesting tasks, such as word maps.

Writing The writing exercises include practical writing tasks that extend and reinforce the teaching points in the unit and help develop students' composition skills. The Teacher's Manual shows how to use these exercises to focus on the process of writing.

Reading The reading passages develop a variety of reading skills, including guessing words from context, skimming, scanning, and making inferences. Various text types adapted from authentic sources are used.

Interchange Activities The Interchange Activities are pair work and group work tasks, information-sharing tasks, and role plays that encourage real communication. These exercises are a central part of the course and allow students to extend and personalize what they have learned in each unit.

From the Authors

We hope that you will like using *Interchange* and find it useful, interesting, and fun. Our goal has been to provide teachers and students with activities that make the English class a time to look forward to and, at the same time, provide students with the skills they need to use English outside the classroom. Please let us know how you enjoyed it and good luck!

Jack C. Richards
Jonathan Hull
Susan Proctor

Authors' Acknowledgments

A great number of people assisted us in writing **Interchange.** We owe particular thanks to the following:

Our **reviewers,** who gave helpful comments on preliminary versions of the course:

Jeffrey Bright, Lúcia de Aragão, Chuck Sandy, Mark Sawyer, Barbara Strodt-Lopez, and Rita Wong.

The **students** and **teachers** in the following schools where the course was pilot tested:

Adult ESL Administrative Resource Centre, Toronto Board of Education, Toronto, Canada; **Adult Learning Skills Program,** Truman College, Chicago, IL, USA; **Alianza Cultural Uruguay-Estados Unidos,** Montevideo, Uruguay; **American Language Center,** Casablanca, Morocco; **American Language Institute,** New York University, New York, NY, USA; **American Language Center,** University of California at Los Angeles, CA, USA; **American Language Institute,** American College in Paris, France; **Associação Alumni,** São Paulo, Brazil; **Centro Boliviano Americano,** La Paz, Bolivia; **Eastdale Collegiate,** Toronto, Canada; **IES,** Okayama, Japan; **Impact Institute,** Santiago, Chile; **Interac,** Tokyo, Japan; **La Guardia Community College,** Astoria, NY, USA; **International House,** Budapest, Hungary; **Kanda Gaigo Gakuin,** Tokyo, Japan; **Kyoto YMCA English Conversation School,** Kyoto, Japan; **New Day School,** Sendai, Japan; **Nihonbashi Women's Junior College,** Chiba, Japan; **Nunoike Language School,** Nagoya, Japan; **Ontario Welcome House,** Toronto, Canada; **Overseas Training Center,** Osaka, Japan; **Seneca College,** Toronto, Canada; **Tokyo Foreign Language College,** Tokyo, Japan; and **University of Pittsburgh E.L.I.,** Tokyo, Japan.

And our **editors** and **advisors** at Cambridge University Press, who guided us through the complex process of writing classroom materials:

Peter Donovan, Adrian du Plessis, Barbara Curialle Gerr, Sandra Graham, Joan Gregory, Colin Hayes, Steven Maginn, Ellen Shaw, and Erica Townsend.

1 Please call me Dave

1 CONVERSATION: Introductions 🔲

1 Listen to people introduce themselves.

Hello. My name is David Johnson.
Please call me Dave.
I am from Toronto, Canada.

Hello. I am Mrs. Kato.
I'm from Kyushu, Japan.

Hi! My name is Antonio Tavares.
I am from Rio de Janeiro, Brazil.
Please call me Tony.

2 *Class activity* Now take turns
and introduce yourself.

Useful expressions

Sorry. What is your first name again?
Excuse me. How do you say your name again?
What is your last name, please?

2 NAMES IN ENGLISH 🔲

1 Use a title with a full name or with a family name. Use a full name, first name, or short name without a title.

"I am Susan Miller." (*not* "I am Miller.")
"I am Susan." *(or)* "I am Sue."
"Hello, Mrs. Miller." (*not* "Hello, Mrs. Sue Miller." *or* "Hello, Mrs. Sue.")
"Hello, Ms. Miller. Hello, Mr. Jones."

2 Now listen to people greet Mr. Kenji Ota, Mrs. Francine Dupont, and Ms. Susan Taylor. Do they use names and titles correctly (**C**) or incorrectly (**I**)?

"I'm Ludwig Carlos Phillip Augustine Louis Arthur Fredric von Hoopsburg, but everybody just calls me 'Your Majesty!'"

a) .... b) .... c) .... d) .... e) .... f) ....

3 WORD POWER: Jobs

1 *Pair work* Look at this word map. Fill in the blanks with words from the list below.

✓architect
bank president
clerk
company director
doctor
engineer
lawyer
receptionist
sales manager
secretary
✓supervisor
✓typist

2 Now add two more jobs to each category.

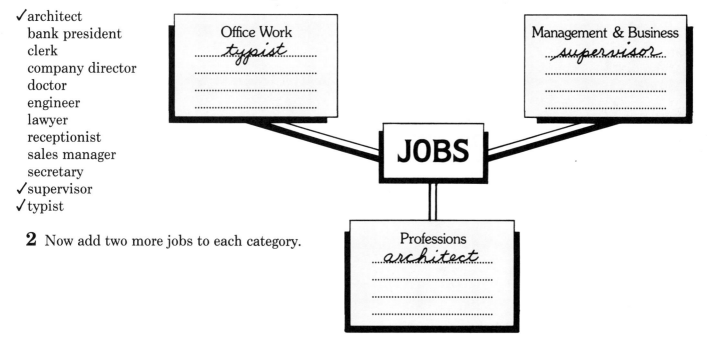

Office Work
typist

Management & Business
supervisor

JOBS

Professions
architect

---

4 CONVERSATION: Meeting someone 📼

1 Listen and practice.

Noriko: Hi! My name is Noriko Sato.
I am from Osaka, Japan. What is your name?
Chuck: I'm Chuck O'Brien.
Noriko: And where are you from, Chuck?
Chuck: I'm from Austin, Texas.
Noriko: Oh, really? Nice to meet you.
Chuck: Nice to meet you, too.
Noriko: By the way, what do you do?
Chuck: I'm a sales manager.
And how about you?
Noriko: I'm a dance instructor.
Chuck: Hey, Noriko, can I join your class?

2 *Class activity* Now go around the class and meet four classmates.

Useful expressions

I am a homemaker.
I am not working right now.
I am retired.

5 GRAMMAR FOCUS: Wh-questions with *be* ▭

What is your name?	My name **is Chuck.**
Where are you from?	I **am** from **Texas.**
What is her name?	Her name **is Noriko.**
Where is she from?	She **is** from **Japan.**
What are their names?	Their names **are Ken and Pat.**
Where are they from?	They **are** from **Ireland.**

Personal pronouns

I	my
you	your
he	his
she	her
it	its
we	our
you	your
they	their

1 Complete these conversations.

A: What is .... name?
B: His name .... Seiji Ozawa.
   .... a conductor.
A: Where .... he from?
B: .... from Japan.

A: .... is .... name?
B: .... name .... Catherine Deneuve.
   She .... an actress.
A: .... is .... from?
B: She .... from France.

A: .... are .... names?
B: Their names are Barbra Streisand and Michael
   Jackson. .... are singers.
A: Where are .... from?
B: They .... the United States.

2 Now practice the conversations. Use these contractions.

what is	= **what's**	he is	= **he's**	they are = **they're**
where is	= **where's**	she is	= **she's**	

3 *Pair work* Take turns and talk about these famous people.
Choose names from the box.

Sylvester Stallone
Yoko Ono
Charles and Diana,
Prince and Princess
of Wales
Dolly Parton
Bishop Desmond Tutu

6 COUNTRIES AND NATIONALITIES

1 *Pair work* Complete this chart.

Country	Nationality	Country	Nationality
Australia	*Australian*	Italy	....
....	Brazilian	....	Japanese
Britain	....	Mexico	....
....	Canadian	....	Portuguese
China	....	Spain	....
....	German	....	American

2 Add five more countries and nationalities.

3 Now take turns and ask questions like this:

A: What's someone from Spain called?
B: Spanish.

7 SPELLING 🔲

Reprinted by permission of UFS, Inc.

1 Listen to people talk to a bank clerk. How do they spell their names?
Check (✓) the correct answer.

a) .... Lewis .... Louis c) .... Roger .... Rodger

b) .... Helen .... Ellen d) .... Catherine .... Kathryn

2 *Group work* **Spelling Contest** Make a list of ten words in this
unit. Then students from two groups take turns like this:

A: How do you spell Portuguese?
B: P-o-r-t-u-g-u-e-s-e.
A: That's right! *(or)* No, that's wrong. It's . . .

Which group spells the most words correctly?

8 SNAPSHOT

English today

English is a first language in 12 countries.
Number of speakers: 350 million

People use English as a second
language in 33 countries.
Number of speakers: 400 million

People study English as a foreign
language in 56 countries.

Number of students studying English
in the USSR: 4 million

Number of students studying Russian in the
United States: 25,000

Write *first*, *second*, or *foreign*. Then compare with a partner.

In India, English is a .... language.
In the USSR, English is a .... language.
In New Zealand, English is a .... language.
In France, English is a .... language.
In my country, English is a .... language.

9 CONVERSATION 📼

1 Listen.

Giovanni: Hello.
Vera: Hi.
Giovanni: Excuse me. Are you from Italy?
Vera: No, I'm from Brazil.
Giovanni: Oh? What city are you from?
Vera: I'm from São Paulo.
Giovanni: Oh, really? By the way, my name's
Giovanni.
Vera: Hi, I'm Vera.
Giovanni: Are you on vacation here?
Vera: No, I'm not. I'm studying English.

2 Now listen to the rest of the conversation. Who says these things?
Write **V** for Vera and **G** for Giovanni.

.... I'm not married.   .... I'm not free tonight.
.... I'm staying with friends.   .... How about tomorrow?
.... I'm here with my sister.

10 GRAMMAR FOCUS: Yes/No questions with *be* 🔊

Are you from Italy?	**No,** I'm **not.**	I am from Brazil.
Are you a student?	**Yes,** I am.	
Is Paul a writer?	**Yes,** he is.	
Is Carol French?	**No,** she isn't.	She is Canadian.

1 Complete these conversations. Then practice them.

A: .... you from the United States?
B: Yes, I .... I'm from Chicago.

A: .... Rosa from Chile?
B: No, she .... She's from Argentina.

A: Is George Michael an actor?
B: No, he .... He .... a singer.

A: Are .... in English 101?
B: No, I'm .... I'm in English 102.

2 Now write five questions like these about classmates or famous people. Then ask your questions in groups.

11 CONVERSATION: Saying goodbye 🔊

1 Listen and practice.

A: Goodbye. See you tomorrow.
B: See you. Take it easy.

A: Bye! See you later!
B: Yeah, bye!

A: Goodbye.
B: Bye-bye. See you on Wednesday.

A: Goodbye. Have a nice evening.
B: Thanks. You, too!

Days of the week
Monday
Tuesday
Wednesday
Thursday
Friday
Saturday
Sunday

▶ **Interchange 1: Press conference**

Take part in a Hollywood press conference! Group A are reporters and look at page 102. Group B are actors and look at page 104.

2 *Class activity* Take turns. Close your books and practice saying goodbye.

2 It's a great job!

1 CONVERSATION: Greetings 📼

1 Listen.

A: Good morning, George.
B: Good morning, Mary.
A: How are you?
B: Fine, thanks.

A: Hello, Mrs. Garcia. How are you doing?
B: Pretty good, thanks. How about you, Pierre?
A: Not bad, thanks.

A: Good morning, Ann. How's everything?
B: OK, thanks. How are you today, Toshi?
A: Just fine, thanks.

2 Now practice greeting classmates. Use "good morning,"
"good afternoon," or "good evening."

---

2 LISTENING 📼

Listen to greetings and choose the correct responses.

a) .... Fine, thanks.   c) .... Good afternoon.
   .... Hi! How are you?   .... Fine, thanks.

b) .... Oh, not bad, thanks.   d) .... Pretty good, thanks. How about you?
   .... Yes, thanks.   .... How about you?

---

3 PRONUNCIATION: Word stress 📼

1 Listen to the stressed syllables in these words. Then practice them.

1st syllable	2nd syllable	3rd syllable
morning	to**day**	after**noon**
evening	to**mor**row	engi**neer**

2 Are these words stressed on the 1st, 2nd, or 3rd syllable? Put them
into three lists. Then check with a partner.

tonight   vacation   language   university   Saturday   conversation

4 SNAPSHOT

Number of years in school	women	men
Fewer than 8 years	$9,828	$14,624
1–3 years of high school	$11,843	$19,120
High school graduate	$14,569	$23,269
1–3 years of college	$17,007	$25,831
College graduate	$20,257	$31,487
Postgraduate	$25,076	$36,836

Education and salary

What are three good jobs for:

a high school graduate?   a college graduate?   a postgraduate?

Compare your answers with a partner.

5 WORD POWER: Workplaces and jobs

1 How many workplaces can you find for each job?

Workplaces

a) a bank
b) a factory
c) a hotel
d) an office
e) a store

Jobs

.... a bank teller   .... a receptionist
.... a cashier   .... a salesclerk
.... a chef   .... a secretary
.... a clerk   .... a supervisor
.... a manager   .... a typist

2 Look at the jobs again and underline the stressed syllable in each word. Then compare with a partner.

3 *Group work*   Now ask about the workplaces like this:

Who works in a bank?
–A bank teller.
–A clerk.

Who works in these places:
a restaurant?   a hospital?   a department store?

6 ALL IN A DAY'S WORK 📼

Listen to five people at work. What is each person's job?
Talk about each job like this.

Job #1   A: It's a secretary.
         B: No, I think it's a clerk.

7 CONVERSATION 🔲

Listen and practice.

A: Where do you work?
B: I work for Thomas Cook Travel.
A: Oh, really? And what do you do there?
B: I'm a guide. I take people on tours to Europe.
A: That sounds interesting!
B: Yes, it's a great job. I love it! And what do you do?
A: I'm a student, and I work part-time, too.
B: Oh? Where do you work?
A: I work in a fast food restaurant. I cook hamburgers.
B: Big Macs?
A: No, Whoppers! I work for Burger King.

8 GRAMMAR FOCUS: Wh-questions with *do;* prepositions 🔲

Where do you work?	I work **for** Thomas Cook Travel. I work **at/in** a fast food restaurant.
Where do you go to school?	I go **to** UCLA.
What do you do?	I am a guide. I take people on tours. I am a student, and I work part-time, too.

1 What do these people do? Match the information. Then describe each person's job like this:

I work in a store. I'm a salesclerk. I sell clothes.

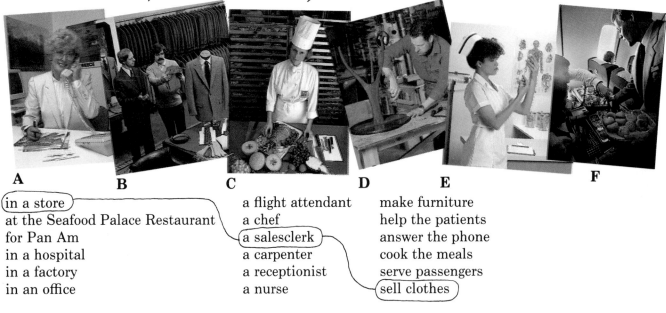

A B C D E F

in a store	a flight attendant	make furniture
at the Seafood Palace Restaurant	a chef	help the patients
for Pan Am	a salesclerk	answer the phone
in a hospital	a carpenter	cook the meals
in a factory	a receptionist	serve passengers
in an office	a nurse	sell clothes

2 Complete these conversations. Then practice them.

A: .... do you work?
B: I work .... Japan Air Lines.
A: Oh, really? And what .... you do?
B: I .... a flight attendant.

A: Where .... you work?
B: I work .... the *Daily News*.
A: Oh, ... do you .... there?
B: .... am a photographer.

A: What .... you .... ?
B: I'm a student.
A: Where .... you .... to school?
B: I go .... Jefferson College.
   I'm studying business.

3 Now take turns talking about where you work and what you do,
or where you study and what you are studying.

9 WRITING

1 Write a description of what you do.

*I'm a student. I go to McGill
University in Canada. I'm a freshman.
I study computer science.
I work part-time in a disco, too.
I'm a disk jockey. It's a great job!*

*I'm a salesclerk. I work at Macy's
department store. I sell toys and games
in the toy department. I hate it!*

2 Pass your papers around the class. Can you guess who wrote them?

10 LISTENING 📼

Listen to three people talk about their jobs. Number the jobs from 1 to 3
in the order you hear them.

11 NUMBERS ▭

1 Say these numbers.

0	1	2	3	4	5	6	7	8	9	10
zero/oh	one	two	three	four	five	six	seven	eight	nine	ten

11	12	13	14	15	16	17
eleven	twelve	thirteen	fourteen	fifteen	sixteen	seventeen

18	19	20	21	22	30	40
eighteen	nineteen	twenty	twenty-one	twenty-two	thirty	forty

50	60	70	80	90	100	1,000
fifty	sixty	seventy	eighty	ninety	one hundred (a hundred)	one thousand (a thousand)

2 Listen to the difference between these numbers.

thir**teen** – **thir**ty   fif**teen** – **fif**ty
four**teen** – **for**ty   six**teen** – **six**ty

3 Now listen and write down the numbers you hear.
Then practice them.

a) ....   b) ....   c) ....   d) ....   e) ....   f) ....   g) ....   h) ....

12 CONVERSATION: Names and addresses ▭

1 Listen and practice.

Clerk: What is your name, please?
Mary: Mary Moore.
Clerk: Is that M-O-O-R-E?
Mary: Yes, that's right.
Clerk: And what's your address?
Mary: 809 Oak Street, Apartment 1201,
        Westwood, California.
Clerk: And what's your phone number?
Mary: It's 732-1465.
Clerk: Thank you very much.
Mary: You're welcome.

2 Now listen to the clerk talking to two more people and complete the information.

Hotel Registration

NAME	STREET	APT. NO.	CITY, STATE	PHONE
Mary Moore	809 Oak Street	1201	Westwood, CA	732-1465

▶ **Interchange 2: Who is it?**
Do you believe in astrology? Find out what zodiac signs can tell you about your classmates on page 103.

13 READING: Job advertisements

1 Read these ads and fill in the blanks with the correct job.

chef	manager	sports instructor
English teacher	nurse	waiter
guide	receptionist	

............................: College grad with degree in English. Work in language school in Italy. Write to Da Vinci School, P.O. Box 234, Rome, Italy.

............................: Part-time or full-time job in doctor's office. Greet patients and answer the phone. Mornings and afternoons. Interesting work. Call Dr. Strangelove at 524-7423.

............................: Part-time job at Asian Garden Restaurant. Cook Chinese and American meals. Work evenings. Call Mr. Chang at 955-6511.

............................: Full-time job in department store in camera and TV section. Supervise 6 salesclerks. No evening work. $22,000. Call Mr. James at 731-8959.

............................: Full-time job in hotel. To help with games and to teach tennis, golf, and swimming. Good English and Japanese needed. Write Mrs. Sato, Pacific Hotel, Honolulu, Hawaii.

............................: Take South American tourists on bus tours in Canada and the U.S. Need good Spanish and English. Call 815-7880.

2 Which jobs need:

a college degree?   good English?   a foreign language?

1 SNAPSHOT

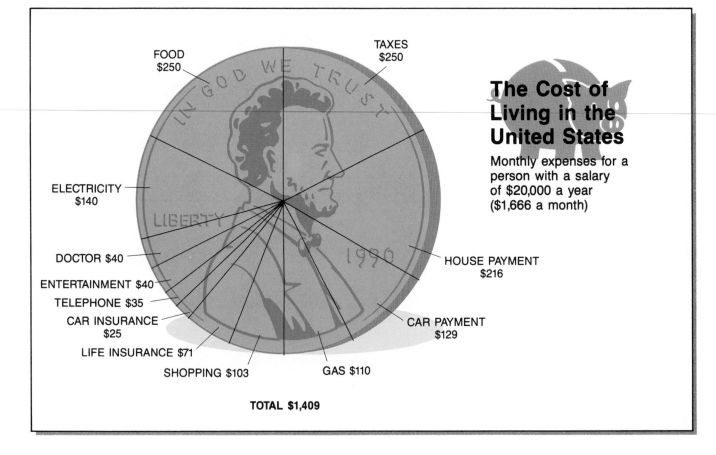

FOOD
$250

TAXES
$250

ELECTRICITY
$140

DOCTOR $40

ENTERTAINMENT $40

TELEPHONE $35

CAR INSURANCE
$25

LIFE INSURANCE $71

SHOPPING $103

GAS $110

CAR PAYMENT
$129

HOUSE PAYMENT
$216

The Cost of Living in the United States

Monthly expenses for a person with a salary of $20,000 a year ($1,666 a month)

TOTAL $1,409

List your five biggest monthly expenses. Then compare with a partner.

2 EXPENSES

1 *Group work* How much do you spend each month on rent, food, shopping, transportation, and entertainment? Ask each member of your group like this:

A: How much do you spend on . . . ?
B: Oh, I spend (about) . . . How about you?
C: Nothing. I live with my parents.

2 *Class activity* Find the average for your group. Compare group averages.

3 LISTENING 🔊

Listen to people compare prices in three cities. Complete the information.

	One gallon of gas	Bus fare	Dinner for two in a restaurant
Honolulu			
Mexico City			
Tokyo			

4 WORD POWER: Possessions

1 *Pair work* Complete the chart with words from the list below.

bag
blouse
bracelet
calculator
folder
✓necklace
ring
skirt
slip
sport shirt
tie
✓trousers

Men's clothing	*Women's clothing*	*School supplies*	*Jewelry*
trousers			*necklace*

2 Now add three more words to each list.

5 YOURS OR MINE?

Class activity Each student puts something (a watch, etc.) on the teacher's desk.

Take turns talking about the objects.

I think this is John's.
It isn't mine.
This is yours, Sue.
I think this is hers . . .
Ah! This is mine.

> *Possessive pronouns*
>
> mine
> yours
> his
> hers
> ours
> theirs
> Sue's
> John's

6 PRONUNCIATION: Plural *s* 🔲

1 We pronounce the plural **s** in three ways. Listen and practice.

s = /z/	**s** = /s/	**s** = /ɪz/
bag → bag**s**	clerk → clerk**s**	dress → dress**es**
pencil → pencil**s**	cook → cook**s**	actress → actress**es**
shoe → shoe**s**	student → student**s**	watch → watch**es**

2 Put these words into three lists: words with /z/, /s/, or /ɪz/.

hotels   books   nurses   glasses   cameras
typists   classes   guides   belts   ties

7 CONVERSATION: Prices 🔲

1 Listen and practice.

Sally: Oh, look at this bracelet, Carlos! It's lovely!
Carlos: Yeah, it's OK.
Sally: Excuse me, please. How much is this?
Clerk: Oh, that's on sale. It's only $75.
Carlos: That's crazy! Come on, Sally...

Carlos: Hey, Sally, how do you like these running shoes?
Sally: Well, they're all right, I guess.
Carlos: Excuse me. How much are these?
Clerk: They're $80.
Carlos: Oh, that's not bad!
Sally: Eighty dollars! Well, thanks, anyway. We're just looking.

2 Now listen to the rest of the conversation. What else do Sally and Carlos ask about?

Item	Price	Do they buy it?
_____	_____	Yes / No
_____	_____	Yes / No
_____	_____	Yes / No

8 GRAMMAR FOCUS: Demonstrative adjectives and pronouns 🔊

How much is	**this** bracelet?	**It** is $75.
	that ring?	(It's)
	it?	
How much are	**these** shoes?	**They** are $80.
	those glasses?	(They're)
	they?	

Complete these conversations. Then practice them.

A: Can I help you?
B: How much .... jeans?
A: .... $60.
B: Sixty or sixteen?
A: Sixty.
B: Sixty dollars! Are you kidding?

A: Good evening.
B: How much .... sunglasses?
A: .... $25.
B: Oh, really?
A: Would you like to buy them?
B: Yes, I'll take them. .... are very nice.

A: Good afternoon.
B: Hi! How much .... backpack?
A: .... $35. Would you like to buy it?
B: Well, I'll think about it.

A: Good morning. Can I help you?
B: How much .... bicycle?
A: .... is on sale. .... only $500.
B: Five hundred dollars! Well, I'm just looking, thanks.

9 ROLE PLAY: In a department store

Put items for sale on the desk (e.g., a ring, a watch, a bag, a pen).

Student A: You are a clerk in a department store.
Answer the customer's questions.

Student B: You are a customer.
Ask about the price of each item.
Say if you want to buy it.

Now change roles and try the role play again.

10 CONVERSATION 🔊

1 Listen and practice.

A: Hello.
B: Hi. I'm calling about the car for sale.
A: Yes, what would you like to know?
B: Well, what kind is it?
A: It's a Toyota Celica.
B: And how old is it?
A: It's about four years old.
B: Oh. How much do you want for it?
A: $5,200.
B: Mmm. I think I'd like to see it. Is 8 o'clock OK?
A: Yes, that's fine. My address is 139 King Street, Apartment 4.
B: OK, thanks a lot. See you later. Bye!
A: Bye.

2 *Pair work* Now take turns calling about the things below.

GARAGE SALE!

CD player   refrigerator
camera   motorcycle

Call 521-6871

Useful expressions

What kind is it?	How old is it?
It's a Honda.	It's new.
It's a Kodak.	It's about six months old.

11 LISTENING 🔊

Three people are calling about things for sale. Complete the missing information.

	For Sale	Kind	Age	Price
1.	_____	*Baldwin*	_____	_____
2.	*TV*	_____	_____	_____
3.	_____	*Volkswagen*	_____	_____

▶ **Interchange 3: Swap meet**

See what kind of deals you can make as a buyer and seller!

Turn to page 105 for the class swap meet.

12 READING: Shopping advertisements

SIMPSON'S Annual Sale

This week only

Men's and women's clothing:
Shoes, coats and sweaters,
swimwear, jeans, shoes

Jewelry: Watches, rings,
earrings, and necklaces

Furniture: Leather sofas,
dining tables and chairs,
and bookcases

Luggage: Bags and briefcases

Simpson's is on the corner
of Main and East Streets.
Open from 9 A.M. to 9 P.M.

FISHER | ON FIRST STREET

Come and see what we have on sale for your office!

30% off all office furniture:
desks and bookcases

20% off office equipment:
typewriters and telephones

And **10% off** office supplies:
pens, paper, and calculators

Open 10 A.M. - 5 P.M. Daily

Sharper Image is having
A BIG WEEKEND ELECTRONICS SALE!

Everything 50% Off!

All stereos, TVs, radios, and
cameras. Open from 10 A.M. to
6 P.M. in Fort Street Mall.

1 You want to buy these things. Which store probably sells them?

	Simpson's	Fisher	Sharper Image
a briefcase	_____	_____	_____
pencils	_____	_____	_____
a bracelet	_____	_____	_____
a CD player	_____	_____	_____
computer paper	_____	_____	_____
headphones	_____	_____	_____

2 Are these statements true (**T**) or false (**F**)?

a) Simpson's is a department store.   T   F
b) Fisher and Sharper Image sell office equipment.   T   F
c) Simpson's sale is for two days only.   T   F
d) Desks are on sale at Fisher.   T   F
e) Sharper Image has photo equipment at 50% off.   T   F

Review of Units 1-3

1 Getting to know you

Pair work You are talking to someone at school. Use the information below and have a conversation.

A: Hi. How are you?
B: ...
A: By the way, my name is ...
B: ...
A: Are you from ...?
B: ...
A: Are you a student here?
B: ...   And how about you?
   What do you do?
A: ...
B: Oh, really? And where are you from?
A: ...
B: Well, nice talking to you.
A: ...
B: Bye.
A: ...

2 Quiz

1 *Pair work*   Write five questions about famous people like this:

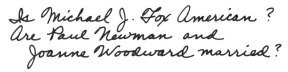

Is Michael J. Fox American?
Are Paul Newman and
* Joanne Woodward married?*

2 *Group work*   Now take turns asking and answering your questions.

A: Is Michael J. Fox American?
B: No, he isn't. He's Canadian.

A: Are Paul Newman and Joanne Woodward married?
B: Yes, they are.

A: Is Mikhail Gorbachev the president of the USSR?
B: Yes, I think so.

20

3 | What's the question?

1 Look at these answers. What are the questions?

No, my apartment isn't on Lewis Street. It's on Black Street.

No, it isn't George's car. It's mine.

Yes, I'm a student. I go to Kansas State University.

The Taylors are from Ottawa.

No, that one isn't mine. The brown one is mine.

I teach at a community college.

No, Carlos isn't from Mexico. He's from Argentina.

I teach business English.

No, my phone number isn't 955–8821. It's 995–8821.

2 Now check with a partner.

4 | Listening

Listen to one side of a conversation and choose the correct answers.

a) .... Yes, I do.
.... At Saxon's Department Store.

b) .... It's on Vine Street.
.... No, I don't know.

c) .... Yes, I'm in the electronics department.
.... Yes, I'm from San Francisco.

d) .... Yes, we do.
.... Oh, that sounds interesting.

e) .... They're on sale. About $65–$200.
.... That's not bad.

f) .... Nice talking to you.
.... Yes, I work on Saturdays.

g) .... OK. See you on Saturday.
.... Well, thanks anyway.

5 | The cost of living

1 *Pair work* Take turns. Ask questions about these things.

How much is . . . ?

a movie ticket   a meal in a fast food restaurant
a gallon/liter of gas   a local phone call
a taxi to the airport   a local bus fare

2 Now ask three more questions about things in your city.

4 What kind of music do you like?

1 SNAPSHOT

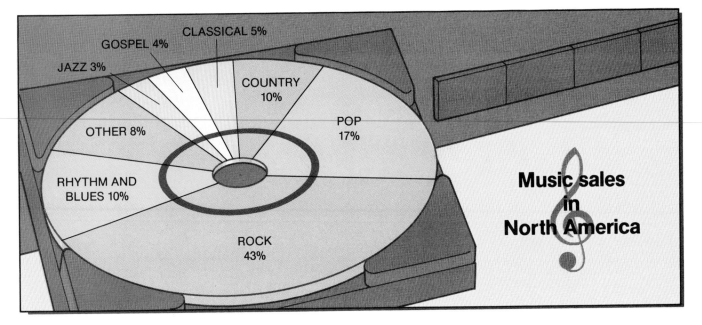

GOSPEL 4%
CLASSICAL 5%
JAZZ 3%
COUNTRY 10%
OTHER 8%
POP 17%
RHYTHM AND BLUES 10%
ROCK 43%

Music sales in North America

Complete the information below. Then compare with a partner.

My favorite kind of music: ....

My favorite music group: ....

My favorite singer: ....

---

2 WORD POWER: Entertainment

1 *Pair work* Complete the chart with words from the list below.

classical   rock
game shows   science fiction
horror films   soap operas
jazz   talk shows
news   thrillers
pop   westerns

ENTERTAINMENT

MUSIC	MOVIES	TV PROGRAMS
jazz	*horror films*	*game shows*

2 Now add three more words to each list.

3 CONVERSATION: Likes and dislikes 🔲

Listen and practice.

Liz: Do you like jazz, Tom?
Tom: No, I don't like it very much. Do you?
Liz: It's OK. What kind of music do you like?
Tom: Well, I like rock a lot.
Liz: What's your favorite group?
Tom: U2. How about you? Do you like them?
Liz: No, I don't. I can't stand them!

4 GRAMMAR FOCUS: Yes/No questions with *do* 🔲

Do you **like** jazz?
  Yes, I do. I like it a lot.
  No, I don't like it very much.
  No, I don't.

Do you **like** U2?
  Yes, I do. I like them a lot.
  No, I don't like them very much.
  No, I don't.

Object pronouns

me
you (singular)
him
her
it
us
you (plural)
them

Complete these conversations. Then practice them.

A: Do you .... disco music?
B: Yes, I really like .... How about you?
A: I .... like it very much.

A: Who's your favorite actress?
B: Jane Fonda. I really like ....
A: Jane Fonda! I can't stand .... !

A: .... you .... Anne Murray?
B: No, I .... like .... very much.
   But I like Whitney Houston. Do you?
A: Yes, I .... She's terrific!

A: What kind of TV programs .... you like?
B: Game shows. I like .... a lot. Do you like
   them?
A: No, I .... like .... very much. I ....
   music videos.

A: .... you like Sly Stallone?
B: He's OK. My favorite actor is Tom Cruise. Do
   you .... ?
A: .... , ... do.

A: What do you think of the Rolling Stones?
B: Well, I .... like them very much.
A: Oh really? I like .... a lot.

23

5 PRONUNCIATION: Question intonation 🔊

1 Yes/No questions usually have rising intonation. Wh-questions usually have falling intonation. Listen and practice.

Do you like pop music?   What kind of music do you like?

Do you like movies?   What kind of movies do you like?

2 Now practice these questions.

Do you like TV?   What programs do you like?
Do you like music videos?   What videos do you like?

6 ENTERTAINMENT SURVEY

Julio Iglesias

1 *Group work*   Talk about entertainment and entertainers like this.

Do you like . . . ?
   (pop music, TV, movies)

What kind of . . . do you like?
   (music, movies, TV programs)

What do you think of . . . ?
   (Cher, horror films, New Age music)

Who is your favorite . . . ?
   (actress, actor, singer)

What's your favorite . . . ?
   (music, movie, TV program)

Frank Sinatra

Liza Minnelli

2 Now complete the information below about your group.

Our Group Favorites

music _____   actor _____

movie _____   actress _____

TV program _____   singer _____

3 *Class activity*   Read your list to the class like this: Our favorite music is . . .

What are the class favorites?

Useful expressions

Most people like . . .
We don't agree on music.
We can't agree on a movie.

7 LISTENING: TV game show 📼

Four people are playing *Who's My Date?* Three men want to invite
Linda on a date. What kinds of things do they like?

	Music	Movies	TV programs
Bill	*classical*		
John			
Tony			
Linda			

Who do you think is the best date for Linda?

8 CONVERSATION: Invitations 📼

Listen and practice.

Dave: There's a jazz concert at the Blue Note
　　　on Friday. Would you like to go?
Joan: Yeah, that sounds good! What time
　　　is the concert?
Dave: It's at 10 o'clock.
Joan: Great! Let's go.

25

9 GRAMMAR FOCUS: *There is;* prepositions 🔲

> **There is** a jazz concert **at** the Blue Note **on** Friday. It's **at** 10 o'clock.
> (There's)

1 Write about the events in town this week.

travel film	the Varsity Theater	Monday	7:00
computer show	the Science Center	Tuesday	6:00
soccer game	the City Stadium	Wednesday	7:45
rock concert	the Civic Hall	Friday	8:30

*THIS WEEK IN **TOWN!***

There's a travel film at the Varsity Theater on Monday. It's at 7 o'clock.

2 *Pair work* Ask and answer questions like these.

Where is the travel film?	It's at . . .
When's the computer show?	It's on . . .
What time is it?	It's at . . .

10 LISTENING 🔲

Listen to the recorded telephone announcements on the "film information number." Complete the information below. Then compare with a partner.

Times:	Times:	Times: ....
Days:	Days:	Days: ....

11 WRITING: Invitations

1 Look at a newspaper. Find three interesting events in your city and write about them like this. Then tell the class about one event.

There is a Japanese movie at the Star Theater. It's on Thursday the 17th at 8 o'clock. The movie is "Tokyo Story."

2 *Pair work* Take turns. Now invite your partner to one of the events you wrote about.

12 READING: Is TV good or bad?

Tube Time

Average TV viewing time in a week for adults:

Age	Men	Women
18–34	24 hours	29 hours
35–54	28 hours	32 hours
55+	39 hours	44 hours

Today, there is a TV set in nearly every home. People watch TV every day, and some people watch it from morning until night. Americans watch TV about 35 hours a week. But is TV good or bad for you? People have different opinions. Read what some American college students say.

a) .... People don't get any exercise. They just sit and watch TV.

b) .... It brings news from around the world into people's homes.

c) .... People just want entertainment today. They don't want to think.

d) .... There's a lot of crime and violence on TV today. The programs are terrible!

e) .... Children learn many useful things from programs like *Sesame Street*. It teaches them to read.

f) .... It helps me relax after a long day.

g) .... Programs on the radio are better. They make you think.

h) .... It's all commercials. I hate it!

i) .... People learn about life in other countries.

j) .... People don't read anymore. It's easier to watch TV.

1 Do the students think TV is good or bad? Write **G** for good and **B** for bad. Then compare with a partner.

2 Do you agree with the opinions above? Write **Yes** or **No** next to each opinion.

▶ **Interchange 4: Can I help you?**

Find out what's happening in town! Student A plays a clerk at a Tourist Information Center and looks at page 106. Student B is a tourist and looks at page 108.

5 Tell me about your family

1 WORD POWER: The family

1 Look at Sam's family tree. Can you add these words to it?

cousins   niece   sister-in-law   uncle   grandmother   father

SAM'S FAMILY TREE

GENERATION

1ST   grandfather & _____

2ND   _____ & mother   _____ & aunt

3RD   Sam   brother & _____   _____

4TH   _____ nephew

2 Now draw your family tree. Then talk about your family like this.

For a single person:

There are 6 in my family.
I have 2 sisters and 1 brother.

For a married person:

There are 4 in my family.
We have a daughter and a son.

2 RELATIVES

1 Complete the sentences with these words:

**aunt   cousin   father   grandmother
grandparents   niece   sister-in-law**

a) My uncle's son is my ....
b) My brother's daughter is my ....
c) My brother's wife is my ....
d) My father's sister is my ....
e) My father's parents are my ....
f) My mother's husband is my ....
g) My mother's mother is my ....

2 *Pair work* Now write three sentences with blanks like the ones above. Can your partner complete them?

3 SNAPSHOT

Families

Average size of a family in the United States and Canada: *3.2 people*

Age when people marry: *men-25.5; women-23.3*

Percentage of people over 60 who live with a relative: *6.3%*

Percentage of families with 1 parent: *26%*

Percentage of people who live alone: *8.3%*

Average age of people who live alone:
men-41.4 years; women-65.5 years

Complete the information below. Then compare with a partner.

Average size of a family in my country: ....
Number of relatives living with me: ....
Average age when people marry in my country: men .... ; women ....

4 CONVERSATION

Listen and practice.

Rita: What do you do, Keiko?
Keiko: I'm a lawyer.
Rita: Really? Tell me about your family.
Keiko: Well, I'm married and have two children.
Rita: And what does your husband do?
Keiko: He has an export business.
Rita: Oh, that's interesting.
Keiko: And how about you, Rita?
 Do you have any brothers and sisters?
Rita: Yes, I have a brother and a sister.
Keiko: Really? And what do they do?
Rita: Well, my brother teaches French, and my
 sister drives a taxi.
Keiko: No kidding.

5 LISTENING: Hollywood lives

Listen to some facts about these famous
people. What do you learn about each
person's family? Take notes. Then compare
with a partner.

Jane Fonda   *Madonna*

6 PRONUNCIATION: Third-person *s* 🔲

1 We pronounce third-person **s** in three ways. Listen and practice.

s = /z/	**s** = /s/	**s** = /ɪz/
lives	makes	manages
sells	works	supervises
owns	likes	teaches

2 Put these words into three lists: words with /z/, /s/, or /ɪz/.

buys	cooks	discusses	helps	takes	washes
comes	designs	exercises	studies	types	writes

7 GRAMMAR FOCUS: Present tense – third person 🔲

What **does** she do?	She **drives** a taxi.
What **does** he do?	He **teaches** French.
What **do** they do?	They **go** to school.

Does your brother go to school?	Yes, he **does**.
Does your sister live here?	No, she **doesn't**.
Do your children work in Chicago?	Yes, they **do**.
	No, they **don't**.

Complete these conversations. Then practice them.

A: Tell me about your parents.
 What .... (does/do) they do?
B: Well, my father is retired, and my
 mother .... (manages/manage) a
 boutique.
A: Oh. Do .... (he/she/they) live with
 you?
B: No, they .... (doesn't/don't). They
 .... (lives/live) in Miami.

A: Do you have any brothers and sisters?
B: Yes, I have two sisters and one brother.
 My older sister .... (works/work) for
 United Airlines, and my younger sister
 .... (goes/go) to UCLA.
A: Oh, really? And what .... (does/do)
 your brother do? Does he .... (goes/go)
 to school, too?
B: No, he .... (doesn't/don't). He is
 married and .... (teaches/teach) in an
 elementary school.

8 INTERESTING PEOPLE

1 *Group work* Take turns talking about your family. Other students ask questions like these.

For a single person:

Where do your parents live?
How old is your sister?
Does your brother go to school?

For a married person:

What's your husband's/wife's name?
Are your children in school?
What grade is your daughter in?

2 *Class activity* Talk about some of the interesting people you heard about like this:

    Helga's sister lives in Kenya, in Africa.
    She takes people on safaris.

9 LISTENING

Listen to Dick and Jane playing "Twenty Questions." Can you guess who they are describing?

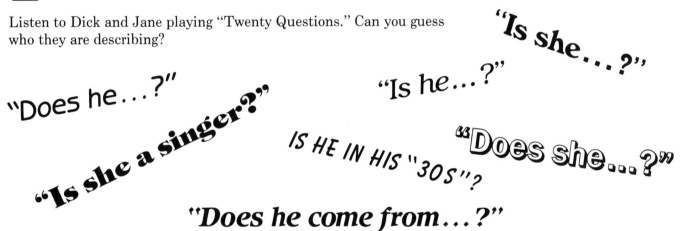

10 TWENTY QUESTIONS

Group work Now you play the game. Take turns. One student thinks of a famous person. The group can ask up to twenty questions like these. The answers are "Yes" or "No."

Is it a man? *(or)* Is it a woman?
Does he live in the United States?
Is she American?
Is he a singer?
Does she wear glasses?
Is he in his 30s?

When you think you know the person's name, say:

Is he . . . (name)? *(or)* Is she . . . (name)?

11 WRITING

1 Write about your family like this.

There are five people in my family. I have an older brother and a younger sister. My brother lives in Vancouver. He sells cars. And my sister...

My wife and I have two children. My wife manages a restaurant. Our older daughter is married. She lives in...

2 Now exchange papers. Do you have any questions about your partner's family?

> ▶ **Interchange 5: Who's who?**
> Help collect some interesting facts about your classmates. Turn to page 107.

Turn to page 107.

12 CONVERSATION 📼

1 Listen and practice.

Greeting someone

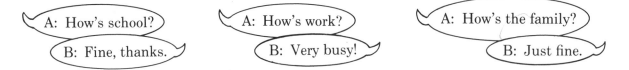

A: How have you been?
B: Just fine, thanks.

A: How are things?
B: Great, thanks.

A: How are you doing?
B: Pretty good. And you?

Making small talk

A: How's school?
B: Fine, thanks.

A: How's work?
B: Very busy!

A: How's the family?
B: Just fine.

Ending a conversation

A: Well, talk to you later.
B: Yeah, bye!

A: Well, nice talking to you.
B: Yeah, see you later.

2 Now cover the expressions above. Listen to people talking to friends and choose the correct responses.

a) .... Pretty good, thanks.
   .... Yeah, see you later.

b) .... Yes, they are.
   .... They are fine, thanks.

c) .... OK, thanks.
   .... How have you been?

d) .... Nice talking to you, too.
   .... Great, thanks.

13 SMALL TALK

Class activity Look at this conversation and then close your books.
Now go around the class and talk to three classmates.

A: Hi! How have you been?
B: Fine, thanks. And you?
A: Pretty good. How's the family?
B: Just fine. And how's work?
A: Good. Very busy.
B: Yes, me too.
　　Well, talk to you later.
A: Yeah, bye!
B: Bye!

14 READING: Touchy topics

In North America when people meet each other for the first time, they talk about things like family, work, school, or sports. They ask questions like "Do you have any brothers or sisters?", "Where do you work?", "What school do you go to?", and "Do you like sports?" They also ask questions like "Where do you come from?" and "Where do you live?" These are polite questions. They are not personal or private.

But some things *are* personal or private, and questions about them are not polite. People don't ask questions about a person's salary. They don't ask how much someone paid for something. It is OK to ask children how old they are, but it is not polite to ask older people their age. It is also not polite to ask people questions about politics or religion unless you know them very well. People don't ask unmarried people "Why are you single?", and they don't ask a married couple with no children "Why don't you have any children?"

1 *Pair work* Look at the following questions. Are they polite or not polite when you meet someone for the first time in North America?

	Polite	Not polite
a) What does your wife do?	....	....
b) Do you believe in God?	....	....
c) How much money do you earn?	....	....
d) How many children do you have?	....	....
e) Why aren't you married?	....	....
f) Do you like baseball?	....	....
g) How old are you, Mr. Lee?	....	....
h) Are you a Democrat or a Republican?	....	....
i) How much was your watch?	....	....

2 Look at the questions again. Are they polite or not polite in your country?

1 SNAPSHOT

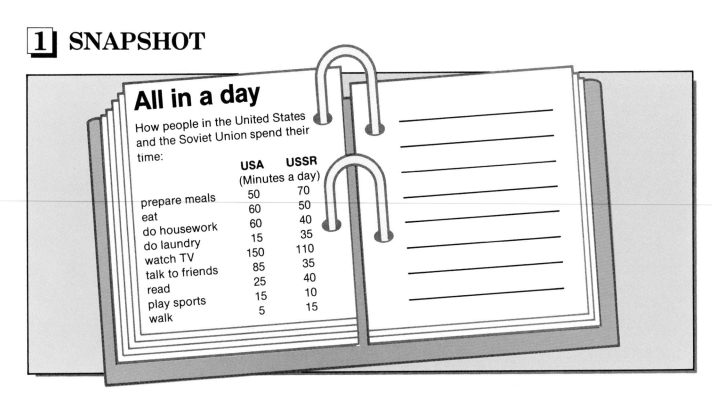

All in a day

How people in the United States and the Soviet Union spend their time:

	USA	USSR
	(Minutes a day)	
prepare meals	50	70
eat	60	50
do housework	60	40
do laundry	15	35
watch TV	150	110
talk to friends	85	35
read	25	40
play sports	15	10
walk	5	15

How much time do you spend each day on the activities above?
Write down your information. Then compare with a partner.

---

2 CONVERSATION: Routines 📼

Listen and practice.

Marie: What do you usually do on your day off, Chuck?

Chuck: Well, I always get up very early, around 5 o'clock. And I lift weights for an hour.

Marie: You're kidding!

Chuck: No, and then I usually run for about 2 hours.

Marie: Wow! You really like to stay in shape.

Chuck: And after that, I come home and eat a big breakfast. How about you?

Marie: Oh, on my day off, I just watch TV all day. I guess I'm a real couch potato!

3 LISTENING

Listen to Mark, Sue, and Liz talk about what they do on their day off.
Who likes to exercise? Who doesn't?

4 GRAMMAR FOCUS: Adverbs of frequency (1) 📼

What do you **usually** do on your day off?

I **always** get up early.
I **usually** run for about 2 hours.
I **often** eat a huge breakfast.
I **sometimes** go downtown in the afternoon.
Sometimes I just watch TV.
I **never** go to discos.
I don't **usually** eat out.

1 Put the adverbs in the correct place. Then practice the conversations.

A: What do you do on your day off?   (usually)
B: Nothing much. I sleep until noon.   (always)

A: Do you go out on Saturday night?   (usually)
B: Yes, I do.   (often)
   I go roller-skating   (sometimes)
   or I go to a movie.

A: Do you drive to school?   (usually)
B: No, I drive to school.   (never)
   I take the bus.   (always)

A: What do you do after class?   (usually)
B: I meet friends for a drink   (often)
   or I go straight home.   (sometimes)

A: Do you get much exercise?   (usually)
B: Yes, I play tennis after work.   (sometimes)
   And on Sundays, I go to the gym.   (often)

2 *Pair work*   Take turns. Ask the questions above,
but this time give your own answers.

3 *Class activity*   Now write four questions like the ones above.
Then go around the class and ask your questions.

5 MY BUSIEST DAY

My busiest
day is
Friday. I
have classes
until 9 P.M.

I hate Mondays! I get up at
5 A.M. I catch the train at 6.
I start work at 7 and finish
around 6 P.M. Then I take a
German class from 7 to 10 P.M.
It's a really long day for me!

Saturday is my busiest day.
In the morning, I always clean
the house. I usually do the
shopping in the afternoon. In
the evening, I work as a waiter.
I usually get home around
midnight.

Pair work   Take turns. Now talk about your busiest day of the week.

A: What's your busiest day?
B: . . .
A: And what do you usually do?
B: . . .

Your partner asks for more information like this:

What time do you usually get up?
Where do you usually have . . . (breakfast, lunch, dinner)?
What do you usually do after . . . (work, school, class)?
What time do you usually go home?
What time do you usually go to bed?

6 WRITING: Writing about a typical day

1 Write about a day in your week (e.g., the busiest day, a day off, or
your favorite day).

2 *Group work*   Now take turns reading your compositions.
Then answer any questions from the group.

7 WORD POWER: Sports and exercise

1 Match the words and the pictures.

.... aerobics

.... baseball

.... bicycling

.... golf

.... hiking

.... karate

.... skiing

.... soccer

A B C

D E F

G H

2 *Pair work*
Now arrange the words above into three lists:

team sports, individual sports, and exercise.

3 Can you add two more words to each list?

8 CONVERSATION 📼

Listen and practice.

Cathy: What great muscles, Pedro! Do you work out in a gym?
Pedro: Yeah, I do.
Cathy: How often do you work out?
Pedro: Every day after work. You're in pretty good shape, too, Cathy.
Cathy: Thanks. I take an aerobics class twice a week.
Pedro: Good for you! Hey! Race you to McDonald's for a chocolate milkshake!
Cathy: OK!

9 PRONUNCIATION: Reduced form of *do* 🔲

1 Listen to how **do you** is reduced in these sentences.

How often **do you** work out?
　　/dəyə/

Where **do you** work out?
　　/dəyə/

2 Practice these sentences using the reduced form of **do you.**

　How often do you play golf?
　How often do you exercise?

10 GRAMMAR FOCUS: Adverbs of frequency (2) 🔲

How often do you exercise? I go to the gym **every day.** I jog about **once a week.** I play tennis **twice a month.** About **three times a year!** I don't exercise **very much/very often.**

1 Write answers to these questions.

a) How often do you exercise?
b) Do you jog or run?
c) Do you work out in a gym?
d) How often do you go swimming?
e) Do you play tennis?
f) What other sports do you play?
g) What other exercise do you get? How often?

2 *Pair work*   Take turns asking the questions. Use the reduced form of **do you.**

11 LISTENING 🔲

Listen to people asking questions about sports and exercise, and choose the correct responses.

a) .... I don't usually do much.
　 .... Yes, I usually do.
b) .... No, I often do.
　 .... Well, I sometimes do.
c) .... Yes, I do.
　 .... About twice a week.

d) .... Yes, once or twice a year.
　 .... How often do you go?
e) .... I play tennis and I swim.
　 .... About twice a month.
f) .... Yes, I often do.
　 .... Golf.

▶ **Interchange 6: Leisure survey**
What do you do in your spare time? Take part in the survey on page 107.

12 READING: Fitness

═ TAKING YOUR FITNESS MEASURE ═

Are you in good shape? How much exercise do you usually get every week?
Many daily activities help keep you fit. Find out how fit you are with this fitness check.

In a week, I usually vacuum, do laundry, cook and clean for:

☐ 1 hour	1 point
☐ 2-4 hours	3 points
☐ 3-5 hours	6 points
☐ 6-8 hours	8 points

I look after children under age 8:

☐ One child	5 points
☐ Two children	7 points
☐ Three children	10 points
☐ Four children	15 points

I usually spend some time in the garden each week:

☐ 1 hour	2 points
☐ 2 hours	4 points
☐ 3 hours	6 points
☐ 4 hours	8 points
☐ 5 hours	10 points

My job keeps me on my feet each day for:

☐ 1 hour	2 points
☐ 2 hours	4 points
☐ 3 hours	6 points
☐ 4 hours	8 points
☐ 5 hours	12 points

I work in a job such as carpentry, construction, farming or delivery, which involves ___ hours a week of physical labor.

☐ 5 hours	5 points
☐ 10 hours	10 points
☐ 20 hours	20 points
☐ 30 hours	30 points

In an average week, I take aerobics, jazzercise or dance classes for:

☐ 1 hour	4 points
☐ 2 hours	8 points
☐ 3 hours	12 points
☐ 4 hours	16 points
☐ 5 hours	20 points
☐ 6 hours	24 points

In an average week, I go out dancing just for fun for:

☐ 1 hour	4 points
☐ 2 hours	6 points
☐ 3 hours	8 points
☐ 4 hours	12 points

In an average week, I play tennis for:

☐ 1 hour	3 points
☐ 2 hours	6 points
☐ 3 hours	8 points
☐ 4 hours	10 points

In an average week, I hike for:

☐ 1 hour	6 points
☐ 2 hours	9 points
☐ 3 hours	12 points
☐ 4 hours	18 points

In an average week, I swim for:

☐ 1 hour	6 points
☐ 2 hours	10 points
☐ 3 hours	15 points
☐ 4 hours	20 points

I walk about ___ mile(s) a day to or from work:

☐ 1 mile	4 points
☐ 2 miles	8 points
☐ 3 miles	12 points
☐ 4 miles	16 points
☐ 5 miles	20 points

In an average week, I spend ___ hours walking.

☐ 1 hour	4 points
☐ 2 hours	7 points
☐ 3 hours	10 points
☐ 4 hours	14 points

In an average week, I run for:

☐ 1 hour	5 points
☐ 2 hours	10 points
☐ 3 hours	15 points
☐ 4 hours	20 points

In an average week, I play squash, handball or racquetball for:

☐ 1 hour	4 points
☐ 2 hours	7 points
☐ 3 hours	10 points
☐ 4 hours	14 points

In an average week, I bike for:

☐ 1 hour	5 points
☐ 2 hours	10 points
☐ 3 hours	15 points
☐ 4 hours	20 points

In an average week, I use an exercise cycle for ___ hour(s):

☐ 1 hour	5 points
☐ 2 hours	10 points
☐ 3 hours	15 points
☐ 4 hours	20 points

In an average week, I play softball for:

☐ 2 hours	4 points
☐ 3 hours	6 points
☐ 4 hours	8 points

In an average week, I play basketball, soccer or volleyball for:

☐ 1 hour	5 points
☐ 2 hours	7 points
☐ 3 hours	10 points

In an average week, I play golf—using a cart—for:

☐ 2 hours	3 points
☐ 4 hours	6 points
☐ 6 hours	9 points

In an average week, I play golf—and walk—for:

☐ 2 hours	5 points
☐ 4 hours	10 points
☐ 6 hours	15 points

═ YOUR FITNESS INDEX ═

1-7 points	You are in very bad shape.
8-16 points	Your fitness level is about average. But your heart needs more exercise. Think about an aerobic activity like jogging, aerobic dance, or swimming.
17-30 points	Your fitness level is above average. You are in good shape.
31-60 points	Congratulations! You are in excellent condition.
61 points or above	Take it easy. Slow down a little. You exercise too much. Be careful.

TOTAL: _____ points

Review of Units 4–6

1 What's on at the movies?

Pair work Take turns. Look at the movie section in an
English-language newspaper and find an interesting movie to see.
Then answer your partner's questions.

A: Are there any good movies on?
B: Yes, there's an interesting movie
   at ... (movie theater)
A: What's the name of the movie?
B: ...
A: What kind of movie is it?
B: ...

A: Who's in it?
B: ...
A: What times is it showing?
B: ... Would you like to see it?
A: ...

2 TV and radio

1 *Pair work* Take turns asking these questions.

TV

Do you watch TV a lot?
How often do you watch TV?
When do you usually watch it?
What kinds of programs do you usually watch?
What's your favorite channel?
What's your favorite program?
When is it on?
Do you ever watch ... (name of program)?

2 Change partners. Now take turns asking these questions.

Radio

Do you listen to the radio a lot?
How much time do you listen to it every day?
When do you listen to it?
What kinds of programs do you listen to?
Do you ever listen to programs in English?

What's your favorite radio station?
What's your favorite radio program?
Do you ever listen to the radio in bed?
What kind of music do you listen to?
Who are your favorite singers and groups?

40

3 An interesting person

1 *Pair work* Who is the most interesting or unusual person you know? First tell your partner about him or her. Then answer any questions your partner may have.

One of the most interesting people I know is my grandfather. He's 75 years old, and he speaks 3 languages. He plays the piano and the trumpet. And he has a great sense of humor.

2 *Group work* Take turns. Now give a short talk about the person.

4 A day in the life of . . .

1 What's a typical day for you? Look at the activities below and fill in the time you spend on each activity in minutes and hours in one day.

....	sleep	....	read	....	do housework
....	eat	....	watch TV	....	take care of children
....	commute	....	listen to music	....	talk to friends
....	work	....	exercise	....	other:
....	study	....	walk		....

2 *Group work* Now talk about each activity and then calculate your group average.

A: I usually sleep about 7 hours a day.
B: Well, I always sleep 8 hours every day.
C: I sleep about 9 hours.

3 *Class activity* Groups report their averages to the class like this:

We usually sleep about 8 hours a day.

5 Listening

People are talking at a party. Listen to their questions. Are they polite or not polite?

	Polite	*Not polite*		*Polite*	*Not polite*
a)	....	....	e)	....	....
b)	....	....	f)	....	....
c)	....	....	g)	....	....
d)	....	....	h)	....	....

7 It was terrific!

1 SNAPSHOT

How people spend the weekend in Canada and the United States:

Watch TV, videos, or listen to music	**51%**
Exercise (walk, jog, or play sports, etc.)	**47%**
Read	**46%**
Go out (go to a movie, disco, restaurant, sports event, etc.)	**43%**
28%	Do other sports (fishing, bowling, etc.)
24%	Spend time with family or friends
21%	Enjoy hobbies
12%	Work in the garden

The Weekend

List four things you like to do on the weekend. Then compare with a partner.

2 CONVERSATION: Monday morning

Listen and practice.

How was your weekend?

1. It was fun. I went out with friends.

2. Oh, not very exciting. I just stayed home and watched TV.

4. Oh, pretty quiet. I didn't do much. I just worked around the house.

3. It was great! My friends and I went dancing. How was yours?

5. It was terrible! My girlfriend didn't call me.

3 GRAMMAR FOCUS: Past tense (1) 🔈

> How **was** your weekend?   It **was** terrific!   It **was** pretty good.
> It **was** OK.   It **was** terrible.
>
> What **did** you **do** on Saturday?   I **watched** the ballgame.
> I **saw** a good movie.
> I **went** to a disco.
> Some friends **came** over.

1 Complete these conversations with the past tense. [See page 133 for past tense forms.] Then practice the conversations.

A: What .... (do) you do on the weekend?
B: I .... (go) to a movie. I .... (see)
   Casablanca. It .... (be) terrific!

A: How .... (be) your weekend?
B: It .... (be) great! I .... (meet) some
   friends on Saturday, and we .... (go)
   to an outdoor concert.

A: What .... (do) you do on Saturday night?
B: I .... (have) friends over and I
   .... (cook) dinner for them. Then we
   .... (watch) a video. And what
   .... (do) you do on the weekend?
A: Oh, I .... (stay) home and
   .... (study).

A: What .... (do) you do on Sunday?
B: I .... (go) to Boston with my friend.
   We .... (take) a tour of the city.
   Then we .... (go) shopping.

2 *Pair work*   Now talk about your weekend.

4 PRONUNCIATION: Past tense 🔈

1 Listen to the past tense ending **-ed.** Then practice the words.

with /d/	*with* /t/	*with* /ɪd/
studied	worked	wanted
played	watched	visited
stayed	liked	added

2 Put these words into three lists: words ending with /d/, /t/, and /ɪd/.

called	waited	listened	talked	tried	looked
cooked	started	invited	phoned	rented	lived

43

5 WORD POWER: Verbs

1 *Pair work* Circle the word that does not belong in each list.

a) walked	typed	ran	climbed
b) studied	wrote	read	bought
c) danced	listened	watched	saw
d) spoke	took	brought	carried
e) cooked	drank	rode	ate

2 What are the present tense forms of the verbs above?

6 LISTENING ▭

1 Three people are talking about their weekends.
Listen and match each person with the correct newspaper headline.

a) Angela

b) John

c) Gary

2 Listen again. What happened to each person?

7 ANY QUESTIONS?

Group work Take turns. One student makes a statement about the
weekend like this:

I went to a movie on Saturday night.

Other students ask questions like these:

Who did you go with?   Where did you go after that?
What time did you go?   What did you do on Sunday?

Each student answers at least four questions.

8 CONVERSATION: On vacation 🔲

1 Listen and practice.

Mike: Hi, Celia! How was your trip to Japan?
Celia: It was wonderful! I really enjoyed it.
Mike: How long were you there?
Celia: I was there for three weeks.
Mike: Great! And did you go to Kyoto?
Celia: Yes, it's a beautiful city.
Mike: What did you do there?
Celia: Well, I visited some temples.
      They're really fantastic!
      And then I went to a sumo match in
      Osaka. That was fun!
Mike: And did you like Japanese food?
Celia: Yes, I did, but I didn't like sushi.
Mike: Oh, really? I love it!
Celia: By the way, do you want to see my
      photos?
Mike: Sure!

(1)............   (2)............   (3)............

2 Now listen to the rest of their conversation. Check (✓) the two photos they talk about. What did Celia say about each one?

Select 2 of the 3 photos. ⟫→

9 GRAMMAR FOCUS: Past tense (2) 🔲

> **Did** you **go** to Kyoto?
>   Yes, I **did**, and I **went** to Osaka.
>   No, I **didn't go** to Kyoto, but I **went** to Tokyo.
> How long **were** you there?
>   I **was** there for three weeks.
>   We **were** there for a month.

Scenes from the Winter Carnival, Quebec

Complete these conversations. Then practice them.

A: Did you .... (go) away for the
   weekend?
B: Yes, I .... (do). My family and I
   .... (go) to Disneyland.
   We .... (have) a great time!

A: Did you .... (enjoy) your trip to
   England?
B: Yes, we .... (do).
A: How long .... (be) you there?
B: We .... (be) there for a month.

A: Did you .... (take) a winter
   vacation last year?
B: Yes, I .... (do). I .... (go)
   to Quebec City for the Winter Carnival.
   I .... (have) a wonderful time, but it
   .... (be) really cold.

10 VACATIONS

Group work Take turns talking about an interesting trip or vacation.
Start like this:

I'd like to tell you about my trip to . . .

Other students ask questions like these.

How did you get there?   Did you enjoy it?
Who did you go with?   Did you like the food?
How long were you there? Did you do any sightseeing?
Where did you stay?   Did you buy anything?

11 WRITING: Writing a postcard

1 Read this postcard.

Dear Cathy,
    I just got back
from London. The
weather was terrible,
but I had a great
vacation. I went
shopping and bought
some clothes at Harrods.
Then I went to the theater
and saw a play called
The Mousetrap. I
loved it!
    Hey! Guess what! I
went to Buckingham Palace
one day and saw Princess
Di and Prince Charles!
Well, that's all for now.
                Love,
                Richard

2 Now write a postcard to a classmate about your last vacation.
Then exchange postcards.

▶ **Interchange 7: Photo album**

Use the pictures in the photo album to help you tell a story. Student A looks at page 109 and Student B at page 110.

12 READING: Vacation postcards

A

Dear Jill,
I just arrived in Corfu in Greece. This is a wonderful place. Nice beaches and interesting architecture. The hotel is great - right on the beach. I toured the island by bus yesterday and bought a leather bag and some jewelry. Two more weeks in Greece and then back to Chicago.
Love,
Margaret

B

Hi, Luis!
I'm in Montreal for a conference. It's a beautiful city. Lots of people speak French here, so I'm glad I took French in college. Great food! And the shops are good. Clothes are quite cheap. I bought a nice winter coat yesterday. I want to go to Quebec City for the weekend. It's not far from here.
Take care,
Sue

C

Keiko,
This is not a good time to visit Washington. It's very hot. It was 102° yesterday. But the city is still crowded with tourists. The museums here are excellent. I went to the Smithsonian and the National gallery yesterday - fantastic! And there's a new musical at the Kennedy Center I want to see. But the heat! Don't come to Washington in August.
See you soon!
Bill

1 Circle **T** (true) or **F** (false).

a) Margaret likes the beaches in Corfu.　T　F
b) Margaret plans to leave Greece in a few days.　T　F
c) Sue speaks French.　T　F
d) Sue likes Montreal.　T　F
e) August is a good month to visit Washington.　T　F
f) Bill likes the museums in Washington.　T　F

2 Find the best place in each postcard for these sentences.

Postcard A: Prices are very good.
Postcard B: Lots of French restaurants, but good Chinese and Italian restaurants, too.
Postcard C: It's called "The Best of Broadway."

1 WORD POWER: Places

1 Match the words and the definitions. Then practice with a partner.

What's a . . . ?   It's a place where you . . .

a) drugstore   .... wash and dry clothes.
b) laundromat   .... have a meal.
c) library   .... get stamps and mail letters.
d) post office   .... buy medicine.
e) restaurant   .... see a movie or play.
f) supermarket   .... buy groceries.
g) theater   .... borrow books and read newspapers.

2 *Pair work*   Now write definitions for these places:
bank, bookstore, bus station, coffee shop, gas station, and gym.

2 LOCATIONS

1 *Pair work*   Match the places and locations like this.

Where's the . . . ?

a) Sheraton Hotel
b) supermarket
c) laundromat
d) library
e) gym
f) bus stop

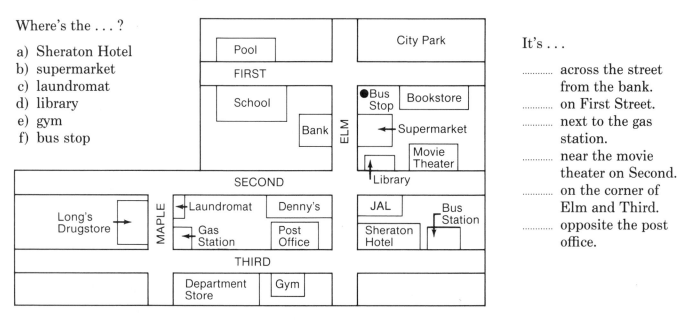

It's . . .

.... across the street from the bank.
.... on First Street.
.... next to the gas station.
.... near the movie theater on Second.
.... on the corner of Elm and Third.
.... opposite the post office.

2 Now take turns asking about these places:

the bus station   Long's Drugstore   Denny's Coffee Shop
Japan Air Lines (JAL)   the school   the bookstore

48

3 LISTENING 🔲

1 Visitors to Vancouver are asking for information. Listen and mark these places on the map.

a) the library
b) Eaton's
c) the Four Seasons Hotel
d) the Orpheum Theatre
e) the YMCA
f) the Art Gallery

2 Now write sentences about six places on the map like this. Then compare with a partner.

Robson Square is on . . .

It's opposite . . .

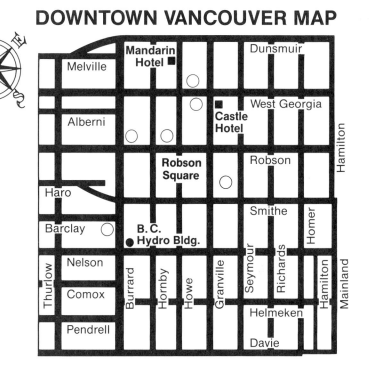

DOWNTOWN VANCOUVER MAP

4 WHERE IS IT?

Pair work Choose an area of your city and draw a street map. Then add some buildings and landmarks and talk about them like this.

A: Where's . . . ?
B: It's . . .

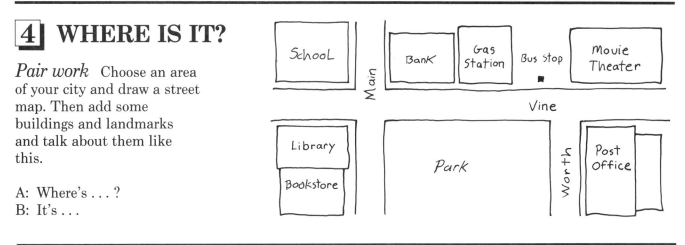

5 PRONUNCIATION: Vowel contrast /ey/ and /ɛ/ 🔲

1 Practice these words.

with /ey/			*with* /ɛ/		
pay	place	neighbor	get	center	rest
eight	station	mail	letter	next	friend

2 Put these words into two lists: words with /ey/ or /ɛ/.

name   spend   went   cake   game   came   met   take

6 CONVERSATION: The neighborhood 💬

Listen and practice.

Jack: Excuse me, ma'am. I'm your new neighbor. I just moved in. My name's Jack.
Woman: Oh, yes.
Jack: Say, are there any grocery stores around here?
Woman: Yes, there are some on Pine Street.
Jack: OK. And is there a laundromat near here?
Woman: Well, I think there's one opposite the shopping center.
Jack: Thanks, ma'am.
Woman: By the way, there's a barber shop in the shopping center.
Jack: A barber shop?

7 GRAMMAR FOCUS: *There is, there are; one, any, some* 💬

> Is there a laundromat near here?
>   Yes, **there is.** There's **one** opposite the shopping center.
>   No, **there isn't,** but there's **one** near the high school.
>
> Are there **any** grocery stores around here?
>   Yes, **there are.** There are **some** on Pine Street.
>   No, **there aren't,** but there are **some** on Third Avenue.

Complete these conversations. Then practice them.

A: Excuse me. Is .... a pay phone around here?
B: Yes, there .... There's .... on the corner .... Jade and King.
A: Thanks a lot.

A: I'm new in town. .... there .... good restaurants near here?
B: No, there .... , but there are .... opposite the shopping center .... Young Street.
A: Oh, great!

A: .... any hotels near the airport?
B: Yes, ... two, the Plaza and the Royal. I like the Plaza.
A: OK, I'll try it. Thanks.

A: .... there a gas station near the school?
B: No, there .... , but there's .... downtown .... Fourth Street .... to the bank. You can't miss it!
A: OK, thanks.

8 IN THE CITY

Group work Take turns asking questions about
your city like this.

A: Is there a good bookstore near the school?
B: ...
A: And are there any coffee shops near here?
B: ...

bookstore   restroom
coffee shops   pay phone
department stores post office
drugstore   restaurants

Useful expressions

Sorry, I don't know.
I'm not sure, but I think ...
Of course. There's one ...

9 SNAPSHOT

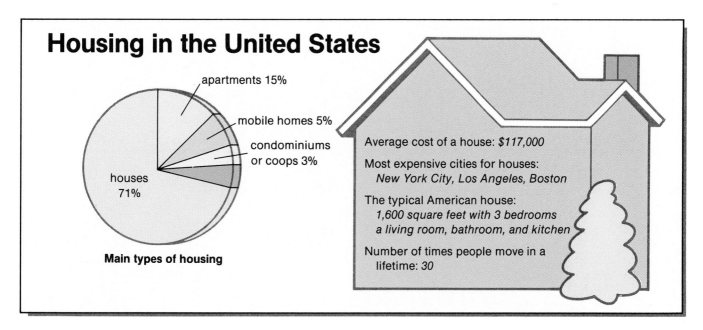

Housing in the United States

apartments 15%
mobile homes 5%
condominiums or coops 3%
houses 71%

Main types of housing

Average cost of a house: *$117,000*

Most expensive cities for houses:
New York City, Los Angeles, Boston

The typical American house:
*1,600 square feet with 3 bedrooms
a living room, bathroom, and kitchen*

Number of times people move in a
lifetime: *30*

Complete the information below. Then compare with a partner.

Main types of housing in my country: ....
A typical house in my country (size, rooms): ....
The kind of place I live in: .... house   .... apartment
                             .... condo   .... other

10 CONVERSATION 📼

1 Listen and practice.

Dan: Where do you live, Kim?
Kim: I just moved into a new apartment on
Bush Street.
Dan: Oh? What's it like?
Kim: It's really nice.
Dan: How big is it?
Kim: Well, it's fairly big. It has two bedrooms, a
living room, and a big kitchen. It also has
a pool.
Dan: Sounds great!
Kim: Yeah. There's a Jacuzzi, too.
Dan: Gee, that's terrific! And what's the
neighborhood like?
Kim: It's very quiet. I really like it.

2 Now listen to the rest of the conversation.
What does Dan say about his apartment?

11 HOUSES AND APARTMENTS

Group work   Talk about where you live.
Ask these and other questions.

Do you live in a house or
an apartment?
Where is it?
How big is it?
What's the neighborhood like?
Is it quiet?
Are there any good shops or
restaurants nearby?
Is there any public transportation
nearby?
Do you like it there?

▶ **Interchange 8:
Just moved!**
Imagine you are about to
move to a new neighborhood.
Find out all the details in
the role play on page 111.

12 READING: For rent

1 Look at these rental ads on a supermarket bulletin board.
Which ads are for "Housing Needed" (mark **N**) and which are for
"Housing Available" (mark **A**)?

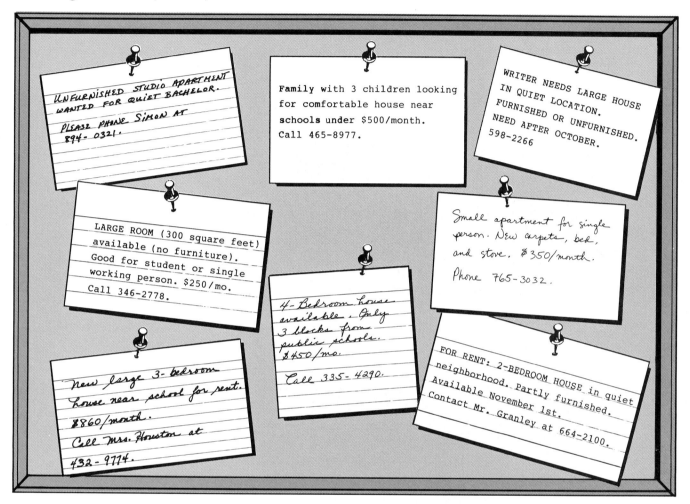

UNFURNISHED STUDIO APARTMENT WANTED FOR QUIET BACHELOR. PLEASE PHONE SIMON AT 894-0321.

Family with 3 children looking for comfortable house near **schools** under $500/month. Call 465-8977.

WRITER NEEDS LARGE HOUSE IN QUIET LOCATION. FURNISHED OR UNFURNISHED. NEED AFTER OCTOBER. 598-2266

LARGE ROOM (300 square feet) available (no furniture). Good for student or single working person. $250/mo. Call 346-2778.

Small apartment for single person. New carpets, bed, and stove. $350/month. Phone 765-3032.

4-Bedroom house available. Only 3 blocks from public schools. $450/mo. Call 335-4290.

new large 3-bedroom house near school for rent. $860/month. Call Mrs. Houston at 432-9774.

FOR RENT: 2-BEDROOM HOUSE in quiet neighborhood. Partly furnished. Available November 1st. Contact Mr. Granley at 664-2100.

2 *Pair work* Look at the ads you marked **N.** Can you find them an
appropriate apartment under the ads marked **A?**

13 WRITING

1 *Class activity* Form two groups.

Group 1: You have a house or an apartment for rent. Write an ad for it.
Give as much information as possible.

Group 2: You are looking for a house or an apartment to rent. Write an
ad for the kind of place you want. Give as much information as
possible.

2 Now put your ads on a bulletin board. How many can you match?

9 Which one is Judy?

1 SNAPSHOT

		Fashion firsts			
Shoemakers first make shoes with different shapes for left and right feet	Levi Strauss makes the first pair of jeans	A Swiss doctor makes the first contact lenses	Nail polish and false eyelashes become fashionable	A French designer introduces the first bikini swimsuit	Miniskirts become popular
1818	1850	1887	1916	1946	1965

Complete the information below. Then compare with a partner.

My usual clothes for school/work: ....

My usual clothes on the weekend: ....

In my wardrobe:

Men:	Number of jeans	....	sweaters	....	suits	....
Women:	Number of jeans	....	sweaters	....	dresses	....

2 CONVERSATION 📼

1 Listen and practice.

Sarah: Hi, good to see you! Where's Margaret? Is she coming tonight?

Raoul: Oh, she couldn't make it. She's working late.

Sarah: Well, why don't you go and talk to Judy? She doesn't know anyone here.

Raoul: Judy? Oh, which one is she?

Sarah: She's standing near the window. She's wearing a black miniskirt.

Raoul: OK! I'll talk to her later.

2 Now listen to the rest of the conversation.
Can you find Kevin, Michiko, Rosa, and John in the picture?

54

3 GRAMMAR FOCUS: Present continuous 🔲

What **am** I **wearing?**	You **are wearing** blue jeans.
Who **is** Kevin **talking** to?	He **is talking** to Michiko.
Where **are** Sarah and Raoul **standing?**	They **are standing** near the table.
Is Margaret **coming** tonight?	No, she **is working** late.

1 Complete these conversations using the present continuous.
Then practice them.

A: Which one is Yoko? What .... she .... (wear)?
B: She .... (sit) on the sofa. She ....
   .... (wear) a green blouse.

A: .... Bill and Helen .... (come) to the party?
B: No, Bill .... (study) for an exam, and
   Helen .... (work) late.

A: Where .... Nick .... (go)?
B: He .... (get) some beer from his car.

A: .... Antonio .... (date) Diane?
B: No, he .... (go) out with Cindy these days.

A: How .... you .... (go) home?
B: Steve .... (give) me a ride, I hope!

2 *Pair work* Look at your partner for five seconds. Then sit
back to back and describe your partner like this.

You're wearing a yellow shirt and orange pants.
You have a purple jacket.

3 Now write five questions like these about your classmates.
Then take turns asking your questions.

Is Angela wearing jeans today?
Where is Satoshi sitting?
What is Helmut doing?
Who is sitting on the left of Carlos?
Are Maria and Kim listening to the teacher?

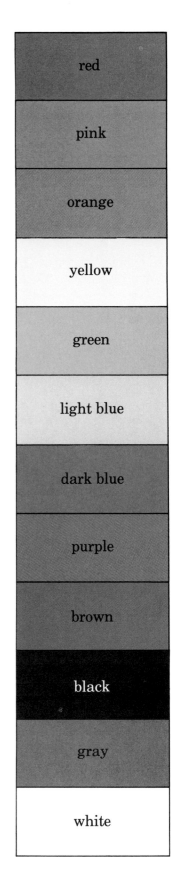

red

pink

orange

yellow

green

light blue

dark blue

purple

brown

black

gray

white

4 WHAT'S GOING ON? 📼

1 Listen to the sounds of five people doing different things.
What is each person doing?

2 *Pair work* Now compare your answers like this.

   #1 A: Someone is mowing the lawn.
       B: Oh, I think somebody is shaving.

5 FIND THE DIFFERENCES

1 *Pair work* Cover each other's pictures. How many differences can
you find? Ask questions like these.

How many people are there in your picture?	What's Dave wearing?
	What color is his T-shirt?
How many are standing? Who?	What is he doing?
How many are sitting? Who?	Who is Kevin talking to?
Does Nick have a drink in his hand?	Is Ann smoking?

Student A

Student B

2 *Class activity* How many differences are there in the pictures?
What are they?

6 PRONUNCIATION: Sentence stress 🔲

1 In conversation, we stress the most important words in a sentence.

Robert is very **short.**   **Mar**garet is in her **twen**ties.
His **fa**ther is pretty **tall.**   She has **long black hair.**

2 *Pair work*   Circle the stressed words.

A: Which one is Sarah?

B: She's standing near the door. She's wearing a red dress.

7 WORD POWER: People

1 Study these words and phrases.

Age

about 20   *in her thirties*   *in his fifties*

Height

short   *medium height*   *tall*
   fairly short   *pretty tall*

Hair

straight black hair   *long red hair*   *curly blond hair*   *short brown hair*

*bald
a beard
a moustache*

2 *Pair work*   Now describe these people like this. Pay attention to the stressed words.

He's about 55.
He's medium height.
He's bald and has a beard.

8 LISTENING: Missing person 📼

1 Listen and take notes.

Who is missing?
What does the person look
like?
What is the person wearing?

2 *Pair work* Compare your
notes. Then listen to the rest of
the conversation. What happened
to the missing person?

9 WHO IS IT?

Pair work Think of someone in the class. Give a clue like this:

I'm thinking of a woman.

Now your partner tries to guess who it is.

How old is she?	What is she wearing?
How tall is she?	Is she wearing a red sweater?
What kind of hair does she have?	Is it . . . (name)?

10 WRITING

1 Cut out pictures of people from
magazines. Two people write their own
descriptions of the same picture. For example:

*The man is in his early 20s. He's tall, and
he has brown hair. He's wearing a red
sweater and dark blue pants, and he's carrying
a black jacket. He's also wearing a watch.*

2 Now compare your description with the
other person's.

> ▶ **Interchange 9:**
> **We Are the World**
>
> How many musicians can you
> recognize from the record
> cover of "We Are the World"?
> Student A looks at page 114
> and Student B at page 116.

11 READING: The Dating Game

Do young people go out on dates in your country?
How old are they when they start dating?
Where do they like to go?
Who usually pays – the man, the woman, or both?

Young people have more freedom in North America than in many other countries. They often start dating around the age of 14, and do not need an older person to go with them. They go in groups or couples to school events (dances, plays, ball games), parties, restaurants, movies, and sports events.

For most teenagers, dating is just for fun. It does not mean that they want to get married. Young people may even date several friends at the same time. They usually choose their own dates. Sometimes, however, someone arranges a date for two people who do not know each other. This is called a "blind date."

Either a man or a woman can invite someone on a date. If there are expenses, the man and woman often "go Dutch"; this means they share the cost. Sometimes, however, one person pays for both people.

Copyright 1969 by Alex Graham.

"It was a very good dance. . . . I enjoyed it . . . I danced with lots of people . . . the food was delicious . . . I got in about three . . . Robin Smith drove me home . . ."

1 *Group work* Is dating the same or different in your country?
Write **S** for same and **D** for different and then discuss your answers.

Young people in my country . . .

.... start dating around 14 .... date for fun, not marriage
.... often go out in couples .... sometimes go out on blind dates
.... date several people at the same time .... sometimes go Dutch

2 *Class activity* Are there any other differences between dating
in North America and in your country?

Review of Units 7–9

1 What can you remember?

1 *Pair work* Take turns asking these questions and talk about what you did yesterday. Give as much information as possible.

What time did you get up yesterday?
What did you have for breakfast?
What did you wear?
Did you meet anyone interesting?
How many phone calls did you make?
Did you drive or take the bus anywhere?
Did you buy anything?
How much money did you spend yesterday?
Did you watch TV? What programs did you watch?
Did you get any exercise?
Where did you have dinner? What did you eat?
What was the best thing that happened to you?
What time did you go to sleep?

2 Now change partners and close your books. How many questions can you ask?

2 Listening

1 A thief robbed a hotel on Saturday. Inspector Dobbs is questioning Frankie. The pictures show what Frankie did on Saturday. Listen to their conversation. Are Frankie's answers true (**T**) or false (**F**)?

2 *Pair work* Now answer these questions.

What did Frankie do after he cleaned the house?
Where did he go? What did he do? When did he come home?

1:00 P.M.   T   F

3:00 P.M.   T   F

5:00 P.M.   T   F

6:00 P.M.   T   F

8:00 P.M.   T   F

10:30 P.M.   T   F

3 | Helping a stranger

Pair work   One student is a visitor in your city, and the other is a resident.
Take turns asking and answering these questions.

A: Excuse me. Can you help me? I'm on
   vacation here. Is there a department store
   nearby?
B: . . .
A: What's it near?
B: . . .
A: Thanks. And I need to go to a travel agency.
   Is there one around here?
B: . . .
A: And how about restaurants? Are there any
   good ones in the neighborhood?
B: . . .
A: Oh, Chinese or Japanese food would be fine.
B: . . .
A: Thanks a lot. That sounds good. And just
   one more thing . . . ?
B: . . .

4 | Charades

Class activity   One student mimes an action. The other students ask
ten questions and try to guess what he or she is doing. Ask questions
like this:

   Are you playing a trumpet?   Are you eating spaghetti?

5 | Role play: Lost at Disney World

Student A: You are visiting Disney World with
your English class. Unfortunately, one of the
students got lost there. You are talking to a
security officer. Answer the officer's questions
and describe one of your classmates. (Don't give
the student's name.)

Student B: You are a security officer at Disney
World. Someone is talking to you about a lost
classmate. Ask questions and complete the
form. Then look around the class. Can you find
the lost student?

LOST PERSON REPORT

Age: ....

Height: ....

Hair: ....

Eyes: ....

Clothing: ....

....

10 Guess what happened!

1 SNAPSHOT

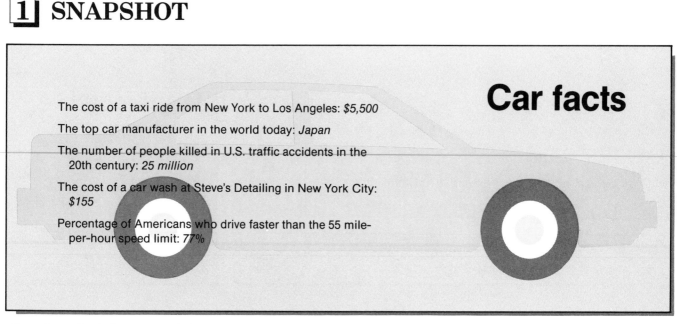

Car facts

The cost of a taxi ride from New York to Los Angeles: *$5,500*

The top car manufacturer in the world today: *Japan*

The number of people killed in U.S. traffic accidents in the 20th century: *25 million*

The cost of a car wash at Steve's Detailing in New York City: *$155*

Percentage of Americans who drive faster than the 55 mile-per-hour speed limit: *77%*

Complete the information below. Then compare with a partner.

The kinds of transportation I have owned:

.... bicycle	.... motorcycle	.... truck
.... van	.... car	.... other

The number of cars I have owned: ....
The number of times I have gotten a speeding ticket: ....
My favorite car: ....

2 CONVERSATION

1 Listen and practice.

Jill: Oh, I love this car! It's so much fun to drive. Have you ever driven a sports car?

Ted: No, I haven't, but please slow down a little, Jill. You're doing nearly 80!

Jill: Am I? Oh, sorry, but don't worry. I've never gotten a speeding ticket.

Ted: Um, how long till we get there? You know, I've never been to Disneyland before.

Jill: Oh, we'll be there in about an hour.

2 Now listen to the rest of the conversation. What happened?

3 GRAMMAR FOCUS: Present perfect 🔲

Have you ever **driven** a sports car?	Yes, I **have.**
Has Jill ever **gotten** a speeding ticket?	No, she **hasn't.**
Has Ted ever **been** to Disneyland?	No, he **has never been** there.
	(he's)

Complete these conversations with the present perfect. (See page 133 for past participle forms.)

A: .... you ever................... (get) a traffic ticket?
B: Yes, I .... Once I got a ticket that cost me $50!

A: .... you ever................... (be) late for an important appointment?
B: Yes, I .... I was 30 minutes late for my wedding.
   Would you believe it!

A: .... you ever................... (lose) your keys?
B: Yes, I .... I lost them twice last month!

A: .... you ever................... (see) a house on fire?
B: No, I .... But I saw a car on fire the other day.

A: .... you ever .... (forget) where you parked your car?
B: No, I .... , but my brother always does. It drives him crazy!

4 PRONUNCIATION: Linking sounds 🔲

We often link consonants at the end of a word with the vowel at the beginning of the next word.

1 Listen and practice.

Have you ever been in a traffic accident?

Have you ever eaten Indian food?

Has your brother ever asked you for a loan?

2 Now practice the conversations in Exercise 3.
Pay attention to the linking sounds.

5 | HAVE YOU EVER . . . ?

1 Think of five interesting or unusual events and write questions for each one like this:

Have you ever met a famous person?

2 *Class activity* Now go around the class and ask your questions. Take notes of the answers. Talk to as many people as you can in five minutes.

A: Have you ever met a famous person, Harry?
B: Yes, I met Mick Jagger at a disco once.
A: Really? Where was that?
B: . . .

3 Tell the class one of the things you found out.

6 | WORD POWER: Verbs

1 *Pair work* Look at the word map. Fill in the blanks with the verbs from the list below.

ask	cook	✓fly	ride	tell
✓buy	drive	✓hike	run	walk
✓clean	✓explain	pay	sell	wash

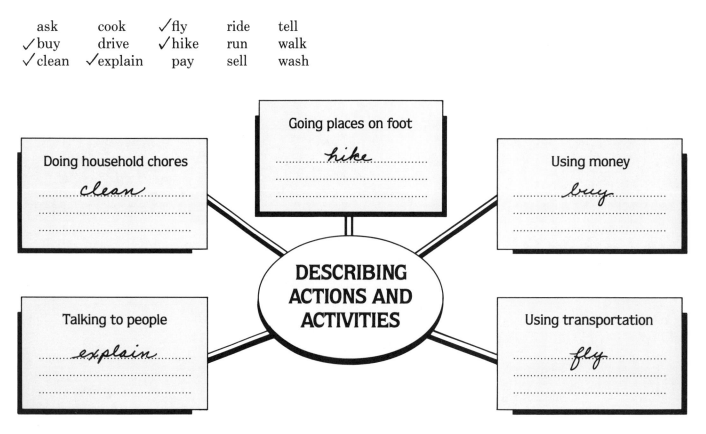

Going places on foot — *hike*

Doing household chores — *clean*

Using money — *buy*

Talking to people — *explain*

DESCRIBING ACTIONS AND ACTIVITIES

Using transportation — *fly*

2 Now write down the past tense and past participle forms for the verbs in the word map. Then compare with a partner.

7 CONVERSATION: An embarrassing situation 🔲

1 Listen and practice.

Bill: Do you know what happened on Sunday?
Rose: No, what?
Bill: I went downtown to do some shopping.
Then I went to a restaurant for lunch. I ate
lunch and asked for the check. But I found I
didn't have enough money!
Rose: How embarrassing! So what did you do?
Bill: Well, first I called my parents, but they were
out. After that I tried my roommate, but he
was out, too. So finally I phoned my boss at
home. He was very nice and brought me
some money.
Rose: That was lucky!

2 *Pair work* Now close your books. Tell Bill's
story in your own words.

8 GRAMMAR FOCUS: Connecting words 🔲

> **First** I called my parents.
> **After that** I tried my roommate.
> **Next** I phoned my boss.
> **Then** he brought me some money.
> **Finally** I paid the check.

1 *Pair work* Read this conversation:

Rick: Have you ever lost your luggage on a flight?
Lisa: Yes, when I went to Spain last summer. It was awful.
Rick: So what did you do?

What happened next to Lisa? Number the events from 1 to 6 in the
order they occurred.

Lisa: .... I went to the airline counter, and they gave me a form to fill in.
.... My luggage arrived at midnight, and the airline brought it to
the hotel.
.... I went out and bought some new clothes.
.... I went to my hotel and checked in.
.... They gave me $50 to buy a few things.
.... I waited for my luggage, but it didn't arrive.

2 Now add a connecting word to each sentence.
Then practice the conversation.

9 LISTENING: And *then* what happened? 📼

1 Ken lost a bag with his passport, money, and airplane tickets while he was on vacation. What did he do? Number the phrases from 1 to 6.

.... called his parents
.... went to the police station
.... sold his camera
.... called the airline company
.... moved to a hostel
.... went to the embassy

2 *Pair work* Take turns. Tell Ken's story.

10 A STRANGE THING HAPPENED TO ME

1 *Group work* Make up an interesting story together. One student gives the first sentence of the story. The next student adds another sentence, and so on. For example:

A: Last week, a strange thing happened to me..
B: The phone rang at 4 o'clock in the morning.
C: First, I jumped out of bed.

Continue around the group until the story comes to an end.

2 *Class activity* Now tell your story to the class. Which group has the best story?

11 WRITING

1 Write down the story your group told in Exercise 10. Use connecting words.

A funny thing happened to me last week. The telephone rang at 4 in the morning on Thursday. First I jumped out of bed...

2 Exchange papers and compare your stories.

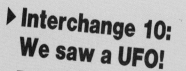

▶ **Interchange 10: We saw a UFO!**

Do you believe in Unidentified Flying Objects? Turn to page 115 for an interesting story about UFOs.

12 READING: To catch a thief

Labor Day was busy for Ann Dresselhaus of Cedar Rapids, Iowa. She finished a quadathlon – a competition which includes running, weight lifting, rowing, and cycling. Then she and her boyfriend went out to dinner.

After dinner, she drove her boyfriend back to his house. When they arrived at the house, they saw his stereo, TV, and computer in boxes in front of the house. And they found a burglar inside! The burglar ran out the back door. Dresselhaus ran after him.

From then on, things went very badly for the burglar. Dresselhaus has a black belt in karate. She chased the burglar for six blocks. Several times he turned to hit her and each time she blocked his blows. Finally, she used her karate skills to stop him. She gave him two quick kicks, and he fell to the ground.

Soon after that, the police arrived and arrested the burglar. For catching him, Dresselhaus, 32, received an award from the state governor. The thief got 10 years in jail.

1 Number these pictures from 1 to 8 in the order each event happened.

2 *Pair work*   Take turns. Cover the magazine article above and tell the story in your own words. Use the pictures to help you.

11 It's an interesting place

1 SNAPSHOT

The ten most interesting cities in the world (according to Jan Morris, travel writer):	The cost of a 2-mile taxi ride:	The cost of a cup of coffee:
New York	Tokyo $4.90	Tokyo $2.80
London	London $3.50	Vienna $2.15
Venice	New York $2.20	Hong Kong $1.20
Cairo	Sydney $1.70	Los Angeles $0.70
Istanbul	Rio de Janeiro $0.80	Madrid $0.60
Rio de Janeiro	Mexico City $0.60	Rio de Janeiro $0.18
Chicago		
Delhi		
Paris		
Beirut		

City living

Complete the information below. Then compare with a partner.

My list of the five most interesting cities in the world: ....

The three most interesting cities in my country: ....

The cost of a 2-mile taxi ride in my city: ....

The cost of a cup of coffee in my city: ....

2 WORD POWER: Adjectives

1 *Pair work* Match each word in list A with its opposite in list B.

A		B
a) beautiful	....	boring
b) big	....	dangerous
c) cheap	....	dirty
d) clean	....	expensive
e) hot	....	dry
f) interesting	....	new
g) old	....	cold
h) quiet	....	small
i) safe	....	ugly
j) wet	....	noisy

2 Now circle four of the adjectives above that describe your city.
Then compare with a partner.

3 CONVERSATION 🔲

1 Listen and practice.

Linda: Whereabouts in Canada are
you from?
Steve: I'm from Toronto.
Linda: Oh, I've never been there.
What's it like?
Steve: It's a great city! It has good
museums and wonderful
restaurants. And the
nightlife is exciting, too.
Linda: Really? Is it expensive there?
Steve: Well, it's not bad, but
apartments are fairly
expensive.

2 Now listen to the rest of the
conversation. What does Steve say
about transportation and shopping
in Toronto?

4 GRAMMAR FOCUS: Adjectives and adverbs 🔲

It's an **exciting** city.	It's a **very** exciting city.
It's **interesting.** **beautiful.** **clean.**	It's **very** interesting. **pretty** cheap. **fairly** clean.
It's not **expensive.** **dangerous.**	It's not **very** expensive. **too** big.

1 Match the questions in column A with the answers in column B.
Then practice the conversations.

A

a) What's Hong Kong like?
   Is it an interesting place?
b) What's your hometown like?
   Do you like it?
c) Tell me about Sydney.
   I've never been there.
d) Is Amsterdam a modern city?

B

.... Oh, really? It's beautiful. It has a great
harbor and beautiful beaches.
.... No, it's very old. It has lots of fascinating
streets, canals, and buildings.
.... Oh, yes, it is. It's very exciting, but it's pretty
crowded.
.... No, I hate it! It's very boring. That's why I
moved away.

2 Now write four sentences about your city. Then compare with a partner.

5 HOME SWEET HOME

Pair work Take turns. Talk about your city or hometown. Ask questions like these and other questions of your own.

What's your city or hometown like?
Is it an interesting place?
Is it safe?
What's shopping like there?
Is it expensive?
Is the transportation good?
Does it have good restaurants?
Do you like it there?

6 LISTENING 🔊

Listen to Joyce, Lou, and Nick talking about their hometowns. What do they say? Write **Y** for yes and **N** for no.

		Interesting	*Big*	*Expensive*	*Beautiful*
1	Joyce				
2	Lou				
3	Nick				

7 MY FAVORITE CITY

Group work Take turns talking about your favorite city. Talk about it like this and answer any questions other students may have.

My favorite city in North America is Santa Fe. It's in New Mexico. It's an old city with lots of interesting Spanish and Indian buildings. It's fairly small, and it's really beautiful . . .

8 CONVERSATION 💬

Listen and practice.

David: Can you tell me a little about Mexico?
Maria: Yes, sure. What would you like to know?
David: Well, when's the best time to visit?
Maria: Mmm, you should go in the winter or spring. The weather is nice then. It's not very hot.
David: Really? And does Mexico have good beaches?
Maria: Yes, the beaches are excellent.
David: Oh, good! And what places should I see?
Maria: Well, you should go to Mexico City. And you shouldn't miss the Mayan ruins. They are very interesting.
David: Great! I can't wait to go there!

9 GRAMMAR FOCUS: Modal verb *should* 💬

What **should** I do there?	You **should** go to Mexico City.
	You **shouldn't** miss the Mayan ruins.
When **should** I go there?	You **should** go in the winter or spring.
	You **shouldn't** go in the summer or fall.

1 Two people are talking about San Diego, California.
Put the words in speaker B's answers in the correct order.

A: When's a good time to visit San Diego?
B: should spring summer the you go or in
A: Where do you think I should stay?
B: in you motel stay should a
A: What places do you think I should see?
B: see San Diego Zoo you the should
A: Anything else?
B: miss yes Sea World shouldn't you
A: And does San Diego have any good museums?
B: to should San Diego Museum of Art yes the go you
A: And how about shopping? Is San Diego good for shopping?
B: Old Town go shopping yes to you for should
A: Gee, thanks, I'm sure I'll have a great vacation.

2 Now practice the conversation.

10 LISTENING 🔲

1 Listen to three lectures about Japan, Argentina, and Italy. Take notes.

2 Listen again. One thing about each country is incorrect. What is it?

11 ON VACATION

Group work Has anyone in your group visited an interesting country or city? Find out more about it. Start like this and ask questions like the ones below.

A: I visited Spain last summer.
B: Did you enjoy it?

What's the best time of the year to visit?
What's the weather like then?
What should tourists see and do there?
What's the food like?
What's the shopping like?
What things should people buy?
What else should visitors do there?

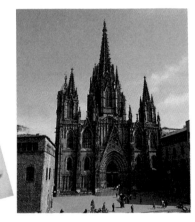

12 WRITING

1 Write about an interesting country, but don't give the name of the country. Give as much information as you can.

This country is in southeast Asia. It's about 3 hours from Hong Kong by plane. It's a very interesting country. There are lots of temples there, and...

▶ **Interchange 11: On tour**
Have you ever planned "the perfect vacation"? Turn to page 117 and plan an unusual tour.

2 Exchange papers.
Can your partner guess the country?

13 READING: Famous cities

1 Read these descriptions of cities and circle the correct city.

The city: Paris   Venice   Rome

#1
This beautiful city in northeastern Italy is built on 100 small islands. This city has no roads. Instead, people use gondolas to travel along the canals. The most famous place to visit is St. Mark's Square, with its wonderful Renaissance buildings and its busy cafes.

The city: New York   San Francisco   Chicago

#2
This American city is the main business and cultural center in the Midwest. It is famous for its music, opera, and theater as well as for its excellent museums and architecture. The world's tallest building, the Sears Tower, is there.

The city: Mexico City   Rio de Janeiro
              Havana

#3
Travelers use many words to describe this South American city: beautiful, glamorous, sunny, friendly, and exciting. People love to visit its fabulous beaches and mountains. It is the city of the Carnival, when everyone dances the "samba" in the streets.

2 Now answer these questions.

Paragraph #1
Why do people use gondolas in this city?
What do tourists do there?

Paragraph #2
Where is this city?
What's it famous for?

Paragraph #3
What do visitors do there?
What do people do there at Carnival time?

12 It really works!

1 SNAPSHOT

The cold facts

Number of people who have a bad cold each year in the
United States: *100 million*

Average number of colds people get each year: *3*

Average length of a cold: *8 days*

Amount spent each year on cold medicines: *$700 million*

Number of days missed each year from work and school
because of colds: *30 million*

Complete the information below. Then compare with a partner.

Number of colds I have a year: ....
Average length of my colds: ....
Number of days I miss from work or school: ....
The cold medicine I usually take: ....

2 WORD POWER: Parts of the body

1 Match the words below to the
numbers in the pictures. Then write
the correct words for numbers 13–20.

.... arm	13	....
.... back	14	....
.... chest	15	....
.... ear	16	....
.... eye	17	....
.... foot	18	....
.... hand	19	....
.... head	20	....
.... leg		
.... mouth		
.... neck		
.... nose		

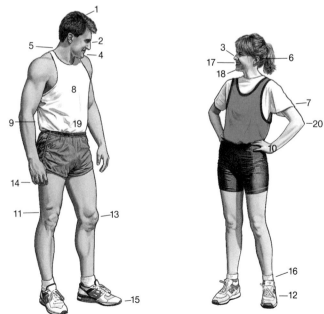

2 Which parts of the body does a
cold affect?

74

3 CONVERSATION 📼

Listen and practice.

Joan: Hi! How are you?
Craig: Oh, not so good.
Joan: Gee, what's the matter?
Craig: I have a terrible cold.
Joan: Really? That's too bad! Have you taken anything for it?
Craig: No, not yet.
Joan: Well, do you know what you should do? Chop up some garlic and cook it in chicken stock. Then drink a cup every half hour. It really works!
Craig: Ugh!

4 GRAMMAR FOCUS: Imperatives 📼

Drink a cup every half hour.
Don't drink coffee or tea.

1 Look at these health problems. Find good advice for each problem.

Problems

a bad headache ....
a sore throat ....
a backache ....
a cough ....
a toothache ....
a fever ....
a burn ....
the flu ....
....
....
....

Advice

a) Drink some orange juice.
b) Take some aspirin.
c) Get some medicine from the drugstore.
d) Take some vitamin C.
e) Don't lift anything heavy.
f) See the doctor.
g) Go to bed and rest.
h) Don't drink a lot of coffee.
i) See the dentist.
j) Don't exercise.
k) Drink lots of liquids.
l) Put some lotion on it.

2 *Pair work* Now compare your advice like this.

A: What should you do for the flu?
B: Take some aspirin and drink lots of liquids.

3 Write advice for these problems. Then compare with a partner.

a cold   stress   insomnia   sore muscles   tired eyes

5 LISTENING 📼

Listen to three people complaining. What are their problems?
What advice do they get?

6 PRONUNCIATION: Consonant contrast /θ/ and /t/ 📼

1 Practice these words with /θ/.

throat	thanks	something	mouth
three	toothache	anything	both

2 Now practice the contrast /θ/ and /t/.

/θ/	/t/	/θ/	/t/
thank	tank	through	true
three	tree	both	boat

3 Listen to eight words. How many words do you hear with /θ/ and how
many with /t/?

7 PROBLEMS AND ADVICE

1 *Group work* Take turns talking about these problems.

an insect bite	indigestion	hiccups
a sore throat	the flu	a hangover

A: What should you do for . . . ?
B: Take a glass of . . .
C: Don't drink . . .
D: I think you should get some . . .

2 *Class activity* Compare your advice around the class.

*"I have an annoying tickle in my throat.
What do you recommend?"*

Drawing by Ross; © 1987 The New Yorker Magazine, Inc.

▶ **Interchange 12:
Keeping in shape**
Have you ever taken an
exercise class in English?
Here's your chance! Turn
to page 118.

8 CONVERSATION 🔲

Listen and practice.

A: How are you, Mrs. Webb?
B: Well, I'm fine. But I'd like something for my husband. He doesn't have any energy these days.
A: Oh, that's too bad.
B: Can I have some multi-vitamins with vitamin E?
A: All right. Do you want a large or small bottle?
B: Could I have two large ones, please?
A: Why yes, Mrs. Webb. Here you are.

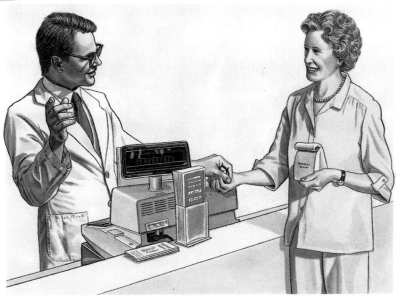

9 GRAMMAR FOCUS: Modal verbs *can, could, may, would* 🔲

Can	I have a bottle of multi-vitamins?
Could	I have something for a sore throat?
May	I have a package of Alka Seltzer?
I **would**	like some Contac 500, please.
I'd	like a bottle of vitamin E.
I'd	like something for a cold.

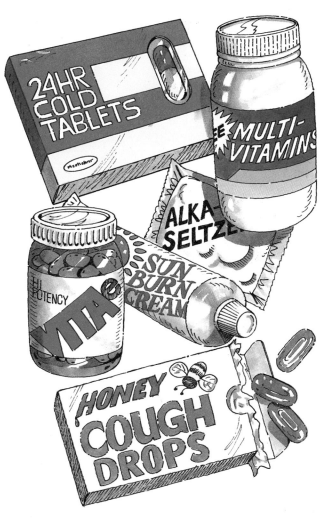

Complete these conversations. Then practice them.

A: . . . (a box of cold tablets)
B: Oh, sure. These are pretty good. Anything else?
A: No, that's all, thanks.
B: OK. That's $5.75.

A: . . . (something for a sunburn)
B: Of course. Try this cream. It's very good.
A: . . . (a stomachache)
B: Here you are. That'll be $8.95 altogether.

A: . . . (a sore throat)
   And . . . (a package of cough drops)
B: OK. Do you want a large or small package?
A: A small one, please.
B: All right. Let me get that for you.

10 CONTAINERS

1 Use these words to complete the expressions below.
Then compare with a partner.

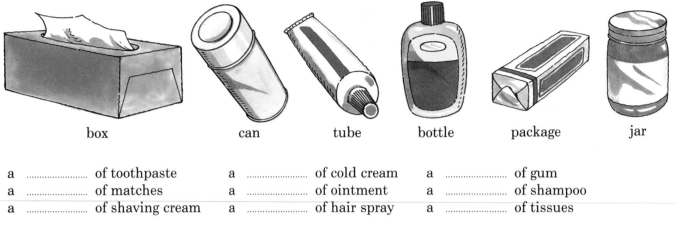

box   can   tube   bottle   package   jar

a .... of toothpaste   a .... of cold cream   a .... of gum
a .... of matches   a .... of ointment   a .... of shampoo
a .... of shaving cream   a .... of hair spray   a .... of tissues

2 *Pair work*   About how much do the things above cost in your country?

11 LISTENING 📼

Listen to people asking questions and choose the correct responses.

a) .... Yes, it really works!
   .... That's too bad!
b) .... Go to bed and rest.
   .... I drink warm lemon juice with honey.
c) .... How many do you want?
   .... Yes, here's some extra-strength aspirin.

d) .... That's all, thanks.
   .... Sure. Do you want a large or small box?
e) .... I'll try these.
   .... All right. Anything else?
f) .... Yes, they're excellent.
   .... Do you want a large jar?

12 ROLE PLAY: In a drugstore

Student A: You are a customer in a drugstore. You need:
           something for a sunburn
           some vitamin C tablets
           a tube of toothpaste
Student B: You are a clerk in a drugstore. A customer needs some
           things. Use this information.

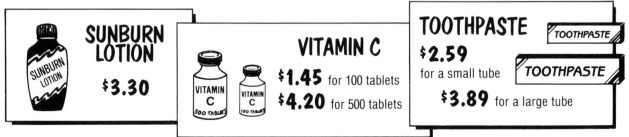

SUNBURN LOTION $3.30

VITAMIN C
$1.45 for 100 tablets
$4.20 for 500 tablets

TOOTHPASTE
$2.59 for a small tube
$3.89 for a large tube

Now change roles and try the role play again. Make up your own information.

13 READING

When you have a minor health problem, do you usually go to the doctor, get something from the drugstore, or use a home remedy?

GRANDMA KNOWS BEST!

When people have a cold, a fever, or the flu, they usually go to the doctor for help or they get some medicine from the drugstore. But many people also use home remedies for common illnesses.

Lots of people drink hot chicken soup when they have a cold. They find it clears the head and the nose. Some people rub oil on the chest for a cold. Other people drink a mixture of red pepper, hot water, sugar, lemon juice, and milk or vinegar. Here are some simple home remedies.

Bee Stings and Insect Bites: Wash the sting or bite. Put some meat tenderizer on a handkerchief and then put it on the bite for half an hour.

Burns: Put the burn under cold water or put a cold handkerchief on it. But don't put ice on the burn.
Coughs: Drink warm liquids or take some honey.
Indigestion: Drink some water with a teaspoon of baking soda in it.
Insomnia: Drink a large glass of warm milk.

1 Cover the passage. Circle **T** (true) or **F** (false).

a) Hot chicken soup is good for a cold. T F
b) Meat tenderizer helps an insect bite. T F
c) Ice is good for a burn. T F
d) Honey helps a cough. T F
e) Hot liquids are good for indigestion. T F
f) Warm milk helps you go to sleep. T F

2 Do you use the same remedies?
What home remedies do you use?

14 WRITING

Write about an interesting home or folk remedy.

This is a home remedy for a sore throat. My grandmother always uses it. Cut slices of meat, put pepper on them, and then tie them around your throat with a flannel cloth. It always works. (my grandmother says!)

2 *Group work* Take turns reading your compositions.
Which home remedy is the most interesting?

Review of Units 10–12

1 What was it like?

Group work Ask these questions around the group.

Have you ever . . .

gone windsurfing?
been on a blind date?
kept a diary?
lost your credit cards?
fainted?
been on a camping trip?
gotten a famous person's autograph?
given first aid to someone?
been in an accident?
had food poisoning?
been abroad?
seen a ghost?

When someone answers "Yes," he or she explains
what happened and the other students ask for
more information like this.

A: Have you ever gone windsurfing?
B: Yeah, I have. I tried it last year in Hawaii.
   It was really fun!
C: What was it like? Was it difficult?
B: Yes, it was hard at first. Has anyone else ever
   gone windsurfing?
D: . . .

2 Listening 📼

1 Listen to Max and Doris talking about unusual things that happened
to them on Saturday. Take notes.

Where were they?   What happened?   What did they do?

2 *Pair work* Take turns. Now use your notes and talk about what
happened to Max or Doris.

3 | Mother Nature

Group work   Take turns talking about your favorite scenic place
(e.g., a national park, a vacation resort, a place in the countryside).
Ask questions like these.

What's your favorite place?   When's the best season to go?
Where is it?   Where should I stay?
What's it like there?   What should I do there?

4 | City tour

1 *Group work*   Plan a one-day tour of your city for visitors. Include
information for morning, afternoon, and evening activities. Describe
places to visit and things to do. Talk about your suggestions like this.

A: First, visitors should take a bus tour of the city in the morning.
B: Yes, and after that, they should go to the zoo. It's really fun to go
   there.
C: And then for lunch, they should . . .

2 *Class activity*   Now groups take turns reading their itineraries.
Which group has the best tour?

5 | Here's how to do it

1 *Group work*   Write complete instructions for doing one of these
things (or something else).

how to change film in a camera
how to use a photocopying machine
how to use a microwave oven
how to use an electric rice cooker

*Here's how to change film
in a camera. First, rewind
the old film. Press the
release button and take
out the film. Don't touch
the lens.*

2 Each group reads their instructions. The rest of
the class listens. Are the instructions correct? Are
they complete?

13 May I take your order, please?

1 SNAPSHOT

The number of people who drink Coke for breakfast in the United States: *965,000*

The favorite meat in North America: *steak*

The most popular orders in restaurants: *hamburgers, fried chicken, roast beef, spaghetti, turkey, baked ham, fried shrimp, beef stew*

The most popular ice cream flavors: *vanilla, chocolate, Neapolitan, chocolate chip, strawberry*

Food facts

Complete the information below. Then compare with a partner.

My typical breakfast: ....

My favorite meat: ....

My favorite order in a restaurant: ....

My favorite ice cream flavor: ....

2 CONVERSATION: Reservations 🔲

1 Listen and practice.

Host: Hard Rock Cafe. May I help you?

Carl: Yes. Can I make a reservation for Saturday the 16th, for two, please?

Host: Certainly. For what time?

Carl: Six o'clock.

Host: All right. And could I have your name and phone number?

Carl: Sure. My name is Carl Moro and the number is 590–3442.

Host: OK, Mr. Moro, that's a table for two at 6 on Saturday, the 16th.

Carl: Thank you. Goodbye.

Host: Goodbye.

2 Now listen to another call and complete the reservation form.

RESERVATIONS

Date	Time	Number in Party	Name	Phone	Special Request
16th	6:00	2	*Carl Moro*	*590-3442*	*none*

3 ROLE PLAY: Calling a restaurant

Student A: You want to eat out tonight. Call a restaurant and make a reservation. Make up your own information.

Student B: You are the host or hostess in a restaurant. Answer the phone and write down the caller's reservation.

Now change roles and try the role play again.

4 WORD POWER: Countable and uncountable nouns

1 Countable nouns have a singular and a plural form (e.g., an apple, apples). Arrange these nouns into the lists below. Then add two more countable nouns to each list.

| an apple | beans | carrots | oranges | potatoes |
| bananas | bowls | a knife | plates | |

Fruit	Vegetables	Tableware
....	....	....
....	....	....
....	....	....
....	....	....
....	....	....

2 Uncountable nouns do not have a plural form (e.g., beef). Arrange these nouns into the list below. Then add two more uncountable nouns to each list.

| beef | yogurt | cream | orange juice |
| rice | pork | flour | water |

Drinks	Meat	Grain and grain products	Milk products
....	....	....	....
....	....	....	....
....	....	....	....
....	....	....	....

5 CONVERSATION: Ordering a meal 🔲

Listen and practice.

Waiter: May I take your order, please?
Customer: Yes. I'd like a hamburger and a large
           order of french fries, please.
Waiter: All right. And would you like a salad?
Customer: Yes, I'll have a small salad.
Waiter: OK. What kind of dressing would you
           like? We have Thousand Island, Italian,
           and French.
Customer: Italian.
Waiter: And would you like anything to drink?
Customer: I'd like a large Coke, please.
Waiter: Thank you.

6 PRONUNCIATION: Reduced forms of *would* and *will* 🔲

1 Listen to how **would** and **will** are reduced in conversation.

What will you have?
What'll

I would like a small salad.
I'd

I will have a 7-Up.
I'll

2 Now practice these sentences with reduced forms of **would** and **will**.

What will you have to eat?
I will have the special.
What will you have to drink?
I would like a glass of water.

7 LISTENING 🔲

1 Listen to Tom and Tina ordering
in a restaurant. What did each of
them order?

2 Now listen to the rest of the
conversation. What happened?

8 GRAMMAR FOCUS: Modal verbs *would* and *will* 🔲

What **would** you **like** to eat? I **would like** a hamburger. **I'd like** a hot dog.	What **will** you **have** to drink? I **will have** a Coke. **I'll have** coffee.
What kind of dressing **would** you **like**? **I'd like** French, please.	What kind of ice cream **will** you **have**? **I'll have** vanilla, please.
Would you **like** anything else? Yes, please. **I'd like** some water.	**Will** you **have** anything else? No, thank you.

1 What are the missing words in these sentences?

Waiter

[ ] What _____ you like to order?
[ ] What flavor _____ _____ like?
[ ] OK. And what will you _____ to drink?
[ ] Would you _____ anything else?
[ ] _____ you _____ dessert?
[ ] What kind of potatoes _____ you
     _____ , mashed, baked, or french fries?
[ ] _____ you like rice or potatoes?

Customer

[ ] I'll _____ chocolate chip.
[ ] I guess I _____ like coffee.
[ ] Yes, I _____ have ice cream, please.
[ ] I _____ have french fries, please.
[ ] No, that'll be all, thanks.
[ ] I _____ have potatoes.
[ ] I _____ like fried chicken, please.

2 Now number the sentences to make a conversation.

3 Compare with a partner. Then practice the conversation.

9 ROLE PLAY: In a coffee shop

Student A: This is what you want to order for lunch:

a hot dog   a large salad
a small order of   Thousand Island dressing
   french fries   coffee

Student B: You are the waiter/waitress. Take your customer's order.

Then switch roles and try the role play again:

Student A: Now you are the waiter/waitress.
Take your customer's order.

Student B: This is what you want to order for lunch:
a turkey sandwich   French dressing
a small salad   a Diet Pepsi

10 CONVERSATION: Thanks and goodbye 🔊

1 Listen and practice.

A: Thank you for inviting me. The dinner was delicious!
B: You're welcome. I'm glad you enjoyed it.
A: Goodbye now! Take care!
B: Thanks. You too. Bye!

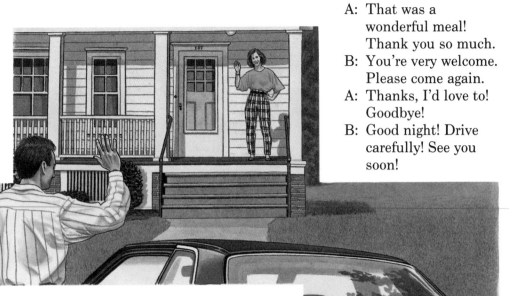

A: That was a wonderful meal! Thank you so much.
B: You're very welcome. Please come again.
A: Thanks, I'd love to! Goodbye!
B: Good night! Drive carefully! See you soon!

2 *Pair work*   Now cover the conversations above and use these cues. Take turns thanking your partner for a meal and saying goodbye.

A: Thank you for . . .
    The dinner was . . .
B: You're . . .
    I'm glad you . . .

A: Goodbye . . .
B: Thanks . . .
A: That was . . .
    Thank you . . .

B: You're . . .
    Please . . .
A: Thanks . . .
B: Good night . . .
    See you . . .

---

11 WRITING: Restaurant reviews

1 Have you eaten out at a restaurant recently? How was it? Write a review of the restaurant and the meal you had there.

> The Surf and Turf Restaurant
>
> I had lunch with a friend at the Surf and Turf Restaurant last week. It is a steak and seafood restaurant on Ward Avenue. The restaurant has about 30 tables and a pleasant atmosphere. I ordered a steak and a salad. For dessert I had chocolate cheesecake and coffee. My meal cost $21 plus a tip.
>
> The food was very good. The salad was delicious, and the steak was tender. The coffee wasn't very good, but the service was excellent. I would go back to the Surf and Turf again.

2 Now put your reviews on the bulletin board. Is there a restaurant you would like to try?

12 READING: To tip or not to tip?

1 Answer these questions and then read the passage.

Do you tip in your country?
In what kinds of places do you give tips?
How much do you usually tip?

Canadians and Americans usually tip in places like restaurants, airports, hotels, and hair salons because people who work in these places get low salaries. A tip shows that the customer is pleased with the service.

At airports, porters usually get a dollar for each bag. Hotel bellhops usually get a dollar for carrying one or two suitcases. A hotel door attendant or parking valet also gets about a dollar for getting a taxi or for parking a car. Many people also tip hotel maids, especially when they stay in a hotel for several days. They usually leave a dollar a day.

The usual tip for other kinds of service – for example, for taxi drivers, barbers, hairdressers, waiters, and waitresses – is between 15 and 20 percent of the check. The size of the tip depends on how pleased the customer is. In most restaurants, the bill does not include a service charge; however, if the group is large, there may be a service charge. There is no tipping in cafeterias or fast food restaurants.

2 How much should you tip someone who:

takes your bag at an airport?
parks your car at a hotel or restaurant?
serves you in a fast food restaurant?

3 What tip should you leave for the following:

a $27 haircut?
a $50 restaurant check?
a $14 taxi fare?

"Do we tip it?"

Drawing by Bernard Schoenbaum;
© 1987 The New Yorker Magazine, Inc.

▶ **Interchange 13:**
Are you ready to order?

Student A plays a waiter/waitress and looks at page 119. Students B, C, D are eating out, and look at page 122.

14 It's the greatest!

1 CONVERSATION: Making comparisons 📼

Listen and practice.

Alan: Gee, Los Angeles is a terrible place to live! I'm glad
I live in New York.
Sue: Come on! L.A. is much nicer than New York! It's
warmer, it's cheaper, and it's cleaner.
Alan: Cleaner? Are you kidding? Anyway, I love New
York. It's much more exciting than L.A. And the
people are friendlier, too.
Sue: Well, you can have New York!
Alan: And *you* can have L.A.!

2 PRONUNCIATION: Intonation – questions of choice 📼

1 Listen to the intonation in questions where there is a choice.

Which is colder, Seattle or Los Angeles?

Which is bigger, Ontario or Alberta?

Which is more exciting, Rio or São Paulo?

2 Now practice the questions.

3 GRAMMAR FOCUS: Comparisons with adjectives 📼

Is New York **bigger than** Miami?
Yes, New York is bigger.
No, Miami is bigger.

Is New York **more expensive than** Miami?
Yes, New York is more expensive.
No, Miami is more expensive.

Which is **warmer,** Miami or New York?
Miami is warmer.

Which is **more crowded,** New York or Miami?
New York is more crowded.

1 Complete these conversations. (See page 133 for comparative forms.) Then practice them.

A: Is Vancouver .... (cool) in winter .... Toronto?
B: No, Toronto is much .... (cold). It's great for skiing.

A: Which city is .... (interesting), London or Paris?
B: I think London is .... (exciting) .... Paris. It has great shopping and good nightlife. But I love Paris in the spring.

A: Is Singapore .... (large) .... Hong Kong?
B: No, it isn't. Hong Kong is .... (big) and .... (crowded). But you know, they are both fascinating places.

A: Which is .... (cheap), Tokyo or Taipei?
B: Taipei is much .... (cheap) .... Tokyo.

2 Now write six questions like these about cities you know. Then take turns asking your questions.

4 TRUE OR FALSE?

1 *Group work* Write five statements comparing cities or places. Some should be true and others false.

San Francisco is much smaller than Los Angeles. (T)
Australia is larger than Africa. (F)

2 Groups read their statements. Other groups say true or false. Which group gets the most correct answers?

5 LISTENING: Radio quiz show

Listen to the radio quiz show.
Listen to each question and check (✓) the correct answer.

1. ....Statue of Liberty .... Eiffel Tower
2. ....747 .... Concorde
3. ....gold .... butter
4. ....Canada .... U.S.
5. ....cat .... horse

6. ....Moscow .... New York
7. ....mile .... kilometer
8. ....Australia .... Brazil
9. ....Amazon .... Nile
10. ....Pacific .... Atlantic

6 WRITING: Comparison of places

1 Choose two cities that are very different and compare them.

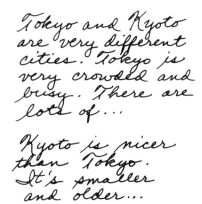

Tokyo and Kyoto
are very different
cities. Tokyo is
very crowded and
busy. There are
lots of ...

Kyoto is nicer
than Tokyo.
It's smaller
and older...

2 Now exchange papers and read each other's compositions.

7 WORD POWER: Geography

1 Circle the word that doesn't belong in each list.
Then compare with a partner.

a) countryside   avenue   forest   valley   c) hill   stream   lake   pond
b) mountain   volcano   canyon   path   d) ocean   beach   desert   sea

2 Make your own list and include one word that doesn't belong.
Then exchange lists. Can your partner find the word that is different?

3 Now add two names to these lists. Then compare with a partner.

Mountains	*Waterfalls*	*Continents*	*Oceans*
Mount Fuji	Niagara Falls	Africa	The Pacific Ocean
....	....	....	....
....	....	....	....

8 SNAPSHOT

Complete the information below about your country.
Then compare with a partner.

The biggest lake: ....
The highest mountain: ....
The longest river: ....
The biggest city: ....
The oldest city: ....

World geography

The world's largest islands:
Greenland, New Guinea, Borneo

The longest rivers:
the Nile, the Amazon, the Mississippi

The largest lakes:
Lake Superior, Lake Victoria, Lake Huron

The largest deserts:
*the Sahara Desert, the Australian Desert,
the Arabian Desert*

The largest countries:
The USSR, Canada, China

9 CONVERSATION 🔲

Listen and practice.

Johnny: Hey, Dad. Can you help me with this crossword puzzle?
Dad: OK, I'll try.
Johnny: What's the largest continent in the world?
Dad: Oh, that's easy. It's Asia.
Johnny: And what's the highest mountain?
Dad: It's Mount Everest, I think.
Johnny: Gee, Dad, you're so smart!
Dad: I know!

10 LISTENING 🔲

Listen to people talking about different places in the world. Circle **T** (true) or **F** (false).

a) The world's largest city is
   Shanghai.   T   F
b) The Pacific is the world's
   largest ocean.   T   F
c) The Paraná in Argentina is
   the longest river in South
   America.   T   F
d) The country with the
   smallest population in the
   world is Monaco.   T   F

11 WORLD KNOWLEDGE QUIZ

1 *Group work* Write five questions about world geography.
(See page 133 for superlative forms.)

What's the largest lake in North America? (Lake Superior)
Which is bigger, the Australian Desert or Alaska? (Alaska)

2 *Class activity* Now groups take turns asking their questions.
Which group gets the most correct answers?

12 READING: Nations of the world

1 Read this information about six different countries.
Then write the correct country in each blank.

Belgium	Canada	Chile	Egypt	France
Italy	Malaysia	Mexico	Switzerland	Thailand

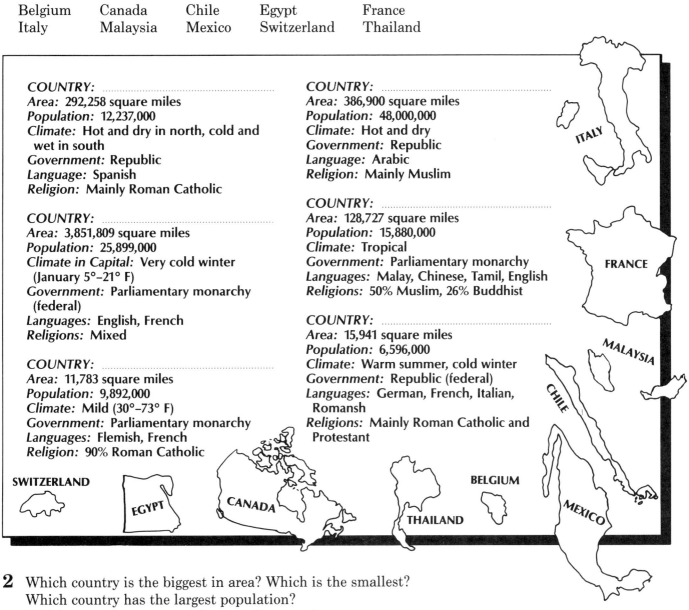

COUNTRY: ....
Area: 292,258 square miles
Population: 12,237,000
Climate: Hot and dry in north, cold and
  wet in south
Government: Republic
Language: Spanish
Religion: Mainly Roman Catholic

COUNTRY: ....
Area: 3,851,809 square miles
Population: 25,899,000
Climate in Capital: Very cold winter
  (January 5°–21° F)
Government: Parliamentary monarchy
  (federal)
Languages: English, French
Religions: Mixed

COUNTRY: ....
Area: 11,783 square miles
Population: 9,892,000
Climate: Mild (30°–73° F)
Government: Parliamentary monarchy
Languages: Flemish, French
Religion: 90% Roman Catholic

COUNTRY: ....
Area: 386,900 square miles
Population: 48,000,000
Climate: Hot and dry
Government: Republic
Language: Arabic
Religion: Mainly Muslim

COUNTRY: ....
Area: 128,727 square miles
Population: 15,880,000
Climate: Tropical
Government: Parliamentary monarchy
Languages: Malay, Chinese, Tamil, English
Religions: 50% Muslim, 26% Buddhist

COUNTRY: ....
Area: 15,941 square miles
Population: 6,596,000
Climate: Warm summer, cold winter
Government: Republic (federal)
Languages: German, French, Italian,
  Romansh
Religions: Mainly Roman Catholic and
  Protestant

SWITZERLAND

EGYPT

CANADA

THAILAND

BELGIUM

ITALY

FRANCE

MALAYSIA

CHILE

MEXICO

2 Which country is the biggest in area? Which is the smallest?
Which country has the largest population?
Which countries use more than one language?
Which country has the coldest winter?
How many different forms of government are there?

▶ Interchange 14:
How much do you know?

You probably know more than you think
you do! Find out with the quiz on page
120.

15 What are you doing Friday night?

1 CONVERSATION: Telephone messages 📼

Listen and practice.

Secretary: Good morning, Parker Industries.
Mr. Kale: Hello. May I speak to Ms. Graham, please?
Secretary: I'm sorry. She's not in. Would you like to leave a message?
Mr. Kale: Yes, please. This is Mr. Kale.
Secretary: Is that G-A-L-E?
Mr. Kale: No, it's K-A-L-E.
Secretary: All right.
Mr. Kale: Please tell her the meeting is on Friday at 2:30.
Secretary: Friday at 2:30.
Mr. Kale: And would you ask her to phone me this afternoon? My number is 356–4031.
Secretary: 356–4031. Yes, Mr. Kale. I'll give Ms. Graham the message.
Mr. Kale: Thank you. Goodbye.
Secretary: Goodbye.

WHILE YOU WERE OUT
Date: August 10
To: Ms. Graham
From: Mr. Kale
Phone: 356-4031   Ext.
MESSAGE
The meeting is on Friday at 2:30.
Please phone him this afternoon.

2 LISTENING: Listening to telephone messages 📼

Listen to telephone calls to Mr. Kawachi and Ms. Carson and write down the messages.

WHILE YOU WERE OUT
Date:
To: Mr.
From:
City
Phone: Ext.
MESSAGE
Call Mrs.

WHILE YOU WERE OUT
Date:
To: Wendy
From:
National
Phone: Ext.
MESSAGE

3 PRONUNCIATION: Reduced forms of *could you* and *would you* 🔲

1 Listen to how **could you** and **would you** are reduced in conversation.

Could you tell Matt the meeting is at 5?
Couldya

Would you ask him to pick me up at 4:30?
Wouldya

2 Now practice these sentences with reduced forms.

Could you ask her to return my dictionary?
Would you tell him there's a picnic tomorrow?

4 GRAMMAR FOCUS: Requests with *tell* and *ask* 🔲

Notice how we ask someone to give a message to someone else.

Messages with statements	*Requests*
The meeting is on Friday.	**Please tell Ann** the meeting is on Friday. **Would you tell her . . . ?** **Could you tell her . . . ?**
Messages with imperatives	*Requests*
Phone me this afternoon.	**Please ask him to** phone me this afternoon. **Would you ask him to . . . ?** **Could you tell him to . . . ?**

1 Make requests from these messages. Use your classmates' names.

Messages

a) The movie is at 7 P.M.
b) There's a class party at The Blue Moon tonight.
c) Come over for dinner on Friday at 6:30.
d) The concert on Saturday is canceled.
e) Meet us in front of the cafeteria at 6:15.

Requests

Please tell Kim the movie is at 7 P.M.

2 *Pair work* You want to give a message to a classmate. Take turns. Write a request and ask your partner to give the message for you.

▶ **Interchange 15: Would you like to leave a message?**

Practice giving and receiving phone messages. Student A looks at page 121 and Student B at page 123.

5 SNAPSHOT

Free time

In a year, the percentage
of people in North
America who...

read a novel, short story, poem, or a play	56%
visit a museum or art gallery	22%
see a musical	19%
go to a classical music concert	13%
go to a play	12%
go to a jazz concert	10%
go to the ballet	4%
go to the opera	3%

Complete the information below. Then compare with a partner.

How often I do things in a year:
read a novel ....
visit a museum or art gallery ....
go to a concert ....
go to a party ....

6 CONVERSATION: Inviting someone out 📼

1 Listen and practice.

Anna: Hello?
Tony: Hi, Anna! This is Tony.
Anna: Hi, Tony! How are you doing?
Tony: Good, thanks. Say, what are you doing
Friday night? Would you like to go out?
Anna: Oh, sorry, I can't. I'm working late.
Tony: Well, how about Saturday night? Are you
doing anything then?
Anna: No, I'm not.
Tony: Well, would you like to see a musical?
Anna: Sure, I'd love to! My treat this time.
Tony: All right! Thanks!

2 Listen to the rest of the conversation.

What musical are they seeing?
What time are they meeting?
Where are they meeting?
What are they doing before the musical?

7 GRAMMAR FOCUS: Present continuous with future meaning 📼

What **are** you **doing** on Friday night?	I'm working late.
Are you **doing** anything on Saturday?	No, I'm not doing anything.
Is your brother **coming** on Sunday?	Yes, he is.

Complete these sentences with the present continuous. Then match invitations in column A with responses in column B and practice the conversations.

A

a) What .... you .... (do) on Friday? Would you like to go to a disco?

b) .... you .... (do) anything on Saturday night? Do you want to see a movie?

c) We .... (have) friends over for a barbecue on Sunday. Would you and your parents like to come?

B

[ ] Well, my mother .... (go) away for the weekend. But my father and I .... not .... (do) anything special. We'd love to come.

[ ] Sorry, I can't. I .... (work) overtime. But how about Saturday?

[ ] I .... (work) till 7 P.M., but I .... not .... (do) anything after that. Can we go to a late show?

8 WORD POWER: Leisure activities

1 Put these words under the correct headings below.

art show	beach party	craft fair	picnic
barbecue	car show	hockey game	play
baseball game	concert	opera	tennis tournament

Exhibitions	*Gatherings with friends*	*Live performances*	*Spectator sports*
....	....	....	....
....	....	....	....
....	....	....	....

2 How many more words can you add to each list?

9 ROLE PLAY

Student A: Choose an activity in Exercise 8 and invite a partner to go with you.

Student B: Your partner invites you out. Either accept the invitation or say you are sorry and give an excuse.

Now change roles and try the role play again.

10 READING: Is that an invitation?

In Canada and the United States, people enjoy entertaining at home. They often invite friends over for a meal, a party, or just for coffee and conversation. Here are the kinds of things people say when they invite someone to their home:

"Would you like to come over for dinner Saturday night?"

"Hey, we're having a party on Friday. Can you come?"

To reply to an invitation, either say thank you and accept, or say you're sorry and give an excuse: "Thanks, I'd love to. What time would you like me to come?" or "Oh, sorry. I have tickets for a movie."

Sometimes, however, people use expressions that sound like invitations but which are not real invitations. For example:

"Please come over for a drink sometime."

"Let's get together for lunch soon."

"Why don't you come over and see us sometime soon?"

These are really just polite ways of ending a conversation. They are not *real* invitations because they don't mention a specific time or date. They just show that the person is trying to be friendly. To reply to expressions like these, people just say: "Sure, that would be great!" or "OK, yes, thanks."

So next time you hear what sounds like an invitation, listen carefully. Is it a real invitation or is the person just being friendly?

1 What is the difference between a real invitation and an expression that sounds like an invitation?

2 Now look at these sentences and check whether the person is giving an invitation (**I**) or just being friendly (**F**).

	I	F
a) Let's go bowling sometime.	....	....
b) How about coming over to watch a video on Saturday?	....	....
c) We'll have to get together real soon.	....	....
d) Please stop by my house anytime.	....	....
e) It's my birthday on Sunday. Would you like to come to my party?	....	....

11 LISTENING 📼

Listen to people talking. Are they giving an invitation (**I**) or are they just being friendly (**F**)? Check (✓) the right answer.

	I	F		I	F		I	F
a)	....	....	c)	....	....	e)	....	....
b)	....	....	d)	....	....	f)	....	....

12 WRITING

1 Make up three invitations to interesting or unusual activities.
Write them on cards.

> *Would you like to go see Godzilla Meets Superman tonight?*

> *There's a dog and cat show on Saturday. Do you want to come with me?*

> *I'm going to the Mud Wrestling Contest tomorrow. Do you want to go?*

2 Write three response cards. One is an acceptance card:

> *That sounds great! What time do you want to meet?*

OR

> *I'd love to, thanks. Where do you want to meet?*

The other two cards are refusals. Think of silly or unusual excuses:

> *I'd like to, but I'm taking my bird to a singing contest.*

> *I'm sorry I can't. I'm taking cooking lessons. We're learning how to boil water that day.*

3 Now use your cards for Exercise 13 below.

13 WHAT AN INVITATION! WHAT AN EXCUSE!

Class activity Put all the invitation cards in one pile and the response cards in another pile face down. Then shuffle each pile. Each student takes three invitation cards and three response cards.

Now go around the class. Use your cards to invite people to do something. Accept or decline any invitations you get.

Review of Units 13–15

1 Favorite restaurant

1 *Group work* Take turns talking about your favorite place to eat.

My favorite place to eat is . . .

Where is it?
What kind of food do they serve?
Does it have a nice atmosphere?
Is it expensive?

How much does it cost for dinner?
When is it open?
How often do you go there?
What do you usually order?

2 Which is the most interesting place? Tell the class about it.

2 Listening 📼

Listen and check (✓) the best responses.

a) .... Yes, this way, please.
.... Yes, please.
b) .... No, I don't.
.... Yes, I'll have tea, please.
c) .... I'd like a steak, please.
.... Yes, I would.

d) .... I'll have a cup of coffee.
.... Thousand Island, please.
e) .... Carrots, please.
.... Yes, I will.
f) .... Yes, I'd like some water.
.... No, I don't think so.

g) .... Thanks, I'd love to.
.... I'm glad you enjoyed it.
h) .... Bye! See you soon.
.... You're welcome.

3 The biggest and the best

1 *Pair work* Talk about places in your city like this.

A: What's the tallest building in . . . ?
B: I think it's the Hilton Hotel.
A: Oh? Well, I think the Shell Building is taller than the Hilton.

Buildings
The tallest building
The oldest building
The most beautiful building

Going Out
The best disco
The best restaurant
The best hotel

Shopping
The best department store
The biggest shopping center
The best place for bargains

Scenic Areas
The most beautiful park
The most interesting street
The best picnic spot

2 *Class activity* Compare your answers around the class.

4 Listening

Listen to radio commercials for three used car dealers and complete the
information below.

Which company has the biggest selection of cars?
Which has the cheapest cars?
Which is closer to downtown, Ajax Motors
or Nixon Autos?
Which has the best financing?

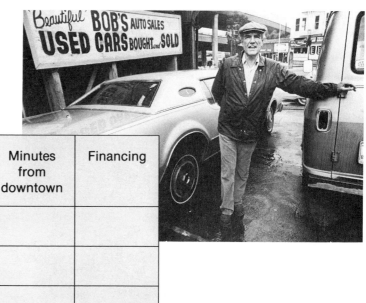

	The number of cars on sale	Prices	Minutes from downtown	Financing
Ajax Motors				
Nixon Autos				
Bob's Used Cars				

5 Inviting a friend

1 *Pair work* Take turns inviting your partner to do something.

A: Hello?
B: Hi, . . . This is . . .   . . . ?
A: Fine, thanks.
B: Say, are you doing anything on . . . ?
A: Well, yes. I'm . . .
B: Oh. Well, how about on . . . ?
   Would you like to . . . or . . . ?
A: Oh, I'd love to, thanks, but I'm . . .
   How about doing something on . . . ?
B: Sure. What would you like to do ?
A: How about . . . ?
B: That sounds great! What time . . . ?
A: . . .
B: And where . . . ?
A: . . .
B: OK. See you on . . . Bye!
A: Bye-bye.

2 Now change roles and try the conversation with a different partner.

Interchange Activities

Class activity You are reporters at a Hollywood press conference for a new James Bond movie. Interview the actors and actresses and complete the information below. Ask questions like these.

Is your first name . . . ? (*or*)
What is your name?
What is your nationality? (*or*)
Are you American (British, French, etc.)?
What is your role in the movie? (*or*)
Are you . . . in the movie?

NAME: *Clint*
NATIONALITY:
MOVIE ROLE:

NAME: *David*
NATIONALITY:
MOVIE ROLE:

NAME:
NATIONALITY: *Austrian*
MOVIE ROLE:

NAME: *Elizabeth*
NATIONALITY:
MOVIE ROLE:

NAME:
NATIONALITY:
MOVIE ROLE: *British Secret Agent*

NAME: *Chase*
NATIONALITY:
MOVIE ROLE:

NAME:
NATIONALITY:
MOVIE ROLE: *Girlfriend #3*

NAME:
NATIONALITY:
MOVIE ROLE: *James Bond's Boss*

NAME: *Murphy*
NATIONALITY:
MOVIE ROLE:

NAME:
NATIONALITY: *Swedish*
MOVIE ROLE:

NAME:
NATIONALITY:
MOVIE ROLE: *Head of the CIA*

Interchange 2 | Who is it?

1 For this activity, you need to know your zodiac sign. Look at this chart, and find your sign.

2 Now make a card about yourself like this and then give it to the teacher.

I'm a Leo.
My hometown is Monterrey, Mexico.
I'm a college student.
My favorite singer is Tina Turner.
My favorite actor is Sylvester Stallone.

3 *Class activity* The teacher will give you one of the cards. Who is it? Go around the class and ask questions like these.

Are you a/an . . . (zodiac sign)?	*or*	What's your sign?
Is your hometown . . . ?		What's your hometown?
Are you a/an . . . (job/student)?		What do you do?
Is your favorite singer . . . ?		Who's your favorite singer?
Is your favorite actor . . . ?		Who's your favorite actor?

When you find out who it is, give your card to the teacher and get another one. How many people can you find in 10 minutes?

Interchange 1 Press conference – GROUP B

Class activity You are actors and actresses in a new James Bond movie. You are at a Hollywood press conference. Choose one of the roles below and answer the reporters' questions.

Name: Clint Eastwood
Nationality: American
Movie Role: James Bond

Name: Eddie Murphy
Nationality: American
Movie Role: American Spy

Name: Grace Jones
Nationality: British
Movie Role: Girlfriend #3

Name: Peter O'Toole
Nationality: British
Movie Role: James Bond's Boss

Name: Vanessa Redgrave
Nationality: British
Movie Role: British Secret Agent

Name: Chevy Chase
Nationality: American
Movie Role: Head of the KGB

Name: David Bowie
Nationality: British
Movie Role: James Bond's Secretary

Name: Brigitte Nielsen
Nationality: Swedish
Movie Role: Girlfriend #1

Name: Arnold Schwarzenegger
Nationality: Austrian
Movie Role: Soviet Spy

Name: Bette Midler
Nationality: American
Movie Role: Head of the CIA

Name: Elizabeth Taylor
Nationality: American
Movie Role: Girlfriend #2

Interchange 3 | Swap meet

1 You want to sell three things at the class swap meet. Make a card for each thing like this.

> Bicycle for Sale
>
> Kind: Schwinn
> Age: 2 years old
> Price: $65

> VCR for Sale
>
> Kind: Toshiba
> Age: 6 months old
> Price: $150

> Hair Dryer for Sale
>
> Kind: Phillips
> Age: 5 years old
> Price: $5

2 *Class activity* Now form two groups – the Sellers and the Buyers – and have a swap meet. The Sellers use their cards first.

Sellers: Use your cards to answer the Buyers' questions. Try to sell all your things.

Buyers: You have $300 to spend. Go around the swap meet and talk to the Sellers. Ask questions like these and write down the things you want to buy.

> What do you have for sale?
> What kind is it?
> How old is it?
> How much is it?

3 Stop after 10 minutes. Tell the class what you want to buy like this.

> I'd like to buy John's stereo. It's $125.
> And I'd like to get Rosa's typewriter. It's only $40.

4 Change roles and have another swap meet.

Interchange 4 **Can I help you?** – STUDENT A

Role play

1 You are a clerk at the Tourist Information Center. Use the chart below to answer questions from telephone callers. Start like this:

"Hello? Can I help you?"

Entertainment Guide

Event	Place	Date	Time
Chinese film festival	Film Center	Thursday the 6th	7:00 P.M.
Fashion show	Hilton Hotel	Friday the 7th	11:00 A.M.
Soccer game	Star Stadium	Saturday the 8th	1:00 P.M.
Movie: *Rocky 12*	Uptown Theater	Sunday the 9th	6:30 P.M.

2 Now you are a tourist. Phone the Tourist Information Center and ask about events in the city. Ask questions from the list below to complete the chart.

What's on at the ... (place)?
What day is the ... (event)?
What time is the ... (event)?
Where is the ... (event)?

Event	Place	Date	Time
	Main Library		
French film festival			
	Campus Hall		
Baseball game			

Interchange 5 | Who's who?

1 Write two or three interesting facts about people in your family. Do not write your name on the paper. The teacher will collect your information and put it on a class chart like this.

My brother is a disk jockey. My younger sister speaks Russian.	My father is a jazz pianist. My aunt lives in Singapore. Her husband is an ambassador.	

2 *Class activity* Try to find the student who wrote the information in each box. Walk around the class and ask questions like these.

Is your brother a disk jockey?
Does your younger sister speak Russian?

Then write the correct person's name in each box on the chart. Stop after 10 minutes. How many names do you have?

Interchange 6 | Leisure survey

1 Interview five people in your class and complete the survey below.

LEISURE ACTIVITIES SURVEY

1. How often do you...

	About once a week	About once a month	About once a year
go to a movie?	....	....	....
eat out?	....	....	....
go to the library?	....	....	....
go to a museum?	....	....	....
go to a sports event?	....	....	....
go to a concert?	....	....	....
go to a disco?	....	....	....

2. What kinds of sports do you play?

.... jog or run	.... play tennis	.... play handball
.... cycle	.... play basketball	.... play volleyball
.... bowl	.... play soccer	.... do karate
.... ski	.... play golf	.... do other martial arts
.... swim	.... play baseball	.... other:

3. What kinds of exercise do you do?

.... do aerobics
.... take a dance class
.... go to a disco
.... work out in a gym
.... work out at home
.... go hiking or backpacking
.... walk
.... go rock climbing
.... work in the garden or yard
.... do calisthenics
.... other:

2 *Class activity* What are the three most popular leisure activities, sports, and exercises in the class?

Interchange 4 | **Can I help you?** – STUDENT B

Role play

1 You are a tourist. Phone the Tourist Information Center and ask about events in the city. Ask questions from the list below to complete the chart.

What's on at the ... (place)?
What day is the ... (event)?
What time is the ... (event)?
Where is the ... (event)?

Event	Place	Date	Time
	Film Center		
Fashion show			
	Star Stadium		
Movie: *Rocky 12*			

2 Now you are a clerk at the Tourist Information Center. Use the chart below to answer questions from telephone callers. Start like this:

"Hello? Can I help you?"

Entertainment Guide

Event	Place	Date	Time
Travel show	Main Library	Wednesday the 5th	2:00 P.M.
French film festival	Savoy Theater	Thursday the 6th	7:15 P.M.
Movie: *My Fair Lady*	Campus Hall	Friday the 7th	8:00 P.M.
Baseball game	Civic Stadium	Saturday the 8th	11:00 A.M.

Interchange 7 | Photo album – STUDENT A

1 You went on an interesting vacation recently and took these photos. First, think about these questions.

Where did you go?
How long were you there?
Who did you go with?
What did you do there?
Did you enjoy it?

Now show the photos to your partner. Use them to tell your partner about the vacation. Give as much information as you can. Start like this:

"I had a really interesting vacation. I went to . . ."

2 Now your partner talks about his or her vacation. Ask questions about his or her photos.

Interchange 7 | Photo album – STUDENT B

1 Your partner is going to show you some vacation photos. First, ask about the vacation like this.

Where did you go?
How long were you there?
Who did you go with?
What did you do there?
Did you enjoy it?

Then ask questions about the photos.

Where did you take this picture?
Who is this/that?
Is this a . . . ?

2 Now it's your turn. Talk about your vacation. Use the photos below and answer your partner's questions. Start like this:

"I had an interesting vacation recently, too. I went to . . . "

Interchange 8 | Just moved!

Role play   Finding out about a new neighborhood

Roles: Clerks (3)
       Apartment manager (1)
       New tenants in an apartment building (rest of the class)

The clerks and the apartment manager sit at the front of the class and answer the tenants' questions using the information on this page. Each tenant uses one of the sets of instructions on pages 112–113 and follows the directions on it.

Clerk at the Greyhound Bus Station

Bus Schedule	**Bus Tickets**
Denver: leaves at 10:00 A.M. & 3:30 P.M.	Reno: $14.00
Portland: arrives at 7:00 A.M. & Noon	Seattle: $21.50

Clerk at the 7-Eleven market

Item	Price
Aspirin	$4.37
Cold medicine	$6.91
Honey	$5.55
Chicken soup	$1.25

Clerk at Robinson's Department Store

Item	Price
CD player	$249
Typewriter	$487
Bookcase	$112
Sofa	$699

Apartment Manager

Laundry room   1st floor

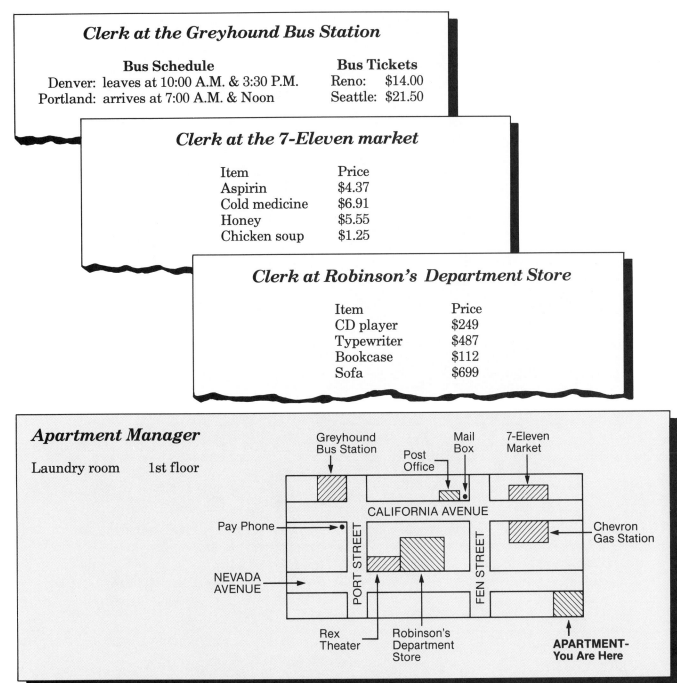

111

Interchange 8 | Just moved! *(continued)*

Tenant 1:

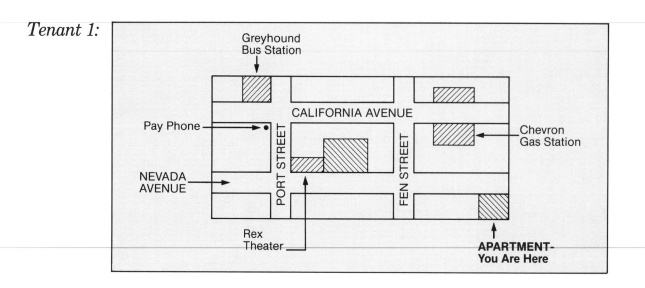

1. Go to the Greyhound Bus Station. Ask what time the bus for Denver leaves. Write the times here:

   ....

2. Ask someone where the 7-Eleven market is. Mark it on your map.
3. Go to the 7-Eleven. Buy a bottle of aspirin. How much is it?

   ....

4. Ask someone where Robinson's Department Store is. Mark it on your map.
5. Go to Robinson's. Buy a CD player. Write the price here:

   ....

6. Ask your apartment manager where the laundry room is. Where is it?

   ....

Tenant 2:

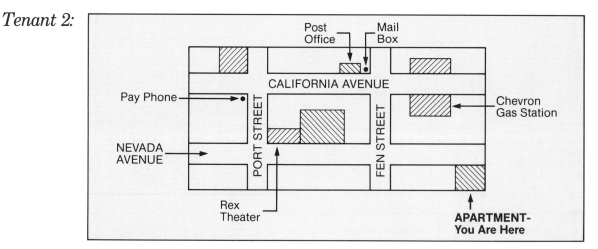

1. Ask someone where the 7-Eleven market is. Mark it on your map.
2. Go to the 7-Eleven. Buy some cold medicine. How much is it?

   ....

3. Ask someone where Robinson's Department Store is. Mark it on your map.
4. Go to Robinson's. Buy a typewriter. Write the price here:

   ....

5. Ask your apartment manager where the Greyhound Bus Station is. Mark it on your map.
6. Go to the Greyhound Bus Station. Ask what time the bus from Portland arrives. Write the time here:

   ....

Interchange 8 **Just moved!** *(continued)*

Tenant 3:

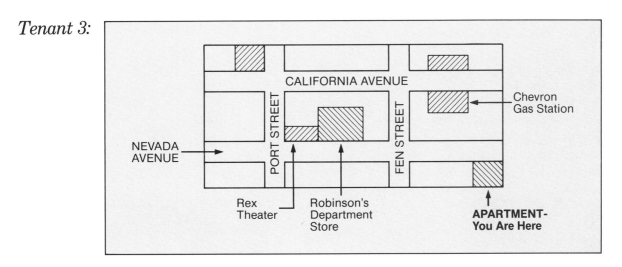

1. Go to Robinson's Department Store. Buy a bookcase. Write the price here:

   ....

2. Ask your apartment manager where the 7-Eleven market is. Mark it on your map.
3. Go the the 7-Eleven. Buy a jar of honey. How much is it?

   ....

4. Ask someone where the Greyhound Bus Station is. Mark it on your map.
5. Go to the Greyhound Bus Station. Ask how much a ticket to Reno is. How much is it?

   ....

6. Ask someone if there is a pay phone nearby. Mark it on your map.

Tenant 4:

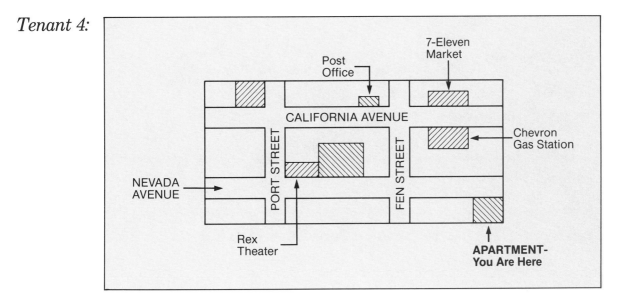

1. Ask your apartment manager where Robinson's Department Store is. Mark it on your map.
2. Go to Robinson's. Buy a sofa. Write the price here: ....
3. Ask someone if there is a mailbox nearby. Mark it on your map.

4. Go to the 7-Eleven. Buy a can of chicken soup. How much is it?

   ....

5. Ask someone where the Greyhound Bus Station is. Mark it on your map.
6. Go to the Greyhound Bus Station. Ask how much a ticket to Seattle is. How much is it?

   ....

Interchange Activities

| Interchange 9 | **We Are the World** – STUDENT A

1 *Pair work* Look at this picture of the artists who recorded "We Are the World" and practice the conversation.

A: Which one is Bette Midler?
B: She's standing in the front row on the right.
A: What's she wearing?
B: She's wearing a black and white dress.
A: Who's she standing next to?
B: She's standing next to a woman in a long jacket. I think she's La Toya Jackson. They're holding hands.

2 Now take turns and ask your partner about these people. You start.

Cyndi Lauper   Ray Charles   Harry Belafonte
Michael Jackson   Paul Simon   Willie Nelson

Interchange 10 We saw a UFO!

1 *Group work* Look at the pictures below.
Can you tell an interesting story about them?
Start like this.

One evening last summer, Jim and Debbie took a drive . . .

2 Now can you finish the story? Tell what happened next and how the story ends.

3 *Class activity* Each group tells its story to the class. Which group has the best UFO story?

Interchange 9 We Are the World – STUDENT B

1 *Pair work* Look at this picture of the artists who recorded "We
Are the World" and practice the conversation.

A: Which one is Bette Midler?
B: She's standing in the front row on the right.
A: What's she wearing?
B: She's wearing a black and white dress.
A: Who's she standing next to?
B: She's standing next to a woman in a long jacket. I think she's
   La Toya Jackson. They're holding hands.

2 Now take turns and ask your partner about these people. Your
partner starts.

Kim Carnes	Kenny Rogers	Tina Turner
Stevie Wonder	Diana Ross	Bob Dylan

Interchange 11 On tour

1 You are a travel agent. Plan an interesting and unusual vacation for the Winkley family. They want to visit your country for one week. Here is some information about the family.

Mrs. Winkley (wife):
   She is an artist and likes music and drama.
Mr. Winkley (husband):
   He collects butterflies and loves nature.
Willie Winkley (older son):
   He is interested in mechanical things.
Fanny Winkley (daughter):
   She loves sports, mountain climbing, and discos.
Bobby Winkley (younger son):
   He loves food, shopping malls, and seashells.

Now plan a one-week vacation for the family. Use the chart below.

Itinerary for the Winkley Family

Day 1: Morning: A city bus tour for the whole family. Afternoon: Mr. Winkley and Fanny go to the botanical gardens. Mrs. Winkley, Willie, and Bobby go to the museum.

Day 2:

Day 3:

Day 4:

Day 5:

Day 6:

Day 7:

---

2 *Pair work* Discuss your itineraries and compare them.

A: On the first day, the whole family should . . .
B: Well, I think Mr. Winkley should . . . ,
   Mrs. Winkley should . . . , and the children should . . .

3 Now work together and make a revised plan using information from your itinerary and from your partner's itinerary.
Then compare your plan with another pair of students. Who has the more interesting itinerary?

Interchange 12 Keeping in shape

1 *Class activity* Your teacher will read these directions for an exercise. Listen and follow the directions.

| Stand up. Put your feet apart and your arms at your sides. | Bend to the left and count to 10. | Stand up straight. | Bend to the right and count to 10. | Stand up straight. |

Now lift your arms up straight. Bend to the left and count to 10. Bend to the right and count to 10. Now put your arms down.

2 Now watch and listen as your teacher demonstrates these actions.

Put your feet together.
  hands behind your back.
  hands over your head.

Touch your toes.
  right ankle.
  left ankle.

Bend forward and touch the floor.
  touch your knees.

Bend your head to the left.

Sit down.

Lift your left foot behind you.
  left arm.
  right knee.

Lower your left arm.
  right knee.

Keep your arms straight.
  back straight.

Hold your hands together.
  left foot with your right hand.

Close your books. Your teacher will call out an action. Can you do it?

3 *Group work* Take turns. One student gives the directions for a simple exercise. The other students do the exercise.

Interchange 13 | Are your ready to order? – STUDENT A

You are the waiter or waitress at Peewee's Corner Cafe. You start.

#1
- Greet your customers.
- Ask what they would like and write down each person's order. (Use the menu below to write down the orders and amounts.)
- Check the orders like this: "You ordered . . . , and you wanted . . . "
- Ask your customers if they want anything else (e.g., to drink, a salad, dessert).
- Go and get their orders.

#2
- Bring the orders to your customers. (You make a mistake. You give one person the wrong order.)
- Go and get the right order and then bring it back.
- Go and wait for the customers to finish eating.

#3
- Give each customer his or her check with a total at the bottom. (You make a mistake. You didn't correctly add up one of the checks.)
- Go and wait for the customers to put the checks and money on the table.

#4
- Go and pick up the checks and money and then take them to the cashier.
- Bring back each customer's change.

PEEWEE'S CORNER CAFE

M·E·N·U

Burgers		**Salads**		**Desserts**	
Hamburger	$3.50	Shrimp Salad	$4.10	Apple Pie	$1.25
Cheeseburger	3.95	Chicken Salad	3.80	Cheesecake	1.50
Chicken Burger	3.70	Side Salad	1.60	Chocolate Cake	1.25

Omelets		**French Fries**		**Ice Cream**	**$1.35**
Mushroom	$4.50	Small	$ .80	Vanilla, Chocolate,	
Cheese	4.25	Large	1.30	Strawberry	

Drinks	Small	Medium	Large	**Drinks**	Medium	Large
Coca-Cola	$.65	$.80	$1.00	Orange Juice	$1.00	$1.60
Diet Coke	.65	.80	1.00	Coffee	.60	.85
Sprite	.65	.80	1.00	Tea	.50	.75
				Milk	.70	1.20

Interchange 14 **How much do you know?**

Pair work Take turns asking and answering these questions. If you agree on the answer, circle the word. If you don't agree, write your initials next to the answer you think is correct.

1. Which is taller, a giraffe or an elephant?
2. Is Mexico closer to the equator than Colombia?
3. Which has more sides, a pentagon or a hexagon?
4. Which weighs the most: the brain, the heart, or the liver?
5. Is the population of Pakistan bigger than the population of Japan?
6. Which is the world's busiest port: Singapore, New York, or Rotterdam?
7. Is the Renaissance or the Middle Ages older?
8. Which has the most calories: a glass of wine, a Coke, or a glass of beer?
9. Does a banana have fewer calories than an orange?
10. Which contains more caffeine, coffee or tea?
11. Does an egg have more calories than a tablespoon of sugar?
12. Which weighs more, gold or silver?
13. Is Venus closer to the Earth than Mars?
14. Which is bigger, the Earth or the Moon?
15. Is London an older capital city than Paris?

How many did you get correct? (See answers on page 134.)

Correct	
15	Perfect! Brilliant! You should be a teacher.
11–14	Very good! Do you watch lots of TV game shows?
7–10	Just OK. How often do you go to the library?
0–6	Oh, dear! You should never be on a quiz show.

Interchange 15 Would you like to leave a message?
STUDENT A

Pair work   You are calling friends or taking messages on the telephone. You start.

#1

You are making a telephone call. Your partner is receiving the call.

- Your partner answers the phone.
- Ask for Carol.
- Give your name and phone number.
- Leave this message:
    There's a school picnic tomorrow.
    The class is meeting at Golden Gate Park at 10 A.M.
    Bring a baseball bat.

#2

This time you are receiving a call. Your partner is making the call.

- The telephone rings. Answer it.
- The caller asks for someone. He/She is not in.
- Ask if the caller wants to leave a message. (Write down the message.)
- Check that your message is correct like this:
    Let me check the message . . . (Read the message aloud.)
    Is that right?

Now change partners and practice #3 and #4.

#3

You are making another call. Your partner is receiving the call.

- Your partner answers the phone.
- Ask for David.
- Give your name and phone number.
- Leave this message:
    There's a baseball practice at 2 P.M. on Sunday.
    Meet us at the stadium at 1:30.
    Bring something to eat after the game.

#4

This time you are receiving another call. Your partner is making the call.

- Answer the phone.
- The caller asks for someone. He/She is not in.
- Ask if the caller wants to leave a message. (Write down the message.)
- Check that the message is correct.

Interchange 13 **Are you ready to order?** – STUDENTS B, C, D

You are hungry customers in Peewee's Corner Cafe.

#1
– Look at the menu below.
– Order something to eat and drink.
– Ask the waiter or waitress to bring you something extra (e.g., an ashtray, a glass of water).

#2
– The waiter or waitress brings your order. Is it correct?
  If not, tell him or her like this:
  "Sorry, I didn't order . . . I ordered . . ."

#3
– The waiter or waitress brings your check. Is it correct?
  If not, tell him or her like this:
  "Excuse me. This isn't right. It should be . . ."
– Put the check and money on the table for the waiter or waitress to pick up.

#4
– The waiter or waitress brings your change.
– Now decide how much to leave for a tip.

PEEWEE'S CORNER CAFE
M·E·N·U

Burgers

Hamburger	$3.50
Cheeseburger	3.95
Chicken Burger	3.70

Salads

Shrimp Salad	$4.10
Chicken Salad	3.80
Side Salad	1.60

Desserts

Apple Pie	$1.25
Cheesecake	1.50
Chocolate Cake	1.25

Omelets

Mushroom	$4.50
Cheese	4.25

French Fries

Small	$ .80
Large	1.30

Ice Cream $1.35

Vanilla, Chocolate, Strawberry

Drinks	Small	Medium	Large
Coca-Cola	$.65	$.80	$1.00
Diet Coke	.65	.80	1.00
Sprite	.65	.80	1.00

Drinks	Medium	Large
Orange Juice	$1.00	$1.60
Coffee	.60	.85
Tea	.50	.75
Milk	.70	1.20

Interchange 15 | Would you like to leave a message?
STUDENT B

Pair work   You are calling friends or taking messages on the telephone. Your partner starts.

#1
You are receiving a call. Your partner is making the call.

- The telephone rings. Answer it.
- The caller asks for someone. He/She is not in.
- Ask if the caller wants to leave a message. (Write down the message.)
- Check that your message is correct like this:
    Let me check the message . . . (Read the message aloud.)
    Is that right?

#2
This time you are making a telephone call. Your partner is receiving the call.

- Your partner answers the phone.
- Ask for Tony.
- Give your name and phone number.
- Leave this message:
    There's a party at Bob's house on Saturday night.
    His address is 4143 Huntington Street, Apartment 202.
    Please pick me up at 8 P.M.

Now change partners and practice #3 and #4.

#3
You are receiving another call. Your partner is making the call.

- Answer the phone.
- The caller asks for someone. He/She is not in.
- Ask if the caller wants to leave a message. (Write down the message.)
- Check that the message is correct.

#4
You are making another call. Your partner is receiving the call.

- Your partner answers the phone.
- Ask for Liz.
- Give your name and phone number.
- Leave this message:
    There's no class on Friday afternoon.
    The class is going to a movie at Westwood Theater.
    Meet us in front of the theater at 4:30.

Unit Summaries

1 Please call me Dave

GRAMMAR

1. BE and subject pronouns

Question		Statement		Contraction	
Am I	...?	I	am (not)	I'm	I'm not
Are you	...?	You	are	You're	You aren't
Is she	...?	She	is	She's	She isn't
Is he	...?	He	is	He's	He isn't
Is it	...?	It	is	It's	It isn't
Are we	...?	We	are	We're	We aren't
Are you	...?	You	are	You're	You aren't
Are they	...?	They	are	They're	They aren't

2. Possessive adjectives

My	name is ...
Your	
Her	
His	
Its	
Our	
Your	
Their	

KEY VOCABULARY

Nouns
actor
actress
architect
bank president
city
class
clerk
company director
conductor
dance instructor
doctor
engineer
homemaker
language
lawyer
name
receptionist
sales manager
secretary
singer
supervisor
typist

Verbs
am
are
is

Wh-words
how
what
where

Adverbs
here
on vacation
retired

Conjunction
and

Titles
Miss
Mr.
Mrs.
Ms.

Prepositions
from
in

Days of the Week
Monday
Tuesday
Wednesday
Thursday
Friday
Saturday
Sunday

Expressions
Hello.
Hi!
Please call me ...
Nice to meet you (too).
What do you do?
Where are you from?
I'm from ...
I'm not working right now.
I'm studying ...

Yeah, ...
OK.

Excuse me.
How do you say ... again?
How do you spell ...?
What's someone from ... called?
Sorry. What is your ... name (again)?
Can I join your ... ?

Oh, really?
By the way, ...
Hey, ...
How about you?

I'm not sure.
I don't know.
I think that's ...
That's right.
No, that's wrong. It's ...

Bye/Bye-bye.
Goodbye.
See you (tomorrow/later).
See you on ...
Take it easy.
Have a nice evening.
Thanks. You, too!

Nationalities
Argentine
Australian
Brazilian
British
Canadian
Chilean
Chinese
French
German
Irish
Italian
Japanese
Mexican
Portuguese
Spanish
American

Countries
Argentina
Australia
Brazil
Britain
Canada
Chile
China
France
Germany
Ireland
Italy
Japan
Mexico
Portugal
Spain
United States

124

2 It's a great job!

GRAMMAR

1. Prepositions

I work **for** Toyota.	FOR + name of company
for Ms. Jones.	FOR + name of person
for a lawyer.	FOR + job
I work **in** a bank.	IN/AT + workplace
at a restaurant.	
I work **in** the sales department.	IN + department/section
in the front office.	
I go **to** Stanford.	TO + name of school

2. Indefinite articles A/AN

I am **a** student.	(**a** before consonant sounds)
He is **an** engineer.	(**an** before vowel sounds)

3. Definite article

I work for **the** *Daily News*.	THE + specific place
I work in **the** sales department.	

KEY VOCABULARY

Nouns
address
apartment
bank
bank teller
business
carpenter
cashier
chef
clerk
clothes
computer science
department store
disk jockey
disco
factory
fast food restaurant
flight attendant
furniture
game
guide
hamburger
hospital
hotel
job
manager
meal
nurse

office
passenger
patient
people
phone
phone number
photographer
receptionist
restaurant
salesclerk
school
secretary
store
street
student
supervisor
tour
toy
typist

Demonstrative Pronoun
that

Adjective
great

Verbs
answer

cook
do
go
hate
help
love
make
sell
serve
study
take
work

Adverbs
part-time
there
too

Wh-words
how
what
where

Prepositions
at
for
in
on
to

Numbers
one
two
three
four
five
six
seven
eight
nine
ten
eleven
twelve
thirteen
fourteen
fifteen
twenty
twenty-one
twenty-two
thirty
forty
fifty
sixty
seventy
eighty
ninety
hundred
thousand

Expressions
Good morning.
Good afternoon.
Good evening.
How are you (today)?
How are you doing?
How's everything?

Where do you work?
What do you do (there)?

Fine, thanks.
Just fine, thanks.
Pretty good, thanks.
OK, thanks.
Not bad, thanks. How about you?

Oh?
Oh, really?
That sounds interesting.

Thank you very much.
You're welcome.

It's a great job.
I love it!

---

3 I'm just looking, thanks

GRAMMAR

1. Possessive pronouns and 's

It's mine.	It's Sue**'s**.
yours.	John**'s**.
hers.	
his.	
ours.	
yours.	
theirs.	

2. Plural nouns

Add **-s**	bag/bag**s**
Add **-ies**	factory/factor**ies**
Add **-s** or **-es**	college/college**s**
	glass/glass**es**

3. Demonstrative adjectives

this bracelet	(**this** and **these** for things near the speaker)
these bracelets	
that bracelet	(**that** and **those** for things away from the speaker)
those bracelets	

KEY VOCABULARY

Nouns
address
bag
blouse
bracelet
calculator
camera
CD player
entertainment
folder
food
garage sale
motorcycle
necklace
nothing
parents
pen
refrigerator
rent
ring

shopping
skirt
slip
sport shirt
swap meet
tie
transportation
trousers
watch

Verbs
guess
live
think

Adjectives
lovely
new
nice
old

Preposition
with

Adverb
very

Other Words
all right
o'clock
on sale

Wh-words
how much
what kind

Pronoun
it

Expressions
Hello?
Excuse me, please.
Can I help you?
What would you like to know?

How do you like . . . ?
Would you like to buy it/them?

I'm calling about . . .
How much do you want for it?
What kind is it?
How old is it?

Yes, I'll take it/them.
I think I'd like to see it/them.

Yes, that's fine.
OK, thanks a lot.

How much do you spend on . . . ?

Ah!
That's crazy!
Come on.
Are you kidding?
Oh, that's not bad.
Yeah, it's okay.

Well, I'll think about it.
I'm/We're just looking.
Well, thanks, anyway.

---

4 What kind of music do you like?

GRAMMAR

1. Pronouns: Review

Subject	Object	Personal	Possessive
I	me	my	mine
you (sing.)	you	your	yours
she	her	her	hers
he	him	his	his
it	it	its	—
we	us	our	ours
you (plural)	you	your	yours
they	them	their	theirs

2. Prepositions

There's a soccer game **at** the City Stadium.	AT + place
It's **at** 8 o'clock.	AT + time
It's **on** Wednesday.	ON + day

KEY VOCABULARY

Nouns
actor
actress
classical music
computer show
disco music
game show
horror film
jazz
movie
music
music group
music video
New Age music

news
pop music
rock music
science fiction
singer
soap opera
soccer game
talk show
thriller
travel film
TV
TV program
video
western

Adjectives
favorite
OK
terrific

Verbs
like
think of

Adverbs
a lot
not very much
really

Wh-words
what kind
when

Conjunction
but

Expressions
I can't stand . . . !
Gee, . . .
That sounds good.

Do you like . . . ?
What do you think of . . . ?
What's your favorite . . . ?
What kind of . . . do you like?

Most people like . . .
We don't agree on . . .
We can't agree on . . .

Would you like to go?
Let's go.

5 Tell me about your family

GRAMMAR

Present simple

Question	Statement	Negative	Contraction
Do I live . . . ?	I live	I do not live	I don't
Do you live . . . ?	You live	You do not live	You don't
Does she live . . . ?	She lives	She does not live	She doesn't
Does he live . . . ?	He lives	He does not live	He doesn't
Does it live . . . ?	It lives	It does not live	It doesn't
Do we live . . . ?	We live	We do not live	We don't
Do you live . . . ?	You live	You do not live	You don't
Do they live . . . ?	They live	They do not live	They don't

KEY VOCABULARY

Nouns
aunt
boutique
brother
brother-in-law
children
cousin
daughter
elementary school
export business
family
father
glasses
grade
grandfather
grandmother
grandparent
husband
lawyer
man
mother
nephew
niece
parent
school
sister
sister-in-law
son
taxi
uncle
wife
woman
work

Adjectives
married
older
younger

Verbs
drive
have
live
manage
teach
wear

Adverbs
too

Preposition
with

Wh-words
how
how old

Expressions
There are four in my family.
Tell me about . . .
Oh, that's interesting.
Really?
No kidding.

How have you been?
How are things?
How's the family?

Well, talk to you later.
Well, nice talking to you.

Great, thanks.
Pretty good. And you?
Very busy!
Bye!
See you later.

6 Do you play tennis?

KEY VOCABULARY

Nouns
aerobics
baseball
bed
bicycling
breakfast
bus
chocolate
class
day
day off
dinner
drink
exercise
friend
golf
gym
hiking
house
karate
lunch
midnight
milkshake
noon
roller-skating
shopping
skiing
soccer
sports
swimming
tennis
train
waiter
weight
work

Adjectives
big
busiest
early
in good shape
long

Verbs
catch
clean
come
eat
eat out
exercise
finish
get home
get up
go home
jog
lift
meet
play
race
run
sleep
start
stay
take
watch
work out

Preposition
until

Other Word
as

Wh-words
how often
what time
where

Adverbs
about
after that
always
around
downtown
ever
every day
home
just
much
never
not very much
not very often
often
once a week
pretty
really
sometimes
straight
then
three times a year
twice a week
usually
very

Expressions
You're kidding.
Nothing much.

Good for you.
Hey!
OK!

7 It was terrific!

GRAMMAR

1. Past tense – regular verbs

Add -ed (most verbs):	want – want**ed**
Add -d (verbs ending in e):	live – live**d**
Add -ied (verbs ending in consonant + y): study – stud**ied**

Question	Statement	Negative	Contraction
Did I want...?	I wanted	I did not want	I didn't
Did you want...?	You wanted	You did not want	You didn't
Did she want...?	She wanted	She did not want	She didn't
Did he want...?	He wanted	He did not want	He didn't
Did it want...?	It wanted	It did not want	It didn't
Did we want...?	We wanted	We did not want	We didn't
Did you want...?	You wanted	You did not want	You didn't
Did they want...?	They wanted	They did not want	They didn't

2. Past tense BE

Question	Statement	Contraction
Was I ...?	I was (not)	I wasn't
Were you ...?	You were	You weren't
Was she ...?	She was	She wasn't
Was he ...?	He was	He wasn't
Was it ...?	It was	It wasn't
Were we ...?	We were	We weren't
Were you ...?	You were	You weren't
Were they ...?	They were	They weren't

3. Past tense – irregular verbs

See page 133 for list of irregular verbs.

KEY VOCABULARY

Nouns
anything
ballgame
city
dancing
disco
friend
girlfriend
outdoor concert
photo
sightseeing
sumo match
sushi
temple
tour

trip
vacation
week
weekend

Adjectives
beautiful
cold
fantastic
fun
great
quiet
terrible
wonderful

Verbs
bring
buy
call
carry
climb
come over
dance
drink
enjoy
go away
go out
have ... over
listen

read
ride
see
speak
stay home
tell
type
visit
walk
want
write

Adverbs
after that
for three weeks
for a month
for the weekend
last year

Wh-words
how long
who

Other Word
some

Expressions
How was your trip to ...?
What did you do there?
Who did you go with?
I really enjoyed it.
Sure!
We had a great time!

8 You can't miss it!

GRAMMAR

1. THERE IS / THERE ARE

Question	Statement	Contraction
Is there ...?	There is (not)	There isn't
Are there ...?	There are	There aren't

2. Prepositions

I live **at** 143 First Street.	AT + address
I live **on** First Street.	ON + street
I live **in** Boston.	IN + city
I live **in** California.	IN + state
I live **in** the United States.	IN + country

KEY VOCABULARY

Nouns
ad
airport
apartment
avenue
bank
barbershop
bedroom
book
bookstore

bus station
clothes
coffee shop
condo
department store
drugstore
gas station
groceries
grocery store
gym

high school
hotel
house
jacuzzi
kitchen
laundromat
letter
library
living room
ma'am

meal
medicine
neighbor
neighborhood
newspaper
pay phone
play
pool
post office
public transportation

restaurant
restroom
shop
stamp
street
supermarket
theater

Adjective
big

Verbs
borrow
dry
get
have
mail
move in
rent
wash

Adverbs	Prepositions	Other Words	Expressions	Sounds great!
also	across from	any	Say, . . .	I'm new in town.
around here	near	one	Well, I think . . .	You can't miss it!
downtown	next to	some	Thanks a lot.	Yeah.
fairly	on		OK, I'll try it.	
for rent	on the corner of	**Wh-word**	Sorry, I don't know.	
nearby	opposite	how big	I'm not sure, but I think . . .	
near here			What's it like?	

9 Which one is Judy?

GRAMMAR

1. Present continuous

Question			Statement		
Am I	standing . . . ?		I	am (not) standing	
Are you	standing . . . ?		You	are	standing
Is she	standing . . . ?		She	is	standing
Is he	standing . . . ?		He	is	standing
Is it	standing . . . ?		It	is	standing
Are we	standing . . . ?		We	are	standing
Are you	standing . . . ?		You	are	standing
Are they	standing . . . ?		They	are	standing

2. BE and HAVE

	BE + adjective		HAVE + noun
I	am 18.	I	have brown hair.
He	is bald.	She	has blue eyes.
She	is tall.	He	has a moustache and a beard.
They	are medium height.	They	have curly black hair.

KEY VOCABULARY

Nouns	party	know	Adverbs	what color	yellow
anyone	people	sit	about 20	what kind of	white
beard	picture	smoke	here	which one	
beer	ride	stand	in her 30s		
blouse	shirt	talk	late	**Colors**	**Expressions**
blue jeans	sofa	wear	later	black	Hi, good to see you!
car	somebody		these days	blue	Oh, she couldn't make it.
dating	someone	**Adjectives**	today	brown	Well, why don't you . . . ?
exam	sweater	bald	tonight	dark blue	I'll talk to her later.
hair	table	blond		gray	
hand	T-shirt	curly	**Preposition**	green	
jacket	window	long	on the left of	light blue	
jeans		medium height		orange	
miniskirt	**Verbs**	short	**Wh-words**	pink	
moustache	give	straight	how many	purple	
pants	go out with	tall	how tall	red	

10 Guess what happened!

GRAMMAR

Present perfect

Question			Statement			Contraction	
Have I	arrived . . . ?		I	have (not)	arrived	I	haven't arrived
Have you	arrived . . . ?		You	have	arrived	You	haven't arrived
Has she	arrived . . . ?		She	has	arrived	She	hasn't arrived
Has he	arrived . . . ?		He	has	arrived	He	hasn't arrived
Has it	arrived . . . ?		It	has	arrived	It	hasn't arrived
Have we	arrived . . . ?		We	have	arrived	We	haven't arrived
Have you	arrived . . . ?		You	have	arrived	You	haven't arrived
Have they	arrived . . . ?		They	have	arrived	They	haven't arrived

(See page 133 for list of irregular verbs.)

KEY VOCABULARY

Nouns
airline
airline desk
appointment
boss
boyfriend
burglar
check
clothes
flight
form
jail
karate
key
luggage
lunch
money
person
phone
roommate
shopping

speeding ticket
sports car
thief
thing
traffic ticket
wedding

Adjectives
awful
enough
famous
important
strange

Conjunction
so

Verbs
arrest
arrive
ask (for)

check in
explain
fill in
fly
forget
happen
hike
hit
lose
park
pay
phone
ring
try
wait (for)
wash

Adverbs
after that
at midnight
before

ever
few
finally
first
just
in about an hour
in the morning
last summer
never
next
once
on fire
out
then
the other day
till
twice last month

Expressions
It's so much fun to drive.
Please slow down a little.
You're doing nearly 80!
Don't worry.

You know, . . .
Would you believe it!
Guess what happened!
Do you know what happened on . . . ?
But I found I . . .
So, what did you do?

It drives him crazy!
How embarrassing!
That was lucky!

---

11 It's an interesting place

GRAMMAR

Modal verb SHOULD

Should I	go . . . ?	I		should (not) go	I	shouldn't go	
Should you	go . . . ?	You	should	go	You		
Should she	go . . . ?	She	should	go	She		
Should he	go . . . ?	He	should	go	He		
Should it	go . . . ?	It	should	go	It		
Should we	go . . . ?	We	should	go	We		
Should you	go . . . ?	You	should	go	You		
Should they	go . . . ?	They	should	go	They		

KEY VOCABULARY

Nouns
beach
building
canal
harbor
hometown
modern
motel
museum
night life
place
ruin
tourist
visitor
weather

Seasons
winter
spring
summer
fall

Adjectives
boring
cheap
clean
cold
crowded
dangerous
dirty
excellent

exciting
expensive
fascinating
favorite
hot
interesting
noisy
safe
small
ugly
wet

Verbs
hate
miss
move away

Modal Verb
should

Conjunction
or

Adverbs
lots of
too

Wh-word
whereabouts

Expressions
Well, it's not bad, but . . .
That's why I . . .
Can you tell me a little about . . . ?
What would you like to know?
When's the best time to . . . ?
Mmm, . . .
I can't wait to go there!
Anything else?

12 It really works!

KEY VOCABULARY

Nouns
advice
aspirin
backache
bed
bottle
box
burn
can
chicken stock
coffee
cold cream
cold tablet
cough
cough drop
cream
cup
dentist
energy
fever
flu
garlic
glass
gum

hairspray
hangover
headache
hiccups
indigestion
insect bite
insomnia
jar
liquid
lotion
match
medicine
milk
multi-vitamin
ointment
orange juice
package
problem
shampoo
shaving cream
something
sore throat
stress
sunburn

tablet
tissue
toothache
toothpaste
tube
vitamin C
vitamin E

Parts of the Body
ankle
arm
back
chest
chin
ear
elbow
eye
finger
foot
hand
head
knee
leg
mouth

muscle
neck
nose
stomach
toe
tooth

Adjectives
heavy
large
sore
tired
warm

Verbs
chop up
exercise
lift
put
rest

Modal Verbs
can
could
may
would

Adverbs
a lot of
every half hour

Expressions
Oh, not so good.
What's the matter?
That's too bad!
Have you taken anything for it?
No, not yet.
Do you know what you should do?

It really works!
Ugh!
Here you are.
No, that's all, thanks.
That'll be $8.95 altogether.
Let me get that for you.

13 May I take your order, please?

GRAMMAR

1. Countable and uncountable nouns

Countable		Uncountable	
Singular	Plural	Singular	Plural
an apple	(**some**) apples	(**some**) beef	—
a bowl	(**some**)bowls	(**some**) water	—

2. SOME and ANY

Question

Would you like **an**	apple?	Would you like	beef?
some	apples?	**some**	beef?
any	apples?	**any**	beef?

Statement
I'd like **some** apples.   I'd like **some** beef.

Negative
I don't want **any** apples.   I don't want **any** beef.

KEY VOCABULARY

Nouns
anything
apple
banana
beef

bowl
broccoli
carrot
chicken
chocolate chip

cream
dessert
Diet Pepsi
dressing
flavor

flour
french fries
hamburger
hot dog
ice cream

knife
orange
order
plate
pork

potato
reservation
rice
salad
sandwich

tip
turkey
vanilla
water
yogurt

Adjectives
baked
delicious
fried
mashed

Expressions
I guess I'd like . . .
That'll be all, thanks.
Certainly.
I'll have . . .

Thank you for inviting me.
Thank you so much.
That was a wonderful meal!
I'm glad you enjoyed it.
Please come again.
Thanks, I'd love to!

Drive carefully!
Take care!
See you soon!

14 It's the greatest!

GRAMMAR

1. Comparative adjectives

Add -er:		cheap – cheaper
Add -r:		nice – nicer
Drop y and add -ier:		dirty – dirtier
Double the final consonant and add -er:	hot	– hotter

2. Superlative adjectives

Add -est:		cheap – cheapest
Add -st:		nice – nicest
Drop y and add -iest:		dirty – dirtiest
Double the final consonant and add -est:	hot	– hottest

(See page 133 for list of adjectives.)

KEY VOCABULARY

Nouns
beach
canyon
continent
countryside
crossword puzzle
desert
forest
hill
island
lake
mountain
ocean
path

pond
river
sea
stream
valley
volcano
waterfall
world

Adverbs
both
busy
more
much

Other Word
than

Adjectives
different
easy
friendlier
highest

Conjunction
or

Expressions
It's great for skiing.
I'm glad I live in . . .

OK, I'll try.
You're so smart!

Anyway, . . .
But you know, . . .
Hey, . . .

Are you kidding?

Wh-words
which
what

15 What are you doing Friday night?

KEY VOCABULARY

Nouns
art show
barbecue
baseball game
cafeteria
beach party
car show
class party
concert
craft fair
hockey game

late show
meeting
message
musical
opera
picnic
play
tennis

Adjectives
canceled

Verbs
ask
tell

Adverbs
then
this afternoon
overtime

Preposition
in front of

Expressions
She's not in.
Would you like to leave a message?
I'll give . . . the message.
Oh, sorry, I can't.
Please tell . . .
Would you ask him/her to . . .

Well, how about . . . ?
My treat this time.
We're not doing anything special.
We'd love to come.

Irregular verbs

Present	Past	Participle
am/is, are	was, were	been
bring	brought	brought
buy	bought	bought
catch	caught	caught
come	came	come
do	did	done
drink	drank	drunk
drive	drove	driven
eat	ate	eaten
fly	flew	flown
forget	forgot	forgotten
give	gave	given
go	went	gone
get	got	gotten
have	had	had
know	knew	known
lose	lost	lost
make	made	made
meet	met	met
pay	paid	paid
put	put	put
read	read	read
ride	rode	ridden
ring	rang	rung
run	ran	run
see	saw	seen
sell	sold	sold
sit	sat	sat
sleep	slept	slept
speak	spoke	spoken
stand	stood	stood
take	took	taken
teach	taught	taught
tell	told	told
think	thought	thought
wear	wore	worn
write	wrote	written

Comparative and superlative adjectives

1. Adjectives with -ER and -EST

big	late	short
busy	light	slow
cheap	long	small
clean	mild	tall
cold	new	ugly
cool	old	warm
dirty	pretty	wet
dry	quiet	young
early	safe	
easy		
fast		
friendly		
heavy		
high		
hot		
large		

2. Adjectives with MORE and MOST

beautiful
boring
crowded
dangerous
delicious
difficult
exciting
expensive
fascinating
interesting
modern

3. Irregular adjectives

bad	worse	worst
good	better	best

Answer Key for Interchange 14 (page 120)

1. A giraffe
2. No
3. A hexagon (a hexagon has 6 sides; a pentagon has 5 sides)
4. The liver (liver = 3.1 pounds; brain = 3.0 pounds; heart = 9.8 ounces)
5. No (Japan = 120 million; Pakistan = 97 million)
6. Rotterdam
7. Middle Ages
8. Beer (beer = 150 calories; coke = 145 calories; wine = 85 calories)
9. No (a banana = 100 calories; an orange = 65 calories)
10. Coffee
11. Yes (an egg = 80 calories; sugar = 45 calories)
12. Gold
13. Yes
14. The Earth
15. No (Paris dates from the 5th century B.C.; London dates from the 1st century B.C.)